MPI Studies on Intellectual Property and Competition Law

Volume 32

Josef Drexl · Moritz Hennemann · Patricia Boshe · Klaus Wiedemann
Editors

Comparative Data Law

The Munich Global Data Law Conference

Springer

Editors
Josef Drexl
Max Planck Institute for Innovation
and Competition
Munich, Germany

Moritz Hennemann
Chair for Private Law, Information Law,
Media Law, Internet Law
University of Freiburg
Freiburg, Germany

Patricia Boshe
African Digital Rights Hub
Accra, Ghana

Klaus Wiedemann
Max Planck Institute for Innovation
and Competition
Munich, Germany

ISSN 2191-5822 ISSN 2191-5830 (electronic)
MPI Studies on Intellectual Property and Competition Law
ISBN 978-3-031-91400-3 ISBN 978-3-031-91401-0 (eBook)
https://doi.org/10.1007/978-3-031-91401-0

This work was supported by Forschungsstelle für Rechtsfragen der Digitalisierung (FREDI), University of Passau, Bavarian State Ministry of Science and Culture and Max Planck Institute for Innovation and Competition, Munich.

This Springer imprint is published by the registered company Springer Nature Switzerland AG
The registered company address is: Gewerbestrasse 11, 6330 Cham, Switzerland

Foreword

It is now widely acknowledged that data is the lifeblood of the global digital economy, shaping production, investment, employment and trade patterns not only in domestic markets, but also in international ones. Its effects extend well beyond markets, into social, political, and psychological spheres. Recognizing its significance, governments around the world implement legal data regimes to harness data's potential while safeguarding against its misuse. These regulatory regimes aim to strike a delicate balance: fostering innovation and competitive advantage through data utilization, while protecting against negative externalities that could diminish social welfare.

Legal data regimes are comprised of laws and regulations that induce, facilitate, or limit activities relating to any or all parts of the data value chain: collection, organization, storage, analysis, and usage. A legal data regime may provide effective means for implementing a positive agenda in a knowledge-based economy by facilitating and inducing the efficient operation of data and data-based markets. It can do so, inter alia, by reducing obstacles to welfare-enhancing data collection, sharing, portability, and interoperability. Conversely, it might inhibit data-based advantages and well-being, if laws are inconsistent, outdated, inefficient, or do not reflect cultural and social preferences.

The rise of Generative AI and the growing recognition of data's role in advancing sustainability initiatives have elevated the importance of creating well-balanced data governance frameworks. These developments underscore the value of learning from diverse regulatory approaches across jurisdictions. By examining how different countries navigate the complexities of data regulation, policymakers can better understand which approaches effectively balance competing interests. By focusing on the comparative experiences of diverse jurisdictions from around the world in regulating different aspects of legal data regimes, the excellent thought-provoking contributions of this book provide invaluable insights and lessons that can guide other jurisdictions in their own path of creating a balanced and effective legal data regime.

The importance of the book is further strengthened by the fact that the effects of a country's data regime often extend well beyond its borders. Cross-border effects can be positive, for example, when a legal data regime in one jurisdiction demonstrates successful approaches to balancing innovation with protection, while others reveal regulatory pitfalls to avoid. Positive effects might also result from bottom-up pressures of citizens in one country, as populations who witness effective data protection measures abroad often pressure their own governments to adopt similar standards. Such effects might also be negative, for example when major jurisdictions implement strict data regulations, multinational corporations may alter their global operations in ways that undermine the carefully crafted policy objectives of other nations. This complex web of regulatory interdependence makes comparative analysis essential – policymakers must understand the international landscape to effectively craft data governance frameworks that enhance both domestic and global welfare.

This book provides an essential resource for understanding the global landscape of data regulation, offering critical insights into how different jurisdictions approach this complex challenge. Through its comparative analysis of diverse regulatory frameworks, the book illuminates both successful strategies and potential pitfalls in data governance. Its comprehensive and critical examination of varied approaches provides guidance for developing balanced data regimes that serve societal interests. The contributors' analysis is ripe with invaluable insights and recommendations that address the interconnected nature of modern data governance, making it an indispensable guide for anyone working to shape effective data policy in our increasingly digital world.

The first part of the book focuses on fundamental aspects of legal data regimes. In "Regulatory Competition in Data Law," Florian Möslein analyzes the behind-the-scene competitive dynamics that shape our data regimes. His analysis reveals how data regulation emerges from a complex interplay between formal state law and the technological architecture implemented by digital firms. By highlighting how companies' technical decisions effectively create and enforce data norms, he builds on Lessig's insight that "Code is Law" in that code functions as a form of law in digital spaces. His analysis leads to the conclusion that "Code Needs Law," emphasizes the necessity for state regulation to actively engage with and shape these technological governance mechanisms. Rather than allowing private firms' technical choices to dominate data governance by default, Möslein argues that public law must evolve to effectively oversee and guide how technology enforces data-related norms. This perspective illuminates the crucial relationship between formal legal frameworks and the practical technological implementation of data governance.

Romandash's analysis in "Data Governance in Fragile Contexts: Ukraine's Dilemma of Security vs. Transparency," explores how extraordinary circumstances can fundamentally reshape the calculus of data governance. Through Ukraine's experience, she demonstrates how national security imperatives can challenge established transparency norms when open data policies potentially expose vulnerabilities to adversaries. Her work illuminates the complex tradeoffs between maintaining democratic values of openness and protecting vital national interests during conflict. By examining various approaches to this dilemma, Romandash provides valuable insights into how states can adjust their data governance frameworks during crisis while preserving core democratic principles. This case study offers crucial lessons for other nations grappling with similar security challenges in their data regimes.

In "Data Processing on Crowdsourcing Platforms: A Comparison Between Germany and the United States," Sina Häusler and Lars Hornuf offer a comparative analysis that illuminates critical differences between Germany and the U.S. in the handling of data on crowdsourcing platforms. They emphasize the importance of data protection standards in situations of structural power imbalance, as exemplified by crowdworkers that often face limited bargaining power against platforms. Their research reveals an interesting paradox: while U.S. platforms initially collect less worker data, German platforms demonstrate superior responsiveness to data access requests, likely due to GDPR enforcement. The study suggests that robust data protection frameworks like the GDPR can help balance these asymmetric relationships by ensuring worker rights to data access and control, despite their subordinate market position.

The second part of the book focuses on data law. Siddharth Peter de Souza and Gargi Sharma suggest "Three Ideas for Data Law from Environmental Law: Harm, Responsibility, and Rights." The authors argue that the emerging field of Global Data Law can learn valuable lessons from International Environmental Law (IEL) to develop core principles that ensure social justice and equity. IEL's frameworks that address to environmental colonialism, transboundary harms, and power imbalances between the global majority and minority, may be useful for global data law to tackle parallel challenges in data governance. In particular, the authors identify three key principles from IEL that could inform GDL: the conceptualization of harm, the allocation of responsibility (including historical and differentiated responsibility), and the development of rights-based approaches. By applying such lessons, GDL can avoid repeating similar mistakes.

Roberta Montinaro focuses on "Responsible Data Sharing for AI: A Test Bench for EU Data Law." Her study focuses on the web of regulatory instruments and market incentives that shape data sharing contracts for the purpose of developing and training AI. Her study identifies a critical weakness in how existing instruments, including the GDPR and the AI Act, fail to adequately promote accountability in data sharing contracts. Her analysis suggests that the current approach, which heavily relies on the contracting parties' autonomy, provides insufficient oversight of how data is shared and used in AI development. By highlighting how EU regulatory instruments fall short of establishing robust governance mechanisms for AI training data, Montinaro points to a crucial regulatory blind spot: the need for more comprehensive frameworks that go beyond basic data protection principles to address the specific challenges posed by data sharing in AI development contexts.

In "User Consent at the Interface of the DMA and the GDPR: A Privacy-Setting Solution to Ensure Compliance with Art. 5(2) DMA" Marco Botta and Danielle Borges study consent requirements under two distinct EU regulations: the Digital Markets Act (DMA) and General Data Protection Regulation (GDPR). Their analysis acknowledges that while both laws require user consent, their underlying objectives differ significantly. To address this, they propose a novel privacy interface specifically for gatekeepers under the DMA: a specialized cookie wall presented at first login that would allow users to specifically consent to different types of data combination activities. This proposal reflects their broader argument that consent mechanisms should be tailored to a law's unique focus on digital market regulation, rather than simply mirroring other laws' consent standards. Their approach aims to create a more nuanced consent framework that serves both the competition-focused goals of the DMA and the privacy protections of the GDPR.

Alexandre Humaine-Lescop offers "A Toolkit for Assessing the Level of Data Subjects' Control in Regulatory Data Sharing Models." His toolkit offers a systematic approach to evaluating different data sharing models. By breaking down data sharing models into their constituent elements, the toolkit enables objective assessment of how effectively different regulatory approaches empower individuals to control their personal data. This novel and thoughtful analytical framework provides a practical method for comparing various data sharing regimes and identifying areas where individual control could be strengthened. The toolkit's parameter-based evaluation system makes it particularly valuable for policymakers and researchers seeking to quantify and compare the effectiveness of different data protection approaches, while also highlighting potential gaps in existing frameworks that might limit individual data control.

Part three provides a comparative perspective. Two of its papers provide interesting and novel analysis of African data regimes. Franziska Sucker and Alexander Beyleveld's study of "African Rules on Cross-Border Data Flows: The Significance of Regulatory Convergence and the African Continental Free Trade Area's Digital Trade Protocol's Potential Contribution" illuminates the evolving landscape of data regulation across Africa, highlighting how multilevel governance structures are shaping the continent's digital future. Their examination of the African Continental Free Trade Area (AfCFTA) Digital Trade Protocol reveals its potential as a unifying force for cross-border data flows, while acknowledging the inherent tradeoff between regulatory harmonization and national autonomy. The authors demonstrate how regulatory convergence serves multiple strategic objectives: strengthening Africa's collective bargaining power in international trade negotiations, fostering the growth of indigenous digital enterprises, and reducing intra-continental disparities. Yet this convergence comes with the conscious sacrifice of some regulatory independence, a compromise they suggest is necessary for achieving broader economic and social benefits. Their work emphasizes how coordinated data governance could help African nations better navigate the global digital economy while promoting internal digital development.

In "Navigating the Data Transfer Maze: Understanding Intra-African Approaches to Data Transfers." Mercy King'ori and Ridwan Oloyede provide a comprehensive analysis of data transfer mechanisms across 39 African nations, which reveals the complex landscape of intra-continental data flows. Their research highlights how diverse regulatory approaches across African jurisdictions create both opportunities and challenges for regional data integration. By mapping out the various frameworks, they provide crucial insights into how different African nations approach cross-border data sharing, illuminating potential pathways towards greater interoperability. Their work addresses the practical challenges of harmonizing data protection standards across a continent with varying levels of digital development and regulatory capacity, while identifying opportunities for creating more seamless data flows that could enhance regional digital commerce and cooperation.

Barbara Lazarotto, writing on "Unlocking Data Sharing Dilemmas: A Comparative Analysis of Business-To-Government Data Sharing Regulations," provides a comparative analysis on the distinct approaches of the U.S. and EU to government access to privately-held data, while also identifying common challenges. Her work highlights an intriguing parallel: despite the different regulatory frameworks, private entities in both jurisdictions show similar resistance to sharing their data with government authorities. Her analysis proves particularly valuable for understanding how different legal systems attempt to balance private sector concerns with government data needs, while also illuminating why certain approaches to mandatory data sharing face similar obstacles regardless of the regulatory context.

Part four of the book explores the way forward. In "Towards Fairer Norm Development for Digital-Rulemaking in the 21st Century," Nelson Otieno Okeyo and Gabriel Zanatta Tocchetto use the hypothetical deductive method to present a critique of the EU's global influence on data regulation through a post-colonial lens. Using experiences from Africa and Latin America, they draw parallels between historical colonialism and the modern extraterritorial effects of EU digital regulations. Their hypothesis examines how the EU's regulatory power, despite its benevolent intentions, can create compliance pressures that echo colonial dynamics. The research suggests that when standardized regulations are exported from developed to developing regions, they risk perpetuating historical inequities rather than addressing unique local needs and contexts. This perspective provides a crucial warning about how well-intentioned regulatory frameworks can inadvertently reinforce existing global power imbalances in the digital sphere, particularly affecting regions still grappling with the legacies of colonialism.

Matt Malone, writing on "Data Localization, Hegemony, and the Popular Will: A View from Canada," adds a nuanced dimension to understanding data localization policies by examining how the complex interplay between state actors, private entities, and the popular will – defined as the aggregate of data subjects that exist in these actors' respective spheres of influence and control – affects the shaping of data localization rules. His analysis of the Canadian experience reveals a critical insight: while hegemonic powers pursue clear objectives of control and surveillance, public sentiment about data governance often remains confused and contradictory. His critique of opinion polling on data localization is particularly significant, highlighting how simplified surveys fail to capture the complexity of public attitudes towards data sovereignty. This research suggests that the apparent confusion in popular will may inadvertently strengthen the position of actors with more focused agendas, whether governmental or corporate.

In "The Need for Emphasis on "Fair Terms" in Data Contracts on a Global Level," Zeynep Ülkü Kahveci's analysis highlights how power imbalances in data ownership and access necessitate implementation of fair terms in B2B data contracts on a global level. Her argument centers on the fundamental issue that localized or regional approaches to enforcing fair contract terms are insufficient given the global nature of data flows and digital markets. Her work implies that without globally coordinated standards for B2B data contracts, stronger market players will continue to exploit their advantaged positions, potentially undermining attempts at creating more equitable data sharing frameworks at local levels.

Mariá Vásquez Callo-Müller, writing on "Future-Proofing the Global CBPR Forum," analyzes the significance of the launch of the Global Cross Border Privacy Rules (CBPR) Forum, which is aimed to facilitate cross-border flows of personal data. She draws crucial insights from the experience of its predecessor, the APEC CBPR System, to strengthen future privacy certification mechanisms. By analyzing the successes and shortcomings of the APEC system, she provides valuable guidance for designing more effective cross-border data flow frameworks. The analysis suggests that understanding historical challenges in privacy certification frameworks is essential for creating more resilient and adaptable systems that can effectively govern cross-border data flows in an increasingly complex global digital economy.

These diverse contributions collectively illuminate the complex landscape of global data governance, offering critical insights into how different jurisdictions navigate the challenges of regulating our digital economy. From Africa's emerging regulatory frameworks to the EU's influential directives, from Canada's struggle with data localization to the intricacies of crowdsourcing platforms' data practices, the analyses reveal both common challenges and unique regional solutions. The authors highlight critical issues including regulatory competition, crisis management, AI governance, consent mechanisms, and the lasting impact of historical power dynamics on modern data regulation. Throughout these varied perspectives, a common thread emerges: the pressing need for thoughtful, balanced approaches to data governance that can protect individual rights while fostering innovation and economic growth. The insights offered here provide invaluable guidance for policymakers and practitioners working to develop effective data regimes that serve both domestic and global interests in an increasingly interconnected digital world.

Michal Gal
Professor of Law
University of Haifa
Haifa, Israel

Doctor Honoris Causa
University of Zurich
Zurich, Switzerland

Preface

In 2021, the Research Centre for Law and Digitalisation (FREDI) at the University of Passau initiated a series of Global Data Law conferences. Their aim was to bring together internationally renowned speakers to analyze global data strategies, different layers of data laws and their underlying political dimensions. The Global Data Law Conference Series was meant to create a platform for discussions on data governance with perspectives from across the globe. The first event, which was held at the University of Passau in 2021, explored Global Data Strategies – with a special focus on fundamentals as well as insights from Europe, the United States, Africa, and China (Hennemann (ed.), Global Data Strategies – A Handbook, C.H. Beck – Hart – Nomos 2023). The second event took place at the University of Ghana School of Law in Accra. The hybrid conference explored the African data (protection) law landscape and the promise of Pan African approaches to data (protection) law, data governance and data policies (Atuguba/Hennemann/Boshe/Dei-Tutu (eds.), African Data Protection Laws – Regulation, Practice, and Policy, De Gruyter 2024).

This volume presents the proceedings of the third and final Global Data Law Conference in Munich, Germany in December 2023. The conference was dedicated to *Comparative Data Law* and was jointly organized by the Max Planck Institute for Innovation and Competition (MPIIC) in Munich, FREDI, and the Institute of Media and Information Law, Dept. I: Private Law, University of Freiburg. The conference was inspired by the substantial legal, regulatory, and policy-related developments that have taken place in the field of data law during the last several years. Academics and experts from all parts of the world analyzed evolution, global spread, normative status, and regulatory implications of data law regimes. They also dived into regional nuances. These proceedings are a compilation of those discussions, which proposed innovative solutions for some of the existing challenges in navigating data law and data governance. It is addressed to scholars, policymakers, legal practitioners, and generally anyone with an interest in the developments and nuances of global data law and data governance.

This book would not have been possible if not for the many speakers who presented papers during the conference and submitted them as written accounts. We are deeply thankful to all those who contributed a chapter to this book. We are most grateful to

Michal Gal for not only delivering a compelling keynote speech, but also for writing a vivid introduction to our book. We also like to express our sincere thanks to the various peer-reviewers involved for their time and their thorough feedback.

We are also most grateful to the University of Passau organizing team, Benedikt Karsten in particular, and the MPIIC organizing team. They underlined the true value of academic cooperation and of a joint event – and made the conference a success.

The conference was also made possible by the generous support of the Bavarian State Ministry for Science and Arts. For this invaluable support, we likewise express our gratitude.

Munich, Germany	Josef Drexl
Freiburg, Germany	Moritz Hennemann
Passau, Germany	Patricia Boshe
Munich, Germany	Klaus Wiedemann
February 2025	

Contents

Surveying the Fundamentals

Regulatory Competition in Data Law

Florian Möslein

Abstract Digital transformation is reshaping societies around the world, underpinned by the proliferation of information technologies. At the heart of this transformation is data, often referred to as the "new oil", which drives innovation, productivity and economic growth. However, realising the full potential of data requires a robust legal framework to govern its creation, processing and exchange. Recognising the critical role of law in unlocking the value of data, legislators around the world are creating legal foundations for its protection and use. This burgeoning field, known as data law, is witnessing the emergence of diverse governance regimes governing data access, localisation and transfer. As such, global and comparative data law is poised to become a discipline in its own right, shaping the competitive landscape of economies and societies. This paper explores the concept of regulatory competition in data law, analogous to similar developments in established legal domains such as corporate law. Unlike traditional sectors, the digital realm introduces a unique dynamic where technology-driven regulatory regimes intersect with state law. Drawing on insights from Lawrence Lessig's "code is law" thesis, this paper examines whether digital regulatory regimes compete independently or operate within broader legal frameworks. Through a three-step analysis, it navigates the complex interplay between regulatory competition and data law. It first outlines the general discourse on regulatory competition, and then examines its nuances in the digital context. Finally, it offers preliminary insights into the competitive dynamics within data law, highlighting its diverse institutional characteristics across subdomains.

Keywords Data governance · Data sharing · Data sharing models · Regulation · Data protection · Personal data · Data subject · Empowerment · Control · Individual control

---

F. Möslein (✉)
Philipps University of Marburg, Marburg, Germany
e-mail: florian.moeslein@jura.uni-marburg.de

J. Drexl et al. (eds.), *Comparative Data Law*, MPI Studies on Intellectual Property and Competition Law 32, https://doi.org/10.1007/978-3-031-91401-0_1

1 Introduction

The current digital transformation is driven by a convergence of technological, social, and economic forces that have reshaped the very fabric of our society.[1] The rapid evolution of information and communication technologies has given rise to the so-called information society, a concept that encompasses profound changes in the way we produce, access, and use information.[2] The information society is characterized by fundamental changes in the nature of economic and social activities, and it is marked by the widespread digitization of information, the spread of the Internet, and the explosive growth of data technologies. In this new era, data has become the lifeblood of our interconnected global community and a key driver of innovation, productivity, and economic growth: "Data is the new oil".[3] While the origins of this often-quoted phrase are not entirely certain, it is typically attributed to Clive Humby, a British mathematician and data science entrepreneur who was the architect of the world's first mass customization loyalty program, Tesco's Clubcard.[4] In a blog post of November 2006, the vice president of the Association of National Advisors, Michael Palmer, expanded on Humby's quote by saying that data, like oil, is valuable, but if it is not refined, it cannot be widely used.[5] While oil has to be turned into gas, plastics, and chemicals to create a valuable entity that drives profitable activity, data has to be broken down and analyzed to have value.[6]

Just as any other economic resource can only be processed, transferred, and used if the law provides the appropriate infrastructure, the resource of data also requires the infrastructure of law in order to be exploited profitably. Recognizing the importance of such a legal infrastructure, many legislators around the world have responded and begun to create legal foundations for the protection, use, and exchange of data. Different governance regimes for data access, data localization and concentration, data transfers between different legal entities, and other data laws have therefore emerged in different jurisdictions. Global and comparative data law is on the verge of becoming a discipline in its own right.[7] As in any other area of the law, a balanced regulatory environment can help protect the public interest and promote economic competitiveness. As data becomes a core resource and production factor in the digital age of our twenty-first century, secure and reliable legal frameworks for data creation, data processing, data use, and data transfer are therefore indeed, "in the words of

[1] See also Möslein (2024), p. 383.

[2] In much more detail Webster (2014); from a historical perspective Feather (2013), pp. 1–38.

[3] For a critique of this analogy from a regulatory perspective, see Scholz (2020), p. 863.

[4] See, for instance Chapdelaine (2020), pp. 1, 9.

[5] Palmer (2006).

[6] In this sense Haupt (2016).

[7] This development is not only evidenced by this book. Cf. also, for instance, the book series "Global and Comparative Data Law", ed. by Hennemann/Kumkar/Kuschel/Steinrötter; cf. also the activities of the Guarini Global Law & Tech Program at NYU Law School: https://www.guariniglobal.org/global-data-law. Accessed 25 February 2025.

data geopolitics inherently linked to the competitiveness of not only economies but also of societies".[8]

With this in mind, the search for an appropriate and balanced legal and regulatory framework for data law can be conceptualized as a competition between different rule-makers, both at the national and the international level, and also including providers of hybrid and soft forms of (self-)regulation: The emergence of global and comparative data law is subject to regulatory competition. States and other regulators, or at least some of them, compete with their data laws to attract data intermediaries and other players in the data economy.[9] Regulatory competition is, of course, a concept that is well-established in many other areas of law, most prominently perhaps in corporate law.[10] One of the best-known cases of regulatory competition is the so-called Delaware effect in US corporate law where it is often argued that Delaware has won the competition as most large US firms incorporate there (with over two-thirds of Fortune 500 company incorporations).[11] Compared to these other, more established areas of law where the debate has deep historical roots, the perspective of regulatory competition seems even more appropriate and important in the area of data law where the race has only recently begun and where its outcome is still largely open: As long as the field is still in its infancy and legal taxonomies are in flux, a Delaware of data law has not yet been established, and a stable competitive equilibrium still seems far off. Data protection law, with its much older roots, can of course be seen as an exception, but only in terms of development: Even if this area of law is already in a more established stage, the perspective of regulatory competition is still appropriate, not least because there is a lot of talk about the Brussels Effect in data protection law.[12] With its claim that the European Union, due to its global influence, can shape and influence data protection law worldwide according to its regulatory ideas,[13] this term ultimately describes nothing else than a specific dynamic of global regulatory competition.

Against this background, this contribution is an attempt to make the discussion on regulatory competition fruitful for data law. It is based on the consideration that regulatory competition has different dynamics in different areas of law simply because the preconditions for this competition are different.[14] In particular, the incentives to choose certain regulatory arrangements depend on the specific characteristics of each area of law. Moreover, regulatory competition in the digital realm follows its own rules, in part because digital technologies are taking over at least some of the

[8] See the announcement of the conference on which this book is based: https://www.ip.mpg.de/en/the-institute/all-events/global-data-law-conference-series-comparative-data-law.html. Accessed 25 February 2025.

[9] See the contributions in Hennemann (2023).

[10] Cf. in particular Murphy (2006), Hornuf (2012); see also Eidenmüller (2013).

[11] For a relatively recent account, including a global perspective, see Moon (2020), p. 1683.

[12] Recently, for instance: á Costello (2023), p. 165; see also Hennemann (2020) p. 864.

[13] Cf. Bradford (2012), p. 1; id. (2020).

[14] Highlighting the need for a sector-specific perspective on regulatory competition even within European company law: Grundmann (2001), pp. 783–832.

functions of the law. For instance, online platforms regulate user behavior, and algorithms and networks operate according to programmed, technology-based rules.[15] More than 20 years ago, Lawrence Lessig addressed the relationship between digital code and state law with his famous "Code is Law" formula.[16] Combining this idea with the concept of regulatory competition raises new questions: Do digital regulatory regimes compete with state legal systems? Or are they embedded in state laws that compete with each other? In order to set the stage for the discussion of regulatory competition in data law, this chapter proceeds in three steps. It starts by briefly outlining the general discussion on regulatory competition and then discusses the specifics in the digital context. In a third step, these conceptual considerations will allow for some initial thoughts on the competitive dynamics in the more specific area of data law. It will be shown that this area of law is itself subdivided into several individual areas, each of which has its own, specific institutional characteristics.

2 Origins and Dynamics of Regulatory Competition

The idea of regulatory competition has played a fundamental role in the academic legal debate ever since U.S. Supreme Court Justice Brandeis remarked in 1933 that there was a "race […] not of diligence but of laxity" between different corporate laws.[17] The discourse originated in political developments that had taken place in two mid-Atlantic states in the United States in the preceding years. The main political protagonist was the former professor of jurisprudence and political economy at Princeton University (and later U.S. president and Nobel laureate), Woodrow Wilson, who had taken office as governor of New Jersey in 1911. In his inaugural address, he declared emphatically that if the law was free to regulate the general conditions of society itself, it was also "at liberty to control these great instrumentalities which nowadays, in so large part, determine the character of society".[18] On his initiative, New Jersey's corporate law, which had been considered particularly liberal because it allowed the creation of monopolies through the acquisition of shares in out-of-state corporations, was replaced with stricter rules. The state, previously known as the "mother of trusts",[19] which had attracted large corporate combinations such as Standard Oil, began to outlaw a whole range of abusive practices.[20] As a result, many leading corporations began to incorporate in Delaware, which had previously copied New Jersey's liberal rules. Instead of controlling the great instrumentalities

[15] In more detail Möslein/Renner (2023), pp. 941, 949.

[16] Lessig (1999), p. 89; see also id. (2000); moreover Reidenberg (1998), p. 553.

[17] Louis/Liggett/Lee (1933), pp. 517, 559 (Brandeis, J., dissenting in part).

[18] Baker/Dodd (ed.) (1925), pp. 273, 275; reprint of the original from (1911), pp. 65, 69.

[19] Cf. Friedmann (2019), pp. 495, 506.

[20] In 1913 the so-called Seven-Sisters Acts were passed, forbidding, among other things, intercorporate stockholding. In more detail: Mahoney (1966), p. 71; cf. also Sanga (2022), p. 369.

that determine the character of society, New Jersey's corporate law lost much of its relevance, and Delaware took over the corporate chartering business.[21]

These historical developments have led to the development of various legal and interdisciplinary theories of regulatory competition that are as controversial as they are presuppositional.[22] Even if the fundamental question of whether law as a product can be the subject to economic competition at all is sometimes being debated, it is hard to deny the possibilities of legal choice in the age of globalization: Gone are the days when the law merely provided a regulatory framework for market participants.[23] Instead, it has become a kind of tradable product: Law is compared to a product and said to be "for sale".[24] Regulatory competition, however, depends on various structural preconditions, the existence of which cannot be taken for granted. Even a mere competition of ideas for comparatively preferable solutions presupposes, in the first place, material differences between the various legal systems: If there is a comprehensive uniform law, regulatory competition cannot develop, and divergent expectations and preferences of the addressees of legal rules cannot be taken into account.[25] Second, genuine competitive dynamics only emerge when these addressees have a choice between different regulatory regimes. If this choice requires physical mobility due to the relevant conflict of laws (e.g. due to the domicile theory in corporate law), the freedom of choice is significantly limited because its exercise depends on extra-legal location factors.[26] The third condition relates to the supply side: There must be financial, political, or at least ideational incentives for rule providers – legislators and governments, but also independent regulatory agencies, courts, and private regulators – to offer attractive legal products.[27] In the absence of a legislative or regulatory response, the choices made by the addressees of legal rules will have no effect in terms of law reform, so that regulatory competition does not arise in any meaningful sense.[28] Whether these three conditions are met depends to a large extent on the respective substantive area of law and its political, economic, and institutional context. For example, the competitive dynamics in contract law are likely to be lower than in corporate law because the freedom of choice of law may be greater, but conversely, there are fewer economic incentives for legislators in contract

---

[21] In more detail: Weitzman (2022), p. 12. In fact, the stricter rules in New Jersey were repealed again in 1917. The report recommending the repeal stated that "those laws now sought to be repealed are harmful to the state because there is much uncertainty as to their meaning, with the result that those who would have otherwise incorporated here or remained here are going to other states", Report of the Commission to Revise the Corporation Laws of New Jersey (1917), p.7.

[22] Cf. for instance O'Hara/Ribstein (2009); from a philosophical perspective Stark (2019); see also references in n. 9 above.

[23] For a closer look at the various market structures and international competitive dynamics that induce states to change their regulations cf. Murphy (2004), p. 84.

[24] Romano (1985), p. 225; Stark (2019); see also Comment without author (1969), p. 861.

[25] Similar Enriques/Gatti (2006), pp. 939–940; see also Stark (2019), p. 18 et seq.

[26] Cf. Stark (2019), pp. 19–25 (distinguishing physical and legal mobility); similar Schön (2005), pp. 331, 333.

[27] For a very differentiated, detailed analysis in an EU context see Gabor (2013), pp. 30–47.

[28] Stark (2019), p. 26; similar Kieninger (2002), p. 17.

law for fiscal reasons, and at the same time greater European harmonization reduces legal diversity.[29]

While the conditions are specific to each particular area of law, the effects of regulatory competition are also controversial. It does not necessarily lead to a downward spiral ("to the bottom") even if corporate law discourse has long feared that managers would exercise their choice of law to the detriment of shareholders, stakeholders, and the community.[30] Conversely, however, increasing attention is being paid to the positive effects of legal competition, which can serve to satisfy different preferences, avoid bad legislation, and promote legal innovation.[31] Accordingly, the fact that Delaware has prevailed can also be seen as an expression of a "race to the top", for example, because Delaware has the greatest expertise in corporate law.[32]

3 Regulatory Competition in Digital Law

The emerging field of digital law, particularly data law, is also likely to follow its own, specific dynamics of regulatory competition. It is important to understand these dynamics in order to predict which jurisdiction will become the 'Delaware of digital law'[33] and, more importantly, whether the race will be to the bottom or to the top. Driven by online platforms, artificial intelligence, and distributed ledger technologies, digital transformation raises myriad new legal questions. These questions often require new legal rules. As a result, the entire field of digital law is currently characterized by a particularly intense legislative dynamic. At the European level, for instance, many new laws are being introduced, such as the Artificial Intelligence Act, the Markets in Crypto Assets Regulation (MiCAR), the Platform to Business Regulation, and the Data Act as well as the Data Governance Act. Regulatory competition in the digital realm is likely to follow its own rules, mainly because digital technologies take over at least some of the functions of the law, thereby substantially changing the

---

[29] In more detail Rühl (2013), p. 61.

[30] This view has most prominently been articulated by Cary (1974), p. 663; see also Easterbrook (2009), p. 685, and the reference n. 13 above.

[31] In this sense Winter (1977), p. 251; for a useful summary of the discussion, see Daniels (1991), pp. 130, 170–9.

[32] More extensively Macey/Miller (1987), pp. 488–489: "For example, the Delaware legislature's drafting committees historically have been staffed with attorneys experienced in corporate law. This expertise means that Delaware is likely to adopt desirable rules to handle complex and technical problems as they arise. Delaware judges, attorneys and legislators have both the expertise to guide the development of corporate law in a way that is consistent with its overall philosophy — thus ensuring stability — and the knowledge of the structure of the law to make needed changes in response to unforeseen circumstances.".

[33] Due to its legislation providing a comprehensive framework supportive of blockchain innovation, the U.S. state of Wyoming has already been declared the "Delaware of digital asset law": Caitlin Long (2019), ('In sum, Wyoming is already the 'Delaware of digital asset law', a reference to Delaware's lead in corporate law'). Here, of course, both the substantive and territorial scope are much broader.

supply side of the market. Before focusing on the subfield of data law, it is important to analyze and understand these particularities of regulatory competition in digital law.

3.1 Digital Technologies as Regulatory Technologies: „Code is Law"

Digital law can be defined as the legal rights and restrictions that govern the use of technology.[34] It is therefore a very broad area of law, the substantive scope of which is not clearly defined, but which covers topics as diverse as digital assets, algorithms, platforms and data exchange. Despite its cross-cutting nature,[35] there is one specific feature that is also relevant to regulatory competition: Digital technologies can both define and enforce rules. Because their technological design can both enable and prevent human behavior, they are sometimes referred to as private legislators, even though they naturally lack formal legislative authority.[36] The phrase "code is law", once coined by Lawrence Lessig,[37] applies not only to the Internet and digital platforms whose terms and conditions regulate usage in a quasi-sovereign manner, but extends to the entire field of digital law, including data law. In analogy to the lex mercatoria, one speaks of a lex cryptographica.[38]

The fact that digital technologies can formulate and enforce rules also has implications for the dynamics of regulatory competition. It opens up additional regulatory options: Instead of relying on state contract law, agreements can be implemented on blockchain protocols; instead of establishing companies in legal forms of state company law, decentralized organizations can be formed; and instead of issuing securities according to the rules of capital market law, security tokens can be issued through initial coin offerings. Some digital platforms even promote themselves as genuine "digital jurisdictions": They (pretend to) offer an alternative to state jurisdictions, including dispute resolution mechanisms such as an "online decentralized court system that isn't bound by traditional artificial barriers such as national jurisdictions".[39] By decoupling themselves from state lawmaking and enforcement, online platforms position themselves as a genuine alternative to traditional legal systems. If digital jurisdictions provide a functional equivalent to state law, new dynamics are likely to emerge on the supply side: Competition between state jurisdictions is likely to turn into a competition between state and digital jurisdictions.

---

[34] For a comprehensive overview, see Martini/Möslein/Rostalski (eds.) (2024).

[35] Similar Martini/Möslein/Rostalski (2024), p. 18: "Querschnittsmaterie des Rechts" (cross-sectional subject matter of law).

[36] More extensively, Möslein (2019), p. 275.

[37] Lessig (1999), p. 89; see also id. (2000), p. 1.

[38] Reidenberg (1998), p. 553.

[39] Cf. Möslein (2019), p. 278, n. 21. The platform Aragon has recently changed its business model and their original offer is no longer available online.

3.2 *Towards Duopolies of Regulatory Supply: A Race to the Code?*

As additional regulatory options become available, the focus of regulatory competition analysis shifts to the supply side. Compared to the corporate law debate, where the focus has traditionally been on the demand side, the competition between different rule providers, including non-state actors, has so far received much less attention, even though regulatory competition between public and private rules is by no means a new phenomenon, even outside the context of digitization.[40] Presumably, non-state regulatory regimes have not been viewed as equivalent competitors to state offerings, mainly because of their enforcement deficits.[41] However, since the intensity of enforcement is a hallmark of digital technologies, a dichotomy with state jurisdictions seems more realistic.[42]

Assuming that digital and state jurisdictions compete as rule providers, the dynamics of competition will depend on the preferences of rule addressees: What are the incentives to prefer digital over state offerings?[43] First, digital offerings may appear to be more cost-effective. For example, the establishment of decentralized organizations does not incur notary or official fees, and there is no minimum capital to be raised. Second, there is a high degree of organizational freedom that exceeds the scope of even the most liberal state legal systems. Third, digital technologies have a global claim that transcends the territorial boundaries of state jurisdictions. Decentralized technologies such as blockchain avoid conflict of law frictions because their digital infrastructure operates uniformly across the globe. Fourth and finally, digital technologies promise effective enforcement: Instead of having to litigate claims, creditors can enforce them through technology. Conversely, the debtor must go to court to contest those claims. Self-enforcement *ex machina* saves creditors time, court costs, and legal uncertainty.[44] On the other hand, a “race to the code” is by no means the necessary outcome.[45] There are good reasons to prefer state laws to technology-based, digital offerings. First, many people still lack experience with such offerings, which means that addressees have greater trust in traditional legal institutions. However, this effect is likely to diminish as the digital transformation progresses. Second, technology-based systems operate more mechanically than legal norms. From an ex-ante perspective, greater potential for differentiation promises to

---

[40] In more detail: Möslein (2013), p. 160.

[41] Similarly, the autonomy of the lex mercatoria has long been the subject of intense debate, not least on the basis of enforceability arguments, cf. Calliess/Zumbansen (2010), p. 31.

[42] For example, it has been suggested that digital technologies could “displace the legal system’s core function of enforcing agreements’, see Werbach/Cornell (2017), pp. 313–314; see also Finck (2019), p. 77.

[43] Cf. for a preliminary discussion, concerning public and private rules in general: Möslein (2013), p. 151.

[44] Similar with regard to smart contracts Werbach/Cornell (2017), p. 331 et seq.

[45] On the limitations of Code as Law, see de Filippi/Wright (2018), pp. 199–201; furthermore cf. again Werbach/Cornell (2017), p. 318.

better address future uncertainty and may therefore prove to be a competitive advantage.[46] Third, the fact that technology-based self-enforcement does not preclude the possibility of legal enforcement, but makes it significantly more difficult, may be a disadvantage, at least in certain circumstances. Fourth and finally, the advantages of digital technologies end at the boundaries of the digital. For example, decentralized organizations may have the advantage of efficient enforcement relative to digital token holders. However, this advantage does not exist for business partners who supply or receive non-digital products. Instead, the lack of legal capacity of such organizations has a negative effect: it undermines their reliability as contractual partners and prevents the effective enforcement of contractual claims. The effectiveness of digital jurisdictions is limited to the virtual world.

3.3 Two-Tier Regulatory Supply: Legal Embeddedness of Regulatory Technologies

Despite all libertarian rhetoric, digital jurisdictions do not exist independently "without the state".[47] Quite the opposite is rightly emphasized: "Code Needs Law".[48] Digital jurisdictions are legally embedded and interwoven with state jurisdictions, even if the autonomy of digital jurisdictions is relatively pronounced due to their effective self-enforcement. While smart contracts do not necessarily require state laws and institutions for their enforcement, state law can counteract their self-enforcement.[49] As a result, state laws have to play a more reactive role: They must respond to the self-enforcement of digital technologies, rather than ensuring that rules are enforced. Despite the additional providers on the supply side, the legal embedding of digital regulatory regimes implies that state jurisdictions still have a predominant role to play. Conversely, legally embedded digital jurisdictions act not only as providers but also as consumers of regulatory supply. Where possible, they will also choose between different regulatory offerings, thus acting as a kind of intermediary in the regulatory supply chain.[50] For instance, the divide between civil law and common law is likely to have an impact on their decision, for example, because these different systems of contract law accommodate smart contracts differently.[51] At the same time, digital players are typically in competition with each other and must therefore be guided by user preferences. In the regulatory supply chain, user preferences may vary and will create tension between legal certainty, enforcement effectiveness, contractual freedom, and global uniformity. All four objectives

[46] Similar de Filippi/Wright (2018), p. 201.

[47] Cf. Hadfield/Weingast (2013), p. 3.

[48] Finck (2019), p. 44.

[49] Cf. again Finck (2019), p. 40.

[50] On the different types of regulation that State laws can choose from see de Filippi/Wright (2018), pp. 173–192.

[51] Extensively Möslein (2021), p. 27.

are attractive, but they can never be achieved simultaneously. Whether a regulatory optimum can be achieved, and whether the competitive race is tilted toward code or law, depends on many different parameters and the complex dynamics of different choices along this regulatory supply chain.

4 Application to Data Law

These general considerations about regulatory competition in the digital realm can be applied to the more specific area of data law, but they must be adapted to the specifics of this area of law and within this area of law. On the one hand, the regulatory nature of data technologies may seem less obvious and less pronounced than in the realm of distributed ledger technologies or online platforms, although it does indeed exist. For example, also data intermediaries can intervene in a regulatory manner by designing the data governance framework on their platform.[52] More specifically, smart contracts which represent a prime example of regulatory technology can also be used for data exchange. In fact, smart contracts are regulated for the first time ever in European law in Art. 36 Data Act. On the other hand, data law itself is very heterogeneous, as it differs in particular between data protection law and data economy law, and more specifically between rules on data access and data intermediation.[53] Respective differences affect the dynamics of regulatory competition. These dynamics cannot be developed in detail here, but can only be hinted at: By pointing out relevant peculiarities, this chapter should (and can) only and primarily encourage a more intensive and differentiated examination of data law from the perspective of regulatory competition.

4.1 Data Protection

In an era where data flows freely across borders and digital providers reign supreme, the General Data Protection Regulation (GDPR) stands as an example of a proactive regulatory strategy.[54] The regulation's start of application in May 2018 marked the beginning of a new era for the protection of information privacy in Europe.[55] Crafted to uphold the fundamental rights and freedoms of individuals, it embodies a robust framework characterized by strong substantive principles and vigorous enforcement

[52] Similar Lis/Gelhaar/Otto (2023), pp. 27, 47.

[53] Cf. for example Streinz (2021), p. 902 (differentiating between Data Protection Law, Non-Personal Data Law, Data Ownership Law and Access to Data Laws).

[54] For a thorough analysis of regulatory competition in data protection law cf. Hennemann (2020), pp. 864–895.

[55] For an overview see, for example, Mitrou (2017), p. 19.

mechanisms.[56] At its core, Art. 5 GDPR champions the principles of lawfulness, fairness, and transparency, setting the stage for a data landscape rooted in accountability.[57] Purpose limitations and data minimization further strengthen this foundation by ensuring that personal data is collected and processed with explicit consent and for legitimate reasons.[58] Such stringent standards not only safeguard individual privacy but also foster trust in digital ecosystems. Enforcement under GDPR includes both public and private means to combat data misuse: The supervisory authorities have the power to impose substantial fines on non-compliant companies, but individual data subjects also have the right to seek redress in the courts, which reinforces the deterrent effect on erroneous data processing.[59]

From the perspective of regulatory competition, however, a delicate balance must be struck amid the quest for a high level of protection. While GDPR advocates for stringent standards, the choice of digital providers naturally tilts toward those offering lower levels of protection, unless they take advantage of data protection as a quality signal to attract additional clients and generate a good corporate reputation.[60] However, their preference is tempered by the extraterritorial reach of GDPR, which invokes in its Art. 3 para. 2 the marketplace principle and forces even foreign companies to comply with its mandates.[61] Thus, the European Union applies its data protection law to market participants outside its borders to ensure its effective enforcement and to limit the risks of circumvention. The pursuit of its data protection regime transcends geographic boundaries to usher in a new era of global accountability. At the heart of the GDPR's regulatory approach is an unwavering commitment to upholding personal fundamental rights and freedoms,[62] even beyond the borders of the European Union. In an age of ubiquitous data collection, the idea is to empower individuals to take control of their personal data and effectively exercise their right to privacy.

Interestingly, this stringent regulatory approach of the GDPR has not proven to be as ineffective as New Jersey's strict corporate law rules long ago due to the so-called Delaware effect. On the contrary, the balance struck by the GDPR is reverberating far beyond the borders of the European Union, giving rise to what scholars call the Brussels effect[63] or even data imperialism.[64] As other jurisdictions align their regulations with GDPR standards to facilitate cross-border data flows, a global consensus

[56] In more detail Truli (2018), pp. 303–329.

[57] For an overview see Voigt/Bussche (2017), p. 31 et seq.

[58] See again Voigt/Bussche (2017), pp. 88–91.

[59] In detail Hess(2016), p. 388, para. 139 et seqs.

[60] Hennemann/Zeiter (2023).

[61] For a much finer analysis see Thon (2020), pp. 24–61.

[62] For an exploration of the steps that led to the emergence of the fundamental right to personal data protection see Fuster (2014).

[63] Bradford (2012), p. 1; id. (2020), p. 132 et seqs.; Scott (2014), p. 87; id. (2014), p. 1343.

[64] Mannion (2020), p. 685; cf. also Bernzen (2023).

on data protection is likely to emerge.[65] The influence of the GDPR transcends legal boundaries and has the potential to shape the contours of data governance worldwide. As we navigate the complexities of the data-driven world, the GDPR seems to be a testament to the power of regulation to protect the rights and dignity of individuals. By balancing the interests of stakeholders and prioritizing fundamental rights, the regulation seeks to pave the way for a digital landscape characterized by trust, accountability, and respect for privacy. The GDPR aims at ensuring a high level of data protection. What is remarkable is that this proactive regulatory strategy has apparently enabled the legal act to prevail in the global regulatory competition, even though potentially to the detriment of regulatory innovation.

4.2 Data Access

After the adoption of important legal acts in the area of data economy law, the key question is whether a similar dynamic of regulatory competition can be expected in this area as in data protection: Will there also be a Brussels effect or is there more of a risk of a Delaware effect leading to a race to the bottom? In particular, the legal rules on data access are currently undergoing a transformative change with the introduction of the Data Act which is in force since January 2024.[66] This new legal instrument forms the centerpiece of the EU data regulation.[67] It aims to improve the availability of data and to promote the exchange of data between different actors in all sectors of the economy.[68] The Data Act presents a complex and nuanced regulatory strategy characterized by ambivalence as it seeks to balance the imperative of fair data access with the need for flexibility in implementation and enforcement at the national level. Central to the Data Act is the mandate for data holders to facilitate fair access to and use of data through connected products, related services, and virtual assistants.[69] By opening up access to valuable data sets, this mandatory obligation aims to promote innovation and competition. However, the flexibility afforded in organizing implementation and enforcement, both at the level of public and private enforcement, allows Member States to tailor approaches to their specific contexts,

[65] However, this global standardization may also be due to effects in the opposite direction, cf. Rustad/Koenig (2019), p. 365 (arguing that the GDPR has adopted US data privacy innovations).

[66] Regulation (EU) 2023/2854 of the European Parliament and of the Council of 13 December 2023 on harmonised rules on fair access to and use of data and amending Regulation (EU) 2017/2394 and Directive (EU) 2020/1828 (Data Act), OJ L 2023/2854.

[67] For an overview see Hennemann et al. (2024).

[68] Similar Recital 3 of the Data Act ("In order to respond to the needs of the digital economy and to remove barriers to a well-functioning internal market for data, it is necessary to lay down a harmonised framework specifying who is entitled to use product data or related service data, under which conditions and on what basis").

[69] In more detail Eckardt/Kerber (2024), p. 133 et seq.

reflecting the diverse regulatory landscapes within the European Union, but also calling into question the effectiveness of data sharing mechanisms.[70]

With regard to the legal embeddedness of regulatory technologies, Art. 36 Data Act is a particularly relevant provision. It contains the first EU-wide regulation on smart contracts, a regulatory phenomenon that is much discussed far beyond data law, as it allows legal (or contractual) rules to be implemented in technology, in particular in DLT networks. However, the provision is not intended to be an overarching, general regulation of the technical phenomenon, but it is limited to the context of data sharing. Moreover, while Art. 36 Data Act, as its title suggests, regulates essential requirements for smart contracts for the execution of data transfer agreements. However, the provision is limited to technical specifications, which are intended in particular to ensure the interoperability of such smart contracts.[71] The provision does not specify the content of the contract and therefore, as such, does not restrict the freedom of contractual design. At most, there are indirect restrictions because in other provisions, the Data Act sets out requirements for fair access to data. As a result, smart contracts can only be technically implemented if they meet these fairness requirements.

For digital providers, the Data Act is a challenge. While they may prefer a less mandatory regime, the extraterritorial scope of the legislation leaves little room for evasion: According to Art. 1 para. 3 Data Act, its territorial scope extends to any connected product or related service placed on the market in the Union, as well as data made available to data recipients in the Union, irrespective of the place of establishment of the respective manufacturers, providers, or data holders.[72] As a result, compliance becomes an imperative for companies operating in the European digital marketplace regardless of their home jurisdiction. In contrast, the preferences of users or data recipients is likely to be less pronounced than in the field of data privacy, even if the choices of commercial users are more likely to be well-thought-out and rational. Given the comparatively low preference for machine data, incentives may be needed to encourage active engagement with the provisions of the Data Act. Education and awareness campaigns, coupled with incentives for data sharing, could encourage greater participation and unlock the full potential of the regulatory framework.

Despite the ambitions of the Data Act, achieving a high level of protection is therefore challenging. Due to weak user preferences, the likelihood of a "Brussels effect" seems less certain compared to the GDPR. In addition, the nuanced regulatory landscape and the flexibility granted to Member States at the level of enforcement may hinder the harmonization of data access standards across the EU. As a result, the emergence of divergent approaches to data regulation could dilute the impact of the Data Act on a global scale. In navigating the complexities of data access and regulatory competition, the balance sought by the Data Act remains elusive. While

---

[70] Similar, for instance, Kerber (2023), pp. 120, 126.

[71] For a detailed account, see Casolari/Taddeo/Turillazzi/Floridi (2023), Möslein (2025).

[72] In more detail Bignami/Resta (2024), p. 10.

the imperative of fair data access is enshrined in law, achieving a harmonized and effective regulatory framework is likely to pose significant challenges.

4.3 *Data Intermediation*

The Data Governance Act (DGA) is another important step in data regulation.[73] It is designed to promote trust in data sharing mechanisms by incentivizing the role of data intermediaries.[74] This legal instrument adopts a regulatory strategy centered on voluntary data sharing, neutrality obligations for data intermediaries, and mechanisms for enforcement aimed at increasing confidence in data exchange processes.[75] At the heart of the DGA lies the concept of incentivizing data intermediaries to act as trustworthy middlemen in the data economy.[76] The regulation of data intermediaries is intended to increase their trustworthiness and ensure the competitiveness of the markets in which they operate.[77] Unlike mandatory sharing models, the DGA opts for a voluntary approach, empowering data intermediaries to engage in data exchange while upholding neutrality obligations. This regulatory approach not only encourages participation but also maintains the autonomy of stakeholders in organizing data exchange according to their preferences. Enforcement mechanisms under the DGA strike a balance between individual and collective interests. While individuals and groups have the right to lodge complaints and seek judicial redress (Art 27 et seq. DGA), penalties for non-compliance are determined by Member States (Art. 34 DGA), reflecting the diverse regulatory landscapes within the European Union. This nuanced approach aims to ensure accountability while accommodating varying national priorities and legal systems, but again, the flexibility granted to Member States may hinder the harmonization of data intermediation standards across the EU.

For data intermediaries, the DGA therefore offers a certain degree of freedom in organizing data exchange, aligning with preferences for flexibility and autonomy, but it also "imposes requirements that not all data intermediaries can satisfy", and it "entrenches a specific techno-organisational form for data intermediation services that may turn out to be economically non-viable".[78] Unlike the marketplace principle observed in other regulations, the establishment of data intermediaries is not

[73] Regulation (EU) 2022/868 of the European Parliament and of the Council of 30 May 2022 on European data governance and amending Regulation (EU) 2018/1724 (Data Governance Act), OJ 2022 L 152/1.

[74] Similar Recital 5 of the Data Governance Act (rules necessary to "increase trust in data sharing by establishing appropriate mechanisms for control by data subjects and data holders over data that relates to them, and in order to address other barriers to a well-functioning and competitive data-driven economy ").

[75] For a practitioners' guide see Schreiber/Pommering/Schoel (2023).

[76] In detail: von Ditfurth (2023).

[77] For a critical assessment see von Ditfurth/Lienemann (2022), pp. 270–295.

[78] Carovano/Finck (2023), 105,830 (questioning whether the rules are necessary and proportionate in light of the freedom to conduct a business).

mandated under the DGA. However, data intermediation services providers that are not established in the Union, but offer their data intermediation services within the Union, have to comply with the requirements of Art. 10 et seq. DGA (cf. Art 11 para. 3 DGA). Moreover, conditions for extraterritorial transfer of non-personal data are delineated, providing guidelines for cross-border data flows within the framework of the DGA.[79] Both data holders and users gravitate towards trustworthy mechanisms of data exchange, reflecting a shared preference for reliability and transparency in the data ecosystem. The DGA's emphasis on incentivizing data intermediaries to uphold neutrality and trustworthiness resonates with stakeholders seeking secure avenues for data exchange.

The dynamics of regulatory competition are difficult to foresee under the DGA. The organizational nature of data intermediaries and the reduced extraterritorial reach introduce complexities that differ from other regulatory frameworks. As such, the DGA serves as a challenging test case for regulatory competition, highlighting the need for adaptive approaches to data governance in a rapidly evolving digital landscape. In sum, the DGA aims to represent a critical step toward fostering trust in data sharing mechanisms by incentivizing the role of data intermediaries. While embracing voluntary data sharing and neutrality obligations, the DGA tries to navigate the complexities of regulatory competition and to present a dynamic framework for data governance in the digital age.

5 Conclusion

In December 2020, Sjef van Erp published an essay entitled "Data Regulation: A Race to…?".[80] Almost 5 years later, the race is still open. The dynamics of regulatory competition in European data law are still difficult to predict, especially with regard to the newly enacted rules of data economy law. As member states seek to attract digital businesses by offering a favorable regulatory environment, there's a delicate balance between harmonization and divergence. Moreover, regulatory competition has different dynamics in different areas of law, including the distinctly different areas of data economy law. The incentives for economic actors to choose particular regulatory regimes depend on the specific characteristics of these different areas of law. In particular, it has been shown that the conditions for regulatory competition are fundamentally different with respect to data access and data intermediation. In addition, regulatory competition in the digital realm follows specific rules because digital technologies take over at least some of the functions of law. To some extent, digital regulatory regimes compete with state legal systems, but they are also embedded in state laws that compete with each other. Legally embedded digital jurisdictions act not only as providers of rules, but also as consumers of rules. Where possible, they

[79] Similar Bignami/Resta (2024), p. 10.

[80] Van Erp (2020), pp. 335–338.

will also choose between different regulatory offerings, acting as a kind of intermediary in the regulatory supply chain. This general observation can be applied to data law, even if it needs to be adapted to the specificities of this area of law and within this area of law.

References

Costello RÁ (2023) The Brussels effect: regulatory stadard setting and constitutional conflicts in post-Brexit privacy law. In: Celeste E, Costello RÁ, Harbinja E, Xanthoulis N (eds) Data protection and digital sovereignty post-Brexit. Hart Publishing, Oxford, p 165

Bernzen A (2023) 'Data Colonialism'? Big Data's Adverse Impact on the (Global) South. In: Hennemann M (ed) Global data strategies. C.H. Beck- Hart- Nomos, München, p 171

Bignami F, Resta G (2024) Extraterritoriality. In: De Gregorio G, Pollicino O, Valcke P (eds) Oxford handbook of digital constitutionalism. Working Paper available at https://papers.ssrn.com/sol3/papers.cfm?abstract_id=4778013, p 10 et seq

Bradford A (2012) The Brussels effect. North-Western University Law Review 107:1

Bradford A (2020) The Brussels effect: how the European Union rules the world. Oxford University Press, Oxford

Calliess G-P, Zumbansen P (2010) Rough Consensus and running code. Hart Publishing, Oxford

Carovano G, Finck M (2023) Regulating data intermediaries: the impact of the data governance act on the EU's data economy. Comput Law Secur Rev 50:105830

Casolari A, Taddeo F, Turillazzi M, Floridi L (2023) How to improve smart contracts in the European Union Data Act. Digital Society 2:9

Cary W (1974) Federalism and corporate law: reflections upon delaware. Yale Law Journal 83:663

Chapdelaine P (2020) Algorithmic personalized pricing. NYU Journal of Law & Business 17:1

Daniels R (1991) Should provinces compete? The case for a competitive corporate law market. McGill LJ130 36:170–179

de Filippi P, Wright A (2018) Blockchain and the law. Harvard University Press, Cambridge

Easterbrook FH (2009) The race for the bottom in corporate governance. Virginia Law Review 95:685

Eckardt M, Kerber W (2024) Property rights theory, bundles of rights on IoT data, and the EU Data Act. Eur J Law Econ 57:113–143

Eidenmüller H (ed) (2013) Regulatory competition in contract law and dispute resolution. C. H.Beck-Hart-Nomos, München

Enriques L, Gatti M (2006) The uneasy case for top-down corporate law harmonization in the European Union. U. Pa. J. Int'l l. 27:939

Feather JP (2013) The information society, 6th edn. Facet Publishing, London

Finck M (2019) Blockchain regulation and governance in Europe. Cambridge University Press, Cambridge

Friedmann L (2019) A history of American Law, 4th edn. Oxford University Press, Oxford

Fuster GG (2014) The emergence of personal data protection as a fundamental right of the EU. Springer, Berlin

Gabor, (2013) Regulatory competition in the internal market. Edward Elgar, Cheltenham

Grundmann S (2001) (2001) Wettbewerb der Regelgeber im Europäischen Gesellschaftsrecht – jedes Marktsegment hat seine Struktur. Zeitschrift Für Unternehmens- und Gesellschaftsrecht (ZGR) 30:783–832

Hadfield GK, Weingast BR (2013) Law without the state. Journal of Law and Courts 1:3

Haupt M (2016) Data is the new oil—a ludicrous proposition, Medium, May 2, 2016. https://medium.com/project-2030/data-is-the-new-oil-a-ludicrous-proposition-1d91bba4f294. Accessed 22 Feb 2025

Hennemann M et al (eds) (2024D) Data act: an introduction. Nomos, Baden-Baden
Hennemann M (2020) Wettbewerb der Datenschutzrechtsordnungen. Rabel J Comp Int Priv Law 84:864–895
Hennemann M (ed) (2023G) Global data strategies. C.H Beck, München
Hennemann M, Zeiter A (2023) The regulatory level playing field(s)—global compliance efforts of and global standard-setting by international corporations. In: Hennemann M (ed) Global data strategies. C.H. Beck, München
Hess B (2016) The private-public divide in international dispute resolution, Recueil des Cours
Hornuf L (2012) Regulatory competition in European Corporate and Capital Markets Law, Intersentia, Cambridge and Antwerp
Kerber W (2023) Governance of IoT data: why the EU data act will not fulfill its objectives. GRUR Int 72:120
Kieninger E-M (2002) Wettbewerb der Privatrechtsordnungen im Europäischen Binnenmarkt. Mohr Siebeck, Tübingen
Lessig L (2000) Code is law: on liberty in cyberspace. Harvard Magazine. https://harvardmagazine.com/2000/01/code-is-law-html. Accessed 22 Feb 2025
Lessig L (1999) Code and other laws of cyberspace. Basic Books, New York
Lis D, Gelhaar J, Otto B (2023) Data strategy and policies: the role of data governance in data ecosystems. In: Caballero I, Piattini M (eds) Data governance. Springer, Heidelberg, p 27
Long C (2019) 'What do Wyoming's 13 new blockchain laws mean?'. Forbes, 4 March 2019. https://www.forbes.com/sites/caitlinlong/2019/03/04/what-do-wyomings-new-blockchainlaws-mean/. Accessed 25 Feb 2025
Macey J, Miller G (1987) Toward and interest group theory of delaware corporate law. Texas L Rev. 65:469
Mahoney JF (1966) Backsliding convert: woodrow wilson and the "seven sisters." Am Q 18:71
Mannion C (2020) Data imperialism: the GDPR's disastrous impact on Africa's E-commerce markets. Vanderbilt J Transnatl Law 53:685
Martini M, Möslein F, Rostalski F (eds) (2024) Recht der Digitalisierung. Nomos, Baden-Baden
Baker RS, Dodd WE (ed) (1925) Minutes of Assembly of New Jersey, Vol. II, in Public Papers of Woodrow Wilson. Reprint of the original from January 17, 1911
Mitrou L (2017) The general data protection regulation: a law for the digital age? In: Synodinou T-E et al (eds) EU internet law. Springer, Heidelberg, p 19
Jn M (2020) Delaware's Global Competitiveness. Iowa L Rev 106:1683
Möslein F (2013) Regulatory competition between public and private rules. In: Eidenmüller H (ed) Regulatory competition in contract law and dispute resolution. C.H. Beck, München, p 160
Möslein F (2019) Conflicts of laws and codes: defining the boundaries of digital jurisdictions. In Hacker P, Lianos J, G Dimitropoulos G, Eich S (eds) Regulating blockchain. Techno-social and legal challenges. Oxford University Press, Oxford, p 275.
Möslein F (2021) Smart contracts and civil law challenges. In: Chiu I, Deipenbrock G (eds) Routledge handbook of financial technology and law. Routledge, London, p 27
Möslein F (2024) Contract governance in the network economy. Eur Bus Law Rev 35:383–402
Möslein F (2025) Art. 36. In: Czychowski C, Lettl T, Steinrötter B (eds) Data act. C.H. Beck, München
Möslein F, Renner M (2023) Systemic failure and systemic change in private and business law. Eur Bus Law Rev 34:941
Murphy DD (2004) The business dynamics of global regulatory competition. In: Vogel D, Kagan R (eds) Dynamics of regulatory change: how globalization affects national regulatory policies. University of California Press, Berkeley, p 84
Murphy DW (2006) The structure of regulatory competition. Oxford University Press, Oxford
Note, (1969) Law for sale: a study of the delaware corporation law of 1967. U Pa l Rev 117:861
O'Hara EA, Ribstein L (2009) The law market. Oxford University Press, Oxford
Palmer M (2006) Data is the new oil. ANA Marketing Maestos, Nov. 3, 2006. http://ana.blogs.com/

Reidenberg JR (1998) Lex informatica: the formulation of information policy rules through technology. Texas Law Rev 76:553
Report of the Commission to Revise the Corporation Laws of New Jersey, 1917
Romano R (1985) Law as a product: some pieces of the incorporation puzzle. JLEO 1:225
Rühl G (2013) Regulatory competition in contract law: empirical evidence and normative implication. Eur Rev Contract Law 9:61
Rustad ML, Koenig TH (2019) Towards a global data privacy standard. Fla L Rev 71:365
Sanga S (2022) The origins of the market for corporate law. Am Law Econ Rev 24:369
Scholz LH (2020) Big data is not big oil: the role of analogy in the law of new technologies. Tenn L Rev 86:863
Schön W (2005) Playing different games? Regulatory competition in tax and company law compared. Common Market Law Review 42:331
Schreiber K, Pommering P, Schoel P (2023) New data governance act. C. Beck, München
Scott J (2014a) 1 Extraterritoriality and territorial extension in EU law. Am J Comp L 62:87
Scott J (2014b) 2 The new EU extraterritoriality. CML Rev. 51:1343
Stark J (2019) Law for sale—a philosophical critique of regulatory competition. Oxford University Press, Oxford
Streinz T (2021) The evolution of European data law. In: Craig P, de Búrca G (eds) The evolution of EU law, 3rd edn. Oxford University Press, Oxford, p 902
Thon M (2020) Transnationaler Datenschutz: Das Internationale Datenprivatrecht der DS-GVO. Rabel J Comp Int Priv Law 84:24–61
Truli E (2018) The General data protection regulation and civil liability. In: Bakhoum M et al (eds) Personal data in competition, consumer protection and intellectual property: towards a holistic approach? Springer, Heidelberg, pp 303–329
van Erp S (2020) Data regulation: a race to…? Eur J Comp Law Gov 7:335–338
Voigt P, von dem Bussche A (2017) The EU general data protection regulation (GDPR). Springer, Berlin
von Ditfurth L (2023) Datenmärkte, Datenintermediäre und der data governance act. De Gruyter, Berlin
von Ditfurth L, Lienemann G (2022) The data governance act:—promoting or restricting data intermediaries? Compet Regul Netw Ind 23:270–295
Webster F (2014) Theories of the information society, 4th edn. Routledge, Abingdon
Weitzman H (2022) What's the matter with delaware. Princeton University Press, Princeton
Werbach K, Cornell N (2017) Contracts ex machina. Duke Law J 76:313
Winter R (1977) State law, shareholder protection, and the theory of the corporation. J Leg Stud 6:251

Prof. Dr. Florian Möslein, LL.M. (London) is a Professor of Law at the Philipps-University Marburg where he teaches Contract Law, Company Law and Capital Markets Law. Before Philipps-University Marburg, he was a Professor at the University of Bremen and an Associate Professor at the University of St. Gallen.

Data Governance in Fragile Contexts: Ukraine's Dilemma of Security vs. Transparency

Anna Romandash

Abstract Prior to the 2022 Russia's invasion, Ukraine made significant progress in open government, Internet Governance, and effective data governance, ranking among the leaders in Open Data and Global Data Barometers. However, in 2022, the country's approach to data governance shifted. During the early weeks of Russia's full-scale invasion, Ukraine's government closed most of its data registries and changed relevant legislation to introduce more data regulations and restrictions. This strategy faced severe criticism from the media, tech sector, and civil society. Under pressure, the government is reversing some of its earlier restrictions, which strongly affected transparency and monitoring capacities of various watchdogs and active citizens in the country; and it is also readjusting its strategy toward open government. However, Ukraine has not returned to its previous approach of transparent and collaborative data governance, and the courts side with the legislators when it comes to access to certain datasets. State vulnerability, extreme conditions, and the usage of open data by the enemy are often cited as the main reasons for such restrictions. This research examines the legal framework for the current state of affairs and compares Ukraine's previous data governance model with the one proposed by the legislators amid the Russo-Ukrainian war. Further, the work analyzes implications for different state institutions and civil society amid the ongoing tensions with the government. The paper provides an overview of approaches recommended by the relevant experts for a better balance between transparency and security. The conclusions of the research highlight important parallels and lessons learned for other similar environments where changing data governance models are being considered under similar conditions, and how inclusivity and privacy are maintained while safety and data regulations are preserved.

Keywords Data maturity · Digital transformation · Martial law · Open data · Registries · Russian war · Transparency · Ukraine

---

A. Romandash (✉)
Carr-Ryan Center for Human Rights Policy, Harvard University, Cambridge, USA
e-mail: arnika4@gmail.com

J. Drexl et al. (eds.), *Comparative Data Law*, MPI Studies on Intellectual Property and Competition Law 32, https://doi.org/10.1007/978-3-031-91401-0_2

1 Introduction

Open governance transformations have been among some of the major successes of Ukraine's reforms from 2015 to 2022. This period was marked by a significant number of legislative and social changes aimed at democratizing the country and paving the way for closer cooperation between the country and the European Union. In less than 10 years, Ukraine introduced a set of laws, practices, and platforms aimed at facilitating the publication and accessibility of public data, as well as simplified procedures for data requests by regular citizens.[1] Data reform, implemented in parallel with other important reforms such as state decentralization, allowed for more transparency[2] in the decision-making process and greater accountability of public bodies on the national, regional, and local levels.

The Russian invasion in 2022 made a profound impact on the state of open data in Ukraine. After February 24, 2022, when Russia launched its full-scale war against Ukraine, Ukrainian authorities decided to close various data registries and limit access to different types of data relevant for public procurement and other tracking and monitoring processes.[3] Due to civil society pressure,[4] different datasets are now being returned to public access, although to a limited extent as before 2022. The purpose of keeping certain datasets closed by the authorities is to protect them from being hacked or stolen by Russia.

The system of open data in Ukraine remains one of the most advanced in Europe even during a full-scale war with Russia. Even with limited access to registries, data processing tools and services are working.[5] However, the arbitrary nature of their closure as well as the initial lack of clear indicators on which data to close and which to continue publishing led to criticisms from civil society – in addition to the fact that different sets of data which were not requested to be taken down have been taken away from public access. Given the discrepancies which exist between the data openness and the legal regulations, this research aims to study the notion of arbitrary data shutdowns and data management, and the legal framework behind it. It provides an overview of the way data is governed in Ukraine and the changes in the legal developments as a consequence of Russian full-scale invasion. With a focus on different actors such as state institutions, the media, and civil society organizations, the research addresses the trade-off between transparency and security, and ways forward in dealing with the controversies which arise regarding state-led data management.

[1] Iuksel (2020), 319–328.

[2] Dickinson (2024).

[3] Ianitskyi (2022).

[4] Institute of Mass Information (2023).

[5] OSCE (2023).

2 Pre-Invasion Open Data

Before the 2022 Russian invasion, Ukraine was among the European leaders in open data. In 2015, Ukrainian authorities initiated an open data reform and launched the Unified State Open Data Web Portal in the following year. The portal marked the official start of local self-government bodies' data disclosure.[6] The portal, as well as relevant reforms, specified a set of data that was to be published by national, regional, and local authorities in an accessible and open way, so interested citizens would be able to track down government spending, monitor public servants' activities, and have a direct channel for communication with relevant authorities on different levels. In 2019, the Ukrainian government created the Ministry of Digital Transformation, which became responsible for open data in Ukraine, overseeing that different government bodies submit and publish the data for public access.[7] Before the Russian full-scale invasion, the concept of open data was governed by the principle of openness by default when all public information can be made available upon request or published in an open data format.

Already in 2020, up to 4.9 million Ukrainians used services based on open data every month such as checking data on public transport (1.2 million users), anti-corruption activities (0.9 million users), and other topics such as legislation.[8]For instance, users were able to verify data on construction companies before purchasing any housing built by them, or get information on water pollution levels in rivers near their residences. During the pandemic, state-led open data was used by Ukrainians to track down alternatives for different medications, locations for finding them, and costs. Additional services and data sets are being added based on the requests from the citizens – for example, Ukraine released data on available shelters which was used by residents to check safe locations near their homes amid the Russian-Ukrainian war.

In 2020, Ukraine entered the Open Data Maturity rating for the first time and was placed 17th in Europe.[9] Its data maturity level was 84% at the time, compared to an average of 78% in Europe. In 2021, Ukraine made the biggest jump among its European competitors and took sixth place in the region.[10] The top five then included France, Ireland, Spain, Poland, and Estonia. The latter, which remains the European leader in the development of a digital state, has been used as a model by Ukraine.

In 2022, despite the full-scale invasion, Ukraine (97%) achieved the second-highest open data maturity rating after France (97.5%), scoring the best in areas such as policy, impact, portal, and quality of data. For the EU countries, the average data maturity rating was 79%.[11] In 2023, Ukraine kept its high position as a country with

[6] Maddison (2018).

[7] Юрій (2023).

[8] Самоходський et al. (n.d.) (2023).

[9] European Data (2022).

[10] Open Stories (2021).

[11] Publications Office of the EU (2023a, b).

the third-highest data maturity in Europe (96%).[12] The high position highlights a decline of Ukraine's data maturity due to data registry closures, but showcases that it still scores highly in comparison to other, less open, European countries.

In Estonia, which is the European leader in the development of a digital state, and which has been used as a model by Ukraine, the field of open data has been regulated since 2012. There is a special catalog of open data in the country, which includes recommendations on the datasets to be published by ministries and state institutions. Open catalogs of municipal data are also available in the largest cities such as Tallinn, Tartu, and Pärnu. In the Estonian capital, an open database contains information on public transport, road works, and planning registers.[13]

3 Open Data in Ukrainian Law

Ukrainian legislation uses the term "public information in the form of open data". The concept of "public information" and its administrators are clearly defined by the relevant law "On access to public information" from 2011. According to the law, public information in the form of open data is public information in a format that allows its automated processing by electronic means, free access to it, as well as its further use.[14]

Managers of information are obliged to provide public information in the form of open data upon request, publish and regularly update it on the unified state web portal of open data and on their websites. Any person may freely copy, publish, distribute, use, including for commercial purposes, in combination with other information or by including it in their own product, public information in the form of open data with a mandatory reference to the source of obtaining such information. The key feature of public information in the form of open data is its digital format and the possibility of automated processing by electronic means. Open data does not include responses to requests in the form of paper letters, scanned documents, tables, graphs, dashboards, interactive maps posted on websites. In accordance with Article 13 of the Law of Ukraine "On Access to Public Information", the managers of the information are subjects of power, in particular, bodies of legislative, executive and judicial power, bodies of local self-government and others; and legal entities financed from the state and regional budgets, and so on. Their key duties are providing public information in the form of open data upon request and publishing and regularly updating it through regional and the national platform.[15]

In 2015, the Cabinet of Ministers, implementing the law "On access to public information", approved the Regulation on data sets that are subject to publication in the form of open data. It has a long list of data that must be published and periodically

[12] Publications Office of the EU (2023a, b).

[13] Ardhaninggar (2023).

[14] Самоходський et al. (n.d.) (2023).

[15] Юрій (2023).

updated, sorted by managers. This list is not exhaustive, and it includes more than 1000 sets for 65 central authorities, state enterprises, local governments, and other administrators.[16] The list is constantly being updated by the Ministry of Digital Transformation, which monitors the Unified State Open Data Web Portal. Various open data initiatives in Ukraine are demanding that access to all data that is not specifically restricted by the law should be available online in a machine-readable format.[17] There is a significant disparity between what is required to be published by the law and the open data that is regularly updated by different authorities; for example, authorities in the regional centers have only published or updated 25.1% of datasets after the 2022 Russian invasion.[18]

4 Open Data Used in Everyday Life in Ukraine

Some of the most popular open-data services in Ukraine were focused on public procurement – such as the system ProZorro, which allowed carrying out all public procurement procedures online through a transparent process accessible to everyone. The service minimized the potential for corruption while spending public money through open data. As a follow-up to this platform, another one was created called DoZorro, which allowed journalists to discuss public procurement procedures and investigate potential violations.[19]

Other practical uses of open data services were focused on public transportation – such as tracking municipal transport in different cities or other transport-related information. Businesses were granted opportunities to minimize corruption risks and financial losses by verifying counterparts, automating document flow, and preparing reports automatically. This progress was made possible through services such as YouControl, Opendatabot, Liga Contr Agent, Ring, Vkursi.Pro, and others. These use the open data provided by government institutions and make it easily accessible for average users as well as showcase links and connections between different datasets. With these tools, journalists and civil society activists were able to conduct investigations and showcase discrepancies in public spending as well as request more information from state authorities. The YouControl and Lex platforms allowed tracking down ownership of different enterprises as well as collect court decisions and different editions of legal acts.[20]

Additionally, many investigative journalistic projects rely on information and data from services like the Clarity Project (verifying participants in public procurement) or services analyzing the use of budget funds and other relevant data. The recent decision to restrict access to such vital information highlights the impact of the

[16] State Statistics Service of Ukraine (n.d.).
[17] Oleksiyuk (2023).
[18] Transparent Cities (2023).
[19] Open Stories (2021).
[20] Самоходський et al. (n.d.) (2023).

ongoing conflict on transparency and open data initiatives in Ukraine. According to the Cabinet of Ministers, the economic impact from the field of open data before the Russian full-scale invasion amounted to about 1% of the GDP and grew annually.[21]

5 Open Data Closures Amid the Full-Scale War

Due to the large-scale war with Russia, the government has chosen to limit access to data that was previously open and widely used by Ukrainians, journalists, and specific industries. This development has raised concerns about the current situation. Citizens expressed criticisms for the lack of ability to check counterparties and difficulties with market analysis and partner search as well as increased costs of data collection and the deterioration of the efficiency of standard business processes due to lack of relevant public data.[22]

In February 2022, the state closed the Unified Open Data Portal for security reasons. Later, on March 12, the Cabinet of Ministers adopted a resolution suspending the operation of information and communication systems, electronic communication systems, and public electronic registers for the period of martial law; the suspension included the operation of the Unified State Open Data Web Portal. Similar measures took place regarding other data registries such as the platform run by the National Agency for the Prevention of Corruption, which had a register of corrupt individuals; or the platform by the Ministry of Justice with a single state register containing information on all business entities. The closures of different datasets were linked to the martial law that came into effect on February 24, 2022 – the launch of the Russian full-scale invasion.[23] According to Article 64 of the Constitution of Ukraine, "In the conditions of war or state of emergency, separate restrictions of rights and freedoms may be established with the indication of the period of validity of these restrictions". Such restrictions may also apply to information rights, i.e. access to public information. In the Law of Ukraine "On the Legal Regime of Martial Law", there are no direct references to restricting access to public information, including in the form of open data. However, the abovementioned resolution from March of 2022 stated that during martial law, the state and other state-related institutions may stop or limit the publication and operation of open data registries and platforms.[24] In December 2022, an amendment was made to this Resolution, which limits such discretion to territories where active hostilities are being conducted or temporarily occupied territories. The Ministry of Reintegration of temporarily occupied territories is the one providing the list of the areas where the data's publication may be limited. With two more resolutions, the government limited the publication of data in the field of procurement, access to the land cadaster, registers and services of the Ministry

---

[21] Економічна Правда (2023).

[22] Огороднік/Балюк (2023).

[23] Вишня (2023).

[24] Балюк/Огороднік (2023).

of Justice and other information systems; these were followed by the April 2022 order from the Ministry of Justice on the suspension of the publication of open data administered by this ministry. The publication of the Ministry's data was restored in January 2023.[25]

Access to the Unified Register of Court Decisions was restored in June of 2022, and access to the Unified State Open Data Web Portal was also restricted until August of 2022. The Ministry of Digital Transformation developed a resolution to better regulate which data can and cannot be published in cases of martial law and state emergency[26]; the Ministry also presented its vision for further developing open data registries. According to it, by 2026, the Ministry plans to add about 100 new data sets that must be made public, conduct training for 5,000 civil servants, and provide grant support to 15 services based on open data.[27] However, as mentioned above, regional and municipal agencies as well as state institutions still abstained from publishing certain datasets citing lack of human resources, lack of understanding of the new regulations, and challenges collecting the data in the war situation.[28]

After the access to the Unified Open Data Portal was restored in August 2022, the Ministry of Digital Transformation opened public discussions on changes to the legislation to clarify which data should and should not be published in the context of war and under martial law. As a result of these discussions, local governments and municipalities were advised not to publish eight sets which contained such information like the data on deputies of local councils, including contact information and reception schedule, the registry of addresses, the data on issued passports, the data on the location of special equipment, which is used for the provision of communal services, landscaping, construction and repair work, the urban cadaster data, in particular geospatial data, the data which contains territory planning schemes of regions, territory planning schemes of districts, general plans of settlements, territory zoning plans, detailed territory plans, urban planning documentation of territorial communities, their projects (in accordance with the powers), the data with the register of town planning conditions and restrictions, and the data on the location of video surveillance cameras that are in communal ownership.[29]

Other data sets were not affected by the changes, and the regional, municipal, and state institutions are required to publish them. However, by the beginning of 2023, only four of the eighteen regional centers posted or updated more than 20 data sets out of 57 mandatory ones. The average indicator of the state of data publication by all regions is 25.1%.[30] Data on local council members are most often published, including contact information and reception schedule; electronic petitions, as well as rollcall voting results of deputies at plenary sessions. Five sets have not been

[25] Огороднік/Балюк (2023).

[26] Федоров (2022).

[27] Юридична Газета (2024).

[28] Захаров (2022).

[29] Латиш (2022).

[30] Балюк/Огороднік (2023).

released (or updated by 2023) by any city council.[31] These are data on the location of charging stations for electric vehicles; operational characteristics of buildings of communal enterprises, institutions and organizations in which energy management systems have been implemented; information about fairs; data on imposed fines for violation of parking rules; issued permits for carrying out improvement and renovation objects. Before the start of the full-scale war, there were about 2.7 million people with disabilities in Ukraine. Due to the ongoing Russian war, their number is constantly increasing. However, only one region published data on the accessibility of buildings for persons with disabilities and other groups with reduced mobility. The city councils of three other regions have partially published the data.[32] At the same time, such information could be useful for people with temporary health problems, pregnant women, elderly people and people with baby carriages.

Despite the urgent need of people to know the addresses of shelters, not all local officials have been able to centrally collect and publicize such information. Data on the location of civil defense protective structures was made public by nine regions. The publication of separate data sets could also facilitate the choice of a new residence for internally displaced persons. For example, the apartment registration data made it possible to monitor the current state of the queue for improvement of living conditions. However, only four regions updated this information by 2023. Importantly, both regions nearer and farther from the frontline showed low levels of data sets publications, so relative distance from the frontline did not contribute to the greater publication of open data.[33] The reasoning for limited publications is different; some stem from the lack of understanding of the legislative changes, and others stem from the lack of collected data itself. For example, there are cases when the needed data is simply not collected, and there are also instances when the data is being collected, but not released publicly. There are also structural problems – such as the necessity to balance openness and transparency with security concerns, which are being addressed through ongoing public discussions between civil society and authorities in Ukraine.

5.1 Challenges to Open Data Publication on the Regional Level

Despite the legal changes and the public debates, many local and regional policymakers cite legal ambiguity and consequential security risks as a reason for not disclosing certain data.[34] The administrators are not ready to take responsibility for the publication of sets that could potentially adversely affect the security situation. For example, the location of special equipment can be used by the enemy for potential

[31] Вишня (2023).

[32] Вишня (2023).

[33] Юрій (2023).

[34] Захаров (2022).

missile strikes, and information about fairs can indicate places where civilians are gathered. Secondly, in connection with the active phase of the war, mass movements of people took place both within the state and abroad. On the ground, there are not always enough qualified specialists to process, publish and update data. The general priorities of cities have also changed: resources have been redirected to support defense capability, social security, infrastructure preservation, etc. Work in the field of open data took a back seat. Lack of regular access to the Internet and electricity is also among the challenges voiced.[35]

5.2 *Improving the Open Data Strategy for Ukraine Amid War*

Coordinated communication between all stakeholders and a clear data handling policy during martial law could improve the situation. Both users and managers must share an understanding of how to work with the data. Temporarily restricting access to certain information during wartime may be justified and must be explained and meet the criteria for determining security-sensitive information. Therefore, it is necessary to review the approach of chaotic closure of access to information and be guided by the following principles outlined by Ukrainian civil society organizations data experts. These can help address chaotic data closures by explaining what datasets need to be disclosed and according to what principles. The principles include **Motivation:** access restriction should be accompanied by a description of specific risks, scenarios of their implementation and ways of managing them. **Proportionality:** only the information that creates the described risks can be restricted. **Completeness and Systematics:** Limitations cannot apply to information available in other public sources or those that have been previously made public. Managers on the ground should also be aware of their responsibility. In order to assess the potential harm from publication, it is important to carry out the three-fold test provided for by Ukrainian legislation. Unreasonable restriction of access or closing of pages of information managers is not about data protection, but about violation of the law. Information managers must urgently restore access to priority data sets to the extent that security is compromised and justify decisions about data that cannot be released during wartime. Open data makes urban communities more resilient to the challenges of war. For example, despite the war, public transport routes appeared in real time in the "Kyiv Digital" application, as well as a new electronic registration system for educational institutions in Drohobych. They became possible thanks to open data.[36] Similarly, people could track the locations of shelters and continue receiving other governmental services and information through open data platforms. Therefore, it is important to return to the principle of "openness by default" today, taking into account all the risks.[37]

[35] Доступ До Правди (2022).

[36] Diya (n.d).

[37] OSCE (2023).

5.3 *How to Resume Work with Open Data*

The existing practice of shutting down data portals without clear guidance and explanations risks decreasing trust and works against a transparent recovery system. Even in the conditions of war, the public expects to be able to check the ownership of the business, government spending, and other crucial information. Therefore, it is crucial to adapt already existing practices of openness to the conditions of war.[38] This includes restoring access to all data that would ensure the transparency of the restoration process. Access must be provided in accordance with the principles set forth in Art. 6 of the Law of Ukraine "On Access to Public Information", i.e., the state can hide only those information and datasets, the harm from the disclosure of which exceeds the public interest in them. Further, it is recommended to implement new recovery management tools using the principle of "openness by default". Such tools include the already established Register of Damaged and Destroyed Property and the Electronic Reconstruction Management System, which is still being developed. In turn, civil society should put pressure on the country's political leadership and call on international partners to do the same. High-ranking officials should realize that greater transparency of state bodies ensures better manageability and the ability to respond to problems in a timely manner. Ukraine needs to restore the infrastructure of transparency in the same way that it needs to restore the infrastructure of energy and transport. Transparency will hold politicians and officials accountable for their actions almost instantly and allow society to monitor potential abuses. The chance for the government to retain the trust of citizens and its legitimacy during reconstruction under such conditions will be much higher. To conclude, it is crucial to understand the dilemma between security and transparency, which puts limitations on data openness in the country. At the same time, there is a need for pushing for more transparency in accordance with the points mentioned above to guarantee data accessibility and continuous data gathering.

6 Conclusion

Ukraine's journey towards open governance reforms from 2015 to 2022 showcased remarkable strides in democratization and transparency. However, the full-scale invasion by Russia in 2022 brought about a significant shift in the state of open data in Ukraine. The government's decision to close various data registries and limit access was driven by security concerns, aiming to protect sensitive information from potential exploitation by the aggressor. Despite civil society pressure, data sets were selectively returned to public access, albeit to a limited extent, and certain datasets remained restricted.

This paper analyzed the legal framework surrounding the changes in data governance during martial law, comparing Ukraine's current model with its pre-invasion

[38] Samokhodskyi (2023).

approach. The study delved into the implications for state institutions, civil society, and the broader public, examining challenges faced in the management and publication of open data during war. Lessons learned from Ukraine's experience offer insights into balancing transparency and security in fragile contexts, emphasizing the importance of clear communication, proportionate restrictions, and adherence to principles of openness.

Recommendations for improving the open data strategy amid war include developing a clear data handling policy, maintaining coordination between stakeholders, and justifying access restrictions based on specific risks. The paper emphasizes the need for local administrators to be aware of their responsibilities and advocates for a return to the principle of "openness by default." Resuming work with open data involves adapting existing practices to the conditions of war, restoring access to crucial datasets, and implementing new recovery management tools.

As Ukraine navigates the challenges of post-war reconstruction, transparency and openness in governance will play a pivotal role in rebuilding trust and ensuring accountability. The successful restoration of the infrastructure of transparency is essential for monitoring government actions, preventing abuses, and fostering public confidence in the reconstruction process.

References

Ardhaninggar N (2023) E-government success stories: learning from Denmark and Estonia. Modern Diplomacy. https://moderndiplomacy.eu/2023/12/05/e-government-success-stories-learning-from-denmark-and-estonia/. Accessed 22 Feb 2025

Dickinson P (2024) Wartime Ukraine ranks among world's top performers in anti-corruption index. Atlantic Council. https://www.atlanticcouncil.org/blogs/ukrainealert/wartime-ukraine-ranks-among-worlds-top-performers-in-anti-corruption-index/. Accessed 22 Feb 2025

State Statistics Service of Ukraine (n.d.) Datasets. https://stat.gov.ua/en/datasets. Accessed 22 Feb 2025

Diya (n.d.) How open data helps Ukrainians during war. https://diia.data.gov.ua/info-center/yak-vidkriti-dani-dopomagayut-ukrayincyam-pid-chas-vijni. Accessed 22 Feb 2025

Ianitskyi A (2022) Ukraine's transparency dilemma. Institute for War and Peace Reporting. https://iwpr.net/global-voices/ukraines-transparency-dilemma. Accessed 22 Feb 2025

Ingram G, Vora P (2024) Ukraine: digital resilience in a time of war. Brookings. https://www.brookings.edu/articles/ukraine-digital-resilience-in-a-time-of-war/. Accessed 22 Feb 2025

Iuksel G (2020) Use of open data in Ukraine: some important aspects. Revista San Gregorio 42(1):319–328. https://avesis.istanbul.edu.tr/yayin/2b6bd801-7343-468f-bb96-883db1927092/use-of-open-data-in-ukraine-some-important-aspects. Accessed 22 Feb 2025

Maddison J (2018) How Ukraine became an open data pioneer. Open Data Institute. https://theodi.org/news-and-events/blog/how-ukraine-became-an-open-data-pioneer/. Accessed 22 Feb 2025

Oleksiyuk T (2023) The importance of transparency: reconstruction in Ukraine. Visegrad Insight. https://visegradinsight.eu/the-importance-of-transparency-reconstruction-in-ukraine/. Accessed 22 Feb 2025

Open Data (n.d.) Open government partnership. https://www.opengovpartnership.org/members/romania/commitments/RO0065/. Accessed 22 Feb 2025

OSCE (2023) How open data helps Ukrainians navigate times of war. https://www.osce.org/oceea/560511. Accessed 22 Feb 2025

Publications Office of the EU (2023) Open data in Europe 2023. https://data.europa.eu/en/publications/open-data-maturity/2023. Accessed 22 Feb 2025

Publications Office of the EU (2023) Open data maturity report 2022: Countries' perspectives on open data quality. https://data.europa.eu/en/publications/datastories/open-data-maturity-report-2022-countries-perspectives-open-data-quality. Accessed 22 Feb 2025

UNDP (2017) Open data readiness assessment Ukraine. https://www.undp.org/ukraine/publications/open-data-readiness-assessment-ukraine. Accessed 22 Feb 2025

Samokhodskyi I (2023) Can open data form the basis for a transparent recovery process in Ukraine? Royal United Services Institute. https://www.rusi.org/explore-our-research/publications/commentary/can-open-data-form-basis-transparent-recovery-process-ukraine. Accessed 22 Feb 2025

European Data (2022) The acceleration of open data practices in Ukraine. https://data.europa.eu/en/publications/datastories/acceleration-open-data-practices-ukraine#:~:text=Despite%20being%20a%20particularly%20new,European%20countries%20(Figure%201). Accessed 22 Feb 2025

Institute of Mass Information (2023) The public demands that the authorities open state registers and restore access to public information. https://imi.org.ua/en/news/the-public-demands-that-the-authorities-open-state-registers-and-restore-access-to-public-i51230. Accessed 22 Feb 2025

OpenStories (2021) Through the power of the people: empowering citizen watchdogs. https://www.ogpstories.org/through-the-power-of-the-people-empowering-citizen-watchdogs/. Accessed 22 Feb 2025

Odessa Journal (2021) Ukraine is among the top 6 European countries in the ranking of open data. https://odessa-journal.com/public/ukraine-is-among-the-top-6-european-countries-in-the-ranking-of-open-data. Accessed 22 Feb 2025

Балюк Б, Огороднік О (2023) Відкриті дані під час війни. Скільки їх оприлюднюють у містах і чому це важливо. Texty. https://texty.org.ua/articles/108805/vidkryti-dani-pid-chas-vijny-skilky-yikh-opryljudnjujut-u-mistakh-i-chomu-tse-vazhlyvo/. Accessed 22 Feb 2025

Вишня Г (2023) Відкриті дані під час війни: що вони дають для розуміння теперішнього і майбутнього. Радіо Свобода. https://www.radiosvoboda.org/a/vidkryti-dani-pid-chas-viyny-vplyv-vykorystannya/32323255.html. Accessed 22 Feb 2025

Економічна Правда (2023) Війна знищила третину ВВП України. Як зараз виглядає економіка? https://www.epravda.com.ua/weeklycharts/2023/05/4/699766/. Accessed 22 Feb 2025

Доступ До Правди (2022) «Закриті» відкриті дані: яка ситуація з даними під час війни. https://dostup.pravda.com.ua/news/publications/zakryti-vidkryti-dani-iaka-sytuatsiia-z-danymy-pid-chas-viiny. Accessed 22 Feb 2025

Захаров К (2022) Відкриті дані під час війни: питання, що потребує відповіді. Vox Ukraine. https://voxukraine.org/vidkryti-dani-pid-chas-vijny-pytannya-shho-potrebuye-vidpovidi. Accessed 22 Feb 2025

Латиш І (2022) "Приходьте після війни". В яких регіонах та містах влада сховалась у кущі? Чесно. https://www.chesno.org/post/5301/. Accessed 22 Feb 2025

Мінцифра презентувала візію розвитку відкритих даних в Україні. (2024) Юридична Газета. https://yur-gazeta.com/golovna/mincifra-prezentuvala-viziyu-rozvitku-vidkritih-danih-v-ukrayini.html. Accessed 22 Feb 2025

Огороднік О & Балюк Б (2023) Відкриті дані міст в умовах війни: результати дослідження. Transparent Cities. https://transparentcities.in.ua/articles/vidkryti-dani-mist-v-umovakh-viiny-rezultaty-doslidzhennia. Accessed 22 Feb 2025

Самоходський І, Лебедєв Д & Ткаченко Р (n.d.). Політика відкритих даних. Офіс фективного Регулювання BRDO. https://brdo.com.ua/wp-content/uploads/2024/06/ZK-Polityka-vidkrytyh-danyh.pdf. Accessed 22 Feb 2025

Transparent Cities (2023) Українські міста публікують лише 25% наборів відкритих даних – результати дослідження. https://transparentcities.in.ua/news/ukrainski-mista-publikuiut-lyshe-25-naboriv-vidkrytykh-danykh--rezultaty-doslidzhennia. Accessed 22 Feb 2025

Федоров М (2022) Відкриті дані зараз та їх роль у післявоєнному відновленні України. Економічна Правда. https://www.epravda.com.ua/columns/2022/12/26/695423. Accessed 22 Feb 2025

Юрій П (2023) Публічна інформація у формі відкритих даних в умовах воєнного стану: специфіка, парадокси, поради. Центр Демократії Та Верховенства Права. https://cedem.org.ua/analytics/vidkryti-dani-voyenyi-stan/. Accessed 22 Feb 2025

Anna Romandash is an award-winning journalist from Ukraine. Romandash is an author of Women of Ukraine: Reportages from the War and Beyond. She is a researcher with expertise in transparency, democratization, and human rights. Romandash is recognized for impactful work by prestigious organizations like UNESCO, G20, and the Council of Europe. She has extensive experience in producing research, media content, and managing international teams for democracy-focused initiatives across Europe and Central Asia. Romandash is a 2024–2025 Tech and Ethics Fellow at the Carr-Ryan Center for Human Rights Policy at Harvard University, and a Research Affiliate at the Mgrublian Center for Human Rights at Claremont McKenna College.

Data Processing on Crowdsourcing Platforms: A Comparison Between Germany and the United States

Sina Häusler and Lars Hornuf

Abstract The processing of personal data has become commonplace in most areas of social life, steadily increasing with the emergence of the Internet of Things and the widespread use of people analytics and artificial intelligence. In many situations, disclosure of personal data is voluntary and individuals often receive something from the data processor that is beneficial to them. For example, there are various payback card programs where individuals disclose their spending habits and receive a discount later when making a purchase. Accepting a company's privacy statement is also often a prerequisite for a customer to be able to use a particular service. Under the privacy calculation model, individuals in such situations either disclose their personal information to achieve an expected benefit or refrain from disclosing it to avoid potential costs associated with a data breach. The individual's decision regarding the disclosure of personal data will then depend on the outcome of this careful cost–benefit analysis.

1 Introduction

The processing of personal data has become commonplace in most areas of social life, steadily increasing with the emergence of the Internet of Things and the widespread use of people analytics and artificial intelligence. In many situations, disclosure of personal data is voluntary and individuals often receive something from the data

This chapter builds on the authors' previous findings and arguments. Particularly worth mentioning here are: Dorfleitner, Hornuf, Kreppmeier, 2023, 33; Hornuf, Mangold, Yang, 2023, 19; Hornuf, Vrankar, 2022, 553. This research project received financial support from the Hans Böckler Foundation.

S. Häusler (✉) · L. Hornuf
Chair of Business Administration, Esp. Finance and Financial Technology, Dresden University of Technology, Dresden, Germany
e-mail: sina.haeusler@tu-dresden.de

L. Hornuf
e-mail: lars.hornuf@tu-dresden.de

J. Drexl et al. (eds.), *Comparative Data Law*, MPI Studies on Intellectual Property and Competition Law 32, https://doi.org/10.1007/978-3-031-91401-0_3

processor that is beneficial to them. For example, there are various payback card programs where individuals disclose their spending habits and receive a discount later when making a purchase. Accepting a company's privacy statement is also often a prerequisite for a customer to be able to use a particular service. Under the privacy calculation model, individuals in such situations either disclose their personal information to achieve an expected benefit or refrain from disclosing it to avoid potential costs associated with a data breach.[1] The individual's decision regarding the disclosure of personal data will then depend on the outcome of this careful cost–benefit analysis.

In certain situations, people do not have the choice to make such a cost–benefit trade-off. For example, disclosing personal data may be necessary for some people to ensure a basic income by engaging in online work, which has become increasingly ubiquitous as a result of recent transformations in online work. In such a situation, an individual's bargaining position vis-à-vis an online platform is even weaker than it usually is. Flexible working conditions have also become more important, especially during the pandemic years and because refugees can no longer do their previous work on-site.[2] In such situations, the privacy calculus model is de facto ineffective and obsolescent.

The present chapter examines the processing of data by crowdsourcing platforms in Germany and the United States. On crowdsourcing platforms, companies (the *crowdsourcers*) publish tasks on a website and ask *crowdworkers* to complete these tasks. The way platforms advertise and process tasks is highly standardized. Data processing is therefore largely comparable across national borders and platforms. Moreover, the fact that European data subjects[3] also fall under the protection of the European General Data Protection Regulation (GDPR, Art. 3) even when they work with service providers outside European borders makes it possible to compare how companies on both sides of the Atlantic implement data privacy.

Germany and the U.S. nevertheless have different approaches to data protection, each shaped by its distinctive legal, economic, and cultural context. Germany, as a member state of the EU, follows a model characterized by strict regulations and is committed to the fundamental right to protection of personal data.[4] In contrast, the U.S. has largely taken a market-driven approach to data protection,[5] emphasizing flexibility and adaptability to address the dynamic nature of the digital landscape. An empirical analysis of data processing on crowdsourcing platforms in the two countries illuminates these differences. We ask the following research questions: How do crowdsourcing platforms deal with data privacy issues in practice and are there

[1] Dinev, Hart, 2006, 25.

[2] Crowdworking has always brought flexibility advantages for certain groups of society. See: Berg, Rani, 2021, 93.

[3] According to the GDPR, data subjects are defined as an identified or identifiable natural person.

[4] Kuner, Bygrave, Docksey, Drechsler, Tosoni, 2021. See also European Union: Council of the European Union, Charter of Fundamental Rights of the European Union (2007/C 303/01), Article 8, 14 December 2007, C 303/1.

[5] Schwartz, Peifer, 2017, 115.

significant differences between crowdsourcing platforms from these two countries? In order to answer these research questions, we first provide a brief, comparative overview of the countries' legal frameworks and enforcement mechanisms. We then describe the data and methods used, and the subsequent section presents the results. The final section concludes.

2 Data Privacy Regulations in Germany and the United States

2.1 Data Privacy Frameworks

The EU and the U.S. differ fundamentally in their legal traditions, and this is particularly evident in the regulation of the digital economy and data privacy. The EU defines the protection of personal data as a fundamental right in the Charter of Fundamental Rights (Article 8, ECFR), which went into force with the Treaty of Lisbon on December 1, 2009. Individuals within the EU hence have a universal right to the protection of their personal data and any violation of this right can be challenged in court. The recognition of the right to the protection of personal data in the Charter reflects the EU's commitment to safeguarding individuals' personal data within the legal framework of the EU. It laid the foundation for subsequent developments in data privacy legislation, including the GDPR, which became applicable on May 25, 2018. Unlike the U.S., the EU has traditionally focused on omnibus regulations, which address multiple regulatory issues such as data protection and data privacy within a single legal framework. Moreover, to some extent, the EU sees threats to data protection and privacy as originating primarily with large digital companies creating profiles of their users and using them for commercial purposes. This viewpoint is reflected in the lawsuits filed by Maximilian Schrems, an Austrian who prominently complained that Facebook had illegally forwarded his data from Ireland to the company's headquarters in the U.S. In the 2020 Schrems II ruling, the Court of Justice of the European Union raised concerns about inadequate protection of EU citizens' data in the U.S. due to extensive surveillance practices.[6] As a result, the Privacy Shield between the EU and the U.S. was terminated.[7]

U.S. law follows a market-driven approach, which manifests in the principle of unhindered information flow and allows for the processing of any personal data unless a specific law restricts this activity.[8] In a similar vein, EU law not only protects privacy and data but also ensures an unhindered exchange of information. This aligns with

[6] Court of Justice of the European Union (2020) Case C-311/18, Judgment of the Court (Grand Chamber) of 16 July 2020: Data Protection Commissioner v Facebook Ireland Limited and Maximillian Schrems.

[7] Note that the Safe Harbor agreement, which was the predecessor of the EU-US Privacy Shield, was already declared void in the 2015 Schrems I ruling.

[8] Schwartz, Peifer, 2017, 115.

its objective of creating an internal market for personal data, characterized by free movement of goods, persons, services, and capital, as already stipulated in the Data Protection Directive of 1995, which the GDPR suspended. Consequently, the dual aims of EU regulation are to facilitate the unrestricted movement of personal data between EU member states and at the same time to establish stringent data privacy standards that safeguard the fundamental rights of EU citizens.[9]

According to Article 88(1) of the GDPR, in the context of employment EU member states can also provide for more specific regulations to ensure data protection. The German Federal Data Protection Act (*Bundesdatenschutzgesetz*, BDSG), the German Telecommunications Act (*Telekommunikationsgesetz*, TKG), and the Telecommunications Digital Services Data Protection Act (*Gesetz über den Datenschutz und den Schutz der Privatsphäre in der Telekommunikation und bei digitalen Diensten*, TDDDG) remain applicable as further relevant sources of law. In their role as internet service providers, crowdsourcing platforms must take the TKG and the TDDDG into account. An important difference between the GDPR and the BDSG is that companies with 20 employees in Germany are required by the BDSG to have a data protection officer (*Datenschutzbeauftragter*), while there is no such specific rule in the GDPR.

In contrast to European law, U.S. law generally does not grant the data subjects a fundamental constitutional privacy right. Instead, it envisions data subjects and companies engaging in a series of voluntary transactions that entail the exchange of personal information.[10] In line with the scholarly law and economics tradition, personal data is thus considered another commodity in the market, and the improvement of human well-being is facilitated when individuals can optimize their decisions regarding data transactions.[11] In the U.S., the focus of data privacy is therefore on ensuring fairness in the commoditization of personal data.[12]

Threats to privacy are also presumed to come primarily from the government.[13] After the terrorist attacks of September 11, 2001, the U.S. passed, among other laws, the Patriot Act, which provides for expanded surveillance options for law enforcement authorities. In 2013, there were high-profile reports in *The Guardian*[14] and *The Washington Post*[15] about global surveillance of domestic and foreign nationals, particularly through programs of the National Security Agency (NSA) such as PRISM and XKeyscore. These reports are based on top-secret documents leaked by former NSA contractor Edward Snowden. The reports revealed the extent to which the U.S. government looked into individuals' data. The NSA scandal exacerbated

[9] Ibid.

[10] Ibid.

[11] Ibid.

[12] Ibid.

[13] Asunción, 2017, 36.

[14] Greenwald, 2013.

[15] Lee, 2013.

the divide between the U.S. and the EU with regard to privacy and national security, with negative consequences for trust in transatlantic data processing.[16]

Data privacy is generally not regulated at the federal level in the U.S. The first California Consumer Protection Act (CCPA) of 2018, which has been in force since January 2020 and was recently amended by the California Privacy Rights Act of 2020, established a data privacy standard that is similar to the GDPR, but still implements lower standards in the most populous U.S. state than in Europe.[17] By the end of 2023, twelve U.S. states—California, Oregon, Montana, Utah, Colorado, Texas, Iowa, Indiana, Tennessee, Virginia, Delaware, and Connecticut—have enacted data privacy laws.[18] There are some industry-specific laws regarding the processing of data, some of which can have an impact on crowdsourcing platforms. For example, the Children's Online Privacy Protection Act regulates requirements for operators of websites that collect personal information from children under 13 years of age. The Electronic Communications Privacy Act restricts the use of electronic communications by public and private entities.[19]

2.2 *Substantive Legal Differences*

Different legal frameworks also lead to substantive differences in data privacy regulation. European citizens have a right to erasure (Art. 17 of the GDPR), also known as the "right to be forgotten."[20] The obligation to remove content when a European user makes such a request applies to data processors worldwide, even if the data is stored on servers located outside the EU.[21] In the U.S., the right to be forgotten exists within bankruptcy law and in creditworthiness reports but not in a general context.[22] Under the CCPA, there is also a general right to correct incorrect personal data[23] and a right to be forgotten that applies specifically to minors.

Although codified in the GDPR, the following rules do not pertain to U.S. data privacy law. According to Article 7 of the GDPR, the data subject has the right to withdraw his or her consent at any time and it shall be as easy to withdraw as to give consent. Even if such a right is not codified in privacy law in the U.S., the data

---

[16] Cole, Fabbrini, 2016, 220.

[17] Pernot-Leplay, 2020, 25.

[18] Stauss, 2023.

[19] Hornuf, Mangold, Yang, 2023, 19.

[20] Klar, Kühling, 2016, 165.

[21] Court of Justice of the European Union (2019) Judgment of the Court (Grand Chamber) of 24 September 2019 Google LLC, successor in law to Google Inc. v Commission nationale de l'informatique et des libertés (CNIL).

[22] Klar; Kühling, 2016, 165.

[23] California Department of Justice (2018) California Consumer Privacy Act (CCPA). https://oag.ca.gov/privacy/ccpa Accessed 23 Jan 2024.

subjects there could potentially rely on an efficient breach of contract.[24] Moreover, unlike in the U.S., according to Article 16 of the GDPR European data subjects have a right to obtain from the controller the rectification of inaccurate personal data. To minimize the transaction costs of such corrections, we presume that European companies could *ex ante* limit the amount of data processed. Finally, European data subjects have more rights with regard to the information obligations of the data controller. For example, Article 13 of the GDPR stipulates that data subjects have the right to obtain information about the identity and the contact details of the controller as well as contact details of the data protection officer. Since the concept of a data protection officer is largely foreign to U.S. privacy law, this right does not exist there.

There are also specific differences with regard to employee privacy protection. In Germany, if data processing is carried out on the basis of the employee's consent, the employee's dependency and the circumstances of the consent must be taken into account under Article 26 of the BDSG. However, if crowdworkers do not have the legal status of an employee, Article 32 of the BDSG does not apply,[25] although in 2020 the German Federal Labour Court (*Bundesarbeitsgericht*, BAG) leaned toward favoring employee status for online workers.[26] There is also a proposed directive aimed at granting employee status and other rights to online workers in the EU.[27] In the U.S., federal law and most state privacy laws do not protect employee privacy from monitoring.[28] However, the U.S. Equal Employment Opportunity Commission prohibits asking personal questions during job interviews to prevent workplace discrimination. In summary, we presume that European companies will place greater restrictions on the amount of data processed, because the protection standards are higher.

2.3 *Privacy Law Enforcement*

Although data privacy is regulated at the EU level with the GDPR, there is no European data protection authority. Rather, the competent supervisory authority is that of the member state in which the controller has its main establishment (GDPR Recital 36). After a comprehensive investigation, on May 22, 2023, the Irish Data Protection Commission issued the highest GDPR-related fine of €1.2 billion to Meta for violating Article 46 of the GDPR. According to the Irish Data Protection Commission, the data transfers by Meta are made in circumstances which "(…) *fail to guarantee a level of protection to data subjects that is essentially equivalent to that*

[24] Zeetony, 2022.
[25] Hornuf, Mangold, Yang, 2023, 19.
[26] Bundesarbeitsgericht Urteil vom 1. Dezember 2020 9 AZR 102/20.
[27] Marketa, Stefano, 2023.
[28] Determann, Sprague, 2011, 979.

provided by EU law."[29] However, compared to the U.S., European fines have been relatively small.[30]

Because the U.S. takes a more market-driven approach[31] to data privacy, it is only fitting that the Federal Trade Commission (FTC) plays a prominent role in its enforcement.[32] Violations of consumer privacy can be pursued by the FTC as unfair competition on the basis of Sect. 5 of the FTC Act (15 USC § 45). Overall, U.S. privacy laws are relatively strictly enforced by government agencies and private plaintiffs, with steep penalties, fines, and damages awarded in class actions often amounting to millions, if not billions, of dollars. The $5 billion fine imposed on Facebook (now Meta) by the FTC in 2019 is still the largest ever imposed on a company for violating consumer privacy and is approximately four times larger than the highest European fine. The total amount of fines in the U.S. is also significantly higher than in Europe,[33] which should have a deterrent effect on data privacy violations by U.S. companies.

Of the 100 highest data privacy fines imposed in Europe and North America between 2018 and 2022, approximately the same number of high-profile fines were imposed in Europe and North America.[34] Although ever-higher GDPR-related fines have been imposed in Europe, especially since 2021, the fines in the U.S. have remained significantly higher. Thus, if the expected fine for a data privacy violation is a combination of the expected amount of the fine and the likelihood of receiving a fine, then it can then be assumed that data privacy enforcement will have a stronger deterrent effect on U.S. companies. This is also to be expected because not only U.S. privacy law but also the GDPR can apply to U.S. companies if they deal with Europeans. This is because, according to Article 3(2), the GDPR has extraterritorial reach and "*applies to the processing of personal data in the context of the activities of an establishment of a controller or a processor in the Union, regardless of whether the processing takes place in the Union or not.*"

2.4 Transparency as a Basic Principle

To make data privacy tractable, the GDPR makes transparency a basic requirement for good data processing and protection (Art. 5(1), Art. 12 GDPR). Transparency is a user-centric principle empowering users to hold data controllers accountable and obtain confirmation as to whether or not their personal data is being processed.[35] Key aspects of transparency under the GDPR include a data subject's right to be informed about the collection, processing purposes, and relevant details of their personal data

---

29 European Data Protection Board, 2018.

30 Freshfields Bruckhaus Deringer, 2021.

31 Schwartz, Peifer, 2017, 115.

32 Solove, Hartzog, 2014, 583.

33 Global Data Risk Report 2021.

34 Global Data Risk Report 2021.

35 Spagnuelo, Ferreira, Lenzini, 2019, 114.

(Art. 13 and 14), the right to receive clear, concise, and easily understandable information about how their personal data is processed (Art. 12), to be informed whether their personal data is being processed and to access that data (Art. 15), to have inaccurate or incomplete personal data corrected or completed (Art. 16), to object to the processing of their personal data in certain situations (Art. 21), and to be notified without undue delay in the event of a personal data breach (Art. 34). We will rely on some of these basic principles in the empirical analysis that follows.

3 Data and Method

3.1 Research Design and Data Collection

In Article 5, the GDPR defines several basic principles for the processing of personal data. The first principle is that personal data shall be processed lawfully, fairly, and in a transparent manner (*principles of lawfulness, fairness, and transparency*). In a narrower sense, lawfulness implies that crowdsourcing platforms must have the user's consent or another legal basis for processing their data. While the definition of fairness differs slightly in the German and English translations of the GDPR,[36] transparency implies that no data may be processed secretly and the data subject shall be adequately informed about the data processed. The next two principles in Article 5 of the GDPR stipulate that the processing of personal data shall be adequate, relevant, and limited to what is necessary in relation to the purposes for which personal data is processed (*principles of purpose limitation and data minimization*). These data processing principles provide the basis for our empirical investigation. In order to examine how crowdsourcing platforms deal with data privacy issues in practice and whether there are significant differences between crowdsourcing platforms from Germany and the U.S., we pursue two different methodological approaches.

First, we registered new user accounts and checked which user data is de facto collected by crowdsourcing platforms. Because not all data is collected through active user input,[37] we have also asked the platforms to inform us about the data processed in connection with our user account. For example, by using tracking services, platforms could collect and process data on the behavior of users on their website or analyze information about user movements in the real world via the GPS chip of their personal device. Our approach allows us to identify differences in data privacy practices in two respects. On the one hand, we can investigate differences with regard to data minimization practices. If European platforms require less user data during the registration process, this would count as proof of better data minimization by European crowdsourcing platforms and implicitly the effectiveness of the GDPR. On the other hand, by creating actual user accounts and requesting our user data from the

---

[36] See: Herbst, 2021, 265.
Bundesarbeitsgericht Urteil vom 1. Dezember 2020 9 AZR 102/20.

[37] Hornuf, Mangold, Yang, 2023, 19.

crowdsourcing platform, we also learn something about how the data subject's right of access is implemented in practice. If U.S. crowdsourcing platforms handle data subjects' requests faster and provide more accurate responses, this would count as evidence that legal deterrence apparently works better in the U.S.

We sought to register on 293 crowdsourcing platforms. These platforms consist of crowd labor markets, crowd contests, crowd complementors, and collaborative community,[38] and include 268 U.S. and 25 German crowdsourcing platforms. The list of platforms comes from a recent publication by Hornuf and co-authors from 2023. On some platforms, registration would only have been possible with a work sample or ID from the respective country. Because we did not want to falsely represent ourselves as U.S. citizens, trained graphic designers or computer scientists, we refrained from registering in these cases. In some cases, registering with a European IP address was not possible from the outset because platforms employ geo-blocking.[39] Consequently, we were able to register on 142 crowdsourcing platforms, including 118 U.S. and 24 German platforms. Registrations on the U.S. platforms were conducted from May 9 to May 13, 2022, and on the German platforms from March 3 to March 4, 2022, respectively with a unique user profile and a unique email address.

Second, we are interested not only in what data is processed and whether crowdsourcing platforms enable effective access to this data, but also in the transparency of the data processing itself. Like others before us,[40] in order to conduct a comprehensive analysis of crowdsourcing platforms' data transparency, we check the content of the privacy statements published by each crowdsourcing platform. In order to make the analysis of privacy statements comparable with data from user registrations, we sought only to obtain privacy statements for the 142 platforms where registration was possible. Overall, we identified 142 privacy statements and subsequently analyzed them. For three platforms, no privacy statement was available. In some cases, platforms have integrated privacy information into the terms and conditions or included additional privacy information in the terms and conditions. In such cases we considered the terms and conditions as well.

3.2 Variables

To measure the amount of data processed by a crowdsourcing platform, we create a data index similar to that developed by Dorfleitner and co-authors.[41] However, unlike in that previous study, the basis for our data index is not the privacy statements of the platforms, but the data that had to be entered when registering on the platform.

---

[38] For a definition see: Boudreau, Lakhani, 2013, 61.

[39] It would have been possible to use a VPN client to circumvent geo-blocking, but the GDPR might then no longer have been applicable.

[40] Hornuf, Mangold, Yang, 2023, 19.

[41] Dorfleitner, Hornuf, Kreppmeier, 2023, 33.

The data processed ranges from general personal data (e.g., name, address, and email address) to specific work-related data (e.g., work experience, highest level of education, place of educational qualification, and salary expectations) to special categories of personal data (e.g., family status). Table 1 provides the full list of data categories from which the data index is composed. Because not all data had to be entered during the user registration process, even if a corresponding field was available, each variable that is part of the data index is a rank variable ranging from 0 to 2. The respective variable takes the value 0 if no field was available to enter the respective information, it takes the value 1 if the field was available, but entering the respective information was not required to register at the platform, and it takes the value 2 if the field was available and entering the respective information was required to register on the platform. The variable *data index* represents the normalized sum over eighteen dummy variables of different data categories. We divide the transparency index by the maximum achievable number of variables to scale it between 0 and 2. Thus, we interpret a higher index value to mean a higher quantity of data processed.

To examine how well platforms handle a request of access, we measured how long it took them to respond to our requests and whether the data was actually

Table 1 Data entry requests on German and U.S. crowdsourcing platforms

	German platform	U.S. platform	Difference p value
Email address	2.00	2.00	
Email address verification/temporary link	2.00	2.00	
Phone number/mobile number	1.70	0.24	< 0.001
Date of birth/age	1.45	0.15	< 0.001
Address/place of residence	1.45	0.10	< 0.001
Time zone in which you live	1.45	0.11	< 0.001
First name	1.33	0.73	< 0.001
Highest level of education	1.33	0.10	< 0.001
Last name	1.29	0.73	< 0.001
Proficient in working languages	1.29	0.04	< 0.001
Gender/form of address	1.12	0.13	< 0.001
General work experience	1.00	0.02	< 0.001
Place of educational qualification	0.75	0.05	< 0.001
Username	0.45	0.31	0.165
Marital status	0.37	0.03	< 0.001
Last job	0.25	0.02	0.001
Salary expectations	0.20	0.09	0.215
Data index	1.14	0.33	< 0.001

provided. The *time to response* variable measures the number of days until the platform responded with the user data, disregarding any simple email confirmation of receipt of the request. It also leaves out Sundays, because it is not a regular working day and no platform responded on a Sunday.[42] The variable *GDPR compliant* has two components. First, according to Article 12(3) of the GDPR, information must be provided without undue delay and within one month at the latest. Second, the response has to contain information about the data being processed or the data itself. If both conditions were met, the variable *GDPR compliant* was coded 1 and otherwise 0.

Finally, to examine how crowdsourcing platforms ensure transparency, we consider the variable *transparency index*. Building on the transparency index developed by Dorfleitner and co-authors,[43] we aggregate eleven variables representing different dimensions of transparent data privacy actions undertaken by the crowdsourcing platforms. The transparency index represents the normalized sum over eleven variables such as *data* (whether a company states in detail which personal data they process), *purpose* (if a company states for what reason or purpose personal data are processed) and *storage* (if a company states how long data are stored or when they are deleted). Based on the study by Urban and coauthors,[44] which argues that "privacy policies should list the rights of the data subjects" and "how these rights can be exercised," we appended several variables to the index by Dorfleitner and co-authors, such as *rights*, which measures whether the platform describes the rights of each data subject as defined in Articles 12–23 GDPR. Table 3 provides a complete list and description of the variables that are part of the transparency index.

The variables that are part of the index equal 1 if a specific dimension of transparency is mentioned in an abstract manner, 2 if the privacy statement concretely describes how a certain dimension of transparency is handled by the specific company, and 0 otherwise. For example, the variable *purpose* is 1 if examples are given of the reason or purpose for which personal data is processed, and 2 if the privacy statement specifically states for what reason or purpose personal data is processed on the platform. We divide the transparency index by the maximum achievable number of variables to scale it between 0 and 2, and interpret a higher index value to mean greater transparency of data processing practices. Table 3 lists in detail the composition of the transparency index. The assumption of the index is that if a company does not explicitly disclose the processing of specific data or certain data-processing practices, then it is assumed that such processing is not taking place.[45]

---

[42] We adapted this approach from: Kröger, Lindemann, Herrmann, 2020, 1.

[43] Dorfleitner, Hornuf, Kreppmeier, 2023, 33.

[44] Urban, Tatang, Degeling, Holz, Pohlmann, 2019, 61.

[45] Dorfleitner, Hornuf, Kreppmeier, 2023, 33.

4 Results

Table 1 shows the results on the data minimization practices of German and U.S. crowdsourcing platforms during the onboarding process. When registering user accounts on crowdsourcing platforms, we find that U.S. platforms request clearly less data than German platforms. As Fig. 1 shows, the data index for Germany is more than three times larger and this difference is statistically significant at the 1% level. The fact that German platforms request more data holds for 14 out of 18 data categories. In line with previous findings by Hornuf and co-authors, privacy statements from both German and U.S. crowdsourcing platforms reveal that it is primarily the users' email addresses that are processed. However, our analysis shows that the email address is not only processed but also verified in all cases. In addition to the email address, the data most frequently requested by German platforms is the phone number, date of birth, and address of the user. U.S. platforms frequently request first and last name, email address, and username.

After registering, we allowed a month to pass before requesting access to our data stored on the platform. We deliberately refrained from making any changes to our account during this period. Subsequently, we sent out a total of 142 requests of access to the crowdsourcing platforms on which we had been able to register. We received responses from 87 platforms. Of these, 39 platforms sent us our data within a month or provided relevant information about the data processed. Out of the responses that

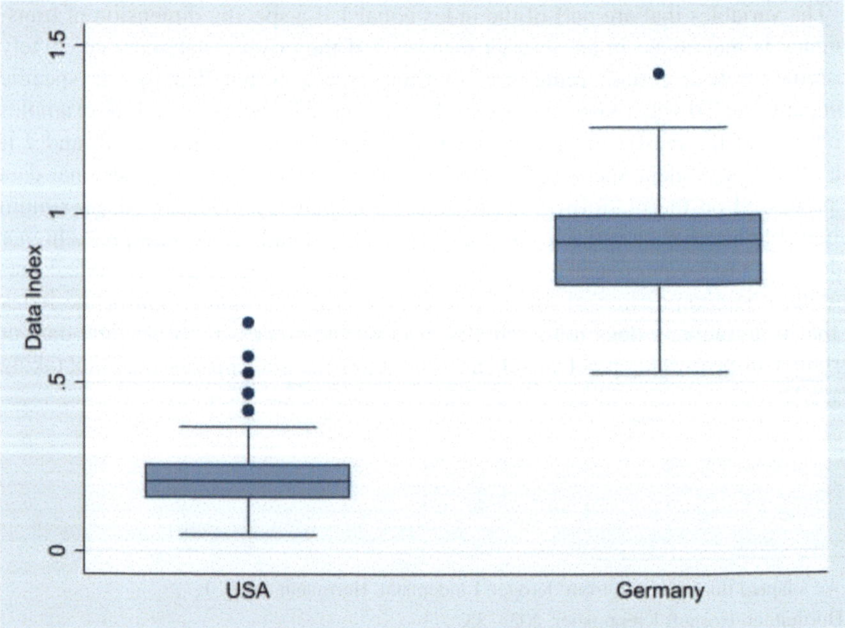

Fig. 1 Data Index for German and U.S. Crowdsourcing Platforms

Table 2 Request of data access

	German platform	U.S. platform	Difference p-value
GDPR compliant	0.58	0.21	< 0.001
GDPR compliant time to response (in days)	3.00	2.65	0.887

transmitted the requested data in a timely manner, 14 responses were from German platforms (out of 24 requests), and 25 were from U.S. platforms (out of 118 requests). As Table 2 shows, the response rate on the German platforms was significantly better. A little more than half of the German platforms sent us the information about our data on time; in the U.S. it was only a little more than one in five platforms. While this is a poor GDPR compliance rate, for Germany it roughly matches the results of a similar study by Urban and co-authors that examined access requests from 39 companies and found that 58% of companies did not respond within the statutory one-month deadline.[46] Moreover, a total of 112 platforms named a specific data protection officer (Germany) or a privacy department representative (U.S.) in their privacy statement. Only in seven cases did we actually receive a response with the signature "legal team" or "data protection team."

A total of 35 platforms responded to our request for information, but without sending us the data. The responses were typically along the lines of "we will take care of your request," but nothing happened. In addition, five platforms sent us a link to our data that did not work. A further five platforms sent us the data, but not within the legally defined time frame. This is consistent with a study by Kröger and co-authors,[47] who found that a very small group of companies responded after more than a month. Furthermore, our data or accounts were deleted on five platforms, even though we did not seek to exercise the right to erasure,[48] but merely wanted to receive information about our data. In five further cases, data privacy statements were sent to us by email or responses contained a mere reference that the processing of our data occurred in accordance with the GDPR. Three platforms responded to the request of access and explained that we should first check our account to see what data was entered. Only then would we be informed about the data processed, which is a clear violation of the GDPR.

On the positive side, the companies that responded in accordance with the GDPR usually did so very quickly, both in Germany and in the U.S. In these cases, the request for access to our data was usually answered within three days. This number is consistent with a study by Kröger and co-authors, in which the vast majority of responses came within five days.[49] In many cases, direct access to the data was granted via a link or email. Our results also show that an appropriate IT process is crucial for a GDPR-compliant request of access. Positive examples included four

---

[46] Urban et al., 2019, 61.

[47] Kröger, Lindemann, Herrmann, 2020, 1.

[48] See Kröger et al., 2020, who have had similar experiences.

[49] Kröger et al., 2020, 1.

Table 3 Data transparency on German and U.S. crowdsourcing platforms

	German platform	U.S. platform	Difference *p*-value
Data (company states which personal data are processed)	1.62	1.53	0.412
Purpose (company states for what reason or purpose personal data are processed)	1.50	1.68	0.167
Storage (company states for how long data are stored or when they are deleted)	1.25	0.82	0.002
Rights (company describes the rights of each data subject in accordance with Art. 12–23 GDPR)	1.37	0.07	0.466
Cookies opt-out (company states that the use of cookies can be denied)	1.25	0.96	0.026
Pseudo (company states that data are processed pseudonymously)	1.08	0.37	< 0.001
Cookies (company explains the use of cookies)	1.67	1.50	0.209
Third parties[1] (company states which personal data are shared with third parties)	1.54	1.42	0.392
Right to erasure (company explains the right to erasure)	1.46	0.91	< 0.001
Payment (company explains the security standards of the payment process)	0.87	0.52	0.058
Marketing purpose (company states that personal data are used for marketing purposes)	1.37	0.89	0.001
Transparency Index	1.36	1.07	0.005

[1]Urban et al. (2019, 71)

U.S. platforms where a ticket system with automated responses was implemented. On these platforms we usually received answers to our access requests much more quickly, often within a day.

We were also interested in how platforms handled data security. Because we generated a separate account and email address that was only used once on the platform, we were then able to investigate whether that email address was shared with third parties. In seven cases we actually received mail from third parties within a year after registration; six times on U.S. accounts and once on a German account. We classified these emails as "external" because the privacy statement did not contain any references to collaboration or involvement with third parties.[50]

Finally, although data minimization worked comparatively poorly in Germany, the transparency in privacy statements worked significantly better there. The privacy statements of German crowdsourcing platforms were significantly clearer in explaining how long data are stored or when they are deleted and that use of

[50] For a comprehensive and longitudinal analysis of data leaks, see: Di Martino, Meers, Quax, Andries, Lamotte, 2022, 95.

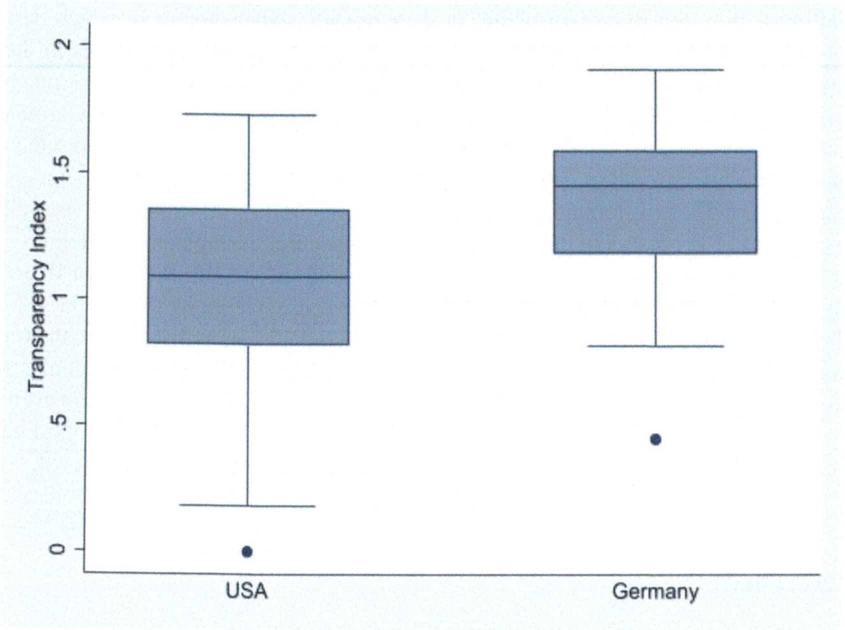

Fig. 2 Transparency Index for German and U.S. Crowdsourcing Platforms

cookies can be denied. Moreover, German platforms more frequently mentioned that user data is processed pseudonymously and that users have a right to erasure. Finally, German platforms were more precise in explaining the security standards of the payment process and made transparent whether personal data are used for marketing purposes. In other respects, for example which personal data are processed, no differences could be found (Fig. 2).

5 Conclusion

In work relationships in which crowdworkers are often structurally inferior to a platform, the privacy calculus model is obsolescent. In these cases, it is even more important that legal standards such as the GDPR are strictly enforced. This chapter examines how German and U.S. crowdworking platforms handle data privacy in practice. Our empirical analysis produces at least three important findings. First, U.S. crowdsourcing platforms request far less data during the onboarding process than German platforms. This is surprising because there is no uniform data protection regulation at the federal level in the U.S. that requires data minimization in a similar vein to the GDPR. On the other hand, we know from previous studies[51] that U.S.

[51] Hornuf, Mangold, Yang, 2023, 19.

platforms are often more transparent in their privacy statements about which data is explicitly not processed and may also see data minimization as an asset in the negotiation process with the data subjects. Second, German platforms are much better on average at handling a request of access. Slightly over half of the German platforms provided our data punctually, whereas in the U.S. only slightly more than one in five platforms did so. The different effectiveness of granting access to personal data could be due to different interpretations of the new data protection laws[52] as well as different IT processes in the respective companies. For example, the guidelines[53] on how to handle a request of access, which the European Data Protection Board has published, could have been more widely observed in Germany than in the U.S. The U.S. platforms, on the other hand, often had a ticket system that helped answer inquiries more quickly. Third, the transparency in the German data privacy statements was in many respects significantly better. In particular, crowdsourcing platforms in Germany provided a notably clearer explanation in their privacy statements regarding the duration of data storage and the circumstances under which data are deleted.

References

Asunción E (2017) The business of personal data: Google, Facebook, and privacy issues in the EU and the USA. Int'l Data Privacy L 7(1):36–47

Berg J, Rani U (2021) Working conditions, geography and gender in global crowdwork. In: Haidar J, Keune M (eds) Work and labour relations in global platform capitalism. Edward Elgar Publishing, Cheltenham, pp 93–110

Boudreau KJ, Lakhani KR (2013) Using the crowd as an innovation partner. Harvard Bus Rev 91(4):61–69

Cole D, Fabbrini F (2016) Bridging the transatlantic divide? The United States, the European Union, and the protection of privacy across borders. Int'l J Const L 14(1):220–237

Determann L, Sprague R (2011) Intrusive monitoring: Employee privacy expectations are reasonable in Europe, destroyed in the United States. Berkeley Tech L J 26:979–1036

Di Martino M, Meers I, Quax P, Andries K, Lamotte W (2022) Revisiting identification issues in GDPR "right of access" policies: a technical and longitudinal analysis. In: Proceedings on privacy enhancing technologies, pp 95–113

Dinev T, Hart P (2006) Privacy concerns and levels of information exchange: an empirical investigation of intended e-services use. E-Service J 4(3):25+. Gale Academic OneFile, link.gale.com/apps/doc/A160812855/AONE?u=anon~fa98e56c&sid=googleScholar&xid=5ef2d50b. Accessed 22 Feb 2025

Dorfleitner G, Hornuf L, Kreppmeier J (2023) Promise not fulfilled: FinTech, data privacy, and the GDPR. Electron Markets 33(1):33

European Data Protection Board (2018) Decision of the Data Protection Commission made pursuant to Section 111 of the Data Protection Act, 2018 and Articles 60 and 65 of the General Data Protection Regulation

[52] Urban et al., 2019, 61.

[53] European Data Protection Board (2022) Guidelines 01/2022 on data subject rights - Right of access Version 1.0. https://edpb.europa.eu/system/files/2022-01/edpb_guidelines_012022_right-of-access_0.pdf. Accessed 23 Jan 2024.

European Data Protection Board (2022) Guidelines 01/2022 on data subject rights - Right of access Version 1.0. https://edpb.europa.eu/system/files/2022-01/edpb_guidelines_012022_right-of-access_0.pdf. Accessed 22 Feb 2025

Global Data Risk Report (2021) Freshfields Bruckhaus Deringer. https://www.freshfields.de/49661d/globalassets/our-thinking/campaigns/digital/cyber-attacks-data-breaches-and-litigation/global-data-enforcement/gpr-report.pdf. Accessed 22 Feb 2025

Greenwald G (2013) XKeyscore: NSA tool collects "nearly everything a user does on the internet." The Guardian. https://www.theguardian.com/world/2013/jul/31/nsa-top-secret-program-online-data. Accessed 22 Feb 2025

Herbst T (2021) Art. 5 Grundsätze für die Verarbeitung personenbezogener Daten. In: Kühling J, Buchner B (eds) Datenschutz-Grundverordnung, Bundesdatenschutzgesetz. Beck, München, pp 265–292

Hornuf L, Mangold S, Yang Y (2023) Data protection law in Germany, the United States, and China. In: Data privacy and crowdsourcing. Advanced studies in diginomics and digitalization. Springer, Cham, pp 19–79

Hornuf L, Vrankar D (2022) Hourly wages in crowdworking: a meta-analysis. Bus Inf Sys Eng 64(5):553–573

Klar M, Kühling J (2016) Privatheit und Datenschutz in der EU und den USA - Kollision zweier Welten? Archiv des Öffentlichen Rechts 141(2):165–224

Kröger J, Lindemann J, Herrmann D (2020) How do app vendors respond to subject access requests? A longitudinal privacy study on iOS and Android Apps. In: Proceedings of the 15th international conference on availability, reliability and security, 2020, pp 1–10

Kuner C, Bygrave L, Docksey C, Drechsler L, Tosoni L (2021) The EU general data protection regulation: a commentary/update of selected articles. SSRN Electron J. https://doi.org/10.2139/ssrn.3839645

Lee TB (2013) Everything you need to know about the NSA's phone records scandal. The Washington Post. https://www.washingtonpost.com/news/wonk/wp/2013/06/06/everything-you-need-to-know-about-the-nsa-scandal/. Accessed 22 Feb 2025

Marketa P, Stefano S (2023) Digital platform workers: EU rules one step closer. European Parliamentary Research Service

Pernot-Leplay E (2020) EU influence on data privacy laws: Is the U.S. approach converging with the EU model? Colo Tech L J 18(1):25

Schwartz PM, Peifer K-N (2017) Transatlantic data privacy. Geo L J 106:115. UC Berkeley public law research paper. Available at SSRN. https://ssrn.com/abstract=3066971. Accessed 22 Feb 2025

Solove DJ, Hartzog W (2014) The FTC and the new common law of privacy. Colum L Rev 114:583

Spagnuelo D, Ferreira A, Lenzini G (2019) Accomplishing transparency within the general data protection regulation. In: Proceedings of the 5th international conference on information systems security and privacy, pp 114–125

Stauss D (2023) Tracking U.S. state consumer data privacy legislation. Husch Blackwell. https://www.huschblackwell.com/2023-state-privacy-law-tracker. Accessed 23 Jan 2024

Urban T, Tatang D, Degeling M, Holz T, Pohlmann N (2019) A study on subject data access in online advertising after the GDPR. In: Data privacy management, cryptocurrencies and blockchain technology: ESORICS 2019 international workshops, DPM 2019 and CBT 2019, Luxembourg, 26–27 Sept 2019, pp 61–79

Zeetony DA (2022) Do people always have the right to withdraw consent? GreenbergTraurig. https://www.gtlaw-dataprivacydish.com/2022/02/do-people-always-have-the-right-to-withdraw-consent/. Accessed 22 Feb 2025

Sina Häusler is a doctoral student and research associate at Dresden University of Technology where she works on the project "platform work and data protection in a national and international perspective". In addition, she teaches EU law and EU politics as a lecturer at the University of Applied Sciences in Bremen.

Prof. Dr. Lars Hornuf received his PhD in economics at the Ludwig Maximilian University and subsequently completed his habilitation in business administration at the University of Regensburg. He has been a visiting scholar at UC Berkeley, Stanford University, Duke University, Georgetown University, the CESifo, and the House of Finance at Goethe University Frankfurt. In 2014, he became assistant professor of law and economics at Trier University. From 2016 to 2021, he was an affiliated research fellow at the Max Planck Institute for Innovation and Competition. In 2017, Lars Hornuf became a full professor of business administration at the University of Bremen. Since spring 2023 he has been a full professor of business administration specializing in financial services and financial technology at Dresden University of Technology. He has worked on numerous projects related to financial technology, financial regulation, and data privacy. Media including The Economist and Foreign Policy have reported on his research findings.

Data Law

Three Ideas for Data Law from Environmental Law: Harm, Responsibility, and Rights

Siddharth Peter de Souza and Gargi Sharma

Abstract The field of data law is in a period of emergence, one where there are different proposals in terms of hard law as well as soft law, and also in terms of ethical and governance models that are being proposed to regulate the digital world. With the fundamentals of data law continuing to be determined, discussing them in a manner that is global in nature, requires studying how different locations influence and shape the making and realizing of law and regulation. With the increased globalization and circulation of legal norms and ideas, of particular importance is the need to situate global data law within the continued coloniality of the circulation of legal knowledge and models from the global Minority to the global Majority. This chapter discusses lessons from International Environmental Law for Global Data Law. We begin by arguing for why International Environmental Law is a useful field of comparison through undertaking a demand-based approach to the regulation of data. The paper focusses on different points in the lifecycle of data where intervention is necessary, in particular, through an examination of how to think about the mitigation of harms, the allocation of responsbility, and the articulation of rights.

1 Introduction

The field of data law is in a period of emergence, one where there are different proposals both in terms of hard law as well as soft law, and in terms of ethical and governance models that are being proposed to regulate the digital world.[1] With the fundamentals of data law continuing to be determined, discussing them in a manner that is global in nature, requires considering aspects of 'cultural, economic

S. P. de Souza (✉)
Centre for Interdisciplinary Methodologies, University of Warwick, Coventry, UK
e-mail: siddharth.de-souza@warwick.ac.uk

G. Sharma
University of Amsterdam, Amsterdam, The Netherlands
e-mail: gargi@climasolutions.org

[1] Global Data Law (2023).

J. Drexl et al. (eds.), *Comparative Data Law*, MPI Studies on Intellectual Property and Competition Law 32, https://doi.org/10.1007/978-3-031-91401-0_4

as well as infrastructural dimensions'.[2] This includes engaging with the increasing transplantation of regulation from the global Minority to the global Majority,[3] with the continued coloniality of the circulation of legal knowledge and models.[4]

As a contribution to exploring the components of Global Data Law (GDL), this chapter aims to discuss how GDL can have a social justice core.[5] This draws from the approach of data justice, which argues for ensuring that people have the ability to choose how visible they are in a digital world, how much control they have over their participation, and how they are treated as a result of their participation.[6] This focus on data justice indicates a shift in how data is understood, from a commodity that can be traded, to one that has implications for people, social relations, and the society at large.[7] Taking data as something that cannot be alienated from personhood, and thereby highlighting its embodiment as a key characteristic, is critical to ensuring that the right to human dignity is paramount in data regulation.[8]

With this in mind, in this chapter, we identify points of intervention where regulation is necessary across the lifecycle of data. In particular, we identify three aspects — the first is the aspect of the mitigation of data related harm, the second is in terms of the allocation of responsibility in response to harms, and the third is in terms of articulation of rights as entitlements that ensure the redressal of harms. These aspects are identified by taking a demand-based approach to thinking about the regulation of data.[9] In this approach, rather than focussing on institutional arrangements, we explore the realisation of justice, as it emerges in different lived realities. A demand-based approach focusses on the identification of grievances, the negotiations and attributions of where these grievances arise, and the pathways to finding satisfactory responses for grievances in different institutional arrangements.[10]

To develop proposals along these three aspects, we suggest looking at developments from International Environmental Law (IEL). We focus on IEL because as a relatively young field in international law, it has emerged incrementally in response to environmental concerns and has also grown institutionally through the creation of multilateral organisations. Studying IEL can be of particular interest to data law and governance scholars as the field of IEL has and continues to grapple with the friction between the economic interests of the few and the rights of the many.

In the second section of the chapter, we will discuss the boundaries of data law, and why we think there is value in identifying foundational principles that focus on social justice. The third section will discuss why learning from IEL can be useful. The fourth section will examine how harm has been conceptualised in IEL, drawing

---

[2] Global Data Law (2023).

[3] Boshe/Caride (2024), Mesquita et al. (2024).

[4] Bradford (2020), Bonilla Maldonado (2018).

[5] Global Data Justice.

[6] Taylor (2017), Dencik/Sanchez-Monedero (2022).

[7] Lopez Solano et al. (2022), Viljoen (2020).

[8] Kukutai/Taylor (2016).

[9] Barendrecht et al. (2008), Genn (1999).

[10] Gramatikov et al. (2011).

from discussions on transboundary harms and the relations between environmental pollution and data pollution, which are not confined to particular jurisdictional or geographical areas, but have cross-border dimensions. The fifth section will explore the notion of responsibility, drawing from the debate on historic burdens in environmental law, and how one can explore these principles in data law by foregrounding the importance of thinking about common but differentiated responsibility, particularly as we are observing how data colonialism is following similar exploitative practices of extraction that are present in environmental colonialism. In the sixth section, we will explore the development of a right to healthy environment under IEL and examine how a human rights-informed approach to data law could be derived from the developments in IEL, in regard to related aspects of protection, justice, and access. We will review how the right to a healthy environment has emerged in IEL and how data law can be informed by this development, including in the formalisation of international law instruments.

2 Regulating the Digital, and the Boundaries of Data Law

Proposals to define law to govern the digital are emerging in different models. These include identifying ways to create data protection regulation and to protect the rights to privacy and personal data of individuals, for instance, in the General Data Protection Regulation in the European Union (EU).[11] Since 2020, as part of its Digital Strategy,[12] the EU has developed a Digital Markets Act,[13] the Digital Services Act,[14] the Data Governance Act,[15] the Data Act,[16] and more recently the Artificial Intelligence (AI) Act.[17] This is part of a new strategy of the EU around governing data, technology, and infrastructure to create competitive markets, as well as balance this with the protection of fundamental rights.[18] With the emergence of these new regulations, the make-up of what constitutes data law, is increasingly multi-layered, with a move beyond looking at data protection law.

With an increasing need to think systemically about data regulation, digital constitutionalism has emerged as a stream of research that as Celeste argues 'advocates

[11] European Commission (2016).

[12] European Union (2023)

[13] Designed to encourage fair competition, challenge gatekeeping by big tech, and ensure that consumers benefit by having better and fairer access to services (European Commission 2022a).

[14] Enacted to combat disinformation, create a fair online environment, through regulating intermediaries such as social networks and online marketplaces (European Commission 2022b).

[15] Promoted to encourage data sharing in trusted ways, as well as enable reuse of data (European Commission 2022b).

[16] Drafted to provide a comprehensive protections for access and use rights(European Commission 2024a, b).

[17] Enacted to promote the regulation of AI to ensure that their development, design and deployment is addresses risks while at the same time promotes innovation (European Commission 2024c).

[18] European Commission (2023).

the perpetuation of foundational principles, such as the rule of law, the separation of powers, democracy, and the protection of human rights, in the mutated scenario of the digital society.'[19] Redeker, Gill, and Gasser argue that digital constitutionalism can be understood as a 'constellation of initiatives that seek to articulate a set of political rights, governance norms, and limitations on the exercise of power on the Internet.'[20] A key concern of governing digital spaces is also the place for digital rights. Tan, in her mapping of digital rights in Southeast Asia, argues that digital rights can be understood as human rights in digital spheres.[21] They can also be data-centric protections, that include the governance of digital spheres and can also include rights concerning access to data, infrastructure or be focussed on competition and intellectual property-related concerns. At a global level, Streinz speaks about the design of an international economic data law, suggesting 'one must ask which issues to address or prioritise and whose interests are being served.'[22] He raises concerns about whether restrictions on data flows are the most pressing issue to address or whether we need to examine the infrastructural control over data when it comes to articulating a framework for international economic data law.

In addition to data, frameworks for regulating digital societies are also emerging with a focus on technology and technology-related harms. International organisations like the United Nations Educational, Scientific and Cultural Organization (UNESCO) have proposed principles to regulate AI, which place an emphasis on putting 'human' rights at the centre, stating that 'the protection of human rights and dignity is the cornerstone of the Recommendation, based on the advancement of fundamental principles such as transparency and fairness, always remembering the importance of human oversight of AI systems.'[23] On matters related to content moderation, private entities like Meta have set up forums for self-regulation like the Oversight Board, which, in their words, is designed to 'promote free expression by making principled, independent decisions regarding content on Facebook and Instagram and by issuing recommendations on the relevant Meta content policy.'[24]

Civil society coalitions like the Non-Aligned Technologies Movement speak to the need to have the 'purposeful implementation of digital technologies in a way that affirms each community's power of self-determination and governance.'[25] Their principles include that data extraction is illegitimate, that in the race for quick solutions, speed should not circumvent ethics, that people should be able to opt out of digital platforms, that there must be alternative platforms, and that communities should be allowed to develop multiple solutions.[26] Indigenous data sovereignty scholars and leaders argue that there is a need to study and understand data not as a commodity

[19] Celeste (2022a), Celeste (2022b), Padovani/Santaniello (2018).
[20] Redeker/Gill/Gasser (2018).
[21] Jun-E (2019).
[22] Streinz (2021).
[23] UNESCO (2021), UNESCO (2022), UNESCO (2023).
[24] Oversight Board (2024)
[25] NATM.
[26] NATM.

but as a living thing, and thereby argue for the need to protect the collective and encourage autonomy, respect, and an ethics of care in terms of how data is regulated.[27] These illustrations demonstrate that models are emerging to govern the digital through multi-cited norm-making processes.[28]

In September 2024, the Global Digital Compact was adopted and positioned as a framework for governing technologies and Artificial Intelligence, with a focus on anchoring the role of international law in safeguarding rights of people in online and offline spaces.[29] Its objectives include addressing the digital divides, creating an inclusive digital economy, enabling human rights in online spaces, ensuring that data governance is responsible, interoperable and equitable, and that the governance of AI benefits humanity. Similarly, the High-Level Advisory Board on Artificial Intelligence argued for the imperative of a global approach to governance stating that "AI's raw materials, from critical minerals to training data, are globally sourced. General-purpose AI, deployed across borders, spawns manifold applications globally. The accelerating development of AI concentrates power and wealth on a global scale, with geopolitical and geoeconomic implications."[30]

These illustrations point to the dynamism and fuzziness in approaches to govern digital societies. In the following section, we will discuss why, in an attempt to build out fundamental principles, drawing from IEL can be valuable.

3 Bringing in the International Environmental Law Perspective

The field of IEL has emerged from the utilisation of treaty law, soft law, and other environment-specific international regulations (such as the Kyoto Protocol), initially, for the determination and resolution of disputes between states on resource preservation and conservation, and presently, to prevent catastrophic and irreversible impacts of climate change.[31]

While the initial considerations at international fora concerned themselves primarily with the environment as an object of protection insofar as it relates to use by humans (an anthropocentric approach), international and regional bodies, state actors, academics, and movement groups increasingly emphasise a balanced

---

[27] Walter/Kukutai/Carroll/Rodriguez-Lonebear (2020), Carroll/Garba/Figueroa-Rodríguez et al. (2020).

[28] de Souza and Taylor (2025).

[29] "This Compact is anchored in international law, including international human rights law. All human rights, including civil, political, economic, social and cultural rights, and fundamental freedoms, must be respected, protected and promoted online and offline. Our cooperation will harness digital technologies to advance all.

human rights, including the rights of the child, the rights of persons with disabilities and the right to development" United Nations (2024a, b).

[30] United Nations (2024a, b).

[31] Van Steenberghe (2023), Freeland (2015).

approach that places the environment as an object of protection in itself and in its relation to all organisms (an eco-centric approach).[32]

IEL scholars are increasingly recognising historical and ongoing climate injustices and inequities within the scope of IEL.[33] Historical and ongoing forms of colonialism ensure the dominance of the global Minority countries at the expense of the global Majority countries with peoples dealing with the past and present effects of environmental subjugation, unbridled resource extraction and extensive environmental destruction to ecosystems, leading to ecocide.[34] The global extractive economy, too, privileges the global Minority, where power, wealth, and industry is concentrated, at the expense of the global Majority, whose land and people are exploited and existence commodified for the benefit of the former.[35]

There are clear intersections between data and the environment. For instance, several international organisations have suggested that data flowing between jurisdictions forms the basis for trade, which overlaps with how the environment is perceived as something that transcends states and, therefore, is boundaryless.[36] Dupuy and Vinuales argue that the initial approach to international environmental regulation was in terms of transboundary harms, shared watercourses, and rules governing the exploitation of natural resources.[37] The need to examine the global nature of data also arises from the fact that the access, control, and governance of the infrastructures that underpin its flow, crosses jurisdictions.[38]

Data, like the environment, is not an intangible commodity. Data is generated through the labour, land, and resource extraction that takes place across the world.[39] The critique that 'raw data is an oxymoron' is important here because it demonstrates how data as a commodity requires large environmental resources to be useful for commerce and business.[40] An example of this are the plans by Google to build a data centre in Uruguay when the country is experiencing its worst drought in 74 years.[41] This has resulted in large protests, especially because, according to researcher Daniel Pena, Google will use 29 hectares of land, and over 2 million gallons of water per day to keep its servers cool, which is equal to the daily usage of 55,000 people.[42]

---

[32] Dupuy/Viñuales (2018).

[33] Kotzé/Du Toit/French (2021); Friend or foe? International environmental law and its structural complicity in the Anthropocene's climate injustices. Oñati Socio-Legal Series, 11(1), 180–206. Gonzalez/Atapattu (2016); International environmental law, environmental justice, and the Global South. Transnat'l L. & Contemp. Probs., 26, 229.

[34] Adeola (2001). Environmental injustice and human rights abuse: the states, MNCs, and repression of minority groups in the world system. Human Ecology Review, 39–59.

[35] Veltmeyer (2013).

[36] United Nations Trade and Development (2021).

[37] Dupuy/Viñuales (2018), p. 27.

[38] Mishra (2024).

[39] Vera/Walker/Murphy et al. (2019).

[40] Gitelman (2013).

[41] Livingstone (2023).

[42] Id.

The extraction of data bears similarities to the exploitation present in environmental colonialism. We have seen how communities have been displaced, Indigenous knowledge and traditions replaced, and the global Majority used for testing experimental methods by the global Minority, without proper safeguards or protections in place. The parallels between environmental and digital colonialism and extraction are visible in the case of Shell in Nigeria, with wanton disregard for people, and the environment[43] and in the approaches by Meta to create walled gardens on the internet through internet.org, which determined how people should be online.[44] Both these projects were designed to dominate how resources were used, and in particular, for people in the global Majority. In the case of Shell's operations in Nigeria, Shell Nigeria had failed to prevent an oil spill in 2005 by not installing a leak detection system. The oil spill reached a cooking area and parts of the village and a nearby mangrove forest erupted in flames, destroying nearly 40 acres of the mangrove forest.[45] The company's actions caused great environmental devastation and it then refused to clean up oil spills,[46] thus evading accountability.[47] In the case of internet.org by Meta, formerly Facebook, which was launched in many global Majority countries, the company offered 'free' internet access but had full control over the content and media that users could access, thus undermining internet neutrality, while whitewashing its actions with a facade of altruism by marketing access to the internet as free.

The emergence of IEL is an important point of comparison and source of inspiration for data law for several reasons. Firstly, this field has incrementally developed over the last 50-odd years. This includes in terms of the recognition of different types of harms and the framing of grievances such as the environmental-related effects on health. As a field, there has been an articulation of principles such as the 'polluter pays principle' or the 'precautionary principle,' which are increasingly being adopted in legal reasoning to adjudicate disputes. Institutions are being developed to determine ways to study, regulate, and monitor the consequences of environmental injustice, such as specialised green tribunals or a dedicated UN agency like the United Nations Environment Programme (UNEP).[48] Secondly, by virtue of developing incrementally, the core of environmental law is dynamic and iterative.[49] This reflects an understanding that the phenomenon that is being regulated needs to closely tie to continuously emerging scientific expertise.[50] Thirdly, as an emergent field of international law, environmental law has also allowed for the re-conceptualisation of concepts such as state sovereignty, corporate liability,[51] as well as benefit and burden-sharing

43 Henshaw/Stuart (2021).

44 Solon (2017).

45 Craig (2022).

46 ECLI:NL:GHDHA:2021:132.

47 Wifa/Adebola (2021).

48 Dupuy/Viñuales (2018), p. 27.

49 Ghaleigh (2016).

50 Fisher (2019).

51 Varvastian/Kalunga (2020).

agreements[52] to name a few. These innovative mechanisms are a consequence of societal transformations and the law having to respond to emergent threats and challenges from environmental destruction. As data regulators and GDL scholars deal with corporate overreach and other harms resulting from the actions of technology companies, they can find guidance in the successes and failures in holding polluting corporations responsible under IEL.

Fourthly, IEL's struggles at building international solidarity and collaboration also have important lessons in thinking about aspects of responsibility. For instance, countries in the global Majority have long been highlighting the disproportionate historic and continuing contributions to environmental degradation, and the need for global regulation that acknowledges this difference. This is typified by the challenges that were faced by negotiators drafting the Kyoto Protocol, which established mandatory commitments amongst the parties to act against climate change and the transition now to a more bottom-up governance approach that is present in the Paris Agreement. The Kyoto Protocol introduced a market-based approach to curbing emissions, an approach that has been disastrous for the planet. The Paris Agreement, on the other hand, while still imperfect, emphasises the interconnectedness of nations and focuses on global cooperation.[53] The different shapes within which such agreements have come to pass are also a reflection of both the successes and failures of institutional mechanisms like the Conference of Parties seeking to build international consensus on the way forward to address environmental and climate injustices. These institutional mechanisms are also important for GDL to consider so as to ensure that the lives and territories of the global Minority are not compromised in favour of the economic interests of the global Minority.

Fifthly, and of particular interest to us in this chapter, is the value of principles that have emerged in IEL. Principles in environmental law have been important legal instruments with their presence in both international soft law instruments, as well as through adoption by national jurisdictions.[54] Scotford discusses how environmental principles act as 'legal connectors across jurisdictions, reflecting the inherent nature of environmental law as a transnational enterprise, these connections are subtler than simply representing the emergence of a common set of identical legal phenomena globally.'[55] Principles thereby are also inherently flexible, and malleable in that they allow for them to be interpreted, bearing in mind different legal cultures, and local specificities. In a dynamic landscape of GDL, with differing market specificities, digital infrastructural capacity as well regulatory institutions, drawing on principles can have value in terms of presenting a global approach to regulating data law.

With these considerations in mind, in the next three sections, we will discuss three fundamental ideas that can govern data law from a social justice standpoint. We group these considerations around firstly, the ways in which the law needs to respond to the emergence of harms, and how these affect people in differentiated

[52] Oberthür (2006).

[53] Denchak (2021).

[54] Scotford (2019).

[55] Scotford (2019).

ways in global contexts. Secondly, we draw a link between the emergence of harm, and the challenges of the allocation of responsibility, and why responsibility need to be constructed in systemic ways. Thirdly, we connect the identification of responsibility to identifying pathways to secure rights and entitlements, by reflecting on the development of a rights-based approach to governance. We organise the analysis by discussing why we are focussing on a particular development (e.g. with regard to harm), what are the ways in which it has emerged in IEL, and finally what we see as value for GDL.

4 Articulation of Harm

Identifying and naming the nature of environmental harms has been key to developing a common vocabulary and a shared understanding of the effects on the environment, and the types of actors who are responsible for it. Recognising harm is also essential for creating a governance and regulatory framework, and ways to seek redressal for those who have been affected.

In order to constitute an understanding of harm for GDL, ideas can be drawn from the no-harm rule. A well-known principle of international law, it states that States are 'duty-bound to prevent, reduce, and control the risk of environmental harm to other States'.[56] The origin of this principle lies in the concept of sovereignty under public international law, wherein states are under an obligation not to inflict damage on, or violate the interests of other states. This principle has been used in the environmental context in the case of regional and international environmental problems. Regional environmental problems include transboundary air and water pollution, impacts of resource extraction, nuclear accidents, and international trade involving hazardous materials. At the international level, environmental issues include ozone depletion, species extinction, biodiversity loss, depleted fish stocks and standing forests, and human-caused climate change, among others.[57]

The no-harm rule has been critical to clarifying aspects, for instance, of territorial integrity at a national level and identifying the ways in which states might cooperate with each other to take measures to prevent harm. It has been useful to define the contours of harm through the development of instruments such as conducting environmental impact assessments or having consultations with populations in different local contexts.[58]The no-harm principle was applied by an arbitral tribunal in 1941 in the Trail Smelter case, a transboundary air pollution dispute between USA and Canada wherein the tribunal, basing its reasoning in the concepts of sovereignty and territorial integrity, held Canada responsible.[59] The tribunal held that Canada's state

[56] Brownlie (2008), pp. 275-285; Birnie/Boyle/Redgwell (2009), pp. 143-152.

[57] Jervan (2014).

[58] Tignino/Bréthaut (2020).

[59] Trail Smelter case (1941).

sovereignty was limited by its obligation to act in within its territory in a manner that does not harm other States and their sovereignty.[60]

Resource extraction and accompanying emissions occurring within the boundaries of one state have an impact on the rest of the planet owing to the interconnected nature of our global commons.[61] Under the present environmental governance mechanisms, national emissions are calculated at the source or the point of production, instead of in the country of use or the point of consumption.[62] This means that emissions resulting from goods produced in countries like China are included in the annual emissions tally of China, instead of European countries, with one of the highest consumption rates in the world, where these goods are sold and used. Similarly, the inability or unwillingness of global Minority countries to contain consumption or recycle trashed goods leads to this waste being sent to countries like Turkey, Chile, and India causing sky-high landfills.[63] This regulatory construction of the emissions, harms, and responsibility system feeds into parochial ideas of who contributes to our planet's disintegration and who should be subject to strict regulation.[64]

As another example of cross-border harms resulting from resource extraction in one jurisdiction, we know that the destruction of the Amazon rainforest within the borders of Brazil has an impact on the air quality, biodiversity, and territory rights of individuals within neighbouring states. As the lungs of our planet, once the Amazon rainforest becomes a carbon source instead of a carbon sink, environmental harms done in one part of the world have an impact everywhere else. Political permissiveness stemming from authoritarianism and a lack of regulation affect the lives of every being on the planet. Thus, the Brazilian state may be said to owe the rest of the world to protect the natural resources within its borders, and, more specifically, owe other states to prevent emissions so as to reduce the environmental protection burden of the latter. However this is not aided by European colonial expansion into Brazil and continuing neocolonial ventures by American and European corporate powers that have played a massive role in the destruction of the rainforest.[65] In the Brazilian example, we have observed a marked change in public policy and outcomes over the last few years following a change in government.[66] We can conclude that authoritarian, market-oriented administrations directly contribute to climate collapse, whereas broad-based, equitable governments have the power to uplift the rights of all peoples and ensure the protection of the planet.

IEL is also developing a justiciable regime for determining the source of harm and holding polluters accountable for compensation. For example, in the 2018 case between Costa Rica and Nicaragua, the International Court of Justice held that activities within Nicaraguan territories caused an adverse environmental impact in Costa

[60] Tignino/Bréthaut (2020).

[61] United States v. Canada, 1938 and 1941, 3 R.I.A.A. 1905.

[62] Steinwehr (2021), McKibben (2023).

[63] European Parliament (2023), Bartlett (2023).

[64] McKibben (2023).

[65] Tavares (2023).

[66] Rodrigues (2023).

Rica. The Court also established that the damage to the environment and the cost of restoration was eligible for compensation under international law.[67] A week later, the Inter-American Court of Human Rights also published its Advisory Opinion on the Environment and Human Rights wherein it stated that states are under an obligation to prevent environmental harms to individuals both within and outside its territory. This advisory opinion affirmed that a healthy environment is essential for the protection of all other human rights, and that cross-border responsibility exists in cases of cross-border environmental harms.[68]

Similar to environmental pollution and harms, many data-related interventions have been seen to create harm in a transboundary fashion, wherein the harms created in one jurisdiction have grave impacts in another.[69] For example, in the case of the Cambridge Analytica scandal, the lack of oversight and regulation in one jurisdiction enabled violations of rights in several other jurisdictions.[70] Facebook's actions, too, in its unwillingness to regulate harmful, incendiary speech in Myanmar, led to the loss of human life, ultimately resulting in war crimes.[71] In these instances, harms are not confined to a single jurisdiction since the inability or unwillingness of one state actor to regulate corporations incorporated under its law creates irreversible repercussions for individuals and communities in other states. Data collection and processing may be hazardous and, if not handled well, can create dangerous data pollution, which should be viewed less as a harm to the privacy interest of individuals and more as a harm to the public sphere. When discussing the management of data spills, Ben-Shahar highlights that since digital matter is infinitely replicable by the touch of a button, unlike in the clean-up of hazardous environmental waste sites, it is not containable.[72] The Data Pollution & Power Initiative defines data pollution in terms of 'the interrelated adverse impacts of the generation, storing, handling, and processing of digital data on the natural, social, and personal environment through unsustainable handling, distribution, and generation of data resources'.[73]

Respecting the global environmental commons and the individual (and community) rights to a safe and healthy environment requires states to act in cooperation. Owing to the international nature of climate harms, it is imperative to move away from the notion of individual-level rights and harms and towards entitlements and harms at the societal level. Even presently, a small minority of states, corporations, and individual actors cause a disproportionate amount of harm to the global environmental commons.[74] Drawing from the concept of global environmental commons, states have a responsibility to cooperate and take coordinated action to protect our global

---

[67] Certain Activities Carried Out by Nicaragua in the Border Area (Costa Rica v. Nicaragua), Compensation, Judgment, I.C.J. Reports 2018, p. 15.

[68] Inter-American Court Of Human Rights Advisory Opinion Oc-23/17 Of November 15, 2017.

[69] The Data Pollution & Power - Initiative.

[70] Humble (2021).

[71] Fink (2018).

[72] Ben-Shahar (2018).

[73] Hasselbalch (2022).

[74] Griffin (2017), p. 8; Evans (2021).

data commons. Similar to rectifying past environmental harms and repairing injury and destruction, in the environmental context, so emerges a concept of historical harms carried out in the digital sphere.

The intersections between the environment and data are also visible in the rampant extraction in both spheres. Technological companies routinely operate with extractive tendencies with disregard for individual and community rights in the absence of a clear framework holding them accountable. These impacts can also be seen in the immense environmental harm posed by large data centres alongside territory rights violations through large-scale land grabs and displacement.[75] As discussed earlier, instances of resources being diverted away from the local populations to benefit large, technology multinationals, such as in the case of the data centres being built by Google, in drought prone areas in Uruguay are increasingly becoming common.[76] There are also cases where digital technology projects have an adverse impact on the political, social, and economic bundle of rights of communities for example through extraction and exploitation in supply chains for raw materials necessary to produce technological products, like in the Congo.[77] The concept of Free, Prior, and Informed Consent (FPIC) allows for community input and governance of projects that relate to them. Deriving from Indigenous rights scholarship and jurisprudence under IEL and domestic environmental and administrative laws, local communities' ability to have FPIC ensures that extraction of resources and knowledge takes place without accounting for power asymmetries. Environmental Impact Assessments (EIA) too are proposed under IEL to prevent, mitigate, and manage any potential adverse impacts of proposed projects. Under the Convention on Biological Diversity, for example, EIAs take into account not just the potential impact on the natural environment, but also social, cultural, and human health impacts at the planning stage to make sure that decision-makers are fully aware of the predictions and can shape projects to suit the local environment. Taking inspiration from environmental policy and including the concepts of FPIC and EIA in GDL would go a long way in ensuring that technological interventions are locally appropriate and locally accountable.

5 Locating Responsibility in GDL

Connected with the concept of harm developed in the last section, in this section, we examine how responsibility can be understood for GDL through examining developments in IEL. As a starting point, we take the fact that studying the impacts of harms requires seeing them in a historical sense. We know that those most affected by our current climate crisis are the ones who have historically contributed the least

[75] Mejias (2022).

[76] Livingstone (2023).

[77] Amnesty International (2016).

to it.[78] Some states have had an outsized impact on the global temperature rise,[79] and ensuing rise in sea levels, increase in instances of natural disasters, loss of habitat, and mass displacement.[80] Historical and ongoing colonialism and extraction, thus, are hugely responsible for the climate crisis we face today.[81] Scholars have called on state powers that have benefitted from colonialism to repair the historical harm their actions have caused.[82] Climate scientists have recognised colonialism as a historic and ongoing driver of climate change, and policy spaces such as the UN IPCC have also named colonialism as a contributor to global heating.[83]

Of relevance here is Principle 7 of the Rio Declaration laying out the principle of common but differentiated responsibility: "*In view of the different contributions to global environmental degradation, States have common but differentiated responsibilities. The developed countries acknowledge the responsibility that they bear in the international pursuit of sustainable development in view of the pressures their societies place on the global environment and of the technologies and financial resources they command.*"[84] The historicity of the common but differentiated responsibility principle is important because it connects thinking about the climate crisis not as a singular event but as an ongoing issue, which needs to be placed along a longer arc of extractivism and dispossession.[85]

This principle has value for GDL because much like the fact that the climate crisis is a result of years of irresponsible industrial and economic expansion that has taken place in the global Minority for the benefit of the global Minority, we are seeing similar extractive logics when it comes to technology, and the growth of technology companies.[86] As a principle, this is significant because it acknowledges differing responsibility on account of environmental degradation and the necessity to consider the different needs, resources, and capacities of States.

In fact, we argue, thinking historically is important because it acknowledges that the colonial ways in which resources have been extracted, lands have been mined, and people have been exploited to foster economic growth are central to the climate emergency.[87] This is apparent in regard to the fact that the largest technological corporations are based in the United States, with a few exceptions in Europe and China. As a consequence, there are emerging epistemological inequities, and thus, asymmetries between priorities for a digital economy between places that have digital technology behemoths and the rest of the world.[88] Internet.org, which we

---

[78] IPCC (2023b), p. 5.
[79] IPCC (2013).
[80] Singh (2023), p. 50.
[81] Crate (2009), p. 190; Voskoboynik (2018).
[82] Chapman/Ahmed (2021).
[83] IPCC (2023a).
[84] United Nations (1992).
[85] Sultana (2022), Bolados/Panez/Jérez (2023).
[86] Kazansky et al. (2022).
[87] Waters (2023).
[88] Mignolo (2011), Ricaurte (2022).

discussed briefly earlier, the free internet basics program from Meta, is one example where Meta, under the guise of offering access to the internet, instead offered a walled garden which determined how people should access the internet.[89] This differentiation between how different countries will be able to shape technology governance requires examining who has the responsibility to challenge big tech power.

Such an understanding of the principle of common but differentiated responsibility is important for the scholars of GDL, since we know that the global Minority States, whether through permissiveness or through disregard, have failed to regulate the private actors (such as Big Tech companies) cementing historical harms and creating new forms of injustice beyond their borders, such as in the case of Cambridge Analytica shared previously. In a bid to make markets more innovative and competitive, there has been a lack of regulation of companies incorporated within global Minority jurisdictions. Taking a lesson from IEL, we argue that global Minority States should fulfil their responsibility owed to the rest of the world to prevent and address harm caused by technology actors and regulate for the common good. If they don't, they risk facilitating digital colonialism following similar trends of extraction, like in environmental colonialism, where countries in the global Majority continue to be grounds for extraction, experimentation, and exploitation.[90]

Related to examining the aspect of temporality in responsibility is also the question of inter-generational equity. The principle of inter-generational equity places the question of responsibility not just in terms of the current generation, but also what these choices hold for future generations.[91] Brown-Weiss discussed three aspects of the principle, the first is in terms of creating options for future generations, the second is in ensuring that there is quality to the resources available, and the third is to ensure access to resources.[92] In doing so, the principle reinforces the idea that responsibility is required to be ongoing, and accounts for material-epistemic changes to the socio-technical environment. This principle assumes importance for GDL because assigning responsibility for data-related harms also requires addressing the fact that many such harms emerge on account of structural and systemic injustices that exist in society. In the Netherlands, for instance, the Dutch tax authorities, while attempting to regulate child benefits, wrongly accused 26,000 parents of fraud. It was found that parents who had dual nationality, or were ethnically non-Dutch, were discriminated against.[93] There are numerous examples of algorithms discriminating on the basis of race, for instance.[94] These examples demonstrate the historicity of how data-related harms emerge. They reflect many of the faultlines in society, and efforts to address such harms, assign responsibility, and ensure accountability must account for the challenges that emerge through inter-generational discrimination.[95]

---

[89] Solon (2017).

[90] Couldry/Mejias (2020), Amrute/Singh/Guzmán (2022).

[91] United Nations (1992).

[92] Brown/Weiss (2008).

[93] Heikkilä (2022).

[94] Benjamin (2016), Forster (2023).

[95] Halsband (2022).

The third aspect of responsibility that we would like to discuss, draws from the the precautionary principle in environmental law. In the Rio Declaration of 1992, Principle 15 states, "*[I]n order to protect the environment, the precautionary approach shall be widely applied by States according to their capabilities. Where there are threats of serious or irreversible damage, lack of full scientific certainty shall not be used as a reason for postponing cost-effective measures to prevent environmental degradation.*"[96] This principle advances the idea that it is critical that those advocating for an activity that has the potential to cause environmental harm should also necessarily take steps to prevent the potential for that harm to be caused. This marks a shift where previously scientific certainty was often used as a reason to not act.

The precautionary principle, coupled with the polluter pays principle, which states that those who have caused environmental damage are required to pay the costs towards mitigating it, presents important pathways to attributing responsibility for data-related harms.

In the regulation of data, emphasis is placed on creating conditions for data to be traded and for it to flow to foster innovation, economic efficiency, and growth. However, underpinning such flows is the material infrastructure that determines the nature with which data is collected, curated, shared, and used.[97]

Data builds upon the labour of people, who work in difficult conditions to do more mundane work such as cleaning, annotating and labelling. This work, which is increasingly being conducted in countries in the global Majority exploiting lower salary requirements, lower forms of compliance, and also dire economic conditions, has created digital sweatshops to enable the functioning of products such as Chat GPT.[98] Not only are workers employed under dire financial conditions, but they are also exploited by being made to label data that has violent gender, sexual, and racial elements, as has been seen in the recent case of Kenyan workers working with Open AI through a partner organisation called Sama.[99]

Companies have in the past exploited legal and financial loopholes to outsource work to places where the financial costs of polluting to them are lower. This, of course, requires caution, because fundamental to such a framing is that there must be responsibility assigned to those that cause degradation and harm.[100] In this particular case, the impacts of doing data work are well known to companies, not only by the fact that these jobs are being outsourced, and companies are taking advantage of people's precarity, by exploiting catastrophic economic conditions.[101] That they do not take the necessary steps to provide conditions to mitigate the effects that might be caused from doing such work is a function of the economic choices being made by companies. Drawing from the precautionary principle and the polluter pays principle

---

[96] United Nations General Assembly (1992).

[97] Vatanparast (2020).

[98] Nyabola (2023).

[99] Perrigo (2023), Dinika (2024).

[100] Choi/Yu (2017); C-477/14, *Pillbox 38 (UK) Ltd v The Secretary of State for Health*, ecli:EU:C:2016:324.

[101] Hao/Hernández.

will ensure that steps are taken to manage risk, as well as to demonstrate that steps are taken to reduce the potential for harm.

6 The Right to a Healthy Environment: Lessons for Global Data Law

In the previous sections, we have seen how international environmental law principles such as the precautionary principle and the common but differentiated responsibility principles have helped developing IEL. Among the contributions of IEL and the international environmental legal regime such as the acceptance of the legal personhood of nature[102] and group rights,[103] we also see the development of a right to a healthy environment. The development of this right could be of interest to GDL scholars and policymakers as they seek to centre 'data subjects' or human beings' interests in data regulation.

The recognition of a right to a healthy environment is important since it strengthens the understanding of the degree of human-caused environmental harm that communities are contending with, while also laying the groundwork for legislative reform in States that are yet to pass environmental protection. A rights-led approach strengthens implementation of environmental regulation and enhances accountability through strengthened environmental mechanisms and institutions.[104] The recognition of this right has helped hold polluters accountable, promote biodiversity conservation,[105] and uplift ecologically sustainable development.[106] A rights-led approach to IEL also has the potential to uplift women's participation in environmental governance[107] and Indigenous sovereignty and self-determination.[108]

The earliest iteration of something resembling a right to a healthy environment can be found in the Article 12 of the International Covenant on Economic, Social and Cultural Rights (ICESCR), which states that State parties to the Covenant "*recognize the right of everyone to the enjoyment of the highest attainable standard of physical and mental health*," and that the steps taken to achieve the full realisation of this right include "*[t]he improvement of all aspects of environmental and industrial hygiene*." In 2021, the United Nations Human Rights Council adopted a resolution (48/13) recognising a human right to a clean, healthy, and sustainable environment. Following this resolution,[109] in 2022, the United Nations General Assembly recognised (A/76/L.75) that a clean, healthy, and sustainable environment is a human right. The Human

102 Łaszewska-Hellriegel (2022).

103 Inter-American Court Of Human Rights Advisory Opinion (2017).

104 OHCHR, UNEP, UNDP (2023).

105 Caso Habitantes de La Oroya Vs. Perú (2023).

106 ECLI:NL:GHDHA:2018:2591.

107 Prior/Heinämäki (2017).

108 Boyd (2024).

109 Gueye/de Meyer (2022).

Rights Council established the mandate for an independent expert on human rights and the environment in 2012 (resolution 19/10). The United Nations Special Rapporteur on Human Rights and the Environment has the mandate to examine human rights obligations, promote best practices, and identify challenges and obstacles to the global recognition and implementation of the right to a safe, clean, healthy, and sustainable environment.

The legal momentum emerging from the incorporation of the aforementioned principles into court judgments and advisory opinions has led to the creation of the human right to a healthy environment. Justice-oriented scholars and movements have placed equity at the centre of the legal response to the climate catastrophe, and within it, the right to a healthy environment. As the international environmental legal system has undergone maturity and formalisation over the past years through international agreements and judicial decisions, this human right to a healthy environment is interpreted and unpacked to be broad, consisting of all life on the planet. From the rights of human beings and communities to be protected from emissions[110] to biodiversity protection,[111] soil health,[112] moratoria on deep seabed mining,[113] and the rights of women,[114] Indigenous Peoples,[115] and farmers[116] specifically, have been recognised and proposed to be within the umbrella of the right to a healthy environment.

This bundle of rights makes it clear that this right is broad and expansive, and that protecting the environment necessitates the protection of ecosystems, food and energy sources, and the rights of those historically marginalised in an extractive system.[117] These approaches interpret climate change beyond simply a ‘crisis of carbon’[118] and take a broad view of the root causes and symptoms of the climate crisis.

The development of GDL is at a critical juncture, as regional entities such as the EU are scrutinising the future of technologies such as AI. The absence of a rights-oriented approach to data would only harm human welfare there exist a number of lessons for GDL from the debates in IEL over the years.

First, GDL can avoid the friction between environmental protection and trade promotion, by recognising that economic growth and human development are not necessarily linked, and that policies that undermine human rights are bound to further solidify power and epistemological asymmetries.[119] Second, GDL scholars ought to be wary of diluting the language of rights to promote profit creation, as has

110 Varvastian (2019).

111 Solon (2012).

112 Claeys (2013).

113 Hamley (2023).

114 Lee (2000).

115 Boyd (2024).

116 Claeys (2013).

117 Borras (2008).

118 Climate Justice Alliance (2018).

119 Sander (2023).

happened in the environmental context. Governments and multinational corporations have co-opted much of the rights language used by environmental civil society organisations to greenwash their reputation, while their actions continue to harm the planet.[120] Third, regulation under GDL would need to move beyond the product liability considerations of laws such as the EU AI Act. This is because risk assessments enshrine a subjective form of risk acceptance.[121] GDL regulations could move towards becoming human rights protecting instruments that incorporate an understanding of the history, reality, and peoples' material conditions, to ensure that no technological innovation or financial gain is placed above the State's responsibility to respect human life and dignity. This approach would be in line with the objectives of the Global Digital Compact, which in turn incorporates the principles underpinning the Charter of the United Nations, international human rights law, and the 2030 Agenda for Sustainable Development.

Following from this, a conclusion can be made that to ensure effective and just data governance, GDL has the opportunity to conceptualise and formalise a human rights-oriented approach to data governance. Following the analysis of a broad right to a healthy environment, this approach will go beyond data protection to creating a governance framework that encompasses the respect, protection, and promotion of the rights people who use of data as individuals and groups. GDL can go one step beyond the IEL framework in making the rights surrounding data justiciable and ensuring respect for individual and community rights. Some of these efforts are evident in recent policy and jurisprudence surrounding content moderation,[122] predictive policing,[123] automated decision-making tools,[124] facial recognition in public spaces,[125] and data scraping by private actors.[126]

7 Conclusion

In this chapter, we set out to explore what core aspects of a GDL could look like if seen from a social justice standpoint. Our interest in carrying out this exercise was to centre questions of equity and dignity into how the interests of people and across contexts could be considered more seriously in data regulation. For several reasons as described above, we argue that IEL can serve as an important benchmark, not just

[120] Guenther (2024).

[121] Hidvegi/Leufer/Massé (2021).

[122] The Republic of the Gambia v. Facebook, Inc., 20-mc-36-JEB-ZMF.

[123] Warso (2022).

[124] Judgement of 7 December 2023, Schufa, C-634/21 EU:C:2023:957.

[125] R v. the Chief Constable of South Wales Police, C1/2019/2670, [2020] EWCA Civ 1058; Rabinowicz (2023).

[126] Injunction order against Clearview AI / Ordinanza ingiunzione nei confronti di Clearview AI, 10 February 2022, 9751362 European Data Protection Board (2022).

in providing examples of dealing with an emergent and dynamic field of law, but also as a source of inspiration to address complex socio-technical realities.

Struggles for environmental justice, in terms of debates around extractivism, transboundary harms, disparities between the global Majority and global Minority, and continuing effects of colonialism, are sites of contestation that see parallels when extrapolated to the digital world.

In order to develop a response that provides fundamental principles to safeguard those most marginalised by technology, we argue for exploring the challenges around harms, responsibilities, and rights as key tenets of a GDL.

This chapter thereby offers a contribution that seeks to shift focus of thinking about regulating data purely as a resource that can be exchanged and traded to one that can materially affect people who use it or are affected by it. In doing so, it argues for paying close attention to engaging with systemic challenges in a data economy between regions, generations, and communities to ensure that regulation truly ensures justice for all.

Acknowledgements The authors would like to thank and acknowledge the valuable insights of colleagues at the Global Data Justice Project at Tilburg Institute for Law, Technology and Society in the development of this research.

References

Adeola O (2001). Digestion and Balance Techniques in Pigs. https://doi.org/10.1201/9781420041842.ch40

Amnesty International (2016) "This is what we die for": human rights abuses in the Democratic Republic of the Congo power the global trade in cobalt

Amrute S, Singh R, Guzmán RL (2022) A primer on AI in/from the majority world: an empirical site and a standpoint. https://datasociety.net/library/a-primer-on-ai-in-from-the-majority-world/

Bartlett J (2023) Fast fashion goes to die in the world's largest fog desert. The scale is breathtaking. National Geographic. https://www.nationalgeographic.com/environment/article/chile-fashion-pollution. Accessed 6 Nov 2024

Barendrecht M, Kamminga P, Verdonschot JH (2008) Priorities for the justice system: responding to the most urgent legal problems of individuals. TISCO Working Paper

Ben-Shahar O (2018) Data pollution. Coase-Sandor Working Paper Series in Law and Economics

Benjamin R (2016) Catching our breath: critical race STS and the carceral imagination. Engag Sci Technol Soc 2:145–156

Birnie P, Boyle A, Redgwell C (2009) International law and the environment, 3rd edn. Oxford University Press, Oxford

Bradford A (2020) The Brussels effect. In: Bradford A (ed) The Brussels effect: how the European Union rules the world. Oxford University Press, Oxford

Bryan K, Hodgson C, Tauschinski J (2024) Amazon, meta and big tech's bid to rewrite the rules on net zero. The Irish Times. https://www.irishtimes.com/business/2024/08/14/amazon-meta-and-big-techs-bid-to-rewrite-the-rules-on-net-zero/. Accessed 6 Nov 2024

Brown Weiss E (2008) Climate change, intergenerational equity, and international law. Georgetown Law Faculty Publications and Other Works

Brownlie I (2008) Principles of public international law, 7th edn. Oxford University Press, Oxford

Bonilla Maldonado D (2018) The political economy of legal knowledge. In: Bonilla Maldonado D, Crawford C (eds) Constitutionalism in the Americas. Edward Elgar, Cheltenham
Borras SM Jr (2008) La Vía Campesina and its global campaign for Agrarian reform. J Agrar Chang 8:258–289. https://doi.org/10.1111/j.1471-0366.2008.00170.x
Bolados P, Panez A, Jérez B (2023) Resistance to dispossession and environmental suffering in territories sacrificed by neoextractivism: the example of Chile. Routledge, London
Boshe P, Caride CG (2024) Is the Brussels Effect Creating a New Legal Order in Africa and Latin America and the Caribbean? Technol Regul 2024:12–18. https://doi.org/10.26116/tecchreg.2024.002
Boyd D (2024) Landmark Court Decision on Right to a Healthy Environment: La Oroya v Peru – GNHRE. https://gnhre.org/?p=17944. Accessed 6 Nov 2024
C-477/14, Pillbox 38 (UK) Ltd v The Secretary of State for Health, ecli:EU:C:2016:324
Carroll SR, Garba I, Figueroa-Rodríguez OL et al (2020) The CARE principles for indigenous data governance. Data Sci J. https://doi.org/10.5334/dsj-2020-043
Climate Justice Alliance (2018) Just transition principles. https://climatejusticealliance.org/wp-content/uploads/2018/06/CJA_JustTransition_Principles_final_hi-rez.pdf. Accessed 6 Nov 2024
Craig J (2022) The village that stood up to big oil – and won. The Guardian. https://www.theguardian.com/environment/ng-interactive/2022/jun/01/oil-pollution-spill-nigeria-shell-lawsuit Accessed 6 Nov 2024
Corte IDH. Caso Habitantes de La Oroya Vs. Perú. Excepciones Preliminares, Fondo, Reparaciones y Costas. Sentencia de 27 de noviembre de 2023. Serie C No. 511
Crate S (2009) Viliui Sakha of Subartic Russia and their struggle for environmental justice. In: Agyeman J, Ogneva-Himmelberger Y (eds) Environmental justice and sustainability in the former Soviet Union. MIT Press, Cambridge
Celeste E (2022a) Digital constitutionalism: the role of internet bills of rights. Routledge, London
Celeste E (2022b) What is digital constitutionalism? The Digital Constitutionalist. digi-con.org/what-is-digital-constitutionalism/. Accessed 6 Nov 2024
Chapman AR, Ahmed AK (2021) Climate justice, humans rights, and the case for reparations. Health Hum Rights 23:81–94
Choi JY, Yu ESH (2017) International outsourcing, environmental costs, and welfare. Asia Pathways. Asian Development Bank Institute. https://www.asiapathways-adbi.org/2017/12/international-outsourcing-environmental-costs-and-welfare/. Accessed 6 Nov 2024
Couldry N, Mejias UA (2020) The costs of connection: how data is colonizing human life and appropriating it for capitalism. Stanford University Press, Redwood City
Claeys P (2013) From Food sovereignty to peasants' rights: an overview of via Campesina's struggle for new human rights. In: La Via Campesina's open book: celebrating 20 years of struggle and hope
C-477/14, Pillbox 38 (UK) Ltd v The Secretary of State for Health, ecli:EU:C:2016:324
De R (2018) A people's constitution: the everyday life of law in the Indian Republic. Princeton University Press
De Souza SP, Sharma G (2023) Resist & reboot: a playbook for solidarity in digital rights work. https://globaldatajustice.org/wp-content/uploads/2023/03/Resist-and-Reboot_280223.pdf. Accessed 6 Nov 2024
de Souza SP, Taylor L (2025) Rebooting the global consensus: norm entrepreneurship, data governance and the inalienability of digital bodies. Big Data Soc 12(2). https://doi.org/10.1177/20539517251330191
Denchak M (2021) Paris climate agreement: everything you need to know. natural resources defense council. https://www.nrdc.org/stories/paris-climate-agreement-everything-you-need-know. Accessed 6 Nov 2024
Dencik L, Sanchez-Monedero J (2022) Data justice. Internet Policy Rev 11
Dinika A (2024) The human cost of our AI-driven future. Noema Magazine. https://www.noemamag.com/the-human-cost-of-our-ai-driven-future/. Accessed 6 Nov 2024

Dupuy PM, Viñuales JE (2018) International environmental law, 2nd edn. University Press, Cambridge
(2018) ECLI:NL:GHDHA:2018:2591, Gerechtshof Den Haag, 200.178.245/01
(2021) ECLI:NL:GHDHA:2021:1825, Gerechtshof Den Haag, 200.126.804/01 200.126.834/01
European Data Protection Board (2022) Facial recognition: Italian SA fines Clearview AI EUR 20 million. https://edpb.europa.eu/news/national-news/2022/facial-recognition-italian-sa-fines-clearview-ai-eur-20-million_en. Accessed 6 Nov 2024
European Commission (2016) Regulation - 2016/679 - EN - gdpr - EUR-Lex. https://eur-lex.europa.eu/eli/reg/2016/679/oj. Accessed 24 Feb 2025
European Commission (2022a) The digital markets act. https://commission.europa.eu/strategy-and-policy/priorities-2019-2024/europe-fit-digital-age/digital-markets-act-ensuring-fair-and-open-digital-markets_en. Accessed 24 Feb 2025
European Commission (2022b) The digital services act. https://digital-strategy.ec.europa.eu/en/policies/digital-services-act-package. Accessed 24 Feb 2025
European Commission (2022b) European data governance act. https://digital-strategy.ec.europa.eu/en/policies/data-governance-act. Accessed 24 Feb 2025
European Commission (2024) Data act. https://digital-strategy.ec.europa.eu/en/policies/data-act. Accessed 16 Oct 2024
European Commission (2024c) AI Act | Shaping Europe's digital future. https://digital-strategy.ec.europa.eu/en/policies/regulatory-framework-ai. Accessed 24 Feb 2025
European Union (2023) A European Strategy for data | Shaping Europe's digital future. https://digital-strategy.ec.europa.eu/en/policies/strategy-data. Accessed 24 Feb 2025
European Parliament (2023) Waste management in the EU: infographic with facts and figures. https://www.europarl.europa.eu/news/en/headlines/society/20180328STO00751/waste-management-in-the-eu-infographic-with-facts-and-figures. Accessed 6 Nov 2024
Evans S (2021) Analysis: which countries are historically responsible for climate change? CarbonBrief. https://www.carbonbrief.org/analysis-which-countries-are-historically-responsible-for-climate-change/ Accessed 6 Nov 2024
Fink C (2018) Dangerous speech, anti-Muslim violence, and Facebook in Myanmar. J Int Aff 71:43–52
Fisher E (2019) Sciences, environmental laws, and legal cultures: fostering collective epistemic responsibility. In: Lees E, Viñuales JE (eds) The Oxford handbook of comparative environmental law. Oxford University Press, Oxford
Freeland S (2015) Addressing the intentional destruction of the environment during warfare under the Rome statute of the international criminal court. Maastricht University
Forster M (2023) Refugee protection in the artificial intelligence era. A test case for rights. Chatham House
Genn H (1999) The landscape of justiciable problems. In: Paths to justice: what people do and think about going to law. Hart Publishing
Ghaleigh NS (2016) Science and climate change law—the role of the IPCC in international decision-making. In: Gray KR, Tarasofsky R, Carlarne CP (eds) The Oxford handbook of international climate change law. Oxford University Press
Gitelman L (ed) (2013) Raw data" is an oxymoron. MIT Press, Cambridge
Global Data Justice Global Data Justice. http://globaldatajustice.org/. Accessed 24 Feb 2025
Global Data Law, Passau (2023) Comparative data law conference (part of the global data law series). https://www.uni-passau.de/en/international/news/news/comparative-data-law-conference-part-of-the-global-data-law-series. Accessed 24 Feb 2025
Griffin P (2017) The carbon majors database: CDP carbon majors report 2017. https://cdn.cdp.net/cdp-production/cms/reports/documents/000/002/327/original/Carbon-Majors-Report-2017.pdf Accessed 6 Nov 2024
Gramatikov M, Barendrecht M, Verdonschot JH (2011) Measuring the costs and quality of paths to justice: contours of a methodology (September 17, 2008). Hague Journal on the Rule of Law 3,

349–379, Tilburg University Legal Studies Working Paper No. 009/2008, Available at SSRN: https://ssrn.com/abstract=1269328

Guenther G (2024) The language of climate politics: fossil-fuel propaganda and how to fight it. Oxford University Press, Oxford

Gueye MK, de Meyer T (2022) UN General Assembly recognizes human right to a clean, healthy, and sustainable environment. International Labour Organization. https://www.ilo.org/global/about-the-ilo/newsroom/news/WCMS_857164/lang--en/index.htm. Accessed 6 Nov 2024

Gonzalez C, Atapattu S (2016) International environmental law, environmental justice, and the global south. https://papers.ssrn.com/sol3/papers.cfm?abstract_id=2992297 Accessed 7 Feb 2025.

Halsband A (2022) Sustainable AI and intergenerational justice. Sustainability 14:3922. https://doi.org/10.3390/su14073922

Hasselbalch G (2022) Data Pollution & Power. White paper for a global sustainable development agenda on AI. The Sustainable AI Lab, Bonn University

Hamley G (2023) The human right to health and marine biodiversity nexus: an integrated approach for a healthy future. Faculty of Humanities and Social Sciences, School of Law, University of Strathclyde

Hao K, Hernández AP. How the AI industry profits from catastrophe. MIT Technology Review. https://www.technologyreview.com/2022/04/20/1050392/ai-industry-appen-scale-data-labels/. Accessed 24 Feb 2025

Heikkilä M (2022) Dutch scandal serves as a warning for Europe over risks of using algorithms. Politico. https://www.politico.eu/article/dutch-scandal-serves-as-a-warning-for-europe-over-risks-of-using-algorithms/. Accessed 6 Nov 2024

Henshaw K, Stuart F (2021). 'Oil companies owe a debt to the lives destroyed'. OpenDemocracy. https://www.opendemocracy.net/en/oureconomy/oil-companies-owe-a-debt-to-the-lives-destroyed/. Accessed 6 Nov 2024

Hidvegi F, Leufer D, Massé E (2021) The EU should regulate AI on the basis of rights, not risks. In: Access Now. https://www.accessnow.org/eu-regulation-ai-risk-based-approach/. Accessed 6 Nov 2024

Inter-American Court Of Human Rights Advisory Opinion Oc-23/17 Of November 15, 2017 Requested By The Republic Of Colombia The Environment And Human Rights (State Obligations In Relation To The Environment In The Context Of The Protection And Guarantee Of The Rights To Life And To Personal Integrity: Interpretation And Scope Of Articles 4(1) And 5(1) In Relation To Articles 1(1) And 2 Of The American Convention On Human Rights)

Humble KP (2021) International law, surveillance and the protection of privacy. Int J Hum Rights 25:1–25. https://doi.org/10.1080/13642987.2020.1763315

Intergovernmental Panel on Climate Change (IPCC) (2013) Climate Change 2013 The Physical Science Basis Summary for Policymakers A report of Working Group I of the IPCC. Part of the Working Group I Contribution to the Fifth Assessment Report of the Intergovernmental Panel on Climate Change. Stocker TF, Qin D, Plattner GK, Tignor MMB, Allen SK, Boschung J, Nauels A, Xia Y, Bex V, Midgley P M (eds). IPCC

Intergovernmental Panel on Climate Change (IPCC) (2023) Climate change 2022 – impacts, adaptation and vulnerability: working group II contribution to the sixth assessment report of the intergovernmental panel on climate change. Cambridge University Press, Cambridge

Intergovernmental Panel on Climate Change (IPCC) (2023b) Summary for policymakers. In: Climate Change 2023: Synthesis report. contribution of working groups I, II and III to the sixth assessment report of the intergovernmental panel on climate change [Core Writing Team, Lee H, Romero J (eds)]. IPCC, Geneva, pp. 1–34. https://doi.org/10.59327/IPCC/AR6-9789291691647.001

Jervan M (2014) The prohibition of transboundary environmental harm: an analysis of the contribution of the international court of justice to the development of the no-harm rule. Thesis, University of Oslo

Judgment of 7 December 2023, Schufa, C-634/21 EU:C:2023:957

Jun-E T (2019) Digital rights in Southeast Asia: conceptual framework and movement building. In Hooi KY, Simandjuntak D (eds.) Exploring the nexus between technologies and human rights: opportunities and challenges in Southeast Asia

Kazansky B, Karak M, Perosa T et al (2022) At the confluence of digital rights and climate & environmental justice: a landscape review. The Engine Room

Kotzé LJ, Du Toit L, French D (2021) Friend or foe? International environmental law and its structural complicity in the Anthropocene's climate injustices. Oñati Socio-Legal Ser 11(1):180–206. https://doi.org/10.35295/osls.iisl/0000-0000-0000-1140

Kukutai T, Taylor J (2016) Indigenous data sovereignty: toward an agenda. ANU Press

Łaszewska-Hellriegel M (2023) Environmental personhood as a tool to protect nature. Philosophia 51:1369–1384. https://doi.org/10.1007/s11406-022-00583-z

Lee J (2000) The underlying legal theory to support a well-defined human right to a healthy environment as a principle of customary international law. Colum J Environ L 25:283

Livingstone G (2023) It's pillage': thirsty Uruguayans decry Google's plan to exploit water supply. The Guardian. https://www.theguardian.com/world/2023/jul/11/uruguay-drought-water-google-data-center. Accessed 6 Nov 2024

Lopez Solano J, Martin A, de Souza S, Taylor L (2022) Governing data and artificial intelligence for all: models for sustainable and just data governance. European Parliament, Brussels

Mesquita H, Garrote MG, Zanatta RA (2024) Regulating Artificial Intelligence in Brazil: the contributions of critical social theory to rethink principles. Technol Regul 2024:73–83. https://doi.org/10.26116/techreg.2024.008

Mishra N (2024) International trade law and global data governance. Hart Publishing

McKibben B (2023) Uncounted emissions: the hidden cost of fossil fuel exports. YaleEnvironment360. https://e360.yale.edu/features/fossil-fuel-export-emissions-climate-change. Accessed 6 Nov 2024

Mejias UA (2022) The plantation, the factory, and the data center. https://www.tierracomun.net/blog/the-plantation-the-factory-and-the-data-center. Accessed 6 Nov 2024

Mignolo WD (2011) The global south and world dis/order. J Anthropol Res 67:165–188

Non Aligned Technologies Movement (NATM) (2022). https://nonalignedtech.net/index.php?title=Main_Page. Accessed 6 Nov 2024

Nyabola N (2023) ChatGPT and the sweatshops powering the digital age. Al Jazeera. https://www.aljazeera.com/opinions/2023/1/23/sweatshops-are-making-our-digital-age-work. Accessed 6 Nov 2024

Oberthür S (2006) The climate change regime: interactions with ICAO, IMO, and the EU burden-sharing agreement. In: Oberthür S, Gehring T (eds) Institutional interaction in global environmental governance synergy and conflict among international and EU policies. MIT Press

Ordinanza ingiunzione nei confronti di Clearview AI, 10 February 2022, 9751362

Oversight Board (2024) Oversight Board | Improving how Meta treats people and communities around the world. https://www.oversightboard.com/. Accessed 24 Feb 2025

Padovani C, Santaniello M (2018) Digital constitutionalism: fundamental rights and power limitation in the Internet eco-system. Int Commun Gaz 80:295–301. https://doi.org/10.1177/1748048518757114

Perrigo B (2023) Exclusive: OpenAI used Kenyan workers on less than $2 per hour to make ChatGPT less toxic. Time. https://time.com/6247678/openai-chatgpt-kenya-workers/. Accessed 6 Nov 2024

Plantin JC (2013) «Raw Data» is an Oxymoron Lisa Gitelman (dir.), Cambridge, MIT Press, 2013.: Communication & Langages N° 177: 155–156. https://doi.org/10.4074/S0336150013013100

Prior TL, Heinämäki L (2017) The rights and role of indigenous women in climate change regime. Arctic Rev Law Polit. https://doi.org/10.23865/arctic.v8.901

R v. the Chief Constable of South Wales Police, C1/2019/2670, [2020] EWCA Civ 1058

Rabinowicz C (2023) Approaches to regulating government use of facial recognition technology. In: Lozano PS (eds.) Jolt Digest. https://jolt.law.harvard.edu/digest/approaches-to-regulating-government-use-of-facial-recognition-technology. Accessed 6 Nov 2024

Redeker D, Gill L, Gasser U (2018) Towards digital constitutionalism? Mapping attempts to craft an internet bill of rights. Int Commun Gaz 80:302–319. https://doi.org/10.1177/174804851875 7121

Regulation (EU) 2016/679 (General Data Protection Regulation). https://eur-lex.europa.eu/eli/reg/2016/679/oj. Accessed 6 Nov 2024

Ricaurte P (2022) Ethics for the majority world: AI and the question of violence at scale. Media Cult Soc 44(4):726–745

Rodrigues M (2023) Politics and the environment collide in Brazil: Lula's first year back in office. Nature. https://www.nature.com/articles/d41586-023-04042-x. Accessed 6 Nov 2024

Sander B (2023) At the Intersection of Climate Change, AI, and Human Rights Law: Towards a solidarity-based approach (part 1). Afronomics Law. https://www.afronomicslaw.org/category/analysis/intersection-climate-change-ai-and-human-rights-law-towards-solidarity-based. Accessed 6 Nov 2024

Scotford EAK (2019) Environmental principles across jurisdictions: legal connectors and catalysts. In: Lees E, Vinuales J (eds) Oxford handbook on comparative environmental law. Oxford University Press, Oxford

Singh N (2023) Climate justice in the global south: understanding the environmental legacy of colonialism. In Global climate justice: theory and practice, 46

Solano JL, Martin A, de Souza SP, Taylor L (2022) Governing data and artificial intelligence for all: models for sustainable and just data governance. STUDY Panel for the Future of Science and Technology EPRS | European Parliamentary Research Service. PE 729.533. https://www.europarl.europa.eu/thinktank/en/document/EPRS_STU(2022)729533. Accessed 6 Nov 2024

Solon O (2017) 'It's digital colonialism': how Facebook's free internet service has failed its users. The Guardian. https://www.theguardian.com/technology/2017/jul/27/facebook-free-basics-developing-markets. Accessed 6 Nov 2024

Solon P (2012) At the crossroads between green economy and rights of nature. Focus on the Global South. https://focusweb.org/at-the-crossroads-between-green-economy-and-rights-of-nature/. Accessed 6 Nov 2024

Steinwehr U (2021) Fact check: what's China's role in climate change? DW. https://www.dw.com/en/fact-check-is-china-the-main-climate-change-culprit/a-57777113. Accessed 6 Nov 2024

Streinz T (2021) Designing international economic data law. https://www.cambridge.org/core/journals/proceedings-of-the-asil-annual-meeting/article/designing-international-economic-data-law/DFB877A0435CEAAA73C11E5D6A894336. Accessed 7 Feb 2025

Sultana F (2022) The unbearable heaviness of climate coloniality. Polit Geogr 99:102638. https://doi.org/10.1016/j.polgeo.2022.102638

Tavares P (2023) The Amazon Forest, A Brazilian Colonial Frontier for Over Two Centuries. The Funambulist. https://thefunambulist.net/magazine/forest-struggles/the-amazon-forest-a-brazilian-colonial-frontier-for-over-two-centuries. Accessed 6 Nov 2024

Taylor L, Floridi L, Van Der Sloot B (eds) (2017) Group privacy: new challenges of data technologies. Springer International Publishing, Cham

Taylor L (2017) What is data justice? The case for connecting digital rights and freedoms globally. Big Data Soc 4:205395171773633. https://doi.org/10.1177/2053951717736335

The Republic of the Gambia v. Facebook, Inc., 20-mc-36-JEB-ZMF

The Data Pollution & Power - Initiative (DPP). https://www.datapollution.eu. Accessed 6 Nov 2024

Tignino M, Bréthaut C (2020) The role of international case law in implementing the obligation not to cause significant harm. Int Environ Agreements 20:631–648. https://doi.org/10.1007/s10784-020-09503-6

Trail Smelter case (United States, Canada) (1938 and 1941) Reports of International Arbitration Awards, III, 1905–1982

United Nations (1992) Report of the United Nations Conference on Environment and Development. Rio Declaration onon Environment and Development. A/CONF.151/26/Rev.1(Vol.I)

United Nations Trade and Development (2021) Digital economy report 2021. https://unctad.org/page/digital-economy-report-2021. Accessed 24 Feb 2025

United Nations Economic and Social Commission for Asia and the Pacific (2019) Global environmental commons https://www.unescap.org/sites/default/d8files/event-documents/Global%20Environmental%20Commons_Layout%20050520.pdf. Accessed 6 Nov 2024
United Nations Educational, Scientific and Cultural Organization (UNESCO) (2021) Recommendation on the ethics of artificial intelligence. SHS/BIO/REC-AIETHICS/2021. https://unesdoc.unesco.org/ark:/48223/pf0000380455. Accessed 6 Nov 2024
United Nations Educational, Scientific and Cultural Organization (UNESCO) (2022) Recommendation on the ethics of artificial intelligence SHS/BIO/PI/2021/1. https://unesdoc.unesco.org/ark:/48223/pf0000381137. Accessed 6 Nov 2024
United Nations Educational, Scientific and Cultural Organization (UNESCO) (2023) Recommendation on the ethics of artificial intelligence: key facts. SHS/2023/PI/H/1. https://unesdoc.unesco.org/ark:/48223/pf0000385082. Accessed 6 Nov 2024
United Nations General Assembly (1966) International Covenant on Economic, Social and Cultural Rights, International Covenant on Civil and Political Rights and Optional Protocol to the International Covenant on Civil and Political Rights. A/RES/2200(XXI)
United Nations General Assembly (1992) Report of the United Nations Conference on Environment and Development (Rio de Janeiro, 3–14 June 1992) Annex I Rio Declaration on Environment and Development. A/CONF.151/26
United Nations General Assembly (2022) The human right to a clean, healthy and sustainable environment. A/76/L.75. www.undocs.org/en/A/76/L.75. Accessed 6 Nov 2024
United Nations Human Rights Council (2012) Resolution adopted by the Human Rights Council 19/10. Human rights and the environment. www.undocs.org/en/A/HRC/RES/19/10. Accessed 6 Nov 2024
United Nations Human Rights Council (2021) Resolution adopted by the Human Rights Council on 8 October 2021 48/13. The human right to a clean, healthy and sustainable environment. A/HRC/RES/48/13. www.undocs.org/en/A/HRC/RES/48/13. Accessed 6 Nov 2024
United Nations Human Rights Special Procedures. Special Rapporteur on human rights and the environment. https://www.ohchr.org/en/special-procedures/sr-environment. Accessed 6 Nov 2024
United Nations Office of the High Commissioner for Human Rights (OHCHR), United Nations Environment Programme (UNEP), United Nations Development Programme (UNDP) (2023) What is the right to a healthy environment? Information Note
United Nations (2024) Global digital compact. https://www.un.org/techenvoy/global-digital-compact. Accessed 24 Feb 2025
United Nations (2024) Governing AI for humanity. United Nations
United States v. Canada (1938 and 1941) 3 R.I.A.A. 1905
van Steenberghe R (2023) International environmental law as a means for enhancing the protection of the environment in warfare: a critical assessment of scholarly theoretical frameworks. In: International Review of the Red Cross
Vatanparast R (2020) The Infrastructures of the global data economy: undersea cables and international law (April 2020). 61 Harvard International Law Journal Frontiers. Available at SSRN: https://ssrn.com/abstract=3583708
Varvastian S (2019) The human right to a clean and healthy environment in climate change litigation. Max Planck Institute for Comparative Public Law & International Law (MPIL) Research Paper, 19
Varvastian S, Kalunga F (2020) Transnational corporate liability for environmental damage and climate change: reassessing access to justice after Vedanta v. Lungowe. Transnatl Environ Law 9:323–345. https://doi.org/10.1017/S2047102520000138
Veltmeyer, (2013) The political economy of natural resource extraction: a new model or extractive imperialism? Can J Dev Stud/revue Canadienne D'études Du Développement 34(1):79–95
Vera LA, Walker D, Murphy M et al (2019) When data justice and environmental justice meet: formulating a response to extractive logic through environmental data justice. Inf Commun Soc 22:1012–1028. https://doi.org/10.1080/1369118X.2019.1596293

Viljoen S (2020) A relational theory of data governance. Social Science Research Network, Rochester

Voskoboynik DM (2018) The memory we could be: overcoming fear to create our ecological future. New Society Publishers

Walter M, Kukutai T, Carroll SR, Rodriguez-Lonebear D (2020) Indigenous data sovereignty and policy. Routledge, London

Warso Z (2022) Human rights requirements for person-based predictive policing: lessons from selected ECtHR case law and its limits. Technol Regul 2022:71–80. https://doi.org/10.26116/techreg.2022.007

Waters S (2023) Opinion: it's time to recognize that colonialism causes climate change – and repair our relationships. UBC Climate Emergency. https://climateemergency.ubc.ca/opinion-its-time-to-recognize-that-colonialism-causes-climate-change-and-repair-our-relationships/. Accessed 6 Nov 2024

Wifa E, Adebola T (2021) Triumph for Farmers and Fisherfolks: The Hague Court of Appeal finds Shell Liable for Oil Spills in Nigeria. Health of Mother Earth Foundation. https://homef.org/2021/02/04/triumph-for-farmers-and-fisherfolks-the-hague-court-of-appeal-finds-shell-liable-for-oil-spills-in-nigeria/. Accessed 6 Nov 2024

Wood L (2015) The environmental impacts of colonialism. BSU Honors Program Theses and Projects. Item 119. https://vc.bridgew.edu/honors_proj/119/. Accessed 6 Nov 2024

Siddharth Peter de Souza is an Assistant Professor in AI & Society and the Centre for Interdisciplinary Methods, University of Warwick. His work explores how data is governed globally in contested, and plural settings, and he is interested in the role that social movements and civil society can play in shaping digital transformations. He is also the founder of Justice Adda, a law and design social venture in India where he works on projects related to access to justice, and legal empowerment. He previously worked as a post doctoral researcher at the Global Data Justice Project, Tilburg Law School, Tilburg University, The Netherlands.

Gargi Sharma is the Communications and Development Manager at the CLIMA Fund and programme coordinator at the critical infrastructure lab at the University of Amsterdam. As a human rights activist, advocate, and lawyer, Gargi focuses on uplifting broad-based, locally-led, and locally-accountable solutions addressing the most pressing crises of our time.

Responsible Data Sharing for AI: A Test Bench for EU Data Law

Roberta Montinaro

Abstract The chapter addresses data sharing contracts for AI development and training, entered into by parties participating in AI value chains, in order to assess the incentives for responsible data sharing set out by European data law. As the governance of AI training data is mainly entrusted to party autonomy and the principles of the GDPR, the analysis first assesses whether contract theory, as it is traditionally conceptualized, is an appropriate tool to promote responsible data sharing. Then the paper delves into the impact of the data protection framework on data sharing contracts, to conclude that the principle of accountability in its organizational dimension requires the parties to 'contractualize' good data sharing practices. Lastly, the analysis comprises a brief overview of the relevant provisions of the AI Act that deal with data governance and AI value chains, to highlight their impact on the relationship between the entities participating in these value chains.

Keywords Data governance · Data sharing · Data protection · Personal data

1 Introduction

Responsible data governance with respect to Artificial Intelligence (hereinafter 'AI') is a field of research that tries to reconcile two perspectives which underpin European Union data law (hereinafter 'EU data law')[1]: on the one hand, fostering innovation by favoring the availability of data and, on the other hand, ensuring protection of personal data and, more broadly, of the fundamental rights of the individuals and groups affected by the deployment of AI applications.

[1] Riis (2023), p. 54. See also Streinz (2021), p. 903.

R. Montinaro (✉)
University of Naples L'Orientale, Naples, Italy
e-mail: rmontinaro@unior.it

J. Drexl et al. (eds.), *Comparative Data Law*, MPI Studies on Intellectual Property and Competition Law 32, https://doi.org/10.1007/978-3-031-91401-0_5

The Regulation of the European Parliament and of the Council laying down harmonized rules on artificial intelligence (Artificial Intelligence Act, hereinafter 'AI Act'[2]) seeks as well to bridge these two perspectives. It states that one of the main purposes of the Regulation is to promote a high level of protection of fundamental rights, according to the Charter of Fundamental Rights of the European Union (hereinafter the 'Charter'), starting from the development phase of AI applications (Article 1 and Recital 1 AI Act). At the same time, the AI Act acknowledges that access to data, namely to data of high quality, plays a vital role in preventing and mitigating any risk of harm to those rights (Recitals 66 and 67 AI Act).

When machine learning techniques are applied, data comes into consideration in view of its function as training data and any lack of data quality or any deficiency in the data generation and management processes can be a source of harm to the fundamental rights of data subjects, particularly when AI is used in decision-making processes that impact individuals or groups.[3]

Data sharing for AI mainly takes place by means of contracts that can be simple arrangements between two parties or multilateral complex agreements. These contracts are often entered into in the context of the so-called AI value chains in which multiple entities may participate, including entities contributing data.

The aim of this paper is to explore data sharing contracts[4] for the purpose of developing and training AI, entered into by parties participating in AI value chains, and to assess the incentives to engage in responsible data sharing for AI under EU data law. Responsible data sharing entails, at the very minimum, compliance with personal data regulations, prevention of bias and discrimination and respect for human rights.

As will be noted in paragraph 2, the normative instruments recently enacted by the EU fall short of promoting the accountability of the parties to a data sharing contract. Regulation (EU) 2022/868 on European data governance (Data Governance Act, hereinafter 'DGA')[5] and Regulation (EU) 2023/2854 on harmonized rules on fair access to and use of data (hereinafter 'Data Act')[6] are both concerned with establishing a 'data economy' and entrust the protection of fundamental rights to Regulation (EU) 2016/679 on the protection of natural persons with regard to the processing of personal data (General Data Protection Regulation, hereinafter

[2] Regulation (EU) 2024/1689 of the European Parliament and of the Council of 13 June 2024 laying down harmonized rules on artificial intelligence and amending Regulations (EC) No 300/2008, (EU) No 167/2013, (EU) No 168/2013, (EU) 2018/858, (EU) 2018/1139 and (EU) 2019/2144 and Directives 2014/90/EU, (EU) 2016/797 and (EU) 2020/1828 (Artificial Intelligence Act).

[3] Suresh, Guttag (2021), p. 1. See also Hacker (2020), p. 12.

[4] Within the present paper, the terms 'supply' and 'sharing' of data will be used interchangeably, to describe a one-way provision of data, as well as a two-way provision of data, where the parties provide data to one another.

[5] Regulation (EU) 2022/868 of the European Parliament and of the Council of 30 May 2022 on European data governance and amending Regulation (EU) 2018/1724 (Data Governance Act) (OJ L 152, 3.6.2022).

[6] Regulation (EU) of the European Parliament and of the Council of 13 December 2023 on harmonised rules on fair access to and use of data and amending Regulation (EU) 2017/2394 and Directive (EU) 2020/1828 (Data Act) - OJ L, 22.12.2023.

'GDPR'[7]), as well as to other relevant EU and national laws.[8] As a consequence, the governance of AI training data is mainly entrusted to party autonomy and to the principles of the GDPR. Data sharing contracts are indeed subject to the applicable contract law regimes of Member States. Against this background the analysis will firstly consider the viewpoint of contract theory (as it is traditionally conceptualized), referencing some relevant soft law instruments which have been devised with the aim to set out model rules on data sharing contracts.

Then paragraph 3 will analyze how the GDPR interacts with contract law, to conclude that the data protection framework constrains the autonomy of the parties to a data sharing agreement by shaping the contractual relationship.

Lastly, the analysis will conclude with a brief overview of the relevant provisions of the AI Act which deal with data governance and AI value chains, to highlight their impact on the relationship between the parties to data sharing contracts (paragraph 4).

The AI Act sets out requirements on the quality of training data and mandates the use of adequate data governance practices. These requirements result in due diligence obligations which only apply to providers of high-risk AI systems. The AI Act Proposal was only intended for providers and deployers of AI systems, not including those who make data available for the development and training of such systems.[9] However, the Regulation also acknowledges the complexity of AI value chains. Consequently, third parties involved in the development of AI systems are mandated to cooperate with providers of high-risk AI systems to enable them to comply with the requirements therein set out (Recital 88).[10]

---

[7] Regulation(EU)2016/679 of the European Parliament and of the Council of 27April 2016 on the protection of natural persons with regard to the processing of personal data and on the free movement of such data, and repealing Directive 95/46/EC (General Data Protection Regulation) (OJ L 119, 4.5.2016, p. 1).

[8] See in this regard Recitals 7 and 8 Data Act.

[9] Proposal for a Regulation of the European Parliament and of the Council laying down harmonized rules on artificial intelligence (Artificial Intelligence Act) 21.4.2021 COM/2021/206 final.

[10] It is worth noting that the AI Act Proposal with the amendments adopted by the European Parliament on 14 June 2023 (hereinafter 'AI Act Proposal of June 2023') contained explicit reference to those providing data for the development of AI systems: "all relevant third parties, in particular those that are involved in the development, sale and the commercial supply of [...] data incorporated into the AI system" shall cooperate with providers of AI systems to enable them to comply with the AI Act (Recital 60 of the AI Act of June 2023).

2 Data Sharing Contracts Seen from the Viewpoint of Traditional Contract Theory

2.1 Recent Evolutions in EU Data Law

As mentioned above, the EU legal framework currently comprises the DGA and the Data Act, which have been added to the GDPR in order to implement the 'European strategy for data'.[11] As clarified by their respective preambles, both the DGA and the Data Act are mainly concerned with fostering the establishment of a European 'data economy'. As a consequence, they do not directly address the role played by data in the context of AI development and training.

The DGA primary objective is to ensure the neutrality and accountability of data intermediaries falling within its scope of application with regard to both non-personal and personal data. It entrusts the protection of the fundamental rights of data subjects to the relevant EU legislation, most notably the GDPR.

There is much evidence to support this. Under the DGA, the data intermediaries only bear a fiduciary duty towards the data subjects – to act in their best interest – when their business model is centered on facilitating the exercise of data subjects' rights (Article 12 (l)). Duties of care of data intermediaries with regard to third parties' rights are only provided for with respect to non-personal data, such as: *i)* taking the necessary legal, organizational and/or technological measures (see Articles 10 and 12 DGA) to avoid transmission and access to non-personal data which is unlawful under Union or national law; *ii)* adopting measures necessary to ensure an adequate level of security for the storage and transmission of non-personal data (Article 10, (1) DGA).

Moreover, the DGA only covers data sharing services which aim to intermediate between an indefinite number of data holders and data users, excluding data sharing services that are designed to be used by a closed group of data holders and users (see Recital 28 DGA). This requirement may leave outside the reach of the DGA several data governance models that are especially suitable for the development and training of AI, for instance, data clearinghouses (which may come in various forms; e.g. data transfer, consent management etc.) and data pools,[12] whenever the governance of the pooled data is entrusted to an intermediary that facilitates data sharing between predefined data holders and users.[13]

The Data Act sets out obligations for data holders to make both personal and non-personal data available to users of connected products and related services; it

[11] See Communication from the Commission to the European Parliament, the Council, the European Economic and Social Committee and the Committee of the Regions. A European strategy for data (COM/2020/66 final).

[12] See Wernick, Olk, Grafenstein (2020), p. 70.

[13] See Recital 28 DGA: "Examples of data intermediation services include […] data pools established jointly by several legal or natural persons with the intention to license the use of such data pools to all interested parties in a manner that all participants that contribute to the data pools would receive a reward for their contribution".

establishes rules for business-to-business and business-to-consumer data sharing, as well as rules on unfair terms related to data access and use between enterprises (see Article 1 Data Act).[14]

Like the GDA, the Data Act is not directly concerned with protecting the rights of third parties that may be impacted by the data sharing agreement, such as the rights arising from the GDPR. Rather, the Data Act simply clarifies that its provisions do not affect the protection of personal data. It also reiterates the need to comply with the GDPR (see Recital 7[15] and Article 4 (12) Data Act[16]).

The Data Act does take into account the quality of the data covered by the data sharing agreement in some of its provisions. In particular, Articles 4 (1) and 5 (1) Data Act stipulate that the data holder must provide the counterparty with data of the same quality that is available to the data holder. The rationale of these provisions, however, seems to lie in the need to regulate the interests of the parties. At the same time, according to Article 13 (4) (g) Data Act, contract terms relating to data quality cannot be unilaterally modified.

Thus, despite these recent regulations that have been added to European data law, data governance for AI remains predominantly in the realm of party autonomy, as will be demonstrated in the following analysis. However, it will also be argued that the GDPR – and, to a lesser extent, the AI Act – can shape data-sharing contracts in ways that will be discussed in paragraphs 3 and 4.

2.2 *Shortcomings of Traditional Contract Theory*

Traditional conceptualizations of party autonomy – whereby the parties to a contract are only bound by what is agreed between them with a view to protecting their own interests – are put 'under strain' when data is the subject matter of the contract. The GDPR, on the one hand, takes into account the private dimension inherent in the circulation of personal data and its use for economic purposes; on the other hand, it also aims to protect the rights and interests of the natural persons concerned by the processing.

The parties to a data sharing agreement regard data as a commodity, but, at the same time, they are aware that the data sharing may involve a number of legally protected interests. As a consequence, they tend to be risk-averse and inclined to design the

[14] Hennemann, Ebner, Karsten (2023), p. 6.

[15] According to Recital 7 Data Act the legal basis for sustainable and responsible data processing, even where data sets include a mix of personal and non-personal data, is provided for solely by the GDPR.

[16] Article 4 (12) of the Data Act: "Where the user is not the data subject whose personal data is requested, any personal data generated by the use of a connected product or related service shall be made available by the data holder to the user only where there is a valid legal basis for processing under Article 6 of Regulation (EU) 2016/679 and, where relevant, the conditions of Article 9 of that Regulation and of Article 5(3) of Directive 2002/58/EC are fulfilled." In this vein, see also Article 5(7) of the Data Act.

contract terms in such a way as to manage the risk of being held accountable or incurring liability for any harm to third parties' rights under tort law regimes enacted at a national level or at the level of EU law. Therefore, it is relevant to consider whether such regimes provide incentives to the parties involved in data sharing to take into account third parties' interests.

If we consider tort law, and namely, the EU product liability regime, as it currently stands, we can find that it only insufficiently contributes to promoting responsible data sharing for AI.

Under the Council Directive 85/374/EEC of 25 July 1985 concerning liability for defective products (Product Liability Directive, hereinafter "PLD"),[17] it is debated whether AI systems and input data, due to their nature as intangible goods, can be regarded as a product (or a component thereof); at the same time, due to the complexity and opacity of AI systems, it is difficult for the injured party to give evidence of the defect.[18]

These obstacles are likely to be overcome if the PLD will be updated by the Proposal for a Directive on Liability for Defective Products (proposal for a New Liability Directive, hereinafter "NLD").[19] Therein, the definition of 'component' appears to be broad enough to include the data supplied to the value chains of an AI system (see Article 4 (2) NLD[20]). A mechanism of disclosure is provided for in Article 8 NLD to alleviate the burden of proof resting on the claimant.[21]

Entrusting the governance of AI training data to party autonomy entails further shortcomings.

First, contract terms providing for limitation or exclusion of liability for breach of contract agreed upon by the parties to a data sharing contract may shift the risk of being held accountable onto one party. Under Article 13 of the Data Act, such contract terms are not binding when they are included in data contracts between

---

[17] Council Directive 85/374/EEC of 25 July 1985 on the approximation of the laws, regulations and administrative provisions of the Member States concerning liability for defective products (Product Liability Directive) OJ L 210/29.

[18] De Meeus (2019), p. 149. See also BEUC The European Consumer Bureau (2020).

[19] European Commission. Proposal for a Directive of the European Parliament and of the Council on Liability for Defective Products. Brussels 24.3.2023 COM (2022) 495 final/2.

[20] Article 4 (2) NLD: "'component' means any item, whether tangible or intangible, or any related service, that is integrated into, or inter-connected with, a product by the manufacturer of that product or within that manufacturer's control". Whether this definition covers, as well, data is a matter of interpretation.

[21] However, the mechanism of disclosure provided for in Article 8 NLD can only be used in the course of the litigation and on condition that the plaintiff has provided sufficient elements to substantiate the plausibility of its claim. In the same vein, under Article 3 of the Proposal for a Directive of the European Parliament and the Council of 28 September 2022 on adapting non-contractual civil liability rules to artificial intelligence (AI Liability Directive) COM(2022) 496 final), the presumption of causation also applies to damage caused by high-risk AI systems whenever the court deems it excessively complex for the injured party to prove the causal link. See Gellert, Janssen (2023), p. 169.

enterprises,[22] but only if the breach of contracts results from intentional acts or gross negligence of the party who imposed the contract term. Therefore, this rule aims to rebalance unequal relationships between economic operators active in data markets. It differs from provisions which prohibit exclusion or limitation clauses contravening public order[23] and, in particular, clauses on the exclusion or limitation of contractual liability for physical harm or harm to personality rights.[24]

Second, liability under contract law does not extend beyond the parties to the contract and, hence, it fails to promote the accountability of all those who share data for AI development (for instance, in the case of a chain of data sharing contracts).

Moreover, the third parties impacted by the deployment of AI applications are not entitled to claim damages under contract law, unless they qualify as end-users that can seek compensation from the seller under Directive (EU) 2019/770 on certain aspects concerning contracts for the supply of digital content and digital services (hereinafter 'DCDS Directive'[25]) or Directive (EU) 2019/771 on certain aspects concerning contracts for the sale of goods (hereinafter 'CSD'[26]). In this case, incentives for developers of AI systems to comply with data protection principles can only arise from the right of redress that the seller can exercise against the entity in the previous links of the transaction chain, whose action or omission resulted in the lack of conformity with the contract (see Article 18 CSD and, in the same vein, Article 20 DCDS Directive).[27]

---

[22] See Article 13 (1) Data Act: "1. A contractual term concerning access to and the use of data or liability and remedies for the breach or the termination of data related obligations, which has been unilaterally imposed by an enterprise on another enterprise, shall not be binding on the latter enterprise if it is unfair". According to Article 13 (2) Data Act: "In particular, a contractual term shall be unfair for the purposes of paragraph 3, if its object or effect is to: (a)exclude or limit the liability of the party that unilaterally imposed the term for intentional acts or gross negligence; (b) exclude the remedies available to the party upon whom the term has been unilaterally imposed in the case of non- performance of contractual obligations, or the liability of the party that unilaterally imposed the term in the case of a breach of those obligations; (c) give the party that unilaterally imposed the term the exclusive right to determine whether the data supplied are in conformity with the contract or to interpret any contractual term".

[23] The Italian civil code qualifies as null and void any terms that exclude or limit liability for breach of contract for intentional acts and gross negligence, irrespective of whether these terms are unilaterally imposed (Article 1229 Italian civil code).

[24] See Claes, Herbosch (2023), p. 475.

[25] Directive (EU) 2019/770 of the European Parliament and the Council of 20 May 2019 on certain aspects concerning contracts for the supply of digital content and digital services (OJ L 136/1).

[26] Directive (EU) 2019/771 of the European Parliament and the Council of 20 May 2019 on certain aspects concerning contracts for the sale of goods, amending Regulation (EU) 2017/2394 and Directive 2009/22/EC, and repealing Directive 1999/44/EC (OJ L 136/28).

[27] Hacker (2020), p. 11.

2.3 *Model Rules on Contracts for the Provision of Data: Fit for AI Training Data?*

The party autonomy logic above described is reflected in some soft law documents aiming to set out uniform model rules and implied terms for the cross-border flows of data.

According to the American Law Institute and the European Law Institute's Principles for a Data Economy: Data Transactions and Data Rights (hereinafter 'ALI/ELI Principles for a Data Economy')[28], in contracts for the 'supply' or 'sharing' of data, the data recipient must be enabled "rightfully to exercise control over the data" (Principle 7(2)(c)(ii)).[29] At the same time, "the data recipient may utilize the data [...] for any lawful purpose and in any way that does not infringe the rights of the supplier or third parties [...]" (Principle 7(2)(c)(iv)).[30]

In the same vein, under the Default rules for data provision contracts (hereinafter 'UN Default rules for data provision contracts') issued by the United Nations Commission on International Trade Law,[31] the data must be provided lawfully (Article 7 (2)(d)). Moreover, the data recipient is entitled to use the data for any lawful purpose (so "that the data recipient can exercise its rights to use the data under the contract"[32]) and in a manner that does not infringe the rights of third parties (Article 8 (1) (a) and (2) (a)).

In a nutshell, the lawfulness of the data provided or made accessible under these contracts pertains to the conformity of the data[33] and covers compliance with any

[28] The American Law Institute and the European Law Institute (2023).

[29] The rationale behind Principle 7(2)(c)(ii) of ALI/ELI Principles for a Data Economy is explained as follows: "the usefulness of data to the recipient would be undermined if the recipient did not obtain rightful control over the data at the time it is supplied". "The supplier must therefore ensure that, for example, there are no legal barriers that would prevent the recipient from rightfully gaining control. Legal barriers could be barriers stemming, e.g., from data privacy/data protection law, from intellectual property law, or from trade secrets law".

[30] From the perspective of the ALI/ELI Principles for a Data Economy, third party rights, including fundamental rights, help to define the data rights conferred on the recipient of the data under the contract. See ALI/ELI Principles for a Data Economy, p. 10: "Among the policy choices recommended by these Principles in the context of supply or sharing of data is the default position that, when the data is fully transferred, the data may be used by the recipient for any lawful purpose that does not infringe the rights of third parties".

[31] United Nations Commission on International Trade Law. Working Group IV on Electronic Commerce (2023).

[32] UN (2023), p. 13.

[33] In this respect, these soft law instruments mirror Article 10 DCDS Directive: Third-party rights: "Where a restriction resulting from a violation of any right of a third party, in particular intellectual property rights, prevents or limits the use of the digital content or digital service in accordance with Articles 7 and 8, Member States shall ensure that the consumer is entitled to the remedies for lack of conformity [...]".

applicable legal requirements[34]; at the same time, lawfully using the data is a contractual obligation towards the data supplier that the data recipient must comply with, to ensure that the data provider is not held liable under the law.

Some conclusions can be drawn from these soft law documents. The contract terms therein devised are shaped by the private interests of the parties. They do not reflect the legal status of data which differs from tradable commodities.[35]

The ELI/ALI Principles for a Data Economy do recognize the existence of third parties' rights, including rights with *erga omnes* effect, which may be affected by data sharing or 'data activities' (e.g. how data are handled, their quality, security, etc.). However, these Principles: *i)* on the one hand, adopt a 'tort law logic' in that they merely reiterate that the data processing activity may be unlawful towards third parties holding *erga omnes* rights; ii) on the other hand, they entrust the determination of legal remedies available to the affected third parties to the applicable law (see Principles 4, 28, 29). Similarly, they do not provide for any direct action by a data supplier towards a downstream recipient (see Part IV, Chapter B, Principles 32 and 33 respectively), only suggesting that a 'model rule' is one that sets out due diligence obligations for the party supplying the data with respect to wrongful activities of other parties in the chain of contracts for the provision of data.

Above all, the soft law instruments already mentioned do not take into account the peculiarities of the data used in the context of AI development/training. As explained by experts in the field of machine learning,[36] the data used for this purpose is not a static artefact; on the contrary, it is the result of choices and practices to be implemented during the phases of data collection and generation and model development. Possible sources of harm to fundamental rights may result from poor choices and practices at these stages.

In order to prevent such harms, the terms of data-sharing agreements should include good practices, such as: *i)* requiring 'data traceability', *ii)* setting forth transparency requirements (for instance, documentation on how input data are generated and managed), *iii)* mandating to identify adequate technical standards/practices.

Soft law alone appears ill-suited to ensure that good practices and technical standards become binding and thus subject to enforcement. It is therefore relevant to identify the incentives offered by European data law to engage in responsible data governance, in particular, with regard to personal data used for the development of AI applications.

---

[34] See Article 7 (2) (d) UN Default rules for data provision contracts.

[35] See Janeček, Malgieri (2020), p. 2.

[36] Suresh, Guttag (2021), p. 6.

2.4 *The Impact of the GDPR on Data Sharing Contracts for AI*

The interaction of the GDPR with contract law challenges the corollaries of traditional contract theory above mentioned.

Owing to the peculiar nature of data, when the subject matter of a contract is the provision of data, several legally protected interests may come into play, including the right to the protection of personal data and other fundamental rights, such as the right not to be discriminated against.

Indeed, the provision of personal data to the recipient of the data pursuant to a data sharing agreement implies a form of processing within the meaning of Article 4 (2) GDPR. Accordingly, the data protection legal framework applies, which aims, inter alia, to protect the fundamental rights and freedoms of natural persons (see Article 1 (2) GDPR).

Under EU data law, where non-personal and anonymized data are processed, and technological developments make it possible to turn this data into personal data, the data protection framework comes into play (see Recital 9 of the Regulation (EU) 2018/1807 on a framework for the free flow of non-personal data in the European Union (hereinafter 'FFDR')[37]). In light of this, the key concept for defining the character of data is 'identifiability' (see Article 4(1) GDPR). As highlighted by legal scholars and case law,[38] identifiability is a dynamic and context-dependent concept. There is a strong argument that the qualification of data as personal must take into account inter alia the 'life cycle' of the data. This can be deduced from Recital 26 GDPR, which refers to anonymous data, i.e. data rendered anonymous in such a manner that the data subject is not or is *no longer* identifiable.

Against this background, the relevant international technical standards (ISO/ IEC 27,701) rely on the concept of *Personally Identifiable Information* (hereinafter 'PII').[39] These standards suggest that any data that *i)* can be used to establish a link between the information and the natural person to whom it relates or *ii)* can be directly or indirectly linked to a natural person should be regarded as PII and managed by taking into account any risk of harm to third parties. Therefore, the substantive scope of application of the data protection framework is not narrow, as some scholars point out.[40]

---

[37] Regulation (EU) 2018/1807 of the European Parliament and of the Council of 14 November 2018 on a framework for the free flow of non-personal data in the European Union (OJ L303). According to Recital 9 FFDR "Recital 9 of the FFDR "If technological developments make it possible to turn anonymized data into personal data, such data are to be treated as personal data, and Regulation (EU) 2016/679 is to apply accordingly".

[38] See European Court of Justice, Judgement of the Court (Second Chamber) of 19 October 2016 in the Case C-582/14, Patrick Breyer vs Bundesrepublik Deutschland. Available at https://eur-lex.europa.eu/legal-content/EN/TXT/HTML/?uri=CELEX:62014CJ0582. See as well, Graef, Gellert, Husovec (2018), p. 7.

[39] Podda, Palmirani (2021), p. 4.

[40] Purtova (2018), p. 40–81.

The public law regime set out by the GDPR entails constraints on party autonomy, since personal data can only be processed in conformity with the principles of lawfulness and fairness enshrined in Article 5 GDPR. The requirements arising from the data protection framework translate into limits on entitlements and rights of the parties to data sharing contracts, as well as into duties for the same parties.[41] These constraints and duties shape the contractual relationship between the parties to such contracts.

For instance, in the Italian legal system, as interpreted by the Supreme Court (no. 15824/2014), compliance with duties of care arising from public law regulations, such as the EU Regulation on food safety, constitutes a contractual obligation resting with both the parties to a sales contract: they are required to proactively comply with the regulation in order to ensure a high level of protection of the rights of consumers; failing to fulfil such obligations may result in liability for breach of contract and/or contract termination. Some legal scholars point out that duties of this kind lie in the grey area between tort and contractual liability, having their origin in the fact that the liable party is entrusted with the protection of the person or property of the other party and/or a third party.[42]

A similar finding holds with regard to Article 16 DCDS Directive: "In respect of personal data of the consumer, the trader shall comply with the obligations applicable under Regulation (EU) 2016/679". This provision can be read as it entails that non-compliance with the GDPR is also relevant from the point of view of contract law.[43]

Moreover, the data protection framework covers automated decision-making that often involves the deployment of AI systems which may have significant adverse impacts on individuals (Article 22 (1) GDPR).[44] Automated decision-making of this sort is per se prohibited, but Article 22 (2) GDPR provides for several exceptions. When one of these exceptions applies, transparency requirements are set out and the adoption of adequate measures is mandated (Article 22 (3)) according to the principles of accountability and privacy by design (see Articles 5, 22, 24 and 25; Recital 71 GDPR), in order to prevent such impacts.[45] These principles interact with party autonomy by establishing duties of care on the parties that share and manage data for the purpose of training/developing AI applications.

As highlighted by some authors, the principle of accountability has an organizational dimension, since it places on controllers the duty to also adopt the 'legal' measures that enable them to comply with the GDPR. Therefore, the parties to these contracts are required to arrange adequate data sharing architectures, starting with the choice of the contract type and contract terms,[46] which should be made taking into

---

[41] Orlando (2023), p. 232.

[42] Castronovo (1995), p. 147. See Nivarra (2014), p. 73.

[43] Resta (2005), p. 281.

[44] European Court of Justice, Judgment of the Court (First Chamber) of 7 December 2023 in Case C-634/21, OQ vs Land Hessen, intervener SCHUFA Holding AG (ECLI:EU:C:2023:957). Available at https://eur-lex.europa.eu/legal-content/EN/TXT/?uri=CELEX%3A62021CJ0634.

[45] Kaminski (2019), p. 7.

[46] Stalla-Bourdillon, Thuermer, Walker, Carmichael, Simperl (2020), p. 5.

account the complexity and severity of the risks entailed in the processing (which are a variable of the purpose of the AI system and type of data needed). As for the choice of contract type, for instance, where there is a large number of data contributors, the creation of data pools instead of a chain of contracts can be considered in line with these principles. In fact, this type of agreement allows each party to monitor whether the other parties comply with data protection requirements. In this way, all the parties to the contract are compelled to responsibly manage the data.

Moreover, when an AI application is meant to be used for decision making purposes, the parties that confer the training data are required to ensure data quality and use adequate processes of data generation and management. This aspect has been underlined by the EDPB-EDPS Joint Opinion on the interplay between the AI Act and the GDPR[47]: AI systems should be conceived and developed having in mind data protection principles and rules, such as the ones which require to adopt adequate safeguards to prevent any harmful impact arising from automated decision making having legal or similarly significant effects on a data subject (Article 22 and Recital 71 GDPR).

One way to comply with the principle of accountability and privacy by design is to choose adequate contract terms. This means that the duties of care arising from the data protection framework can be 'contractualized' and turned into due diligence contract terms included in the data sharing contracts.

Contract terms of this sort may compel the parties to such contracts to adopt: i) technical and procedural standards and practices on matters such as the ones mentioned in Paragraph 2.2 ii) mechanisms to oversee compliance with these standards/practices by all the parties (for instance, mandating to carry out internal audits or reporting) and iii) enforcement mechanisms (for instance, penalty clauses, contract termination clauses etc.) in the event of non fulfilment of these duties. Along the same lines are contract terms requiring the parties to monitor whether sub-suppliers comply with data protection requirements.

As a consequence, the adoption of good practices and standards is not left to market drivers.[48] On the contrary, it is triggered by the public law provisions at play and notably by the principle of accountability which is a regulatory model for the protection of personal data based on a hybrid form of enforceable self-regulation.[49]

The GDPR already provides for some form of private enforcement. According to Article 82 GDPR, data controllers (and processors) are liable for damage resulting from a processing that does not comply with the rules and principles laid down in the GDPR. However, a right to compensation is only afforded under certain conditions, i.e. an infringement of the Regulation, the existence of a material or non-material damage and a causal link between these two elements (Article 82(1) GDPR). Furthermore, when a processing is complex and involves multiple parties and processing operations, these parties may qualify as *i)* processors or separate and independent controllers (or a combination of the two) or *ii)* as joint controllers. The claimant must

[47] EDPB-EDPS (2021), see point 58.

[48] Peterkova Mitkidis (2014), p. 7.

[49] Spina (2016), p. 148. See also Comandé (2019), p. 184.

therefore prove the existence of all such conditions. An easing of the burden of proof is provided for in Article 82 (4) GDPR, according to which all the parties involved in the same processing may be held jointly and severally liable can only provided that the requirements of Article 82 (2) and (3) GDPR are met.

Above all, the one just described is a form of tort liability having a compensatory function.[50] A further policy objective is to prevent infringements of data protection regulations and the resulting harm to data subjects. This objective underpins Article 26 GDPR which mandates joint controllers to clarify their roles and responsibilities in an agreement (Article 26 GDPR). The agreement to be adopted by the joint controllers under this provision is intended to ensure the lawfulness of joint data processing activities and, therefore, to perform an ex ante protection function, whereas liability under Article 82 GDPR only comes into play once damage has occurred.

However, providing evidence of the existence of joint control in a concrete case can be arduous and generate uncertainty. In this respect, the EDPB Guidelines on the concepts of controller and processor in the GDPR are emblematic when they state that "The fact that several actors are involved in the same processing does not mean that they are necessarily acting as joint controllers of such processing. Not all kind of partnerships, cooperation or collaboration imply qualification of joint controllers as such qualification requires a case-by-case analysis of each processing at stake and the precise role of each entity with respect to each processing".[51] The decisive factor is the existence of purposes and means of processing determined jointly by the controllers. In this respect, it is added that "the exchange of the same data or set of data between two entities without jointly determined purposes or jointly determined means of processing should be considered as a transmission of data between separate controllers[52]". Being well aware of these challenges, the French CNIL felt the need to provide guidance that specifically addresses where joint controllers can be involved in the use of personal data for the development and training of AI applications.[53]

On the contrary, good practices/standards on data governance, once turned into contract terms, become binding on all parties to a data sharing contract, regardless of how these parties qualify under the data protection legal framework. Furthermore, they can be enforced through the contractual remedies available under the applicable contract law regime, such as contract termination and/or penalty clauses. These remedies may thus contribute to promoting the accountability of all those who share data for the training and development of AI applications.

[50] See European Court of Justice, Judgment of the Court of 4 May 2023 in the Case C-300/21 Österreichische Post AG. Available at https://eur-lex.europa.eu/legal-content/IT/TXT/?uri=CELEX%3A62021CJ0300.

[51] European Data Protection Board (2021), point 69.

[52] Ibidem, point 70.

[53] See CNIL (2024).

2.5 The AI Act: Data Governance and AI Value Chains

The AI Act aims to establish a legal framework that is mainly addressed to providers of high-risk AI systems (which may not coincide with data controllers) and deals with all the stages (input data collection, design and development of models etc.) leading to the deployment of AI systems. Inter alia, it mandates providers of high-risk AI systems to adopt adequate data governance practices and to ensure the quality of training data (Article 10 AI Act). It also sets out transparency and documentation duties for providers of systems of this kind with reference, as well, to data governance and data quality (see Articles 11 and 13 (3) (vi) AI Act). These requirements, however, only apply to high-risk AI systems.

Moreover, the AI Act Proposal did not take into account the fact that the provider of an AI system rarely coincides with its developer and almost never carries out in-house all the steps leading up to the AI system being placed on the market or put into service. As a result, the Proposal left to AI providers to promote the accountability of the other participants in the value chain, also by adopting contract terms under which the latter are required to guarantee compliance with the AI provisions on data quality, documentation etc. This policy option relied on the assumption that the AI provider is the economic operator in a dominant position vis-à-vis these participants. This assumption, however, was criticized for being too simplistic and failing to take into account that possible imbalances of economic power between the parties do not always see AI providers assuming the role of 'strong' parties in the relationship with participants in the AI value chain.[54]

Conversely, the AI Act acknowledges the complexity of AI value chains, which may include multiple third parties involved in the development and in the supply of components. Hence, it prescribes that these third parties must cooperate, as appropriate, with providers of AI systems to enable them to monitor compliance with the requirements set out by the AI Act. To this end, third parties are required to disclose in writing to AI providers all information necessary for this purpose (Article 25 (4) AI Act).[55]

This obligation to cooperate sets an incentive for AI providers and value chain participants to 'contractualize' and document how they share responsibility for complying with requirements on high-risk AI systems, including data governance. However, the implementation of such a policy has the potential to bring certain benefits but also raises concerns.

AI providers and value chain participants can theoretically agree on a fair distribution of the responsibilities between them. On the other hand, risks arise from possible imbalances of bargaining power among the contracting parties, for instance, where

[54] Engler, Renda (2022), p. 7.

[55] Article 25 (4) AI Act: "The provider of a high-risk AI system and the third party that supplies an AI system, tools, services, components, or processes that are used or integrated in a high-risk AI system shall, by written agreement, specify the necessary information, capabilities, technical access and other assistance based on the generally acknowledged state of the art, in order to enable the provider of the high-risk AI system to fully comply with the obligations set out in this Regulation".

AI providers are in a position of economic dominance vis-à-vis the other participants in the value chain, such that the former can impose contractual terms under which the costs of compliance with the requirements of the AI Act or the fines provided for therein are passed on to the latter.

In order to address possible inequalities in bargaining power within AI value chains, the AI Act Proposal of June 2023 explicitly qualified contract terms unilaterally imposed by AI providers on an SME or start-up providing for an exclusion or limitation of liability of the party imposing the term for intentional acts and gross negligence (or excluding or limiting access to remedies available to the other party) as unfair and non-binding.[56] In addition, the AI Act Proposal of June 2023 stated that "*A contractual term is also unfair if it has the effect of shifting penalties referred to in Article 71 or associated litigation costs across parties to the contract, as referred to in Article 71(8)*" (Article 28a).

These provisions have not been included in the final text of the AI Act. Instead, Article 28 (4) AI Act empowers the AI Office to develop and recommend voluntary model terms for contracts between providers of high-risk AI systems and those involved in the value chain. The fact that such model terms can be adopted on a voluntary basis is further evidence that the governance of AI value chains is left to national regulations on unfair terms in business contracts. Likewise, the validity of clauses on penalties or claims arising from non-compliance with the AI Act included in contracts between suppliers and participants in AI value chains must be assessed under national contract law.[57]

3 Conclusion

The paper addressed data sharing contracts for AI development and training, entered into by parties participating in AI value chains, in order to assess the incentives for responsible data sharing under European data law.

The normative instruments recently enacted by the EU, such as the DGA and the Data Act, are concerned with establishing a 'data economy' and fall short of

[56] See Article 28a AI Act Proposal of June 2023. See, as well, Recital 62 AI Act Proposal of June 2023: "In order to ensure a high level of trustworthiness of high-risk AI systems, those systems should be subject to a conformity assessment prior to their placing on the market or putting into service. *To increase the trust in the value chain and to give certainty to businesses about the performance of their systems, third-parties that supply AI components may voluntarily apply for a third-party conformity assessment*".

[57] In reality, the AI Act Proposal of June 2023 contained a provision (Article 71 (8a)) under which: "*The penalties referred to in this article as well as the associated litigation costs and indemnification claims may not be the subject of contractual clauses or other form of burden-sharing agreements between providers and distributors, importers, deployers, or any other third parties*". Although clarifying, this provision merely reasserted a principle common to many legal regimes, i.e. that private autonomy is not allowed to alter the allocation of liability between the parties, which is established by public law remedies.

promoting the accountability of the parties to a data sharing contract. As a consequence, the governance of AI training data is mainly entrusted to party autonomy and to the principles of the GDPR.

As demonstrated, the terms included in data sharing contracts tend to be exclusively shaped by the private interests of the parties. These terms may not reflect the legal status of data which differs from tradable commodities, nor do they take into account the peculiarities of the data used in the context of AI development/training. The data used for this purpose is not a static artefact. On the contrary, it is the result of choices and practices to be implemented during the phases of data collection and generation and model development. Therefore, adopting responsible data management practices helps to prevent harm to the rights of natural persons. The analysis showed that leaving the governance of AI training data to party autonomy entails several shortcomings. The parties are incentivized to comply with mandatory regulations, such as those which protect personal data and the right to privacy, only if the public law and tort law regimes at play show an adequate level of effectiveness. Moreover, liability under contract law does not extend beyond the parties to the contract and, therefore, it fails to promote the accountability of all those who share data for AI development.

However, it was demonstrated that the interaction of the data protection framework with contract law challenges the corollaries of traditional contract theory. The legal regime set out by the GDPR entails constraints on party autonomy, since data can only be processed in conformity with the principles of lawfulness and fairness enshrined in Article 5 GDPR. Moreover, the data protection framework also covers automated decision-making that often involves the deployment of AI systems which may have significant adverse impacts on individuals. In these cases, transparency requirements are set out and the adoption of adequate measures is mandated according to the principles of accountability and privacy by design (see Articles 5, 22, 24 and 25; Recital 71 GDPR), in order to prevent such impacts. These principles interact with party autonomy by establishing duties of care on the parties that share and manage data for the purpose of training/developing AI applications.

As highlighted in the paper, the principle of accountability has an organizational dimension and places on data controllers the duty to take the 'legal' measures that enable them to comply with the GDPR. Therefore, the parties to these contracts are required to arrange adequate data sharing architectures, starting with the choice of the contract type and contract terms.

The duties of care stemming from the data protection framework are, as a result, 'contractualized' and turned into due diligence contract terms included in the data sharing contracts. Contract terms of this sort may compel the parties to such contracts to adopt: *i)* technical and procedural standards and practices *ii)* mechanisms to oversee compliance with these standards/practices by all the parties (for instance, mandating to carry out internal audits or reporting) and *iii)* enforcement mechanisms (for instance, penalty clauses, contract termination clauses etc.) in the event of non fulfilment of these duties. Along the same lines are contract terms requiring the contracting parties to monitor whether sub-suppliers comply with data protection requirements.

As a consequence, the adoption of good practices and standards for the distribution of responsibilities among participants in complex value chains for AI development is not left to market forces. On the contrary, it is prompted by the principle of accountability and is enforced by recourse to contract law remedies.

Lastly, the analysis comprised a brief overview of the relevant provisions of the AI Act that deal with data governance and AI value chains. This new body of legislation acknowledges the complexity of AI value chains, which may comprise multiple entities, such as parties involved in the supply of data. It is therein prescribed that these third parties must cooperate, as appropriate, with providers of AI systems to enable them to monitor compliance with the requirements set out by the AI Act. However, the AI Act does not address inequalities of bargaining power between the various economic actors involved. This gap risks undermining the policy objective of making all those participating in value chains for high-risk AI systems accountable.

References

Castronovo C (1995) L'obbligazione senza prestazione. Ai confini tra contratto e torto, in Le ragioni del diritto. Scritti in Onore di Luigi Mengoni (Giuffré Milano) I:147–240

Claes H, Herbosch M (2023) Artificial intelligence and contractual liability limitations: a natural combination? ERPL 31(2–3):497–518

Comandé G (2019) Intelligenza artificiale e responsabilità tra liability e accountability. Il carattere trasformativo dell'IA e il problema della responsabilità. Analisi Giuridica Dell'economia 1:169–188

de Meeus C (2019) The product liability directive at the age of the digital industrial revolution: fit for innovation? EuCML 8(2):149–154

Engler A C, Renda A (2022) Reconciling the AI value chain with the EU's artificial intelligence act. In: CEPS in-depth analysis. September 2022. https://www.ceps.eu/ceps-publications/reconciling-the-ai-value-chain-with-the-eus-artificial-intelligence-act/. Accessed 22 Feb 2025

Gellert R, Janssen AU (2023) The impact of artificial intelligence on European contract law: talking stock to an ongoing process. In: Janssen A, Lehmann M, Schulze R (eds), The future of European Private Law Nomos 2023, 169–194

Graef I, Gellert R, Husovec M (2018) Towards a holistic regulatory approach for the European data economy: why the illusive notion of non-personal data is counterproductive to data innovation. (September 27, 2018) TILEC Discussion Paper No. 2018-029. Available at SSRN: https://ssrn.com/abstract=3256189 or https://doi.org/10.2139/ssrn.3256189

Hacker P (2020) A Legal Framework for AI Training Data - From First Principles to the Artificial Intelligence Act. Law, Innovation and Technology. Available at SSRN: https://ssrn.com/abstract=3556598 or https://doi.org/10.2139/ssrn.3556598

Hennemann, M, Ebner G, Karsten B (2023) Part I (Art. 1–13, 35). In: Hennemann M, Karsten B, Wienroeder M, Lienemann G, Ebner G (eds). The Data Act Proposal – Literature Review and Critical Analysis. University of Passau Institute for Law of the Digital Society Research Paper Series No. 23-01. https://www.jura.uni-passau.de/irdg/publikationen/research-paper-series/

Janeček V, Malgieri G (2020) Data extra commercium. In: Lohsse S, Schultze R, Staudenmayer D (eds) Data as counter-performance—contract law 2.0? Hart Publishing/Nomos 2020, 93–122. Available at SSRN: https://ssrn.com/abstract=3400620. Accessed 22 February 2025

Kaminski ME (2019) The right to explanation, explained. Berkeley Technol Law J 34(189–218):201. https://doi.org/10.2139/ssrn.3196985

Nivarra L (2014) Alcune precisazioni in tema di responsabilità contrattuale. Eur Dirit Priv 1:45–108

Orlando S (2023) Il coordinamento tra la direttiva 770/2019 e il GDPR. L'interessato-Consumatore. Persona e Mercato 2:222–241

Peterkova Mitkidis K (2014) Sustainability clauses in international supply chain contracts: regulation, enforceability and effects of ethical requirements' 1. Nord J Comm Law, 7. https://www.researchgate.net/publication/299269785_Sustainability_Clauses_in_International_Supply_Chain_Contracts_Regulation_Enforceability_and_Effects_of_Ethical_Requirements. Accessed 22 August 2024

Podda E, Palmirani M (2021) Inferring the meaning of non-personal, anonymized, and anonymous data. In: Rodríguez-Doncel V, Palmirani M, Araszkiewicz M, Casanovas P, Pagallo U, Sartor G (eds) AI approaches to the complexity of legal systems XI–XII. AICOL 2020, AICOL 2018, XAILA 2020. Lecture notes in computer science, vol 13048. Springer, Cham

Purtova N (2018) The law of everything. Broad concept of personal data and future of EU data protection law. Law Innov Technol 10(1):40–81. https://doi.org/10.1080/17579961.2018.1452176

Quintais JP, Appelman N, Fathaigh RÓ (2023) Using terms and conditions to apply fundamental rights to content moderation. German Law J 24:881–911

Resta G (2005) Autonomia privata e diritti della personalità (Jovene Editore Napoli) 281

Riis N (2023) Shaping the field of EU data law. JIPITEC 14:54–65

Spina A (2016) Alla ricerca di un modello di regolazione per l'economia dei dati. Commento al regolamento (Ue) 2016/679. Rivista della Regolazione Dei Mercati. 1:143–152

Stalla-Bourdillon S, Thuermer G, Walker J, Carmichael L, Simperl E (2020) Data protection by design: building the foundations of trustworthy data sharing. Data Policy 2:1–10

Streinz T (2021) The evolution of European data law. In: Craig P, de Búrca G (eds) The evolution of EU data law, 903. Oxford University Press, Oxford

Suresh H, Guttag J (2021) A framework for understanding sources of harm throughout the machine learning life cycle. In: Equity and access in algorithms, mechanisms, and optimization (EAAMO '21), 5–9 Oct 2021. https://doi.org/10.1145/3465416.3483305. Accessed 22 Feb 2025

Wernick A, Olk C, Grafenstein M (2020) Defining data intermediaries. A clearer view through the lens of intellectual property governance. Technol Regul. https://doi.org/10.26116/techreg.2020.007

American Law Institute and the European Law Institute's principles for a data economy: data transactions and data rights (2023). https://www.europeanlawinstitute.eu/fileadmin/user_upload/p_eli/Publications/ALI-ELI_Principles_for_a_Data_Economy.pdf. Accessed 22 Feb 2025

BEUC The European Consumer Bureau (2020) How to make product liability fit for consumers in the digital age (Ref: BEUC-X-2020-024—07/05/2020). https://www.beuc.eu/sites/default/files/publications/beuc-x-2020-024_product_liability_position_paper.pdf

Communication from the Commission to the European Parliament, the Council, the European Economic and Social Committee and the Committee of the Regions. A European strategy for data (COM/2020/66 final)

European Data Protection Board, Guidelines 07/2020 on the concepts of controller and processor in the GDPR, adopted on 07 July 2021, point 69. https://www.edpb.europa.eu/system/files/2023-10/EDPB_guidelines_202007_controllerprocessor_final_en.pdf. Accessed 22 Feb 2025

EDPB-EDPS Joint Opinion 5/2021 on the proposal for a Regulation of the European Parliament and of the Council laying down harmonised rules on artificial intelligence (Artificial Intelligence Act)—21 June 2021. https://edpb.europa.eu/our-work-tools/our-documents/edpbedps-joint-opinion/edpb-edps-joint-opinion-52021-proposal_en. Accessed 22 Feb 2025

United Nations Commission on International Trade Law. Working Group IV on Electronic Commerce (2023) A/CN.9/WG.IV/WP.183 - Default rules for data provision contracts (first revision), Vienna, 16–20 Oct 2023. https://documents-dds-ny.un.org/doc/UNDOC/LTD/V23/064/75/PDF/V2306475.pdf?OpenElement. Accessed 25 Feb 2025

CNIL, Déterminer la qualification juridique des acteurs (8 April 2024). https://www.cnil.fr/fr/determiner-la-qualification-juridique-des-fournisseurs-de-systemes-dia. Accessed 22 Feb 2025

Prof. Roberta Montinaro is a full Professor at the Department of Humanities and Social Sciences, University of Naples L'Orientale, where she teaches Private Law and Private Law of the Digital Economy, Data Law and Artificial Intelligence Regulation. She is also the scientific coordinator of the Jean Monnet Centre of Excellence "AI-CoDED – Artificial Intelligence and Communication in a Digitized European Democracy" established at the University of Naples L'Orientale. Since 2023 she is a member of the teaching board of the Italian PhD in Artificial Intelligence.

User Consent at the Interface of the DMA and the GDPR: A Privacy-Setting Solution to Ensure Compliance with Art. 5(2) DMA

Marco Botta and Danielle Borges

Abstract The EU Digital Markets Act (DMA) aims at improving the 'fairness' and 'contestability' of digital markets. Art. 5(2) DMA prohibits gatekeepers from combining and cross using the end user's data collected from different sources within its own eco-system. However, data combination is possible if the end-user provides his 'consent' to such data combination. The users' consent should comply with the requirements of the General Data Protection Regulation (GDPR). The chapter discusses the relationship between the DMA and the GDPR, focusing on the users' consent as a lawful basis to the processing activities of data combination and cross-use under Art. 5(2) DMA. The chapter argues in favour of a 'privacy setting' solution: at the first log in, the user would face on his other screen a cookie wall, asking the user to opt-in to specific types of data combination activities by the gatekeeper. Secondly, the chapter argues that the DMA represents a *lex specialis* in comparison to the GDPR. Therefore, while respecting the general criteria indicated by Articles 4(11) and 7 GDPR, the user's consent under Art. 5(2) DMA should be 'adjusted' to the special features of the Digital Markets Act.

Keywords Digital markets act · General Data Protection Regulation · Data combination · Data cross-use · Personal data · Consent

1 Introduction

The digital transformation has enabled the emergence of new business models, generating an economy based upon data processing power, storage, communication, and networks. In the last decade, digital platforms have been able to grow exponentially by collecting, accumulating, analysing, and delivering new personalised products and

M. Botta (✉) · D. Borges
Centre for a Digital Society at the European University Institute, Florence, Italy
e-mail: Marco.botta@eui.eu

D. Borges
e-mail: Danielle.borges@eui.eu

J. Drexl et al. (eds.), *Comparative Data Law*, MPI Studies on Intellectual Property and Competition Law 32, https://doi.org/10.1007/978-3-031-91401-0_6

services.[1] The recognition of the increasing economic power of digital platforms' business models has resulted in new political responses, with a shift towards more governmental intervention *vis-à-vis* practices and business strategies of digital platforms.[2] In different parts of the world, we have thus been observing regulatory and legislative changes aiming at building a more comprehensive regulation of digital platforms' activities.[3]

The Digital Markets Act (DMA) represents the best example of the new sector regulation of digital platforms.[4] By imposing asymmetric regulation on 'large' digital platforms (i.e. gatekeepers), the DMA aims at improving the 'fairness' and 'contestability' of digital markets.[5] The 'digital gatekeepers' are platforms that provide at least one of the core platform services mentioned in the DMA, and fulfil the DMA thresholds of application, in terms of number of users and turnover/market capitalization.

The DMA is fully applicable since 2nd May 2023. On 6th September 2023, the EU Commission designated six firms as having 'gatekeeper' status. At the beginning of March 2024, each designated gatekeepers submitted a compliance report to the EU Commission, explaining the measures adopted to comply with the DMA obligations. Following the publication of the reports, the Commission has opened investigations concerning a potential lack of compliance with the DMA obligations by *Google, Apple* and *Meta*; the investigations should be completed by March 2025.[6]

Art. 5(2) DMA prohibits a gatekeeper from combining and cross-using end users' data collected from different sources within its own eco-system. However, Art. 5(2) DMA offers an exception to this general prohibition in case the end-user provides his or her 'consent' to such data combination and cross-use, to benefit from more personalized services or advertisements from the gatekeeper.[7] In particular, the users' consent should comply with the requirements of Article 7 of the General Data Protection Regulation (GDPR).[8]

The chapter discusses the 'complex' relationship between the DMA and the GDPR, to clarify the scope of the user's consent to data combination under Art. 5(2) DMA. The chapter first analyses the content of Art. 5(2) DMA. Secondly, the chapter discusses the GDPR concept of consent and its requirements, in the light of

---

[1] Davola and Malgieri (2022), p. 67-92.

[2] Cioffi, Kenney and Zysman (2022), p. 820–836.

[3] Botta (2021), p. 500–512.

[4] Regulation (EU) 2022/1925 of the European Parliament and of the Council of 14 September 2022 on contestable and fair markets in the digital sector and amending Directives (EU) 2019/1937 and (EU) 2020/1828 (*Digital Markets Act*). OJ L-265/1, 12.10.2022.

[5] *Ibid,* Para 33–34 DMA Preamble.

[6] European Commission. https://digital-markets-act.ec.europa.eu/latest-news_enlast. Accessed 19 July 2024.

[7] *Ibid.*

[8] Regulation (EU) 2016/679 of the European Parliament and of the Council of 27 April 2016 on the protection of natural persons with regard to the processing of personal data and on the free movement of such data, and repealing Directive 95/46/EC (General Data Protection Regulation). OJ L-119/1, 4.5.2016.

the case law of the EU Court of Justice, as well as the guidelines adopted by the Article 29 Working Party. Finally, the chapter proposes a 'privacy-setting' solution that would allow the gatekeepers to comply with the requirements under Art. 5(2) DMA.

The chapter aims at contributing to the on-going policy debate on the challenges faced by gatekeepers in implementing the DMA obligations, a topical subject after the entry into force of this Regulation. Secondly, the chapter aims at contributing to the on-going debate on the relationship between the DMA and GDPR.

2 DMA and the Obligations for Gatekeepers: Article 5(2)

One of the competitive advantages enjoyed by gatekeepers, in comparison to other platforms, is their ability to collect, combine and process end users' data from a variety of different sources within its own eco-system.[9] A gatekeeper can match the personal data provided by the end user when signing up for a digital service (e.g. signing up for a social network) with the 'traces' left by the end user while using the services provided by the gatekeeper within its own eco-system (e.g. web navigation history; apps downloaded; geo-location information; ads and videos watched…).[10] Owning to data combination, the gatekeeper can 'profile' the end user, and provide more targeted services to the end user.[11] For instance, via profiling, the gatekeeper may automatically adjust the default app feature based on the user's expected preferences. Similarly, the gatekeeper can provide a higher ranking to certain types of content (e.g. specific videos, songs, apps, pictures, posts on social networks) that are considered 'more relevant' for the end user. On the other hand, the gatekeeper may also rely on data combination for targeted advertising and to carry out price discrimination[12]: Based on the end user's behaviour within the eco-system, the gatekeeper may target the end user with specific ads and offers, which are considered (by the platform) to best match the end user's interests and willingness to pay.

Personalized services, ads and prices should not be considered as per se against the interests of end users; several consumers enjoy more personalized offers and services, which decrease their search costs.[13] However, users should be duly informed about data combination, and should be able to freely provide their authorization (i.e. 'consent') to such use of their personal data. The GDPR requires the user's consent for 'data processing' – a broad expression that also includes 'data combination'.

[9] Krämer, Schnurr and Broughton Micova (2020), p. 55. https://cerre.eu/publications/data-digital-markets-contestability-case-studies-and-data-access-remedies/. Accessed 2 August 2024.

[10] *Ibid*.

[11] Article 29 Working Party, 'Guidelines on Automated Individual Decision-Making and Profiling for the Purposes of Regulation 2016/679', WP 251 rev.01, 6 February 2018. https://ec.europa.eu/newsroom/article29/items/612053. Accessed 22 February 2025.

[12] Botta and Wiedemann (2020), p. 381–404.

[13] *Ibid*.

However, consumers are often unaware that platforms collect and cross-use their personal data and tend to accept the general terms and conditions provided by the platforms without fully understanding the effective scope of data combination within the platform's eco-system. Secondly, data combination represents a major competitive advantage for gatekeepers in comparison to smaller platforms, which provide a single service to consumers (e.g. via a single app or a website, rather than via an eco-system including different digital services), and therefore have a limited ability to engage in data combination activities.

Art. 5(2) DMA prohibits a gatekeeper from combining personal data within its own eco-system upon the lack of the user's consent. The Art. 5(2) prohibition may be considered in line with the DMA's 'contestability' goal: since the DMA's obligations are applicable only *vis-à-vis* digital gatekeepers, third platforms will be able to continue combining and cross-using personal data, by improving their market position. At least in theory, Art. 5(2) should therefore reduce one of the main competitive advantages enjoyed by gatekeepers, by fostering inter-platform competition. It could also be argued that Art. 5(2) reflects the DMA's fairness goal, remedying the current in transparent way in which data combination is carried out by some gatekeepers. This is the interpretation recently followed by the Bundeskartellamt in its *Google* Decision adopted under Sec. 19(a) *Gesetz gegen Wettbewerbsbeschränkungen* (GWB).[14] Under Sec. 19(a)(2)(1)(4a) GWB, the Bundeskartellamt may prohibit a firm 'having paramount significance for competition across markets' from "making the use of services conditional on the user agreeing to the processing of data from other services of the undertaking or a third-party provider without giving the user sufficient choice as to whether, how and for which purpose such data is processed."[15]

Art. 5(2) is the first of the 23 obligations included in the Digital Markets Act. The provision is framed in the form of four 'negative obligations' – i.e. the gatekeeper "shall not do any of the following". First, the gatekeeper shall not "process" personal data collected from third party apps and websites (e.g. news chapters and merchants' websites) together with the data collected within its own eco-system "for the purpose of providing online advertising services". Secondly, the gatekeeper shall not "combine" personal data collected from different core platform services within its own ecosystem, as well as with personal data collected from non-core platform services provided by the gatekeeper, as well as with personal data collected from third parties. Third, the gatekeeper shall not "cross-use" personal data collected within the core platform service with the user's data collected from other services provided by the gatekeeper. Finally, the gatekeeper shall not force end users to "sign in" to additional services, by thus forcing them to accept data combination requirements. The four prohibitions may be considered, collectively, as a general prohibition on 'data combination' from the side of the gatekeeper.

[14] German Competition Act in the version published on 26 June 2013 (Bundesgesetzblatt (Federal Law Gazette) I, 2013, p. 1750, 3245), as last amended by Article 2 of the Act of 19 July 2022 (Federal Law Gazette I, p. 1214).

[15] Sec. 19(a)(2)(1)(4a) GWB.

Art. 5(2) provides four possible exceptions to the prohibitions mentioned above. First, the prohibitions are not applicable if the gatekeeper has provided a "specific choice" to the end user, and the latter has provided his orher "consent" to the data combination. As further discussed in the following section, the consent should be expressed by the end user in accordance with the GDPR conditions for a valid consent (Art. 4(11) and Art. 7 GDPR). Secondly, even in the absence of the user's consent, the gatekeeper may also combine or cross-use personal data in case the data processing is "necessary for the compliance with a legal obligation to which the controller is subject;" is "necessary to protect the vital interests" of the end user; or is "necessary for the performance of a task carried out in the public interest or in the exercise of official authority" vested in the gatekeeper.[16]

In terms of enforcement, Art. 5(2) will be applicable as soon as a platform is designated by the EU Commission as having the status of a digital gatekeeper. Art. 5 obligations are considered 'self-executing', and thus the EU Commission is not expected to adopt specific Decisions clarifying how each gatekeeper should comply with the data combination obligation.[17] Every gatekeeper, however, will have the burden of showing that it has duly complied with Art. 5(2) by providing a report to the EU Commission within 6 months after the gatekeeper designation.[18] In the report, the gatekeeper will have to specify the measures adopted to comply with the DMA obligations referring to the GDPR provisions, such as the user's consent under Art. 5(2) DMA.[19]

3 Consent as a Legal Basis for Data Processing Activities Under the GDPR and the DMA

3.1 The Relationship Between the DMA and the GDPR

Departing from the different terminology used by the GDPR and the DMA, which respectively use the terms "data subject" and "end user" to refer to the 'owners' of personal data processed by either the 'controllers' or the 'gatekeepers', the two regulations considerably differ in terms of their objectives and scope. While the empowerment of data subjects in terms of strengthening control over their personal data is one of the main objectives pursued by the GDPR,[20] the DMA focus is on 'fairness' and 'contestability' in digital markets.[21] In other words, in the GDPR, the

[16] Art. 5(2) DMA refers to Art. 6(1) (c) (d) and (e) GDPR as possible legal bases for lawful data combination.

[17] Art. 8 (2) DMA.

[18] Art. 11 DMA.

[19] Recital 68 DMA.

[20] Art. 1(1) GDPR.

[21] Art. 1(1) DMA.

protection of the individuals' right to personal data protection is the main objective of the legislation, whereas in the DMA the protection of end users' personal data arises as an 'indirect objective', connected to the DMA compliance obligations for the gatekeeper.

A second difference between the two regulations concerns the scope of data portability – i.e. the user's- ordata subject's right to request the gatekeeper or data controller to transfer his or her personal data to a third party. Data portability is present both in the GDPR and in the DMA. In both legislations, the data controller and gatekeeper are required to share the data with third parties "free of charge."[22] Nevertheless, the scope of the two legislations is quite different. On the one hand, under Art. 20(1) and (2) GDPR, data portability is limited to 'personal data' that have been voluntarily and actively provided by data subjects to the controller.[23] On the other hand, within the DMA, data portability covers both 'personal' and 'non-personal data' generated by the end-user while using the core platform service.[24] Therefore, the DMA data portability obligation covers a wider range of data generated within the core platform service, such as raw data processed by connected devices, activity logs, web browsing history or web search activities. Finally, while the GDPR data portability is applicable only where it is "technically feasible",[25] the gatekeeper is requested to ensure "continuous and real-time access" to the data.[26] The DMA emphasis on "real-time access" shows a broader data portability obligation in comparison to the limited scope of Art. 20 GDPR.[27]

The different objectives and scope of the data portability right are good examples of the differences between the DMA and the GDPR. According to its Preamble, the Digital Markets Act is applicable "without prejudice" to the General Data Protection Regulation, as well as consumer and competition law.[28] As recently argued by Bania, the expression "without prejudice" means that the DMA obligations would be applicable without detriment to any existing right enshrined in the other legislations.[29] In line with this line of reasoning, one may conclude that the GDPR should always take precedence over the DMA in case of a conflict between the two regulations.

Despite its reference to the expression "without prejudice", the DMA's Preamble fails to clarify which legislation would prevail in case of a conflict or divergent interpretation between the DMA and other sector legislation. By contrast, both the

---

[22] Art. 12(5) GDPR: "Information provided under Articles 13 and 14 and any communication and any actions taken under Articles 15 to 22 and 34 shall be provided free of charge."; Art. 6(9) DMA.

[23] Krämer (2020), p. 263-308.

[24] Art. 6(9) DMA.

[25] Art. 20(2) GDPR.

[26] Art. 6(9) DMA.

[27] Botta (2023), p. 26. https://www.digitalsociety.eui.eu/publication/the-principle-of-frand-in-b2b-data-sharing/. Accessed 22 February 2025.

[28] Recital 12 DMA.

[29] Bania (2023), p. 117.

Data Act[30] and the Data Governance Act[31] stress the relevance of the GDPR in the interpretation of their provisions. The DMA and the GDPR are two EU Regulations: they have equal status within the hierarchy of EU legal norms. However, the two legislations have different objectives; even when dealing with the same issue (e.g. data portability), they follow rather different approaches. According to Bania, the DMA regulates a "more specific" subject than the GDPR, which is horizontally applicable to every type of personal data processing. In other words, the DMA includes a limited number of obligations, which are applicable only to a limited number of firms (i.e. digital gatekeepers), while the GDPR is horizontally applicable to every firm and public institution engaged in the processing of personal data. Therefore, in view of the principle *lex specialis derogat generali,* in case of conflict between the DMA and the GDPR, the first legislation should prevail.[32]

Alternatively, we would argue that the DMA and the GDPR are separate legislations that aim to achieve different objectives and follow different logics. When it comes to data combination, Art. 6(1) GDPR provides six possible legal bases for lawful data processing, including the data subject's consent. By contrast, Art. 5(2) provides only four possible legal bases to authorize data combination by the gatekeeper, including the user's consent. While designated gatekeepers will have to comply with the Art. 5(2) requirements when carrying out data combination activities within their own eco-system, Art. 6(1) GDPR will be applicable to non-gatekeepers firms when they decide to combine, and thus process, collected personal data. To sum up, even without referring to the principle of *lex specialis,* we come to a similar conclusion: although the user's consent under Art. 5(2) DMA should be collected by the gatekeeper in light of the GDPR requirements for lawful consent, some adaptations would be advisable in view of the GDPR peculiarities, considering that the two legislations are rather different in terms of objectives, logic and scope. Keeping this important point in mind, the chapter now turns to the analysis of the concept of consent according to the GDPR and DMA provisions.

3.2 Consent Under the GDPR

The European Union model of data protection regulation is an example of how consent may be specifically regulated. The GDPR in Article 4(11) establishes that:

> "Consent of the data subject means any freely given, specific, informed and unambiguous indication of the data subject's wishes by which he or she, by a statement or by a clear

[30] Regulation (EU) 2023/2854 of the European Parliament and of the Council of 13 December 2023 on harmonised rules on fair access to and use of data and amending Regulation (EU) 2017/2394 and Directive (EU) 2020/1828 (Data Act). OJ L-2023/2854, 22.12.2023. Preamble, para. 7.

[31] Regulation (EU) 2022/868 of the European Parliament and of the Council of 30 May 2022 on European data governance and amending Regulation (EU) 2018/1724 (Data Governance Act). OJ L-152/1, 3.6.2022. Preamble, para. 4.

[32] Bania (2023), p. 148.

affirmative action, signifies agreement to the processing of personal data relating to him or her."

Therefore, the elements of consent are those enumerated in Article 4(11) GDPR. However, the GDPR also establishes 'conditions for consent' in its Article 7. In short, according to Article 4(11) GDPR, the elements of valid consent are the following: a) freely given; b) specific; c) informed; and d) unambiguous, with the indication of the data subject's will, according to which he or she agrees to the processing of his or her personal data.

The EDPB has provided further guidance on how to assess the elements of a valid consent.[33] According to its guidelines, in order for consent to be freely given, there must be real choice and control for data subjects.[34] Therefore, "[I]f consent is bundled up as a non-negotiable part of terms and conditions it is presumed to not have been freely given."[35]

Moreover, other issues must be considered when assessing whether consent is freely given. According to Recital 43 GDPR, when there is an imbalance of power between the data subject and the controller, consent should not be used as a legal basis for the processing of personal data, as it might prevent data subjects to exercise their free will. For instance, this can be the case where public authorities or employers are processing personal data concerning citizens and employees.

Another important issue for the assessment of freely given consent is 'conditionality'. In this regard, Recital 43 and Article 7(4) GDPR indicate that consent should not be tied with the performance of a contract or the provision of a service. In other words, "consent and contract cannot be merged and blurred."[36] Hence, consent is not an adequate legal basis to the processing of personal data when the requested data is necessary for the performance of a contract. In this case, the adequate legal basis will be the one in Article 6(1) (b). On the other hand, if the personal data for which consent is sought is not necessary for the performance of a contract and its accomplishment is conditional on the data subject's consent, then consent is possibly not considered to be freely given.

Therefore, there should always be a choice for the data subject to have either a contract performed, or a service delivered without having to consent to further data processing activities that are not essential for the performance of the contract in question. To avoid this type of 'conditionality', different contracts or services for data subjects must be proposed to data subjects by the provider or data controller: one including consent to the processing of personal data for further data processing purposes, and an alternative option, genuinely equivalent to the first contract or service offered by the same data controller that does not contemplate consenting to

---

[33] European Data Protection. Board (2020), Guidelines 05/2020 on consent under Regulation 2016/679. Adopted on May 2020. https://www.edpb.europa.eu/sites/default/files/files/file1/edpb_guidelines_202005_consent_en.pdf. Accessed 22 February 2025.

[34] *Ibid*, p. 7.

[35] *Ibid*.

[36] *Ibid*., p. 10.

additional data processing activities.[37] For instance, the EDPB when first assessing the requirements of consent, considered it to not be freely given when the controller uses 'cookie walls', conditioning consent on the storing of a data subject's information or upon gaining access to information already stored in the data subject's device, as provided for in Article 5(3) of the ePrivacy Directive (Directive 2002/58/EC).[38]

Cookie walls as a form of obtaining consent were indeed further analysed by the CJEU in *Planet49*. The Court ruled that the consent referred to in Article 6(1)(a) GDPR is not valid "if, in the form of cookies, the storage of information or access to information already stored in a website user's terminal equipment is permitted by way of a pre-checked checkbox which the user must deselect to refuse his or her consent."[39]

This initial general ban on the use of 'cookie walls' for obtaining consent has been further developed by national courts and national data protection authorities leading to a more flexible approach to the use of 'cookie walls'. In this regard, in France, for example, the *Conseil d'État* by a decision from 19 June 2020, which discussed the French data protection authority (CNIL) guidelines on 'cookie walls' from 4 July 2019,[40] ruled that the requirement of free consent could not justify a general ban on the practice of 'cookie walls'.[41] According to this decision, the assessment of whether consent has been freely given must be done on a case-by-case basis, considering the existence of effective alternatives available to users in the event of refusal of cookies. In this specific ruling, however, the French Court concluded that the consent architecture used by *Google* for the creation of an account necessary for the use of the Android operating system provided concise, but very general information on the nature and purposes of the data processing activities carried out by *Google,*and therefore could not be regarded as informed and consequently not valid.[42] In view of this ruling, CNIL reviewed its guidelines and recommendations on 'cookie walls'.[43] In 2022, CNIL provided further guidance on how to assess the legality of using 'cookie walls', clarifying the criteria upon which the alternatives available to users to access websites without consenting to the processing of their data must be assessed. According to the 2022 CNIL guidelines, (1) web providers must make available to users 'a real and fair alternative' to walled content or services; (2) a alternative service upon cost must have a reasonable price; (3) user account creation

[37] *Ibid.*, p. 11.

[38] EDPB guidelines 5/2020, p. 12.

[39] Case C-673/17, *Bundesverband der Verbraucherzentralen und Verbraucherverbände - Verbraucherzentrale Bundesverband e.V. v Planet49 GmbH* [2019] ECLI:EU:C:2019:801. Para 44.

[40] Commission nationale de l'informatique et des libertés (CNIL) (2019) Délibération n° 2019-093 du 4 juillet 2019.

[41] Conseil d'État decision n° 430810 [2020] ECLI:FR:CECHR:2020:430810.20200619.

[42] *Ibid.*, paras. 22 and 23.

[43] Commission nationale de l'informatique et des libertés (CNIL) (2020) Délibération n° 2020-092 du 17 septembre 2020 portant adoption d'une recommandation proposant des modalités pratiques de mise en conformité en cas de recours aux «cookies et autres traceurs». https://www.legifrance.gouv.fr/jorf/id/JORFTEXT000042388197. Accessed 22 February 2025.

must correspond to specific and transparent purposes; (4) paywalls and cookie walls must correspond to specific purposes; and (5) cookies may only be deposited in limited circumstances when an alternative to cookie walls is selected.[44]

Along the same lines, other data protection authorities, such as the Italian and the Spanish authorities, have also issued guidelines on cookie walls in the last two years, specifying that cookie walls can only be considered a valid form of consent when the site owner offers the user the possibility of accessing an equivalent content or service without him or her giving consent to the installation and use of cookies or other tracking tools, to be verified however on a case-by-case basis.[45] However, there are still national data protection authorities in the EU, such as the Belgian data protection authority, which impose a general ban on cookie walls arguing that they prevent obtaining free consent.[46]

This leads to the second important requirement for a valid consent: it must be 'specific'. This means that when consent is the chosen legal basis for data processing, it needs to be as granular as possible in order to be valid, making clear and specific to the data subject the purpose(s) for which consent is being sought. Therefore, if the data processing activity involves more than one purpose, all of them need to be specified and consented by the data subject. In other words, rather than bundling up all purposes in one mode of information, the data controller must seek several different agreements from the data subject when there are different purposes for data processing activities.

The third essential requirement for consent to be valid is that it must be 'informed'. This is indeed part of the transparency principle that governs the GDPR. According to the EDPB, the minimum content requirements for consent to be informed comprise the following elements[47]: the controller's identity; the purpose of each of the processing operations for which consent is sought; which (type of) data will be collected and used; the existence of the right to withdraw consent; information about the use of the data for automated decision-making in accordance with Article 22 (2)(c) GDPR where relevant; and on the possible risks of data transfers due to the absence of an adequacy decision and of appropriate safeguards as described in Article 46 GDPR.

In case controllers do not comply with the minimum requirements for informed consent, the latter will be 'invalid', causing a possible breach of Article 6 of the GDPR. Furthermore, the general transparency requirements of Articles 13 and 14 of

[44] Commission Nationale de l'Informatique et des Libertés (CNIL) (2022), Questions-réponses sur les lignes directrices modificatives et la recommandation « cookies et autres traceurs de la CNIL. https://www.cnil.fr/fr/cookies-et-autres-traceurs/regles/cookies/FAQ. Accessed 22 February 2025.

[45] Garante per la Protezione dei Dati Personali (2021), Linee guida cookie e altri strumenti di tracciamento - 10 June 2021. https://www.garanteprivacy.it/home/docweb/-/docweb-display/docweb/9677876. Accessed 22 February 2025.

Agencia Española de Protección de Datos (AEPD) (2023), Guía sobre el uso de las cookies. https://www.aepd.es/guias/guia-cookies.pdf. Accessed 22 February 2025.

[46] Autorité de protection des données - APD (2023), Cookies et autres traceurs. https://www.cnil.fr/fr/cookies-et-autres-traceurs. Accessed 22 February 2025.

[47] EDPB guidelines 5/2020, p. 15.

the GDPR should also be complied with when it comes to informed consent. In this regard, the Article 29 Working Party has clarified that when processing is based on consent (or explicit consent), information should include, for example, how consent may be withdrawn since it should be as easy for a data subject to withdraw consent as to give it according to Article 7(3) GDPR.[48]

The last essential requirement of consent concerns the unambiguous declaration of the data subject's will. In this regard, for consent to be valid it requires either a statement or a clear affirmative action from the data subject, who must consciously take action to consent to a certain data processing activity. According to Recital 32 GDPR, this deliberate action of consenting may, for instance, take the form of a written or oral statement, including by using electronic means.[49]

Following up on *Planet49*, the CJEU has further reiterated in *Orange Romania* the requirements for consent to be freely given and informed.[50] According to the Court, the burden is on the data controller to demonstrate that the data subject has, by an active behaviour, consented to the processing of his or her personal data.[51] This includes demonstrating that the data subject was informed, in an intelligible and easily accessible form, and in clear and plain language, that allows the data subject to understand the meaning and consequences of his/her consent. Moreover, the ruling clarifies that consent is not valid, for instance, for the collection and storage of ID documents, if it is included as a clause in a contract for the provision of telecommunications services which states that the data subject has been informed of, and has consented to, the collection and storage of their IDs, and where: (i) the box referring to that clause has been ticked by the data controller before the contract was signed, or (ii) the terms of that contract are capable of misleading the data subject as to the possibility of concluding the contract in question even if he or she refuses to consent to the processing of his or her data, or iii) the data subject's choice to object to the collection and storage is unduly affected by an additional form that they must fill to express their refusal to consent to those processing activities.[52]

Therefore, the GDPR provides for a complex framework in relation to consent as one of the lawful bases to process personal data. Yet, it is neither the sole legal ground for the processing of personal data, nor hierarchically superior to the other legal bases provided by Article 6 GDPR. The use of consent should follow specific requirements in order to be considered adequate. In effect, in certain cases, obtaining consent may be inadequate and the controller must rely on the other lawful bases provided in Article 6(1) GDPR for non-sensitive data or in Article 9(2) GDPR for sensitive data. Hence, consent is an appropriate legal basis in situations where serious data

[48] Article 29 Working Party (2018) Guidelines on consent under Regulation 2016/679. Adopted on 28 November 2017 as last Revised and adopted on 10 April 2018.

[49] EDPB guidelines 5/2020, p. 15 and p.18.

[50] Case C-61/19, *Orange Romania SA v Autoritatea Națională de Supraveghere a Prelucrării Datelor cu Caracter Personal (ANSPDCP)* [2020] ECLI:EU:C:2020:901.

[51] *Ibid.* Para. 52.

[52] *Ibid.*

protection risks emerge, requiring, consequently, a high level of choice and control from data subjects over how their data is used.[53]

The chapter now moves to the analysis of the use of consent as a lawful legal basis for the data processing activities provided for in Art. 5(2) DMA.

3.3 Consent Under Art. 5(2) DMA—A Privacy-Setting Solution

As discussed in Sect. 2, Art. 5(2) DMA prohibits the gatekeeper from combining and cross-using the user's data collected within its own eco-system. However, data combination is possible in case the end user has provided his or her consent, in accordance with the GDPR requirements. Article 5(2) DMA explicitly defines 'consent' "within the meaning of Article 4, point (11), and Article 7 of Regulation (EU) 2016/679."

As discussed in the previous section, the GDPR gives a special protection to consent as an appropriate legal basis in situations where serious data protection risks emerge, considering the high level of choice and control that it requires for data subjects. However, the power imbalance present in the relationship between end users or data subjects and gatekeepers (digital online platforms) may end up in converting the granting of consent under the DMA a difficult task, considering all the requirements connected to consent established by the GDPR: that consent should be freely given, be specific, informed and unambiguous.

As a preliminary point, we should discuss whether and to what extent the relationship between the user and the gatekeeper is per se 'imbalanced' within the meaning of Recital 43 GDPR, and thus the user's consent to data combination would be per se invalid. Ribera Martinez has recently defined this issue as the 'circularity problem' between the concept of consent under the DMA and the GDPR.[54] In its ruling in the *German Facebook* case, the EU Court of Justice has pointed out that, even if the data controller is a dominant online platform, this does not make the data subject's consent invalid per se.[55] According to the CJEU, the consent validity should be assessed on a case by case basis, in relation to the degree of effective freedom enjoyed by the online user to reject a specific request of data processing, rather than linked to the dominant position of the platform.[56] Although the *German Facebook* ruling concerns a competition law case, the CJEU interpretation could be applied *mutatis mutandis* to the concept of consent under Art. 5(2) DMA. Such interpretation is also supported by a literal interpretation of Art. 5(2) DMA, which explicitly grants the possibility to continue its data combination or cross-use activities to the gatekeeper after having collected the user's consent.

---

[53] EDPB guidelines 5/2020, p. 20.

[54] Ribera Martinez (2023), p. 191-212.

[55] Case C-252/21, *Meta Platforms v. Bundeskartellamt* [2023] ECLI:EU:C:2023:537. Para. 147.

[56] *Ibid.* Para. 150.

It is worth pointing out that the DMA Preamble has further specified the scope of the consent exception provided for in Art. 5(2). First, the 'specific choice' requirement implies that the gatekeeper should provide to the end user "to freely opt-in" to such data combination, especially via a "user-friendly solution."[57] Therefore, the gatekeeper should not force the end user to provide his or her consent to the data combination. For instance, the gatekeeper should not threaten the end user that the service would not be provided upon the lack of consent to a data combination. Secondly, when collecting consent, the gatekeeper should provide to the end user with a choice between a more personalized service, resulting from providing consent to the data combination, and a "less personalised but equivalent alternative."[58] The DMA Preamble points out that the "less personalised alternative should not be different or of degraded quality compared to the service provided to end users who provide consent."[59] Third, at the time of collecting the consent on the data combination, the gatekeeper should inform the end user about the features of the "less personalised offer" resulting from not providing the consent.[60] Finally, the end user should always remain free to either modify or withdraw its consent to a data combination any time.[61]

From a theoretical perspective, providing a "less personalised service" implies that the service features provided by the gatekeeper may not be influenced by the consent to data combination; only the 'user experience', when navigating the platform service, may be affected by the lack of data combination. From a practical perspective, it is quite hard to imagine how the gatekeeper could provide a "less personalized but equivalent" service: personalization is the main added value of the services provided by a gatekeeper in comparison to competing platforms, which have access to a lower variety of data, and thus they can provide only 'less personalized' services. In the digital world, service 'personalization' and 'quality' are often intertwined concepts. Making a digital service 'less personalized' while keeping the same quality is one of the main challenges that the gatekeepers will have to face in the context of the compliance with Art. 5(2) requirements. Recital 37 of the DMA Preamble, however, seems to recognize this challenge, pointing out that the gatekeeper is not required to provide an equivalent service when "….a degradation of [service] quality is a direct consequence of the gatekeeper not being able to process such personal data…".

The concept of consent has thus been considered under the DMA Preamble. On the other hand, the DMA does not provide for indications on the design of consent by the gatekeeper. This might open the door for different experiments that could hinder the capacity of users to fully exercise their free choice and their capacity of granting consent in an informed, specific, and unambiguous manner. In particular, the problem might rise by the fact that Art. 5(2) DMA is, in theory, a self-executing obligation – i.e. the EU Commission is not expected to adopt a separate Decision to clarify how each gatekeeper should in practice collect the users' consent under

---

[57] Recitals 36–37 DMA.

[58] Recital 36 DMA.

[59] Recital 37 DMA.

[60] *Ibid.*

[61] *Ibid.*

Art. 5(2). This uncertainty also opens the door for future legal disputes around the appropriate architecture design of consent.

In view of the DMA Preamble requirements and considering the consent conditions under Art. 7 GDPR, we would argue that the gatekeeper could design a specific 'privacy setting' tool within its platform service to collect the users' consent to data combination and cross-use. In line with the DMA Preamble, the data combination consent should be based on a free opt-in system, designed in an understandable manner for the user (i.e. non-technical language). In other words, the user should be fully aware that, by authorizing the gatekeeper to carry out data combination and cross-use activities, he or she will receive a personalised service, as well as he/she will be subject to targeted advertising. On the other hand, in case the user decides to opt out of data combination, he/she would receive a 'less personalised' service, as well as general advertising. Since several gatekeepers deliver 'free' online services to their users due to the revenue generated by targeted advertising, opting out of a data combination might also imply that the gatekeeper could ask the user for monetary compensation to continue using the service.[62] Although this possibility is not explicitly mentioned in the DMA preamble, this interpretation is supported by the recent *German Facebook* ruling. In the judgment, the CJEU has pointed out that the online user should never be forced by the dominant online platform to grant his/her consent to a specific data processing activity.[63] However, in case of consent refusal, the platform should grant to the user the possibility to continue using the service subject to "an appropriate fee."[64]

In our view, the privacy-setting solution would guarantee that the consent provided by the user is 'freely given', 'specific', 'informed' and 'unambiguous', in accordance with Art. 4(11) GDPR. To be 'specific', the privacy setting solution should not include a general opt-in, granting to the gatekeeper a 'free cheque' in terms of different typologies of data combination. The new platform setting should include a 'granular' list of data combination activities carried out by the gatekeeper; the user should be free to select which types of data combination activities to opt in.[65] Finally, the user should be free to modify the settings at any time, in terms of opting-in and out to/from specific data combination activities.[66]

A critical point to discuss concerns the 'number of times' in which the gatekeeper may or must ask for consent to data combination from its user. As argued in the previous section, Data Protection Authorities in Europe and the CJEU case law have generally considered cookie walls as incompatible with the requirements of consent under Art. 4(11) GDPR. Data Protection Authorities have emphasized that the data

[62] In November 2023, Meta started to offer its Facebook and Instagram users in Europe the option to pay for an ad-free version. https://about.fb.com/news/2023/10/facebook-and-instagram-to-offer-subscription-for-no-ads-in-europe/. Accessed 22 February 2025.

[63] Case C-252/21, para. 150.

[64] *Ibid.*

[65] For a discussion on the opt-in v. opt-out systems in relation to management of personal data on the Internet, see Thomas Dreier (2010), p. 144–150.

[66] *Ibid.*

subject should provide his or her consent to every processing of his/her personal data. In the online world, the emphasis on 'individual' consent to data processing has caused the so-called 'consent fatigue'.[67] The latter expression refers to the situation where the data subject is repeatedly asked to provide his/her consent to a specific type of data processing. Although the data subject might initially decide to deny his/her consent, in the long term, due to the repeated requests and the complexity of the privacy terms, he/she might finally grant the consent, by thus nullifying the user's decision-making autonomy. The consent fatigue may be considered one of the 'side effects' of the GDPR, which requires the data subject to provide his/her consent to every data processing. Consent fatigue is often referred to as the emotional effects caused by the overload of too many consent requests that may create a state of mind in individuals capable of watering down the real choice implied in consent.[68]

To prevent consent fatigue, Art. 5(2) provides that, in case the end user has either refused or withdrawn his/her consent, the gatekeeper should not repeat the consent request "more than once within a period of one year."[69] In addition, a repeated request of the user's consent by the gatekeeper could also be considered a breach of the DMA anti-circumvention rule. According to Art. 13(6) DMA, the gatekeeper should not make the exercise of the rights provided by the DMA to end users "unduly difficult", in particular "...by subverting end users' autonomy, decision-making, or free choice via the structure, design, function or manner of operation of a user interface."[70] Generally speaking, Art. 13(6) DMA sanctions the so-called 'dark patterns' – i.e. deceptive online practices that mislead consumers, pushing them to specific types of unwanted behaviours.[71] The classical example of dark patterns is where an online intermediation platform creates time pressure on an end user to conclude an online purchase, claiming that the product price will increase if the purchase is not concluded within a limited period of time. Such time pressure reduces the ability of the consumer to compare different online offers, and thus limits the consumer's decision-making autonomy. It could be argued that repeated consent requests to data processing, common in the online world, may also be considered as 'dark patterns' that limit the user's decision-making autonomy. Therefore, a repeated consent request by the gatekeeper to authorize data combination may be considered both in breach of Art. 5(2) DMA, as well as a breach of the anti-circumvention rule under Art. 13(6) DMA.

In view of these considerations, we could argue that consent under Art. 5(2) DMA should be 'adjusted' to the peculiarities of the Digital Markets Act. In view of Art. 13(6) DMA, the privacy setting solution discussed above could be designed as a cookie wall, popping up on the user's screen at the first log in to the platform service after the gatekeeper implements the Art. 5(2) obligation, and thus introduces the new

[67] Wein (2022), p. 307-336.

[68] Schermer, Custers and van der Hof (2014), p. 171–182.

[69] Art. 5(2) DMA.

[70] Art. 13(6) DMA.

[71] Graef (2023) The EU Regulatory Patchwork for Dark Patterns: An Illustration of an Inframarginal Revolution in European Law? Forthcoming in Woodcock R. (ed.), *Toward an Inframarginal Revolution: Markets as Wealth Distributors,* Cambridge University Press.

privacy setting. The user would thus be required only once by the gatekeeper to adjust the privacy setting of the platform service, by opting in and out for different types of data combination and cross-use. The settings defined by the user at the first log in would remain in place, without the need for the gatekeeper to collect the user consent every time he/she accesses the platform service. In case the gatekeeper decides to introduce new types of data combinations and cross-uses within its own eco-system, the user should be informed, and he/she should be asked whether he/she would like to opt-in. Finally, as mentioned above, the user could always modify the privacy settings of the platform service, by opting in and out for specific typologies of data combination and cross-use.

The privacy setting-solution would represent an 'adjustment' of the concept of consent in the GDPR to the peculiarities of the Digital Markets Act, complying at the same time with all the consent requirements set out by the GDPR - and its interpretation by data protection authorities, EDPB, national courts and the CJEU – as previously discussed in Sect. 3.2. Such an adjustment would be possible because, as argued above, the DMA may be considered a *lex specialis* in comparison to the GDPR. Secondly, the privacy-settings solution would be in line with Art. 13(6) DMA and would prevent the consent fatigue that has characterized the GDPR enforcement in the online world.

Finally, it is important to note that Art. 5(2) DMA provides for three 'alternative' legal bases that the gatekeeper could rely upon to combine personal data within its eco-system without collecting the user's consent. However, the legal bases mentioned in Art. 6(1)(c)(d)(e) GDPR have been 'strictly' interpreted by the CJEU and by the EDPB. The recent joint contribution by the EDPS-EDPB on the draft template relating to the description of consumer profiling techniques recommends that when gatekeepers believe that the processing can rely on an alternative lawful legal basis, they should provide the reason(s) for relying on Articles 6(1)(c), (d) or (e) GDPR.[72] Therefore, it will not be an easy task for gatekeepers to rely on these legal bases. The collection of the user's consent thus remains the main reasonable justification that gatekeepers could rely upon to continue its data combination activities under the DMA.

[72] EDPB-EDPS, Comments on the draft template relating to the audited description of consumer profiling techniques pursuant to Article 15 of the Digital Markets Act ('DMA') Adopted on 20 September 2023. https://www.edpb.europa.eu/system/files/2023-09/edps-edpb_comments_on_article_15_dma_template_report_for_plen_formatted.pdf. Accessed 2 August 2024.

4 Complying with Art. 5(2) DMA: Challenges Ahead for the Gatekeepers

The DMA obligations often derive from remedies previously adopted by competition authorities and by the EU Commission in the context of previous antitrust investigations.[73] This is also the case for Art. 5(2) DMA, inspired by the 'data silos' remedy imposed by the *Bundeskartellamt* in its 2019 decision in the *German Facebook* case.[74] However, it is worth stressing that *Meta* will not be the only addressee of the Art. 5(2) obligation; the latter provision will affect most of the designated gatekeepers. Data combination is a common practice among the gatekeepers: it is a practice implemented by platforms that follow a targeted advertising business model (e.g. *Meta, Tik Tok, Google*), but also by online marketplaces (e.g. *Amazon*) as well as by apps, video and music stores (e.g. *Apple*) to personalize the search results of the end user. Therefore, the Art. 5(2) obligation is likely to impact the business models followed by most of the gatekeepers.

In March 2024, the first six designated gatekeepers submitted their compliance reports with the DMA obligations.[75] Generally, the designated gatekeepers have opted to comply with Art. 5(2) by requesting the users' consent, rather than stopping the combination and cross-use of personal data across the eco-system. From this point of view, it is worth mentioning that only Apple has declared in its compliance report not to engage in data cross-use.[76] This choice shows the relevance of personalized advertising in the business models of most of the gatekeepers.

Secondly, it is worth noticing that most of the gatekeepers have implemented a privacy-setting solution like that one presented in the previous pages. In other words, gatekeepers have generally introduced a cookie wall to implement Art. 5(2), forcing the user, at the first log in, to either give or refuse the consent to data combination, specifying for which digital services the gatekeeper could combine the user's personal data (i.e. granular choice). In the case of Alphabet, the user would indicate for each designated core platform service whether he or she would authorize data combination. Alphabet, for instance, would engage in data combination only among the core platform services within its eco-system for which the user has provided his or her consent.[77] On the other hand, Alphabet would not engage in data combination for non-registered users, since they would not be able to provide their consent.[78] All

[73] Bostoen (2023), p. 263–306.

[74] *Bundeskartellamt* decision in the *German Facebook* case, adopted on 6th February 2019, case number B.6/22-16.

[75] https://digital-markets-act-cases.ec.europa.eu/reports/compliance-reports. Accessed 22 February 2025.

[76] Non-confidential version of Apple's compliance report with DMA obligations, published in March 2024. Page 12. https://www.apple.com/legal/dma/dma-ncs.pdf. Accessed 22 February 2025.

[77] Non-confidential version of Alphabet's compliance report with DMA obligations, published in March 2024. Pages 8–19. https://transparencyreport.google.com/report-downloads. Accessed 22 February 2025.

[78] *Ibid.*

gatekeepers have ensured that, after the first log in, the user could modify the initial choice in the 'settings', and thus could be free to revoke the initial consent at any time.

At the moment of writing this chapter, the main controversy in relation to the compliance with Art. 5(2) concerns the possibility for gatekeepers to charge a 'fee' to the users who do not provide their consent to the data combination, since according to the DMA Preamble they are entitled to receive an 'equivalent, but less personalized' digital service. In *Meta Platforms*, the European Court of Justice (ECJ) ruled that digital platforms cannot process the users' data by relying on the contract performance as valid legal basis under Art. 6 GDPR.[79] According to the Court in Luxembourg, the users should be free either to accept personalized advertisements, giving their consent to the processing of their personal data, or to opt for an ads-free version of the social network by accepting to pay an "appropriate fee" for receiving the service.[80] By relying on this paragraph of the ECJ ruling, in November 2023, Meta introduced an ads-free version of Instagram and Facebook for users who accept to pay a monthly subscription fee of € 12,99.[81] Meta has further extended the subscription fee to the users who do not provide their consent to data combination.[82] Following the introduction of the subscription-fee model, the Data Protection Authorities from Hamburg, the Netherlands and Norway have submitted a complaint to the EDPB, arguing that, by introducing a subscription fee, Meta has made 'invalid' the consent provided by end users to data processing.[83] According to the DPAs, users are subject to the "pay v. consent" dilemma, which does not make the consent 'free' in accordance with the GDPR requirements. Following the publication of the DMA compliance report, in March 2024 the European Commission has also opened investigations against Meta concerning its choice to charge a subscription fee to the users who do not provide their consent to data combination.[84]

On 17 April 2024, the EDPB has adopted Opinion 08/2024 on "Valid Consent in the Context of Consent or Pay Models Implemented by Large Online Platforms".[85] According to the EDPB, the offering of only a 'consent or pay' model as an alternative to the processing of personal data for targeted/behavioural advertising prevents users (i.e. data subjects) from exercising their free choice. Therefore, in the view of the EDPB, besides the paid alternative, gatekeepers should also provide users with an

[79] Case C-252/21. Para. 149.

[80] Case C-252/21. Para. 149.

[81] https://about.fb.com/news/2023/10/facebook-and-instagram-to-offer-subscription-for-no-ads-in-europe/. Accessed 22 February 2025.

[82] Non-confidential version of Meta's compliance report with DMA obligations, published in March 2024. Page 16. https://transparency.fb.com/sr/meta-compliance-report-2024. Accessed 22 February 2025.

[83] https://noyb.eu/en/28-ngos-urge-eu-dpas-reject-pay-or-okay-meta. Accessed 22 February 2025.

[84] https://ec.europa.eu/commission/presscorner/detail/en/ip_24_1689. Accessed 22 February 2025.

[85] European Data Protection Board (2023) Opinion 08/2024 on Valid Consent in the Context of Consent or Pay Models Implemented by Large Online Platforms. Adopted on 17th April 2024. https://www.edpb.europa.eu/system/files/2024-04/edpb_opinion_202408_consentorpay_en.pdf. Accessed 22 February 2025.

'equivalent alternative' that does not involve the payment of a fee.[86] For this purpose, the Board proposes a "free alternative without behavioural advertising" without the processing of personal data for targeted/behavioural advertising. The latter would consist in "a version of the service with a different form of advertising involving the processing of less (or no) data, - e.g. contextual or general advertising or advertising based on topics the data subject selected from a list of topics of interest."[87] Even if the EDPB has not banned the use of an alternative to the processing of data for targeted/behavioural advertising that entails the payment of a fee, it concluded that a further alternative (i.e. free of charge), which should be also offered to users of very large online platforms, would be necessary to comply with the requirements of valid consent under the GDPR. However, it is still to be seen how gatekeepers will adapt to this interpretation of the EDPB and which type of 'no fee alternative' will be offered to users.

Following the publication of the EDPB opinion, on 1st July 2024 the European Commission sent a statement of objections to Meta, arguing that the consent v. pay model does not comply with Art. 5(2) DMA.[88] At the moment of writing the case is open and thus it is difficult to foresee its outcome. In case the European Commission decided to sanction Meta for breach of Art. 5(2) DMA, the decision is likely to be appealed to the EU General Court and later to the European Court of Justice. The possibility for gatekeepers to charge a fee to the users who do not accept data combination thus represents the major open legal question, and the major challenge faced by gatekeepers in terms of compliance with Art. 5(2) DMA.

References

Bania K (2023) Fitting the digital markets act in the existing legal framework: the myth of the without prejudice clause. Eur Compet J 19(1):116–149

Bostoen F (2023) Understanding the digital markets act. Antitrust Bull 68(2):263–306

Botta M (2021) Sector regulation of digital platforms in Europe: Uno, Nessuno e Centomila. J Eur Compet Law Pract 12(7):500–512

Botta M, Wiedemann K (2020) To discriminate or not to discriminate? Personalised pricing in online markets as exploitative abuse of dominance. Eur J Law Econ 50:381–404

Botta M (2023) Shall we share? The principle of FRAND in B2B data sharing. EUI-RSCAS Working Chapter 2023/30, p 26. https://www.digitalsociety.eui.eu/publication/the-principle-of-frand-in-b2b-data-sharing/. Accessed 2 Aug 2024

Cioffi J, Kenney M, Zysman J (2022) Platform power and regulatory politics: Polanyi for the twenty-first century. New Polit Econ 27(5):820–836

Davola A, Malgieri G (2022) Data-powerful. Un'Indagine sulla Nozione di Potere e il suo Rapporto con la Vulnerabilità nel Mercato Digitale. Concorrenza e Mercato, pp 67–92

[86] *Ibid*, p. 20.

[87] *Ibid*.

[88] https://digital-markets-act.ec.europa.eu/commission-sends-preliminary-findings-meta-over-its-pay-or-consent-model-breach-digital-markets-act-2024-07-01_en. Accessed 22 February 2025.

Graef I (2023) The EU regulatory patchwork for dark patterns: an illustration of an inframarginal revolution in European Law? In: Woodcock R (ed) Toward an inframarginal revolution: markets as wealth distributors. Cambridge University Press, Cambridge
Krämer J, Schnurr D, Broughton Micova S (2020) The role of data for digital markets contestability. CERRE Report, September 2020, p 55. https://cerre.eu/publications/data-digital-markets-contestability-case-studies-and-data-access-remedies/. Accessed 22 Feb 2025
Krämer J (2020) Personal data portability in the platform economy: economic implications and policy recommendations. J Compet Law Econ 17(2):263–308
Ribera Martinez A (2023) The circularity of consent in the DMA: a close look into the prejudiced substance of Articles 5(2) and 6(10). Concorrenza e Mercato: 191–212
Schermer BW, Custers B, van der Hof S (2014) The crisis of consent: how stronger legal protection may lead to weaker consent in data protection. Ethics Inf Technol 16:171–182
Wein T (2022) Data protection, cookie consent and price. Economies 10(12):307–336

Prof. Marco Botta is a Professor at the European University Institute, in Florence (Italy), where heads the Centre for a Digital Society. In addition, he is a senior lecturer at the Law Faculty of the University of Vienna and visiting professor at the Department of Legal Studies of the Central European University, in Vienna (Austria). Between 2017 and 2022, Prof. Botta was a senior research fellow, and later an affiliated research fellow, at the Max Planck Institute for Innovation and Competition, in Munich (Germany). His current research focus is on data sharing modalities in the context of the emerging EU digitalization acquis.

Dr. Danielle Borges is currently a Research Associate at the Centre for a Digital Society (CDS) at the European University Institute (EUI). She has a PhD in Law and a master's degree in International, Comparative and European Law from the European University Institute (EUI).

A Toolkit for Assessing the Level of Data Subjects' Control in Regulatory Data Sharing Models

Alexandre Humain-Lescop

Abstract Facilitating safe data sharing within the private sector is a major economic challenge for governments around the world. Various regulations are therefore emerging to encourage this sharing through different patterns we call "*data sharing models*", i.e., for different data, through different modalities and between different stakeholders acting as data holders or data users. *GDPR, ePrivacy, DGA, DMA, DSA, Data Act, eIDAS 2.0, PSD2, PSD3, PSR, FIDA, EHDS*, etc., European laws progressively establish many different examples of such data sharing models, promising in particular to enhance individual control. But do these models really improve our control over our data, or could this development of data sharing have the opposite effect by increasing already existing data protection issues? The purpose of this chapter is to propose a method to evaluate each data sharing model in terms of how much control it gives to an individual over the sharing of his or her personal data. It will do this by identifying a series of essential elements ("*parameters*" classified into six "*parameters families*") found in most data sharing models and by estimating what degree of control each one can offer. From this list of parameters emerges a "*toolbox*" that can be used to evaluate the level of individual control in any existing or future data sharing model, thus also permitting comparison between them.

Keywords Data governance · Data sharing · Data sharing models · Regulation · Data protection · Personal data · Data subject · Empowerment · Control · Individual control

---

A. Humain-Lescop (✉)
University Institut Polytechnique de Paris (IP Paris), Palaiseau, France

J. Drexl et al. (eds.), *Comparative Data Law*, MPI Studies on Intellectual Property and Competition Law 32, https://doi.org/10.1007/978-3-031-91401-0_7

1 Introduction

1.1 From Economic Interest to Data Protection Risks

Data sharing is a strategic issue for governments around the world, notably within the private sector.[1] To encourage this sharing many regulatory initiatives are emerging, oriented towards all economic sectors[2] or towards specific economic sectors.[3] Thus, among legislators' motivations many issues emerge, particularly of an economic nature.[4]

In addition to these issues, others arise when personal data are concerned. Many states have already adopted forms of data protection in response to, or even inspired by[5] the European Union (EU) General Data Protection Regulation (GDPR).[6] While a source of inspiration, the GDPR is however far from having fully achieved its initial objective, particularly in terms of delivery of information to individuals.[7]

Consequently, with the prospect of increased data sharing also comes the possibility of an increase in data protection risks. In line with the Organisation for Economic Co-operation and Development (OECD) recommendations,[8] the EU is committed to a policy that "*puts people at the centre*" and "*empowers individuals*",[9] attaching significant importance to "*control by individuals on how their personal data are used and with whom they are shared*".[10]

However, the concept of control hides many subtleties, and sometimes contradictory objectives.[11] Thus, can the various regulatory initiatives aiming at increasing data sharing really improve our control over the sharing of our data, or might they have the opposite effect? The aim of this work is to find a way of verifying this objective, i.e. more control by individuals on how their personal data are used and with whom they are shared. To do so, this chapter analyzes various existing data sharing models to extract key parameters impacting the control of the individual *in abstracto*. These parameters will form a toolbox to help evaluate the level of control

---

[1] OECD, 2019, Enhancing Access to and Sharing of Data - Reconciling Risks and Benefits for Data Re-use across Societies, 121–127.

[2] For a comparison of data portability in several legal systems, see Nakashima, 2022.

[3] For a comparison of financial data sharing in several legal systems, see Remolina, 2019, 13 ff.

[4] OECD, 2019, *op. cit.*, 59–71.

[5] Bradford, 2020.

[6] Regulation (EU) 2016/679 of the European Parliament and of the Council of 27 April 2016 on the protection of natural persons with regard to the processing of personal data and on the free movement of such data, and repealing Directive 95/46/EC (General Data Protection Regulation).

[7] Dorfleitner, 2023, 32–33.

[8] OECD, 2021a, b, Recommendation of the Council on Enhancing Access to and Sharing of Data, section III.(d).

[9] EU, 2022, European Declaration on Digital Rights and Principles for the Digital Decade, whereas 6.

[10] *Ibid.*, chap. V, §17.

[11] OECD, 2022, Going Digital Guide to Data Governance Policy Making, 21–55.

granted to individuals in any existing or future regulations relating to the sharing of personal data.[12]

1.2 From a Data Sharing Model to Its Parameters

The GDPR's right to data portability[13] is widely studied in the literature[14] and sometimes even precisely on the issue of control.[15] Studies on other very specific data sharing regulations are progressively proposed.[16] Through the notion of governance, other studies propose a more general reflection on how to organize the relationships between stakeholders processing data. Over the last two decades, the use of the notion "*models of data governance*"[17] may therefore imply the question of data sharing, but does not necessarily make it the central focus of this study. The present chapter distinguishes itself by proposing both the control of the individual as the main object of study and a general approach that goes beyond the study of a single regulation or model.

The various regulatory models of governance of personal data sharing (models) will be understood as the set of legal requirements that establish rules for certain specific sharing. The common denominator to any models is that there are at least three types of entities involved. First, the individual, a natural person to whom the personal data relates, i.e., the data subjects (DSs) whose control will be examined (DSs' control). Then, an entity that generated the data or already collected it, and that will share it or give access to it, i.e., the data holders (DHs). Finally, an entity wishing to access the data or to receive it as a recipient, for any purposes, i.e., the data users (DUs). Thus, both DHs and DUs are independent legal entities with different interests and managing their own respective data processing.[18] Furthermore, for the sake of clarity the study will not take into consideration if DHs or DUs use any subcontractors[19] or not. Finally, this work will focus on a single data sharing action.

---

[12] In line with the OECD impact assessment guide work cited *ibid.*, cf. chap. 2, table 2.1. "*Checklist for data governance policies*", mentioning the issue of control without aiming to make it the main object of study.

[13] GDPR art. 20.

[14] See in particular the bibliography listed in OECD, 2021a, b, Mapping data portability initiatives, opportunities and challenges, 41–50.

[15] Graef et al., 2019 1359–1398.

[16] See footnotes 14 and 48.

[17] Micheli et al., 2020, see also variants such as "*data governance models*" in Wernick et al., 2023, 65–77, focusing on the issue of data sharing, but via the specific study of sharing intermediaries.

[18] So DHs and DUs are independent data "*controllers*" in the meaning of GDPR art. 4.7. But the term "*data controller*" will not be used in this work to avoid any confusion with the goal of this chapter to assess DSs' control.

[19] Data processors in the meaning of GDPR art. 4.8.

Thus, it will not give importance to whether DHs are the original sources of the data[20] or if they themselves have received the data via a previous sharing from another DH upstream.

A first way to estimate DSs' control could be to study each existing model consecutively, independently of each other. However, this approach would have limits in terms of feasibility and reproducibility since it would require a new study for each model identified or to come. In terms of methodological approach, the study develops a series of questions such as: "*What data is affected? Which DHs/DUs are affected, under what conditions is the sharing triggered,* etc.*?*". Based on these questions, a series of "*parameters*" emerges. It is the set of these parameters from a given regulation that constitutes the model and makes it unique (even if some models may be remarkably similar to each other when several parameters are identical or highly comparable between them). To estimate the impact of each of these parameters on DSs' control, the study proposes a list and studies them through six "*families of parameters*". This approach generates a list of essential control parameters constituting the toolbox.

1.3 From Data Protection to Control

The concepts of data protection and control are interdependent but not interchangeable. Data protection is an objective enshrined in fundamental texts such as the European Convention on Human Rights (ECHR),[21] Council of Europe Conventions 108[22] and 108 + ,[23] and the Charter of Fundamental Rights of the EU (CFR).[24] Achieving this protection can be fulfilled through various measures. Some paternalistic measures[25] do not give individuals complete freedom with regard to their protection, protecting individuals against themselves. Other measures, on the contrary, propose an active role to the individual in its protection by strengthening its control, even if this can sometimes turn out to be counter-productive in terms of data protection.[26]

The notion of control can be conceptualized regarding the final objectives pursued. It can be considered as a means serving other objectives, in particular data protection, as mentioned above. However, the concept of "*informational self-determination*"[27] proposes to consider control not as a means, but as an objective in itself, regardless of the cause it ultimately serves. This second conception of control could arise from

---

[20] That can be named "*first-time collector*" (« *primo collectant*») as in Commission Nationale de l'Informatique et des Libertés (CNIL), Délibération SAN-2023-015, §27–28.

[21] Council of Europe, 1950, European Convention on Human Rights, art. 8.

[22] Council of Europe, 1981, Convention 108.

[23] Council of Europe, 2018, Convention 108 + .

[24] UE, 2020, Charter of Fundamental Rights of the EU, art. 8.

[25] Quelle, 2017, Sect. 3.2.

[26] Brandimarte et al., 2013, 340–347.

[27] Rouvroy, Poullet, 2009.

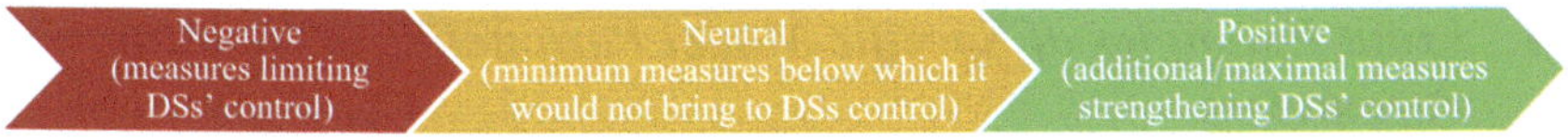

Fig. 1 Colors used throughout the chapter to simplify the representation of possible levels of DSs' control in each parameter studied

the notion of human autonomy and is recognized as an element of other rights such as human dignity. But unlike data protection, control as an expression of individual agency is not directly mentioned as a fundamental right. The toolkit proposed in this chapter takes a neutral approach and can be used to verify control both from an instrumental point of view (to enhance protection) and as a possible objective in its own right (an element of human agency).

But beyond these possible objectives, and the many names given to this notion,[28] another difficulty is to define how control manifests itself in practice, and how its existence can be observed or even quantified. The related concepts of "*personal agency*" and "*empowerment*" point us to two key elements which are the individual's "*ability to envisage options and make a choice*" and "*the capacity to transform choices into desired actions*".[29] However, in terms of data protection, through the various data subjects' rights and effective means of exercising them, a certain duality can appear between, on the one hand, the decision and the mastery over a processing upstream of it, and on the other hand, the verification and intervention over a processing downstream or during it.[30] Although these two components of control are not perfectly hermetic to each other, it is more towards the question of the a priori decision to share or not to share that this chapter will focus on.

Thus, in essence, the chapter will focus more on the aim of enabling individuals to "*make decisions about their own data*" than to "*become an agent of the way their decisions are implemented*". This is in an attempt to maximize the "*range of different options to be open to the individual*"[31] and to minimize the external hindrances to its will to share or not its personal data. Despite the difficulty of quantifying this definition of control, an estimation of three different degrees of DSs' control will be schematized in order to synthesize and simplify the results for each essential control parameter constituting the toolbox. This will result in a graduation of three possible levels of impact on DSs' control. The red level will be assigned to negative measures that limit DSs' control. The orange level will be assigned to the basic measures constituting the minimum in terms of control, i.e., below which the measure would not bring DSs' control. The green level will be assigned to the maximum or additional measures that strengthen DSs' control (Fig. 1).

---

[28] Maxwell, 2022, 4.

[29] Alsop and Heinsohn, 2005, 3 and 6, as quoted and explained in Anciaux et al., 2021, 3.

[30] Picart-Cartron, 2023, §35.

[31] Mainly focusing on the first of the two pillars identified in Anciaux et al., *op. cit.*, dealing with the similar issue of data management by individuals.

1.4 From Examples of Specific Model Parameters to General Parameters

Concrete examples will be given throughout this work to highlight the different essential parameters and the level of DSs' control that constitute the toolkit. The chapter will mainly focus on data sharing in the economic interest of the private sector, as opposed to data sharing for the benefit of the public sector (e.g., Business to Government or Government to Government) or data sharing imposed for a mainly collective interest (e.g., research or anti-money laundering and countering the financing of terrorism). Furthermore, as the EU has already largely inspired other legal systems in the field of data protection,[32] and it has just experienced an unprecedented phase of regulation aiming at stimulating data sharing, it seems to be not only a relevant source of examples of data sharing models, but also a sufficient one regarding feasibility matters.

Because GDPR data portability (GDPR)[33] already exists, at least in the law, and has been studied, the parameters from this model will be used. The ePrivacy Directive (ePrivacy)[34] will also be used with regard to its provisions applicable to cookies. Less studied in the literature, and sector-specific, an article from a regulation relating to vehicles (VehiclesReg)[35] will be studied in that it obliges manufacturers to provide vehicle on-board diagnostic information and vehicle repair and maintenance information to certain DUs. Similarly, some parameter examples will come from a sector-specific directive, relating to the electricity market (ElectricityDir),[36] which notably requires the sharing of DSs' consumption data. Still sector-specific but more famous,

[32] Bradford, 2020, *op. cit.*

[33] Even if focusing on the right to data portability mechanism from its art. 20.

[34] Directive (EU) 2002/58/EC of the European Parliament and of the Council of 12 July 2002 concerning the processing of personal data and the protection of privacy in the electronic communications sector (Directive on privacy and electronic communications) as amended by Directive 2009/136/EC of the European Parliament and of the Council of 25 November 2009 amending Directive 2002/22/EC on universal service and users' rights relating to electronic communications networks and services, Directive 2002/58/EC concerning the processing of personal data and the protection of privacy in the electronic communications sector and Regulation (EC) No 2006/2004 on cooperation between national authorities responsible for the enforcement of consumer protection laws, (ePrivacy - Directive on Privacy and Electronic Communications), mainly art. 5. Which, by applying our DSs/DHs/DUs classification, assume that the website and the browser can be considered both DHs and DUs respectively depending on the phase in which the cookie is stored or accessed.

[35] This term is not consecrated but will be used for simplicity to refer to Regulation (EU) 2018/858 of the European Parliament and of the Council of 30 May 2018 on the approval and market surveillance of motor vehicles and their trailers, and of systems, components and separate technical units intended for such vehicles, amending Regulations (EC) No 715/2007 and (EC) No 595/2009 and repealing Directive 2007/46/EC, mainly art. 61.

[36] This term is not consecrated either but will be used for simplicity to refer to Directive (EU) 2019/944 of the European Parliament and of the Council of 5 June 2019 on common rules for the internal market for electricity and amending Directive 2012/27/EU (recast), mainly art. 23.

the open banking part of 2nd Payment Services Directive (PSD2)[37] will also give some good examples of parameters about the sharing of DSs' payment data.

Many of the other parameters will be derived from models recently developed in regulations from the European Commission's Digital Strategy.[38] This is the case of the Data Governance Act (DGA),[39] which notably enshrines the role of a neutral data intermediation service between DSs/DHs/DUs. The Digital Markets Act (DMA)[40] will also be mentioned because of its requirement over gatekeepers to share data they hold about their users' activity, including potential DSs. The Digital Services Act (DSA) will be mentioned too, with regards to the ability offered to DSs to object in some ways to the sharing of data concerning him or her.[41] Other interesting parameters will be taken from the Data Act (DA),[42] notably obliging the sharing of data generated by connected products used by DSs. Another cross-sectoral source of parameters will be the European Digital Identity Wallet (EUDIW) from the revision of the eIDAS regulation (eIDAS 2.0),[43] which allows DSs to share certain data between DHs and DUs of their choice.

Even more prospective, and back to a sector-based approach, the health sector will provide a reliable source of examples of parameters via the European Health Data Space Regulation (EHDS),[44] notably aiming at facilitating the sharing of DSs' health data for the purpose of providing health care. Coming back to the financial sector, the proposal to revise the aforementioned PSD2 open banking regulatory framework,

---

[37] Directive (EU) 2015/2366 of the European Parliament and of the Council of 25 November 2015 on payment services in the internal market, amending Directives 2002/65/EC, 2009/110/EC and 2013/36/EU and Regulation (EU) No 1093/2010, and repealing Directive 2007/64/EC, (2nd Payment Services Directive), mainly art. 66 and 67.

[38] European Commission, 2020, Shaping Europe's digital future.

[39] Regulation (EU) 2022/868 of the European Parliament and of the Council of 30 May 2022 on European data governance and amending Regulation (EU) 2018/1724, PE/85/2021/REV/1, (Data Governance Act), chap. III.

[40] Regulation (EU) 2022/1925 of the European Parliament and of the Council of 14 September 2022 on contestable and fair markets in the digital sector and amending Directives (EU) 2019/1937 and (EU) 2020/1828, PE/17/2022/REV/1, (Digital Markets Act), mainly art. 6.9 and art. 6.10.

[41] Regulation (EU) 2022/2065 of the European Parliament and of the Council of 19 October 2022 on a Single Market For Digital Services and amending Directive 2000/31/EC, (Digital Services Act), mainly via the broad notion of "*illegal content*" including "*non-consensual sharing of private images*" (whereas 12) and a notice and action mechanisms (art. 16). Although this measure concerns post-sharing control, some of the interesting parameters proposed by the DSA could be applied to DSs' control in general.

[42] Regulation (EU) 2023/2854 of the European Parliament and of the Council of 13 December 2023 on harmonized rules on fair access to and use of data and amending Regulation (EU) 2017/2394 and Directive (EU) 2020/1828, (Data Act), chap. II and III.

[43] Regulation (EU) 2024/1183 of the European Parliament and of the Council of 11 April 2024 amending Regulation (EU) No 910/2014 as regards establishing the European Digital Identity Framework.

[44] Regulation (EU) 2025/327 of the European Parliament and of the Council of 11 February 2025 on the European Health Data Space and amending Directive 2011/24/EU and Regulation (EU) 2024/2847, (European Health Data Space), "*Primary*" use of data, mainly corresponding to certain provisions of chap. II of the EHDS.

through a 3rd Payment Services Directive (PSD3) proposal[45] and a Payment Services Regulation (PSR) proposal[46] functioning together, will also be mentioned. Finally, the ambition of an open finance regulatory framework through the Financial Data Access Regulation (FIDA) proposal[47] will also provide useful parameter examples. Indeed, FIDA aims to facilitate the sharing of more DSs' financial data such as loans, insurance, investment data, etc.(Table 1).

As these models are only used as examples to illustrate the parameters constituting the toolbox, this study is not aimed at establishing a typology of these various regulations according to their respective detailed objectives. Nor does it aim to exhaustively classify all the parameters from these models, or to describe in detail the overall functioning of each model, their context, or their nuances, which is generally already studied in the literature model by model.[48]

2 The Families of Essential Parameters Impacting DSs' Control

To facilitate the reading of this chapter, various parameters influencing DS control by theme are classified into six families. Although this structure facilitates their study, some of these families and their parameters may in fact be linked with each other or even interdependent.

2.1 *The Nature of the Stakeholders*

Although a common denominator of all models is the presence of at least one DH, one DU and one DS, details can be provided for each category.

[45] Proposal for a Directive of the European Parliament and of the Council on payment services and electronic money services in the Internal Market amending Directive 98/26/EC and repealing Directives 2015/2366/EU and 2009/110/EC, 2023/0209(COD), (3rd Payment Services Directive), mainly certain provisions of title II.

[46] Proposal for a Regulation of the European Parliament and of the Council on payment services in the internal market and amending Regulation (EU) No 1093/2010, 2023/0210(COD), (Payment Services Regulation), mainly title III, chap. 3.

[47] Proposal for a Regulation of the European Parliament and of the Council on a framework for Financial Data Access and amending Regulations (EU) No 1093/2010, (EU) No 1094/2010, (EU) No 1095/2010 and (EU) 2022/2554, 2023/0205(COD), (Financial Data Access).

[48] See footnote 14 for GDPR, but also notably Carovano, Finck, 2023, for the DGA, Ibáñez Colomo, 2021, for the DMA, Casolari et al.,2023, for the DA or even Li, Quinn, 2024, for the EHDS.

Table 1 List of the given examples of EU legislation implementing specific data sharing models (in chronological order by date of final vote, or publication of the initial proposal when it has not yet been voted yet)

Abbreviation	Detail of the abbreviation (/legislation establishing the model)	Legislation reference	Main title/ chapter/ article	Type of personal data shared (simplified)
ePrivacy	Directive on privacy and electronic communications	Directive (EU) 2002/ 58/EC as amended by Directive (EU) 2009/ 136/EC	Art. 5	Cookies (via the broader regulation of "*communications*")
PSD2	2nd Payment Services Directive (open banking part)	Directive (EU) 2015/ 2366	Art. 66 and 67	Payment account information (especially DS's payment history)
GDPR	General Data Protection Regulation (right to data Portability part)	Regulation (EU) 2016/ 679	Art. 20	Personal data in general (provided by the DS or observed)
Vehicles Reg	Regulation on the approval and market surveillance of motor vehicles and their trailers, and of systems, components and separate technical units intended for such vehicles	Regulation (EU) 2018/ 858	Art. 61	Data about vehicle on-board diagnostic information and vehicle repair and maintenance information
ElectricityDir	Directive on common rules for the internal market for electricity	Directive (EU) 2019/ 944	Art. 23	Electricity metering and consumption data as well as data required for customer switching
DGA	Data Governance Act (data intermediation services part)	Regulation (EU) 2022/ 868	Chap. III	Personal data in general
DMA	Digital Markets Act	Regulation (EU) 2022/ 1925	Art. 6.9 and 6.10	Data provided by a DS or generated through its activity on a gatekeeper's service
DSA	Digital Services Act	Regulation (EU) 2022/ 2065	Art. 16	Data published on an online platform (such as social networks), including ones about a DS and considered as illegal

(continued)

Table 1 (continued)

Abbreviation	Detail of the abbreviation (/legislation establishing the model)	Legislation reference	Main title/ chapter/ article	Type of personal data shared (simplified)
DA	Data Act (connected product part)	Regulation (EU) 2023/ 2854	Chap. II and III	Data generated by the use of a connected product
EUDIW (from eIDAS 2.0)	EU Digital Identity Wallet, from the regulation establishing the European Digital Identity Framework	Regulation (EU) 2024/ 1183	(All the regulation)	Person identification data (linked to DS's identity such as its name, date of birth, etc.), but possibly any other personal data too
EHDS	European Health Data Space, (*"primary"* use of data part)	Regulation (EU) 2025/ 327	Chap. II	Health Data
PSD3 and PSR	3rd Payment Services Directive and Payment Services Regulation (open banking part)	2023/0209 (COD) directive proposal and 2023/0210 (COD) regulation proposal (initial versions)	Title II for PSD3, and title III, chap. III for PSR	Payment account information (especially DS's payment history)
FIDA	Financial data access regulation	2023/ 0205(COD) regulation proposal (initial version)	(All the regulation)	Other financial information (DS's loans, insurances, investments, etc.)

2.1.1 The Data Holders (DHs)

The question addressed in this paragraph relates to DSs' control over the choice of possible DHs. In this regard, a model can offer DSs maximum choice by theoretically applying to any entity as DHs *(GDPR art. 4.7)*. A more restrictive approach may be based on specific existing entities *(in sectorial regulations such as health professionals from EHDS art. 2.1.b), account servicing payment service provider from PDS2 art. 4.17, vehicle manufacturers from VehiclesReg art. 3.40)* or by creating a new legal category of entities *(i.e., gatekeepers from DMA art. 2.1*[49]*)*. However, the method of determining DHs may vary, from self-certification or reporting *(mandatory such as electronic health record system in EHDS art. 39 or optional such as*

[49] Defined as "*an undertaking providing core platform services*" and designated according to the terms of the text.

labelling of wellness applications in EHDS art. 47) to a licensing process *(payment institutions in PSD2 art. 5)* or a mandatory designation by the competent authorities *(gatekeepers in DMA art. 3 and 4)*.

Beyond this general or specific nature of DHs, additional restrictions can be settled in a model. A first possibility is the exclusion directly in the law of entities from the scope of possible DHs, generally companies of small size, for compliance reasons *(DA art. 7.1)*. The second is to allow DUs to choose DHs from which they agree to obtain the data or not and to impose this pre-selection on DSs *(DGA chap. III not preventing this possibility)*.

2.1.2 The Data Users (DUs)

Here the study focuses on DSs' control over the choice of possible DUs. The possible model approaches regarding DUs are comparable to those relating to DHs. A model can maximize DSs choice by applying to any entity as DUs without distinction *(GDPR art. 20, DGA art. 10, DMA art. 6.9 and 0.10)* or can adopt a more restrictive approach by applying to specific entities. They may also already exist *(same health professionals from EHDS art. 2.1.b), independent operators from VehiclesReg art. 3.45)* or be created in the same regulation *(payment initiation service provider and account information service provider from PSD2 art. 4.18 and 0.19)*. In the same way as for DHs, there may be different approaches in the law in the methods of designating DUs.

With the same logic, additional restrictions may limit DSs' control over the choice of DUs. It can also be done by the exclusion in the law of certain entities from the scope, this time generally large companies for competitive reasons *(exclusion of gatekeepers in DA art. 5.3 and 6.2.d))* or via the possibility for DH to preselect DUs to which they accept to send the data *(DGA chap. III does not prevent this possibility)*. Both hypotheses limit DSs' choice regarding the scope of possible DUs.

2.1.3 The Data Subjects (DSs)

The question of this subsection is to know whether DSs must manage their control alone, or if they can better exercise their control by being accompanied by another entity. The main rule is that DSs are conceptualized as single, isolated entities. But although models do not explicitly provide for it, DSs can normally be accompanied in their rights through ad hoc mandate mechanisms on their own initiatives.[50]

---

[50] In terms of GDPR's DSs'rights, for example, a DS can ask an authorized representative to exercise a right on his/her behalf with a targeted data controller. See in particular the CNIL Deliberation n° 2021-070 detailing this possibility. However, because of its formalism and/or lack of harmonization at the EU level, but also because of the length of time required for all stakeholders to communicate with each other, this mechanism alone does not seem to be adapted to a real-time data-sharing economy.

Fig. 2 Summary of possible DSs' control levels in the "*nature of the stakeholders*" parameters family

However, certain model parameters propose to facilitate this idea of a mandate via explicit mechanisms, so that a mandate can easily be granted by DSs to other natural persons of their choice *(EHDS art. 4.2).* An approach also related to this idea of a mandate is the possibility for DSs to give a kind of mandate to DUs, to directly request the data from DHs.[51] Approaching the concepts of fiduciary models[52] or data trusts,[53] it is also possible to offer DSs support of third parties ensuring a certain neutrality with regard to the interests of DHs/DUs *(data intermediation services from DGA art. 12.m) assumed to "act in the data subjects' best interest" or the supposed neutrality of the eIDAS 2.0 EUDIW, indirectly or directly provided by the State art. 1.5 creating a new article 5a.2).* This conception of non-isolated DSs can also be found in various remedies or modalities relating to out-of-court or judicial settlements (*DGA art. 27.1, DMA art. 42 or DSA art. 22*) (Fig. 2).

2.2 *The Scope of the Data Concerned*

The object of sharing, personal data,[54] is our second family of parameters impacting DSs' control. A possible pitfall on this topic is the question of the quality of the data.[55] Even mentioned in some models *(DMA art. 6.10, DA art. 5.1),* this quality aspect will indirectly be studied through other parameters of this section.[56]

---

[51] Detailed in subsection 2.4.1 "*The request method*".

[52] Balkin, 2020, 13–15.

[53] Delacroix, Lawrence, 2018, 12–13.

[54] In the broad sense of this definition such as GDPR art. 4.1 comparable as in OECD, 2021a, b, Recommendation of the Council on Enhancing Access to and Sharing of Data, *op. cit.,* II, where "*Personal data' refers to information relating to an identified or identifiable individual (data subject)*".

[55] See the seven dimensions of data quality determined in OECD, 2011, Quality Framework and Guidelines for OECD Statistical Activities, 7–11.

[56] And also via the format in which the data is sent or presented to DUs, studied in subsection 2.6.3 "*The quest for interoperability*".

2.2.1 The Nature of the Initial DHs' Processing

For the sake of proportionality, models often concern a delimited scope of data. Thus, the more the scope of data eligible to be shared is limited, the more the possibility of sharing for DSs is reduced, as well as their potential of control.

A model can thus be restricted to data linked to a specific legal basis of the DHs' initial processing *(such as consent*[57] *or performance of contract*[58] *only, as for GDPR art. 20.1.a))*. Another method is to cover data that have been initially used by DHs for a specific purpose *(vehicle on-board diagnostic information in VehicleReg art. 3.49, metering and consumption data in ElectricityDir art. 23.1, priority categories of personal electronic health data in EHDS art. 14.1, payment data from PDS2, PSD3 and PSR, various financial data listed in FIDA art. 2.1)*.

2.2.2 The Level of Processing on the Data Held by DHs

Another essential parameter to consider is the level of work that has already been done on the data before its sharing, and therefore, its originality and potential scarcity. Four distinct levels can be distinguished.[59] The first level is the most basic, i.e., the data is actively and knowingly "*provided*" by DSs such as the data entered in a form, for example. The second level is that of the "*observed*" data, which can transcribe DSs' behavior such as the time spent on a browsing session on a web page. In the third level, the data is said to be "*derived*", it is created, in a way guessed, from other known information, such as the probable DSs' domicile based on their telephone prefix codes, or the probable DSs' genders based on their first names. The last category is that of "*inferred*" data, which is also created from other data, but has undergone more complex processing by DHs. The fine lines between the first two and the last two categories respectively are not disturbing. Indeed, regulations generally treat provided and observed data under the same legal regime on the one hand and derived and inferred data under one other legal regime on the other hand.[60]

A model can thus be limited to provided and observed data *(GDPR art. 20.1, PSD2 in particular art. 67.2.d))*, or grant more control to DSs by allowing them to share more data, including all or part of the derived and inferred data about them *(certain health data covered in EHDS art. 14 and certain financial data in FIDA art. 2.1)*.

[57] GDPR art. 6.1.a).

[58] GDPR art. 6.1.b).

[59] See notably OECD, 2019, *op. cit.*, chap. 2, table 2.1. "*Data categories based on origin*".

[60] Sometimes respectively referred to as "*raw*" data for provided and observed data and "*processed*" data for derived and inferred data, as a misuse of language that emphasizes the origin of the data rather than its use, but which actually involve a future data processing in any cases.

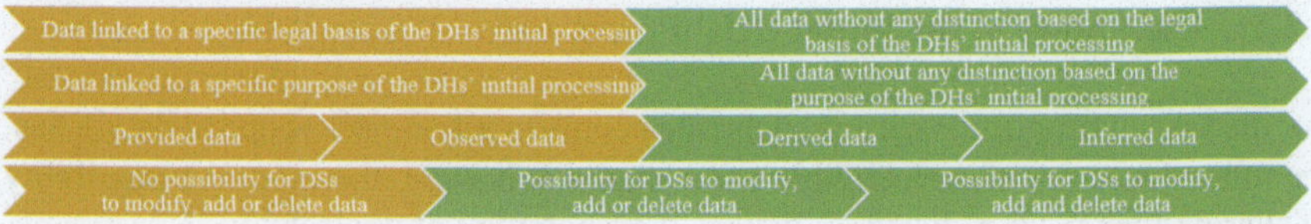

Fig. 3 Summary of possible DSs' control levels in the "*scope of the data concerned*" parameters family

2.2.3 The Granularity of Choice Left to DSs

By maximizing the scope of the data, the two previous subsections can positively influence DSs' control. But the opposite may also be true. For example, a model with the widest possible scope of data, but requiring DSs to either share everything, including data they do not want to share, or to give up sharing altogether, would limit its control. Possible reminders of the general principle of minimisation[61] of processing *(EHDS art. 66 and in PSD2*[62]*)* are laudable but do not really fight the possible "*take it or leave it*" policies[63] *(in particular the practice of "cookie walls" which ePrivacy does not directly prohibit).*[64]

On the contrary, a model can offer real granularity in the choice to be made by DSs via cumulative options. The first is to provide within the sharing mechanism the possibility for DSs to rectify data that they consider to be erroneous, making the general right to rectification[65] more effective *(EHDS art. 6).* The second is the possibility for DSs to select precisely which data will or will not be transmitted to DUs, without the obligation to transmit the entire batch *(EHDS whereas 17).* The third is the possibility for DSs to add data to the batch of data that will be shared (*EHDS art. 5*) (Fig. 3).

2.3 The Justification for Sharing

Another essential parameters family impacting DSs' control relates to the motivations of each stakeholder and the elements that legitimize the sharing.

---

[61] GDPR art. 5.1.c).

[62] European Data Protection Board (EDPB), Guidelines 06/2020, title 6 and in particular §63.

[63] Zuiderveen Borgesius et al., 2018, see some parameters in response to the risk of *take-it-or-leave-it* policies in subsection 2.5.3 "*The prohibition of unfair information practices*".

[64] A "*cookie wall*" is the situation where "*access to services and functionalities […]* [is] *made. conditional on the consent of a user to the storing of information, or gaining of access to information already stored, in the terminal equipment of a user*" EDPB, 2020a, b, Guidelines 05/2020 on consent under Regulation 2016/679, § 39. See the case of France where the Conseil d'Etat (decision n° 434684 of 19 June 2020) overturned the CNIL guidelines that tried to prohibit these practices.

[65] GDPR art. 16.

2.3.1 The Voluntary or Mandatory Sharing for DHs

Participating in the sharing can be voluntary for DHs' *(DGA or eIDAS 2.0)* or, on the contrary, imposed[66] *(GDPR art. 20, DMA art. 6.9 and 0.10, DA art. 3.1, VehiclesReg art. 61.1).*

If the second option seems to grant better control to DSs, who then do not depend on the goodwill of DHs, regulations may set limits and exceptions under certain circumstances, especially when DS's freedom to share could cause certain harms *(for fraud suspicion as in PSD2 art. 68.5, trade secrets as in the DA art. 4.6 et seq, for security reasons as in DA art. 4.2 considering this hypothesis if the sharing could undermine the security requirements of the connected product).*

2.3.2 The Free or Regulated Use of Data by DUs

On DUs side too, the receipt of data can be voluntary *(GDPR, DA, PSD2, PSD3/PSR, FIDA)* or mandatory *(eIDAS 2.0 art. 1.5 creating a new article 5f.2 and 0.3 imposing the sharing in case of strong user authentication or for the very large online platforms,*[67] *or EHDS art. 15.4, 7.2 and 0.4, and 12.5 and 0.6 imposing healthcare professionals to access to data).*

Although the second option offers more control to DSs, who then do not depend on the goodwill of DUs, both options can be restricted by the legislator by looking at the purpose for which DUs access the data. This restriction can be made by allowing only certain processing operations or by specifying their modalities *(repair and maintenance of vehicles in VehiclesReg art. 61)* or by prohibiting certain processing *(advertising purposes except for direct marketing in FIDA art. 6.4.e), prohibition for DUs from developing products competing with DHs in DA art. 6.2.e)).*

2.3.3 The Agreement of DSs

Although rare, parameters can allow DUs to override the will of DSs or to directly bypass their consent *(via the protection of vital interests' legal basis*[68] *in EHDS art. 10.1, or the form of legitimate interest*[69] *in ePrivacy art. 5 for certain types of cookies without the need to ask for DSs' consent).*

While some models are more neutral by not directly addressing the issue of DSs' agreement *(VehiclesReg art. 61, ElectricityDir art. 23)*, others mention the need for DUs to base their processing (including access to the data and the subsequent use that

66 Sometimes also named "*access rights*" or "*right of access*" granted to DSs/DUs to DHs' data, but not to be confused with DSs' right of access within the meaning of GDPR art. 15 (not having a purpose of data sharing but of verification on the data held by a given entity processing data).

67 Designated under DSA art. 33.

68 GDPR art. 6.1.d).

69 GDPR art. 6.1.f).

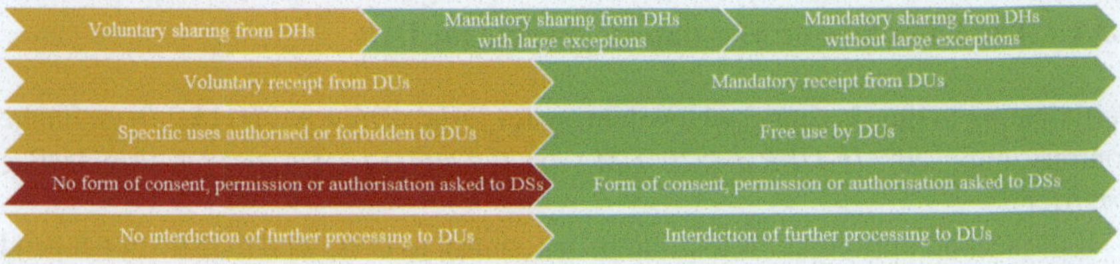

Fig. 4 Summary of possible DSs' control levels in the "*justification for sharing*" parameters family

is made of that data) on the basis of DSs' consent *(ePrivacy art. 5 with the consent rule for the storage of cookies, DMA art. 9.10 and 13.5 even providing that DHs must help DUs to obtain this consent from DSs).* A variation lies in the use by DUs of other legal basis such as performance of a contract, which also makes it possible to ensure a form of consent from DSs, although it then has a "*contractual nature*" *(PSD2).*[70]

Some models try a complementary original approach, although lacking clarity in its exact functioning. In addition to the need for DUs to base their entire processing (access to data plus use of this data) on a legal basis, some models create an additional mechanism applicable to the data access phase only (and not applicable to the use that will be made of this data by DUs) requiring to obtain a form of DSs' permission/authorisation[71] *(DMA art. 6.9, DA whereas 27 and art. 5.6, PSR art. 46.1.b) and 47.1.a), FIDA art. 5, 6 and 8).*

Well after this access phase exists an eventuality of further processing[72] by DUs. Such future processing would drastically damage DSs' control as this mechanism, although regulated, offers the possibility of dispensing with the DSs' consent. This possibility may thus be directly or indirectly prohibited for DUs *(PSR art. 45.2 c), 46.2 c), 47.2.b), FIDA art. 6.2, 6.4 a))* (Fig. 4).

2.4 *The Request Process Imposed on DSs*

Directly related to the previous subsection on DSs' agreement, another key parameters family emanates from the process imposed on DSs to initiate the sharing.

---

[70] This point must have been interpreted by the EDPB guidelines, 2020, *op. cit.*, see notably § 44 and 57.

[71] Without clearly explaining the exact interaction between these new authorisation/permission mechanisms and the GDPR legal basis mechanism.

[72] Possibility, via GDPR art. 5.1 b) and 6.4, for an entity processing the DSs' data to reuse it without their consent, under certain conditions notably of compatibility between the two processing operations.

2.4.1 The Request Method

A model may refer to the DSs' request without specifying precise modalities *(GDPR art. 20)* or, on the contrary, provide for an obligation for DHs to set up an electronic procedure *(DSA art. 16.1 and 0.2, FIDA art. 4 and 5.1)*.

In addition, while some models provide as a general rule that DSs are at the origin of the request *(GDPR art. 20, FIDA* via *art. 4 and 5.1)*, they can also provide for a possibility similar to the idea of a mandate,[73] generally made by DSs to DUs to access the data directly *(resulting from PSD2 art. 66 and 67, FIDA whereas 10 applicable to art. 5.1, DA art. 5)*, thus limiting the risk of power asymmetry between DHs and DSs.

2.4.2 The Facilitation Through Tools

Always with the objective of facilitating the expression of DSs' will, a model can integrate various tools.[74] These tools can be referred to via generic formulations *(just the mention of "tools" in DMA art. 6.9, or "tools for obtaining consent" in DGA art. 12.n))* or via more precise terms *(concept of "permission dashboards" in FIDA art. 8 and PSR art. 43, provided by DHs in order to give DSs an overview of the access permissions he has given to various DUs, and with the ability to remove these permissions and then to reestablish them)*. More directly, a model can itself be considered as a tool *(such as the eIDAS 2.0 EUDIW)*.

Beyond the DSs' request phase, these tools can also facilitate the provision of information for DSs[75] and further facilitate DSs' control after the sharing by integrating various of the DSs' digital rights.[76]

2.4.3 The Limitation for Security Reasons

DHs may be given the possibility to restrict the sharing requested by DSs, at least temporarily, for reasons of fraud, as already mentioned,[77] but also to take the time to verify the DSs' identity in case of reasonable doubts *(GDPR art. 12.6[78])*. For example, verification can be done by sending a copy of DSs' identity cards to DHs.

[73] In line with subsection 2.1.3 on the nature of "*The Data Subjects (DSs)*".

[74] Related to the concept of Privacy Enhancing Tool (PETs) or Personal Information Management System (PIMS). See Fischer-Hübner, Berthold, 2017, 759–778, for PETs and Bergman et al., 2003, 872–878, for PIMS.

[75] In relation to Sect. 2.5 "*The information provided to DSs*".

[76] Notably the DSs' rights within the meaning of GDPR chap. III such as the right of access, of rectification and erasure, to object, etc.

[77] See subsection 2.3.1 "*The voluntary or mandatory sharing for DHs*".

[78] Mentioning that "*where the controller has reasonable doubts concerning the identity of the natural person making the request [...], the controller may request the provision of additional information necessary to confirm the identity of the data subject*".

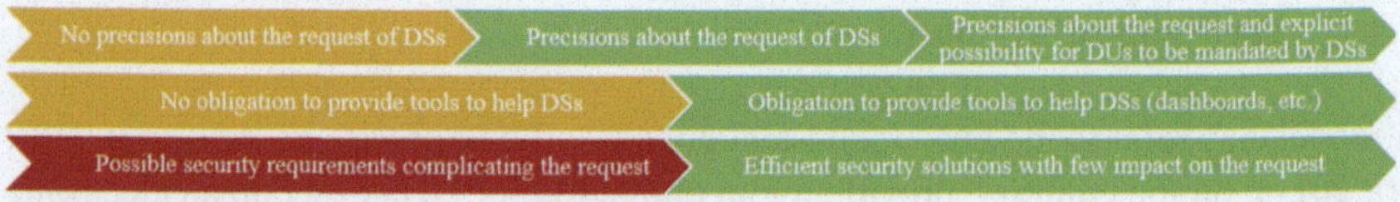

Fig. 5 Summary of possible DSs' control levels in the "*request process imposed on DSs*" parameters family

This procedure is not only heavy for DSs, but potentially counterproductive in terms of security via the risk of identity theft, it implies depending on whether DHs can be trusted or not.

Regarding this situation, parameters may provide for specific identity verification procedures to ensure a process that combines maximum security for DSs with as little interference as possible with their control *(such as the eIDAS 2.0 EUDIW setting up an "electronic identification scheme with assurance level hight"* via *art. 1.5 creating a new article 5a.11, or the "strong customer authentication" process of PSD2 art. 4.30)* (Fig. 5).

2.5 *The Information Provided to DSs*

Going beyond the request phase, another family of parameters arises from the provision of information, which is essential to DSs' control. Although this may be a general duty applicable to any processing,[79] it is possible to find additional parameters within some models.

2.5.1 The Information Friendliness Aspect

The basic requirements of transparency requiring information to be "*concise, easily accessible and easy to understand, and that clear and plain language*"[80] can thus be specified by certain parameters. A first solution is the possible use of tools (already mentioned in subsection 2.4.2 on the facilitation of the request via tools, which will therefore not be taken up again in the summary of this subsection, although the logic can be perfectly taken up here).

Other solutions proposed in some models take up the idea[81] of using distinct levels of information *(in particular* via *concise and easily readable summary in the DSA whereas art. 48)* or icons and logos *(DSA whereas 45, DGA art. 11.9)*, both potentially reinforcing the DSs' good understanding and their control.

[79] GDPR art. 13 and 14, and especially when processing is based on the legal basis of consent (GDPR art. 6.1.a)), requiring, in particular, to be informed (GDPR art. 4.11).

[80] GDPR whereas 58 and art. 5.1.

[81] Already present in GDPR, notably whereas 58 and 60.

2.5.2 The Additional Information Options

In line with the idea of the above-mentioned duty to provide information but also of records of processing activities,[82] some models provide for additional information options. The latter may take the form of an activity log (*such as a log record of the data intermediation activity in DGA art. 12.o)),* a database *(fed by the providers of online platforms and managed by the Commission in DSA art. 24)* or periodic activity reports *(from gatekeepers to the Commission in DMA art. 11 with a public version of it).*

All these measures, which potentially contribute to improving the proper DSs' understanding, can be complemented by the implementation of periodic audits *(DSA art. 37, DMA art. 15)* which also helps to reduce the asymmetry of information between data entities processing data, on the one hand, and public supervisory authorities and DSs, on the other.

2.5.3 The Prohibition of Unfair Information Practices

In addition to both the principle of transparency and the principle of fairness,[83] a model may include parameters to prevent attempts by DHs/DUs to manipulate DSs. Indeed, both DHs being obliged to share data could try to discourage DSs from initiating sharing, and DUs being granted a possible access could, on the contrary, influence DSs to initiate it.

A model can thus explicitly prohibit DHs/DUs from using *dark patterns*[84] by preventing the use of misleading behavioral and interface techniques or more generally prevent to unduly influencing DSs *(notably against the above-mentioned take-it or leave-it practices*[85] *or against obstacles to sharing that could have been put in place. See DSA art. 25, DMA art. 5.7 et seq., 6.3 et seq. and 13.4 and 0.6, DA art. 4.4 and 6.2.a), and PSR art. 44).* Although some of these provisions go beyond the question of informing DSs, all of them seem to be positioned as safeguards, attempting to limit possible external hindrances to the will of DSs (Fig. 6).

---

[82] GDPR art. 30.

[83] GDPR art. 5.1.a).

[84] Also called "*deceptive design patterns*" which can be defined "*interfaces and user journeys implemented on social media platforms that attempt to influence users into making unintended, unwilling and potentially harmful decisions, often toward a decision that is against the users' best interests and in favour of the social media platforms interests, regarding the processing of their personal data*" EDPB, 2022, Guidelines 03/2022 on Deceptive design patterns in social media platform interfaces: how to recognise and avoid them, p. 3. These practices are already supposed to be banned, as detailed in Leiser et al., 2022, 240–269.

[85] Cf. subsection 2.2.3 "*The granularity of choice left to DSs*".

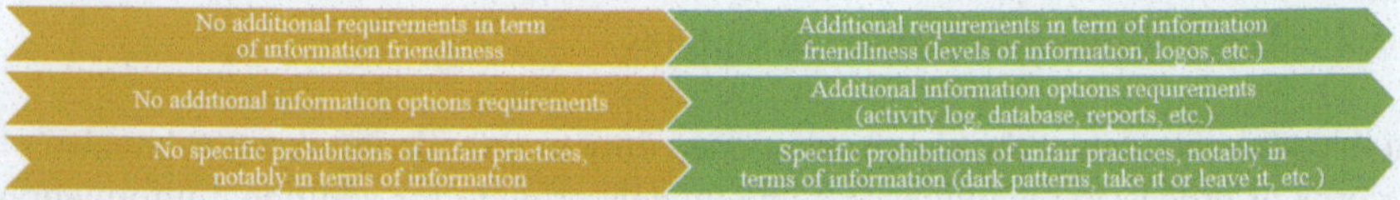

Fig. 6 Summary of possible DSs' control levels in the "*information provided to DSs*" parameters family

2.6 *The Sharing/access Phase*

In particular because of the voluntary or mandatory nature of sharing,[86] DHs may position themselves as a driving force behind the sharing or may not have a particular interest in the sharing to be effective.[87] A final family of parameters impacting DSs' control thus seems to emerge from the modalities of execution of the sharing by DHs.

2.6.1 The Cost, the Frequency, and the Response Time

Cost, frequency[88] and response times are studied together in that these parameters are not only often strongly interdependent, but also because they are the result of a search for a compromise between the DSs' interest and the burden on DHs in terms of compliance.

Unlike the eventuality of financial compensations between DHs and DUs, it is rarely foreseen that DSs can directly be charged *(although this is the case in DGA art. 12.f))*. In principle, sharing is often free of charge, thus not constituting a barrier to the exercise of DSs' control *(DMA art. 6.9, EHDS art. 3.1, eIDAS 2.0 art. 1.5 creating a new article 5a.13, ElectricityDir art. 23.5)*. A possible exception is to allow DHs to refuse the sharing or to charge DSs a reasonable fee in relation to the sharing when DSs' requests are considered to be "*manifestly unfounded or excessive, in particular because of their repetitive character*" *(GDPR art. 12.5)*. This sanction of the repetitive nature of the requests is an interesting factor in terms of control limitation. On the contrary, a model can provide for a continuous access to data *(FIDA art. 4 and 5.1, DMA art. 6.9 and 0.10, DA art. 4.1)*, thus maximizing DSs' control.

Another element of temporality to consider in terms of control is the time allowed to DHs to respond. Sharing can thus potentially take several months *(GDPR with up to three months art. 12.3)* or maximize DSs' control by being done "*in real time*" *(FIDA art. 4 and 5.1, DMA art. 6.9 and 0.10, DA art. 4.1)*.

[86] Cf. subsection 2.3.1 "*The voluntary or mandatory sharing for DHs*".

[87] As supposed for the PSD2 experience, in European Commission, 2023 A study on the application and impact of Directive (EU)2015/2366 on Payment Services (PSD2), in particular p. 14.

[88] Cost and frequency could just as easily have been considered in the light of Sect. 2.4 "The request process imposed on DSs".

2.6.2 The Path and Means of Sharing

A model can propose different paths for sharing the data.[89] If DSs can be considered as receivers of the data, then free to transmit it to DUs of their choice *(GDPR 20.1 or FIDA art. 4),* this role of intermediary can also be performed by a third party *(such as the data intermediation services of the DGA or the eIDAS 2.0 EUDIW).* However, many models mention the possibility for DUs to directly access DHs' data *(GDPR art. 20.2, PSD2 art. 66 and 67, FIDA art. 5.1, DA art. 5),* notably via application programming interfaces (API).

Beyond the path, the question of the sharing means can also be an obstacle to DSs' control. Some parameters could indeed leave the possibility for DHs to respond via a physical means such as paper, CDs, or DVDs *(GDPR[90]),* thus limiting DSs' control, particularly in terms of interoperability.

2.6.3 The Quest for Interoperability

The characteristics of the sharing or access phase need to be studied further than the mere physical or dematerialized nature of the means of sharing. It is in this sense that the question of the format of the sharing and thus the question of its interoperability must be mentioned.[91] The implementation of a model without any interoperability could indeed undermine its effectiveness and thus indirectly impact DSs' control.

A model can thus only invite DHs to use machine-readable and commonly used format, without really defining this standard *(GDPR art. 20.1),* relying on good practices and possible recommendations from authorities.[92] A complementary approach may be to oblige DHs to communicate their standards *(DMA art. 6.7),* without any certainty that interoperability will result from it.

Another possibility in this quest for interoperability may be to rely on data sharing intermediaries, in particular via possible conversion services between DSs/DHs/DUs within and between various sectors of activity *(DGA art. 34 and art. 12.d),.e) and.i)).* Another bet may be to force the stakeholders to come together to agree on common standards *(notably the obligation to join "data sharing scheme", i.e., "collective contractual agreement" as in FIDA whereas 26 and art. 9 and 10).*

However, with a more direct approach, a model can directly delegate the implementation of standards to public bodies *(such as standardisation bodies or the Commission in DMA whereas 96 and art. 48,* via *the European Data Innovation*

[89] In relation to subsection 2.1.3 on the nature "*The Data Subjects (DSs)*", and to subsection 2.4.1 "*The request method*". Therefore, not included again in the summary of this section.

[90] EDPB, 2017, Guidelines on the right to "*data portability*", p. 14 mentioning this possibility.

[91] This can be compared to both the previous subsection notably concerning API standard, and the subsection 2.2.2 "*The level of data held by DHs*".

[92] Such as the CNIL recommendation on API, 2023.

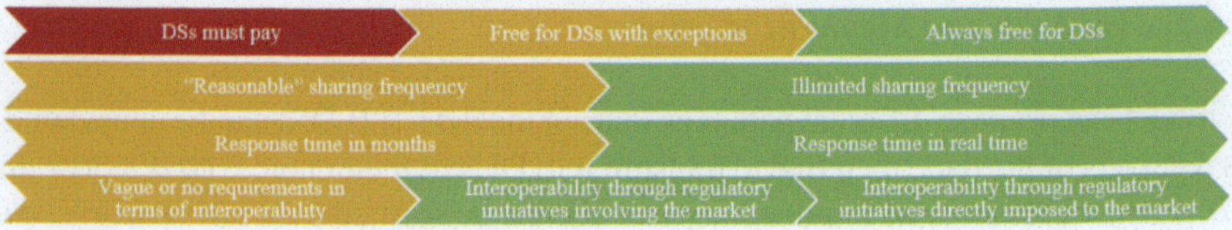

Fig. 7 Summary of possible DSs' control levels in the "*sharing/access phase*" parameters family

Board of the DGA art. 29, via *the Commission and the European Committee for Standardisation in VehiclesReg art. 61.2)* thus limiting the risk of a lack of interoperability that could block the model's effectiveness (Fig. 7).

3 Synthesis

Through various concrete examples of parameters extracted from regulatory data sharing models, this chapter has identified six families of essential parameters in terms of DSs' control, which are *1) the nature of the stakeholders, 2) the scope of the data concerned, 3) the justification for sharing, 4) the request process imposed on DSs, 5) the information provided to DSs, and 6) the sharing/access phase.* This list of essential parameters, therefore, constitutes a "*toolbox*" for estimating the level of DSs' control in data sharing models.

As a result, Fig. 8 displays the different levels of DSs' control studied in this chapter that can be achieved by each parameter (without the six families classification appearing for a better readability). This template makes the toolbox easier to use as shown in Fig. 9 below, that illustrates the assessment of the GDPR data portability model (as envisaged in GDPR art. 20.1). The template could also be used for all the existing models taken as examples in this chapter, but also for any other present or future EU or non-EU legislation aimed at introducing a new data sharing model.

This toolbox should nevertheless be used sparingly. Indeed, as mentioned in the introduction, the complex concept of DSs' control is naturally difficult to grasp by a quantitative approach such as the one proposed via theses three levels of possible impact on DS's control (reminder: red for negative measures, orange for neutral/minimum measures and green for positive/maximum measures). Furthermore, as each essential parameter is presented independently of the others, they are not compared with each other and the effect of specific combinations of different parameters is not estimated. Also, as mentioned in the introduction to this chapter, the objective of better DSs' control may naturally conflict with other objectives of a given model, of economic nature, of public interest or even sometimes of DSs' protection.

Thus, achieving good results through this toolkit should not be seen as an absolute goal, but only as a set of criteria that permit evaluators of data sharing models to look at one dimension of a model, which is the level of DSs' control it provides.

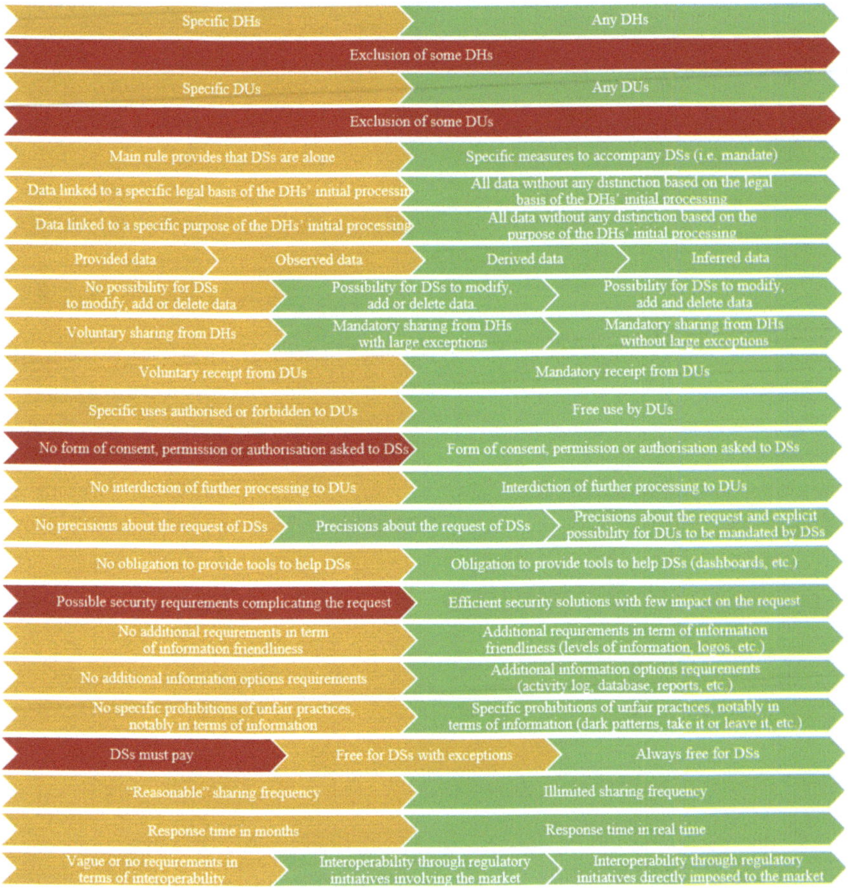

Fig. 8 Constitution of the toolbox through all parameters studied and the different levels of control each one could achieve

This toolbox can therefore be seen as a decision-making tool when establishing a new model in future legislation. It can also be used to compare in detail several models with each other, or simply as a means of checking whether the objective of DSs' control is verified in a given existing data sharing model, revealing which parameter(s) increase(s) or limit(s) DSs' control.

Fig. 9 Example of using the toolbox for assessing the GDPR right to data portability model (as envisaged in GDPR art. 20.1)

References

Alsop R, Heinsohn N (2005) Measuring empowerment in practice: structuring analysis and framing indicators. https://doi.org/10.1596/1813-9450-3510

Anciaux N et al. (2021) Empowerment and big personal data: from portability to personal agency. Global Privacy Law Rev (in press) hal-03140409

Balkin JM (2020) The fiduciary model of privacy. Harvard Law Review Forum 134(1) (2020). Yale Law & Economics Research Paper Forthcoming, 13–15, already available at https://harvardlawreview.org/wp-content/uploads/2020/10/134-Harv.-L.-Rev.-F.-11.pdf

Bergman O et al (2003) The user-subjective approach to personal information management systems. J Am Soc Inf Sci Technol 54(9):872–878. https://doi.org/10.1002/asi.10283

Bradford A (2020) The Brussels effect: how the European Union rules the world. Oxford University Press, Oxford. https://doi.org/10.1093/oso/9780190088583.003.0003

Brandimarte L et al (2013) Misplaced confidences: Privacy and the control paradox. Soc Psychol Person Sci 4(3):340–347. https://doi.org/10.1177/1948550612455931

Carovano G, Finck M (2023) Regulating data intermediaries: the impact of the data governance act on the EU's data economy. Comput Law Secur Rev. https://doi.org/10.1016/j.clsr.2023.105830

Casolari et al (2023) The EU data act in context: a legal. Assessment. https://doi.org/10.2139/ssrn.4584781

CNIL (2021) Deliberation n° 2021-070 of 27 May 2021 adopting a recommendation on the exercise of rights through a mandate

CNIL (2023) Deliberation SAN-2023-015 of 12 October 2023

CNIL (2023) technical recommendation on the use of application programming application programming interfaces (API) for the secure sharing of personal data

Council of Europe (1950) European Convention on Human Rights, signed on 4 November 1950

Council of Europe (1981) Convention for the Protection of Individuals with regard to Automatic Processing of Personal Data, 2 adopted on 8 January 1981, (STE N°108 - convention 108)

Council of Europe (2018) Convention for the Protection of Individuals with regard to Automatic Processing of Personal Data, adopted on 18 May 2018, (STCE n°223 - Convention 108+)

Delacroix S, Lawrence N (2018) Bottom-up data trusts: disturbing the 'one size fits all' approach to data governance, pp 12–13. https://doi.org/10.2139/ssrn.3265315

Directive (EU) 2002/58/EC of the European Parliament and of the Council of 12 July 2002 concerning the processing of personal data and the protection of privacy in the electronic communications sector (Directive on privacy and electronic communications) as amended by Directive 2009/136/EC of the European Parliament and of the Council of 25 November 2009 amending Directive 2002/22/EC on universal service and users' rights relating to electronic communications networks and services, Directive 2002/58/EC concerning the processing of personal data and the protection of privacy in the electronic communications sector and Regulation (EC) No 2006/2004 on cooperation between national authorities responsible for the enforcement of consumer protection laws, (ePrivacy - Directive on Privacy and Electronic Communications)

Directive (EU) 2015/2366 of the European Parliament and of the Council of 25 November 2015 on payment services in the internal market, amending Directives 2002/65/EC, 2009/110/EC and 2013/36/EU and Regulation (EU) No 1093/2010, and repealing Directive 2007/64/EC, (PSD2 - 2nd Payment Services Directive)

Directive (EU) 2019/944 of the European Parliament and of the Council of 5 June 2019 on common rules for the internal market for electricity and amending Directive 2012/27/EU (recast), (ElectricityDir)

Dorfleitner G et al (2023) Promise not fulfilled: FinTech, data privacy, and the GDPR. Electron Markets 33:32–33. https://doi.org/10.1007/s12525-023-00622-x

EDPB (2017) Guidelines on the right to "data portability" (wp242rev.01) as revised and adopted on 5 April 1997

EDPB (2020) Guidelines 05/2020 on consent under Regulation 2016/679

EDPB (2020) Guidelines 06/2020 on the interplay of the Second Payment Services Directive and the GDPR

EDPB (2022) Guidelines 03/2022 on Deceptive design patterns in social media platform interfaces: how to recognise and avoid them

European Commission (2020) Communication from the Commission to the European Parliament, the Council, the European Economic and Social Committee and the Committee of the regions - Shaping Europe's digital future, published on 19 February 2020, COM/2020/67 final

European Commission (2023) A study on the application and impact of Directive (EU)2015/2366 on Payment Services (PSD2), FISMA/2021/OP/0002, Publications Office of the European Union.

EU (2000) Charter of Fundamental Rights of the European Union, proclaimed on 7 December 2000, (2000/C 364/01)

EU (2022) European Declaration on Digital Rights and Principles for the Digital Decade, signed on 15 December 2022

Fischer-Hübner S, Berthold S (2017) Privacy-Enhancing Technologies. In: Computer and information security handbook, 3rd ed, pp 759–778. https://doi.org/10.1016/B978-0-12-803843-7.00053-3

French Conseil d'Etat (2020) Decision n° 434684 of 19 June 2020

Graef I et al (2019) Data portability and data control: lessons for an emerging concept in EU law. German Law J 19(6):1359–1398. https://doi.org/10.1017/S2071832200023075

Ibáñez Colomo P (2021) The draft digital markets act: a legal and institutional analysis. J Eur Compet Law Pract 12(7):561–575. https://doi.org/10.1093/jeclap/lpab065

Leiser MR et al (2022) Dark patterns: the case for regulatory pluralism between the European Union's consumer and data protection regimes. Research Handbook on EU Data Protection Law. https://doi.org/10.2139/ssrn.3625637

Li W, Quinn P (2024) Health data space: an expanded right to data portability? Comput Law Secur Rev. https://doi.org/10.1016/j.clsr.2023.105913

Maxwell W (2022) Le contrôle humain des systèmes algorithmiques - un regard critique sur l'exigence d'un "humain dans la boucle". HDR, Law, University Paris 1 Panthéon- Sorbonne, France

Micheli M et al (2020) Emerging models of data governance in the age of datafication. Big Data Soc. https://doi.org/10.1177/2053951720948087

Nakashima M (2022) Comparison of legal systems for data portability in the EU, the US and Japan and the Direction of Legislation in Japan. In: Kreps D, Davison R, Komukai T, Ishii K (eds) Human choice and digital by default: autonomy vs digital determination. HCC 2022. IFIP advances in information and communication technology, vol 656. Springer, Cham. https://doi.org/10.1007/978-3-031-15688-5_14

OECD (2012) Quality Framework and Guidelines for OECD Statistical Activities, Version 2011/1, published on 17 January 2012

OECD (2019) Enhancing access to and sharing of data—reconciling risks and benefits for data re-use across societies. https://doi.org/10.1787/276aaca8-en

OECD, 2021, Mapping data portability initiatives, opportunities and challenges, OECD Digital Economy Papers, No. 321, OECD Publishing, Paris, https://doi.org/10.1787/a6edfab2-en

OECD (2021) Recommendation of the council on enhancing access to and sharing of data, adopted on 06 October 2021. OECD/LEGAL/0463

OECD (2022) Going digital guide to data governance policy making. https://doi.org/10.1787/40d53904-en

Picart-Cartron E (2023) Le contrôle de la personne à l'utilisation de ses données personnelles, Thesis, Law, University of Rennes, France, not published yet, §35

Proposal for a Directive of the European Parliament and of the Council on payment services and electronic money services in the Internal Market amending Directive 98/26/EC and repealing Directives 2015/2366/EU and 2009/110/EC, 2023/0209(COD), (PSD3 - 3rd Payment Services Directive)

Proposal for a Regulation of the European Parliament and of the Council on payment services in the internal market and amending Regulation (EU) No 1093/2010, 2023/0210(COD), (PSR –Payment Services Regulation)

Proposal for a Regulation of the European Parliament and of the Council on a framework for Financial Data Access and amending Regulations (EU) No 1093/2010, (EU) No 1094/2010, (EU) No 1095/2010 and (EU) 2022/2554, 2023/0205(COD), (FIDA - Financial Data Access)

Quelle C (2017) Not just user control in the general data protection regulation. In: Lehmann A et al (eds) Privacy and identity management—facing up to next steps, IFIP AICT 498. Section 3.2. https://doi.org/10.2139/ssrn.2925410

Regulation (EU) 2016/679 of the European Parliament and of the Council of 27 April 2016 on the protection of natural persons with regard to the processing of personal data and on the free movement of such data, and repealing Directive 95/46/EC, (GDPR - General Data Protection Regulation)

Regulation (EU) 2018/858 of the European Parliament and of the Council of 30 May 2018 on the approval and market surveillance of motor vehicles and their trailers, and of systems, components and separate technical units intended for such vehicles, amending Regulations (EC) No 715/2007 and (EC) No 595/2009 and repealing Directive 2007/46/EC, (VehiclesReg)

Regulation (EU) 2022/868 of the European Parliament and of the Council of 30 May 2022 on European data governance and amending Regulation (EU) 2018/1724, PE/85/2021/REV/1, (DGA - Data Governance Act)

Regulation (EU) 2022/1925 of the European Parliament and of the Council of 14 September 2022 on contestable and fair markets in the digital sector and amending Directives (EU) 2019/1937 and (EU) 2020/1828, PE/17/2022/REV/1, (DMA - Digital Markets Act)

Regulation (EU) 2022/2065 of the European Parliament and of the Council of 19 October 2022 on a Single Market For Digital Services and amending Directive 2000/31/EC, (DSA - Digital Services Act)

Regulation (EU) 2023/2854 of the European Parliament and of the Council of 13 December 2023 on harmonized rules on fair access to and use of data and amending Regulation (EU) 2017/2394 and Directive (EU) 2020/1828, (Data Act)

Regulation (EU) 2024/1183 of the European Parliament and of the Council of 11 April 2024 amending Regulation (EU) No 910/2014 as regards establishing the European Digital Identity Framework, (eIDAS 2.0)

Regulation (EU) 2025/327 of the European Parliament and of the Council of 11 February 2025 on the European Health Data Space and amending Directive 2011/24/EU and Regulation (EU) 2024/2847, (EHDS - European Health Data Space)

Remolina N (2019) Open finance: regulatory challenges of the evolution of data sharing arrangements in the financial sector. SMU Centre for AI & Data Governance Research Paper No. 2019/05, 13 ff. https://doi.org/10.2139/ssrn.3475019

Rouvroy A, Poullet Y (2009) The right to informational self-determination and the value of self-development. In: Reinventing data protection. Springer, Dordrecht. https://doi.org/10.1007/978-1-4020-9498-9_2

Wernick A (2020) Defining data intermediaries: a clearer view through the lens of intellectual property governance. Technol Regul 2020:65–77. https://doi.org/10.26116/techreg.2020.007

Zuiderveen Borgesius F et al (2018) Tracking walls, take-it-or-leave-it choices, the GDPR, and the ePrivacy regulation. Eur Data Prot Law Rev 3(3):353–368. https://doi.org/10.21552/edpl/2017/3/9

Alexandre Humain-Lescop is a PhD researcher specializing in digital law and data protection law at the University Institut Polytechnique de Paris (IP Paris - France). His research explores data-sharing regulatory frameworks and ecosystems, focusing on models, tools, and interfaces that empower data subjects to exercise meaningful control over their information.

The Comparative View

African Rules on Cross-Border Data Flows: The Significance of Regulatory Convergence and the African Continental Free Trade Area's Digital Trade Protocol's Potential Contribution

Franziska Sucker and Alexander Beyleveld

Abstract Data regulation is evolving rapidly across Africa, with national, regional, and international developments shaping the continent's digital landscape. While many African countries have enacted data protection and cybersecurity laws, regulatory divergence remains a concern, particularly in cross-border data flows (CBDFs). At the continental level, the adoption of the Protocol on Digital Trade (DTP) under the African Continental Free Trade Area (AfCFTA) introduces new CBDF rules, raising questions about the extent to which they contribute to regulatory convergence. Regulatory convergence—the process by which different legal systems independently evolve towards similar standards—can strengthen African countries' positions in trade negotiations, empower digital firms, particularly African ones, and foster a more level playing field, though potentially at the expense of regulatory autonomy. In this chapter, we examine the current state of regulatory alignment in CBDFs across African countries and assesses the DTP's potential to enhance convergence. While notable progress has been made, particularly in areas like data protection and cybersecurity, divergence persists in enforcement practices and data localisation mandates. The DTP offers a unique opportunity for African countries to develop a coordinated approach to digital trade and data governance, strengthening their influence in international negotiations. However, its effectiveness will depend on how State Parties interpret and implement its provisions, particularly in balancing legitimate public policy objectives with the principle of free data flow. Rather than advocating for uniformity, we argue for a flexible, evidence-based approach that ensures regulatory alignment while addressing Africa's diverse policy needs.

F. Sucker (✉)
School of Law, University of the Witwatersrand, Johannesburg, South Africa
e-mail: Franziska.sucker@wits.ac.za

A. Beyleveld
Mandela Institute, School of Law, University of the Witwatersrand, Johannesburg, South Africa
e-mail: alex.beyleveld@gmail.com

J. Drexl et al. (eds.), *Comparative Data Law*, MPI Studies on Intellectual Property and Competition Law 32, https://doi.org/10.1007/978-3-031-91401-0_8

Keywords AfCFTA Protocol on Digital Trade · Cross-border data flows · Cross-border data transfer · Cybersecurity · Data governance · Data localisation · Data protection · Malabo Convention · Personal data · Regulatory convergence

1 Introduction

Data regulation is expanding rapidly on the African continent. At the national level, many countries have enacted data protection and cybersecurity legislation and are implementing these laws to varying degrees. At the regional level, the African Union (AU) Convention on Cyber Security and Personal Data Protection (Malabo Convention) entered into force in 2023. Moreover, at the international level, certain African countries are actively engaged in bilateral and plurilateral preferential trade agreement negotiations, with implications for data regulation. The United States (US)-Kenya Strategic Trade and Investment Partnership (STIP) of June 2022, for example, is expected to eventually lead to a fully-fledged Free Trade Agreement (FTA), likely to include rules on digital trade and data flows. Further, on 26 July 2024, after 5 years of negotiations under the plurilateral Joint Statement Initiative on Electronic Commerce (JSI) within the World Trade Organization (WTO), 82 WTO member, including 9 African countries,[1] announced a stabilised text for the first-ever global rules on e-commerce (AEC).[2] More African countries may participate once negotiations resume on the issues that were temporarily set aside, including cross-border data flows (CBDFs).[3]

Concurrently, in February 2024, at the continental level, the State Parties to the African Continental Free Trade Area (AfCFTA) have adopted the Protocol on Digital Trade (DTP).[4] Given that the DTP introduces CBDF rules, we examine whether these rules steer towards regulatory convergence among African countries in their approaches to CBDFs (Sect. 3). Regulatory convergence refers to the process by which different legal systems or regulations independently evolve to adopt similar standards or rules, often due to global trends, shared challenges, or harmonisation efforts,[5] without necessarily being designed to work together, as is the case with interoperable provisions.[6] We start by highlighting the significance of regulatory convergence in strengthening African countries' positions in trade negotiations, empowering African digital firms, and levelling the playing field within the continent, albeit

[1] Benin, Burkina Faso, Cabo Verde, Gambia, Kenya, Côte d'Ivoire, Nigeria, Mauritius, Cameroon.

[2] WTO (2024).

[3] In Art 35 of the AEC, the parties acknowledge that future negotiations may address unresolved issues listed in the longer, previously consolidated negotiating text (WTO (2019)), or any other issues that the Parties may introduce.

[4] Protocol to the Agreement Establishing the African Continental Free Trade Area on Digital Trade.

[5] Harmonisation directs a change of rules or standards to avoid conflicts and bring convergence/equivalence, while unification is a common set of rules that is applied for all jurisdictions (Alarashi (2021), p. 20).

[6] On the diverse meanings of regulatory convergence Tominaga (2020).

at the cost of reduced regulatory autonomy (Sect. 2). Throughout this discussion, we apply a distributional lens.

2 Significance of Regulatory Convergence

In the context of digital trade agreements (DTAs),[7] we contend that the greater the alignment in the governance of CBDFs, generated by a Pan-African strategy consolidated in the DTP, the more likely is (i) an increased impact of African countries in global digital trade rule making, (ii) the interoperability of CBDF rules across Africa, which can strengthening especially African digital firms, and (iii) the prevention of a race to the bottom and regulatory arbitrage, while (iv) reducing State Parties regulatory autonomy.

2.1 Increasing African Countries' Impact in Global Digital Trade Rule Making

From a digital trade law perspective, the greater the alignment of CBDF rules across the continent, the more likely is that African countries will have an increased impact on global digital trade rule-making. This alignment can promote more equitable conditions within data regulation frameworks by (i) enabling meaningful and increased participation in trade negotiations and (ii) strengthening the ability to withstand external pressure, ensuring that outcomes align with shared African goals and not compromise relevant policy space.

2.1.1 Meaningful and Increased Participation in Trade Negotiations

Currently, a small group of primarily developed countries leads the creation and shaping of digital trade rules, significantly influencing the present landscape and positioning themselves to steer the evolution of these rules at the multilateral level. This is evident from the fact that, of the 106 FTAs with digital trade chapters, 70 (ie two-thirds) involve just six countries: Australia, Chile, China, Singapore, the US, and the UK.[8]

While African countries recognise the potential benefits of digital trade for economic growth,[9] such as enhanced trade facilitation, improved infrastructure cooperation, and increased foreign direct investments (FDI), many have hesitated to engage in multilateral and plurilateral negotiations. Their reluctance is largely due

---

[7] Acknowledging that there are many non-trade law rationales for convergence.

[8] Burri/Vasquez/Callo-Müller/Kugler (2022).

[9] Eg AU (2020), (b).

to concerns that binding rules could constrain their developmental strategies, effectively 'kicking away the ladder' before they reach more advanced economic stages. Consequently, African countries have been largely absent from formative discussions shaping digital trade rules,[10] despite being among those most affected by the global digital divide.

The leaked, consolidated JSI negotiating text, which had been prepared under the responsibility of co-convenors Australia, Japan and Singapore, illustrates this. It reveals that the co-convenors had largely taken on board textual proposals from developed Members and large developing ones, such as Brazil and China.[11] Most notably for the current discussion, there is nothing to indicate meaningful African participation of any kind.

This concentration of rulemaking power among a few countries, alongside the underrepresentation of African countries, has resulted in DTAs that favour the 'digital haves' with minimal input from the 'digital have nots'.[12] While these agreements often include rules that promote the liberalisation of CBDFs, provisions that address the diverse levels of digital development such as Special and Differential Treatment provisions, competition rules, technical assistance and capacity building, and relevant regulatory autonomy are frequently absent.[13] This omission limits the ability of developing countries to harness digital trade for growth.

For a more equitable digital trade framework, the active participation of developing countries, including those in Africa, is crucial. The more regulatory convergence the DTP fosters at the national level, the more unified and effective African countries will be in trade negotiations. By consolidating their position and negotiating as a single bloc rather than as 54 individual voices, African countries can increase their collective bargaining power and advocate for their interests more effectively and, thus, participate meaningful.[14] This is likely to increase their confidence in participating in bilateral, plurilateral, and multilateral negotiations, allowing them to push for developmental-focused agreements, thereby amplify their influence trade discussions, including on digital infrastructure, capacity building, and equitable access to technology in forums such as the JSI or future negotiations with other regions or countries.

Such increased participation is crucial for ensuring that global digital trade rules reflect the developmental needs of all nations. In the context of the JSI negotiations, broader participation would increase the legitimacy of the discussions and promote the adopting rules that are globally representative. By presenting a collective voice early on, African countries can help shape DTAs that address their needs, avoiding the imposition of frameworks that do not consider their capacities. Early engagement is critical for securing inclusive agreements that reflect the diverse interests of

---

[10] Not one of the 106 FTAs assessed in TAPED had an African country party (*ibid*).

[11] WTO (2019).

[12] Agrawal/Mishra (2022), p. 284.

[13] On all these Beyleveld/Sucker (2022), pp. 66–76.

[14] Requires the capacity and resources to contribute, see eg Côte d'Ivoire WTO (2019).

all participating countries, particularly those historically marginalised in the digital economy.

2.1.2 Navigating External Pressure in Digital Trade Negotiations: Aligning Outcomes with Shared Goals and Preserving Policy Space

As technology and digital trade increasingly become geopolitical battlegrounds, African countries are emerging as a key focus in this arena. However, they are not yet fully integrated into global digital trade discussion, having only recently finalised continental rules. As a result, they face mounting external pressure to engage in negotiations on binding digital trade rules, often on an individual basis rather than collectively. While Morocco's FTA with the US, negotiated way back in 2006, was an early instance of such negotiations, more recently Kenya's STIP talks with the US and the ongoing EU–ESA EPA negotiations, both of which include provisions on digital trade, reflect African countries increasingly yielding to this pressure.

More specifically, African countries are increasingly pressured to align with the approaches to data governance of dominant players such as the US, EU, and China,[15] whose frameworks may not align with Africa's needs,[16] particularly concerning development-oriented issues. Increased bargaining power enhances the ability to resist this growing pressure. The greater the regulatory convergence among African State Parties, the more likely they are to present a Pan-African position in third-party negotiations. This is relevant not only in the multilateral JSI talks, which have already highlighted issues like digital inequality, but also in regional, plurilateral, and bilateral discussions.

By advancing positions that reflect Africa's priorities, negotiation outcomes can be aligned with shared continental goals, enhancing international cooperation and policy dialogue.[17] Full participation in these discussions is crucial to reaching a multilateral consensus that accommodates the diverse conditions across countries, ensuring universal benefit.

Moreover, as AfCFTA State Parties must adhere to agreed Pan-African rules, the greater regulatory convergence the DTP achieves, the better State Parties will be equipped to engage in third-party negotiations without compromising their policy space, crucial for pursuing collective African goals. This is particularly important for avoiding binding commitments on CBDF rules that could limit their ability to regulate CBDFs within Africa based on their preferences. Back in 2020, the AU

---

[15] On existing data realms, eg, Bradford (2023), part 1.

[16] Beyleveld/Sucker (2022), pp. 18–44, pp. 56–76; Boshe/Hennemann/von Meding (2022), pp. 56–88.

[17] Mishra (2022), p. 11.

Assembly acknowledged this risk and urged Members to review their bilateral negotiation approaches to CBDF regulation to safeguard their flexibility required for implementing the DTP effectively.[18]

A chronological, bottom-up approach[19] to policy development would not only streamline cross-border digital trade but also align with strategies to secure local stakeholder support. Engaging stakeholders to recognise the benefits of a robust digital ecosystem is essential to creating a conducive environment for digital trade across Africa.

2.2 *Interoperability and Strengthening African Digital Firms*

The greater the alignment of national laws relating to CBDF rules and standards, the more their compatibility increases, i.e., their interoperability across the continent.[20] Interoperability goes beyond simple standardisation, involving mutual recognition and coordination among diverse legal systems, enabling them to function together with reduced friction.

At one end of the spectrum, minimal interoperability arises from significant differences in rules, practices, and legal traditions, complicating cross-border legal matters. At the other end, high interoperability features closely aligned rules and mechanisms that ease interactions, often driven by international efforts like model laws or agreements such as the DTP. Despite these efforts, jurisdictional differences remain, even in the most interconnected legal environments.

Improved intra-Africa interoperability would increase legal certainty and predictability, transforming fragmented markets into a cohesive continental one. It would also facilitate smoother cross-continental data flows without requiring identical regulations. The easier and more seamlessly data can be transferred intra-Africa, the lower compliance costs for cross-border transactions, especially benefitting micro, medium and small enterprises (MSMEs). For example, if personal data rights (e.g., access, correction, deletion) are consistent across jurisdictions, firms can adopt data protection policies that comply with multiple legal systems simultaneously. Streamlined CBDFs would also enhance access to regional and global supply chains, foster inter-jurisdictional collaboration, and build online trust among firms and consumers.

This enables African digital firms and startups to expand across the continent more effectively and possibly disrupt oligopolistic market structures, promoting equal competitive conditions among African firms. It may also attract international

[18] AU (2020), (a).

[19] Beyleveld/Sucker (2022), p. 55.

[20] Also acknowledging the need of aligning African standards with global ones to simplify market access and mitigate compliance difficulties, while international collaboration advances common regulatory frameworks.

firms to establish local operations, which, under the right circumstances, could yield developmental benefits.

In the CBDF context, high interoperability would require the DTP to steer the development of national data regulatory frameworks that facilitate smooth CBDFs across State Parties, ensuring that cross-border data management is conducive, in a practically compatible sense, to the creation of intra-African value chains or the integration of African firms into existing mostly global value chains.

2.3 *Preventing a Race to the Bottom and Regulatory Arbitrage: Levelling the Playing Field*

In the absence of common standards and regulations, firms may be incentivised to engage in regulatory arbitrage, i.e., choosing to operate in jurisdictions with less stringent regulations to reduce costs and increase profits. This can undermine specific policy goals. For example, some State Parties might lower their data protection standards to attract FDI, thereby compromising user privacy rights.

The more regulatory convergence that is achieved, the fewer divergent standards are permitted. Thus, greater convergence reduces the likelihood of a race to the bottom or instances of regulatory arbitrage. This would facilitate a level playing field among State Parties and promote competition for FDI based on development orientated policies, such as investing in a skilled workforce. Notably, convergence can also support broader goals associated with CBDF regulation, such as data protection and cybersecurity, by encouraging State Parties to maintain high regulatory standards.

2.4 *Reducing Regulatory Autonomy*

Regulatory convergence may, however, significantly reduce the policy space of State Parties, eroding their regulatory autonomy.[21] This could limit their ability to address emerged regulatory issues in digital trade, such as data sovereignty, the protection of privacy, cybersecurity, and other domestic interests,[22] which go beyond traditional trade law concerns like market access and non-discrimination.

As an example, a domestic interest is likely to be facilitating the competitiveness of domestic industries because integrating the African digital market may exacerbate, the unequal distribution of benefits, both internationally and within or between State Parties, particularly given the outcomes of the negotiated CBDF rules.[23] First, like other market integration frameworks, several AfCFTA provisions, including those in the DTP, aim to dismantle state-imposed barriers to digital trade through

[21] In general on regulatory autonomy in digital trade agreements, see Burri/Kugler (2024).

[22] Eg Chander/Schwartz (2023), (a); Chander/Sun (2023), (b); Mishra (2020).

[23] Sucker (2025).

enforcing market access and non-discrimination rules, while restricting protectionist policies. This provides private operators more leeway to create their own barriers.[24] For example, the DTP establishes a general rule of free data flow, with personal data transfers and data localisation restrictions allowed only under specific circumstances.[25] This could limit African countries' ability to fully control their citizens' personal data, concentrating data control in the hands of large digital MNEs operating in Africa. Second, State Parties may negotiate trade agreements with third parties,[26] such as the US via the STIP. This could trigger a 'race to the bottom', where countries compete for foreign investments by creating 'data havens'. Such hubs would enable MNEs to dominate regional markets, with significant economic consequences across the AfCFTA. Near-unrestricted data flows could amplify the power of dominant MNEs, increasing the likelihood of abuses of dominant positions and deepening inequality in the region.

Overall, digital markets, more so than others, tend to be dominated by a few major firms.[27] This concentration can hinder competition,[28] reduce market diversity, and negatively impact smaller firms.[29] These effects may be even more pronounced in Africa, where non-digital markets have traditionally been far more concentrated than those in developed economies. African technology firms could find it particularly difficult to compete with larger, well-established foreign firms, worsening inequalities between African countries and between Africa and other regions.

To address these disparities, complementary policies will be required in areas like competition law, taxation,[30] and infrastructure development, alongside Special and Differential Treatment provisions.[31] Additionally, fostering workforce skills within AfCFTA State Parties will be essential to ensuring that digital market integration promotes equitable development across the continent and in relation to global counterparts.

Thus, excessive convergence of digital trade rules might impede the balance needed between enabling data flows across borders for a cohesive African digital market and preserving the regulatory autonomy of states. Maintaining this balance is crucial for allowing State Parties to adopt and maintain measures that reflect their public policy interests.

---

[24] Sucker (2020).

[25] Arts 20 & 22 DTP.

[26] Permitted in Art 7.3 DTP.

[27] Mishra (2024), pp. 164–166; Sucker (2025).

[28] Sucker/Klaaren (2021), pp. 567–568.

[29] See generally Brown (2020).

[30] Banga/Beyleveld/Munu (2025).

[31] On most aspects Beyleveld/Sucker (2022), pp. 66–76.

3 Towards Regulatory Convergence Through the AfCFTA Digital Trade Protocol?

Given the described significance and the fact that the DTP introduces CBDF rules, we address how these rules might impact regulatory convergence among African countries. We specifically distinguish between protection of personal information and cybersecurity (3.1), data localisation and cross-border data transfer (3.2) and other rules in the DTP that may influence convergence (3.3). Notably, we discuss aspects of data protection and cybersecurity rules that could lead to de facto data localisation under 'data localisation'. We begin in each sub-section with a brief overview of the current state of convergence at regional and national levels.

3.1 Protection of Personal Information and Cybersecurity

3.1.1 Current State of Convergence

Malabo Convention

Adopted in 2014 and coming into effect in June 2023, the Malabo Convention sets out guidelines to secure digital interactions, safeguard personal data, and combat cybercrime.[32] It encapsulates the collective view of Members, aiming to balance the use of information and communication technologies with the imperative of protecting citizens' privacy, 'while guaranteeing the free flow of information'.[33] The Convention's primary focus is on harmonising data protection and cyber security laws across AU Member. It seeks to develop robust systems for addressing privacy challenges associated with the management of personal data, ensuring that these processes respect individual rights and freedoms. Moreover, it strives to consider broader concerns, including state interests, community rights, and business needs, while aligning with globally recognised best practices.[34]

To achieve these goals, the Convention stipulates that Members must create appropriate legislative frameworks aligned with the Convention and establish national data protection authorities,[35] among others, to enforce data protection principles like consent, lawfulness, fairness, and transparency.[36] This does not only signify a commitment by Members to uphold certain minimum standards in national personal

[32] Malabo Convention, Preamble.

[33] *Ibid.*

[34] *Ibid.*

[35] Malabo Convention, Arts 8.1 & 11.1(a).

[36] Malabo Convention, ch II, sec III.

data protection and cybersecurity legislations, but establishes foundational parameters for convergence in these areas among AU Members, independent of specific AfCFTA rules in these domains.

National Level

At the national level, many State Parties have implemented data protection and cybersecurity laws. Specifically, 36 State Parties have enacted data protection laws, with three more in draft stages, and 39 countries have established cybersecurity laws.[37] A discussion of each law is beyond this chapter's scope.[38] For our purposes, it suffices to note that many of these laws include provisions relevant to CBDFs, generally aiming for similar outcomes.

While varying in substance, they align notably in objectives and principles, influenced in part by the Malabo Convention. Data protection laws, for example, are commonly rooted in the right to privacy, incorporating conditional transfer for CBDFs to protect data subjects' rights, typically allowing CBDFs under specific conditions like consent or adequate protection by the receiving jurisdiction. Cybersecurity legislation focuses on combating cybercrime, protecting critical ICT infrastructure, and enhancing user security. They do not necessarily prohibit CBDFs but leave it to the governments' discretion to restrict them, including for national security reasons and critical ICT infrastructure protection.

An example is the Kenyan Data Protection Act (KDPA), enacted to uphold constitutionally guaranteed privacy rights.[39] It establishes the Office of the Data Protection Commissioner, provides for personal data processing and data subject rights, and stipulates data controllers and processors' obligations. It specifically addresses cross-border transfer of personal and sensitive data, further expanded on in the Data Protection (General) Regulations (KDPA Regulations), requiring either adequate protection in the receiving jurisdiction or consent from the data subject.[40] The Commissioner is also empowered to regulate these transfers, including the authority to prohibit, suspend or condition them to protect data subject rights.[41]

Furthermore, the KDPA calls for data localisation in instances linked to strategic state interests or revenue protection, requiring certain data processing activities to occur only through servers or data centres located in Kenya or 'store at least one serving copy of the concerned personal data' within Kenya.[42] Data for strategic interests includes personal data related to 'protected computer systems' as defined by the Computer Misuse and Cybercrime Act, 2018 (CMC Act) designated by

---

[37] Data Protection Africa (2024).

[38] In detail Hlomani/Ncube (2023).

[39] Sec 31.c & d KDPA.

[40] Secs 25.h & 49 KDPA; further restrictions in sec 48 KPDA.

[41] Secs 49.b & c KDPA.

[42] Sec 50 KDPA.

the ICT Cabinet Secretary as critical for maintaining Kenya's security, infrastructure integrity, and public safety across various sectors, including communications, banking, financial services, public utilities, and transportation.[43] This highlights the KDPA's focus on safeguarding data linked to the nation's strategic operations and security in CBDFs.

Kenya's approach to data protection and cybersecurity, focusing on strategic regulation of CBDFs and critical infrastructure, reflects a broader trend among State Parties, including South Africa and Nigeria,[44] demonstrating regulatory convergence on these issues, at least in relation to laws as they are written. However, the enforcement of most of these laws presents a divergence risk, especially regarding CBDFs, where enforcement practices significantly impact the effectiveness of data regulation. The potential for further convergence exists, raising questions about the DTP's role in influencing or standardising enforcement practices.

3.1.2 Art 21: Protection of Personal Data

Art 21 addresses the protection of personal data for individuals engaged in digital trade. It aligns its structure and content of its first two paragraphs, for example, with Art 17.2 of the Australia Singapore Digital Economy Agreement (Australia-Singapore DEA) and Art 19.8(2) of the United States Mexico Canada Agreement (USMCA). Paragraph 1 requires each State Party to establish a legal framework for protection of personal data in digital trade. Paragraph 2 mandates that these frameworks be developed with consideration of principles and guidelines from relevant regional, continental, and international organisations, such as those outlined in the Malabo Convention.

The convergence potential of paragraphs 1 and 2 is limited. If 'State Parties shall commit itself' in Art 8.1 of the Malabo Convention is interpreted as an obligation to act, meaning the act of committing is still required, Art 21.1 essentially reiterates the commitment to establish data protection laws, albeit with a specific focus on digital trade. If interpreted in this way, Art 21.1 would cover aspects already addressed by Art 8.1, potentially limiting its impact on existing legislative frameworks or enforcement practices. Moreover, paragraph 2's directive for State Parties to consider various principles, without prescribing a specific regulatory model, lacks the prescriptiveness needed to promote regulatory convergence. This approach allows State Parties to design their national laws according to their specific legal contexts and needs.

Paragraph 3 echoes the essence of Art 17.5 of the Australia-Singapore DEA and Art 19.8(5) of the USMCA by addressing transparency in digital trade. It mandates the publication of information regarding laws and regulations related to personal data protection, including details on individual remedies and enterprise compliance requirements. This stipulation has the potential to drive regulatory convergence, particularly in countries where digital trade regulations lack transparency.

[43] Sec 20 CMC Act.

[44] In detail Beyleveld/Sucker (2022), pp. 26–37.

The AfCFTA's institutional structure could be instrumental in achieving such convergence. By introducing this transparency provision, Art 21 represents a significant step toward more uniform standards and clearer practices across jurisdictions, potentially streamlining the digital trade landscape for stakeholders.

Paragraph 4 introduces a novel obligation for State Parties, requiring them to ensure that enterprises within their jurisdiction adopt, maintain, and publicly disclose their personal data protection policies. This obligation extends beyond the encouragement approach seen in Art 17.6 of the Australia-Singapore DEA, aiming to set a new baseline standard for African national data protection laws, potentially fostering new forms of regulatory convergence. While this obligation seeks to enhance data protection standards, when implementing, there is a general risk of overregulation, which could be especially challenging for MSMEs if it leads to increased compliance requirements and associated cost. They often struggle with the resources and expertise needed to manage complex regulations, face higher relative costs, encounter significant administrative tasks, and have limited access to advanced compliance tools. Addressing this challenge, possibly through the Committee on Digital Trade, is essential for achieving paragraph 4's objective to balance effective data protection with the operational realities of smaller businesses.

Paragraph 5 marks a crucial shift from the previous confidential draft's non-mandatory 'shall endeavour' stance to a mandatory requirement. It compels State Parties to actively develop cross-border collaboration mechanisms for handling complaints related to personal data protection. This shift may ensure a more cohesive and effective response to such complaints, highlighting a significant move towards enhancing regulatory convergence in an area previously marked by limited cooperation.

In conclusion, the personal data protection provisions of Art 21 could lead to some convergence among State Parties, potentially enhancing trust and, thereby, facilitating CBDFs. However, their impact largely depends on how they intersect with data localisation and transfer policies, as discussed below. The discretion granted to State Parties in shaping these protections might pave the way for GDPR-like equivalence requirements, influencing future regulatory landscapes.

3.1.3 Art 25: Cybersecurity

Art 25.1 mirrors the structure of the first two paragraphs of Art 21 by mandating each State Party in sentence 1 to adopt or maintain measures for ensuring cybersecurity and combating cybercrime within its jurisdiction. This provision aligns with Art 24 of the Malabo Convention, reinforcing the commitment to national cybersecurity laws. Furthermore, State Parties are advised in sentence 2 to consider standards and guidelines from regional, continental, and international instruments such as the Malabo Convention, when developing these measures. This approach aligns national cybersecurity frameworks with global standards.

Paragraph 2 adopts a 'shall endeavour' approach, urging State Parties to promote collaboration and capacity building in cybersecurity. This involves enhancing national authorities' capabilities in incident management, developing technical assistance collaborations, addressing cybersecurity incidents promptly, and engaging stakeholders from industry, civil society, and academia to foster a cybersecurity culture. It also encourages continuous dialogue and the exchange of best practices.

This strategy promotes cooperation and convergence through mechanisms like the AfCFTA institutional architecture and the Committee on Digital Trade but does not establish enforceable minimum standards. It reflects the approach seen in other regional trade agreements, such as Art 14.16 of the Comprehensive and Progressive Agreement for Trans-Pacific Partnership (CPTPP), Art 19.15(1) of the USMCA, and Art 8 of the ASEAN Agreement on E-Commerce (ASEAN AEC), which all underscore the importance of capacity building and collaborative in cybersecurity without imposing legally binding requirements.

Paragraph 3 introduces a requirement for State Parties to ensure that enterprises within their jurisdiction adhere to cybersecurity best practices for risk identification, protection, incident detection, response, and recovery. Similar to Art 21.4's data protection standards, this sets a minimum standard for enterprises, reflecting a nuanced regulatory approach under the AfCFTA. While enterprises are not direct AfCFTA participants, their compliance is essential for effective cybersecurity, underscoring their significant role in upholding cybersecurity standards and protecting individuals and firms.

Arts 25.1 to 25.3 contribute subtly to the converge of cybersecurity standards among State Parties, potentially enhancing trust in digital trade and indirectly facilitating CBDFs. However, the impact on CBDFs will largely depend on the interplay between cybersecurity measures and data localisation and transfer policies, a topic explored in subsequent discussions.

3.2 Cross-Border Data Transfers and Data Localisation

3.2.1 Current State of Convergence

Malabo Convention

The Malabo Convention provides limited guidance on data localisation and transfer rules, which may either impede or facilitate CBDFs. It outlines the oversight role of DPAs in overseeing cross-border personal data transfers but offers only one a single specific rule for legislative action related to sensitive personal data.

The Convention tasks DPAs with ensuring that personal data processing complies with its provisions, particularly to prevent information and communication technologies (ICTs) from infringing on public freedoms or individual privacy.[45] Regarding legislative requirements, the Convention's focus on CBDFs is mainly confined to Art

[45] Malabo Convention, Art 12.1–2, esp 2(k).

14, which addresses 'sensitive data'.[46] It requires Members to prohibit the collection and processing of sensitive data,[47] with certain exceptions.[48] Specifically, Art 14.6 mandates that personal data transfer to non-AU-Members is only permitted if those states provide an adequate level of privacy, freedom, and fundamental rights protection or the data controller obtains prior approval from the national protection authority.[49]

Overall, the Convention provides general guidelines for data processing, including consent requirements and specific rules for sensitive data. It offers flexibility in restricting CBDFs but does not strongly indicate an intention for Members to align their domestic laws on CBDFs consistently. The Convention also shows limited focus on non-personal data, suggesting minimal effort towards regulatory convergence among Members, and, by extension, among AfCFTA State Parties.

National Level

National data protection and cybersecurity laws, while not explicitly targeting data localisation, often indirectly prompt it through commonly adopted conditional flow regimes. They permit CBDFs only under specific conditions, thus implying a need for data localisation. Moreover, certain cybersecurity laws explicitly require data localisation for certain data types. Countries like Nigeria and South Africa provide illustrative examples for requiring data localisation to support their domestic digital economy growth.

In Nigeria, data hosting requirements mandates that ICT firms within the country store data locally. This strategy aims to enhance local and indigenous digital technology businesses, shift economic power from global to local players, support economic development, enhance the domestic data centre industry, create jobs, and ensure national self-reliance in accessing data and online services.[50]

South Africa's National Data and Cloud Policy (NDCP), adopted in May 2024, addresses key data governance challenges, including data protection, cross-border data transfers, and data localisation. The policy aims to unlock the socio-economic potential of data, align existing regulations, support MSMEs, and encourage research, innovation, and human capital development.[51]

---

[46] Relating 'to religious, philosophical, political and trade-union opinions and activities, as well as to the sex life or race, health, social measures, legal proceedings and penal or administrative sanctions' (Art 1) and to 'ethnic and regional origin, parental filiation, … genetic information or … health' (Art 14.1).

[47] Malabo Convention, Art 14.1.

[48] *Ibid*, Art 14.2.

[49] Art 14.6(a) and (b). In this context, we read 'personal data' as referring to the subset of sensitive data.

[50] 2021 National Policy for the Promotion of Indigenous Content in the Nigerian Telecommunications Sector; National Digital Economy Policy and Strategy 2020–2030; Guidelines for Nigerian Content Development in Information and Communication Technology (2019), 12.1(4).

[51] NCDP, 8 & 10.

In the 2021 draft version, South Africa proposed a stringent approach to data localisation, mandating that all critical information infrastructure, including citizen data, be stored and processed within South Africa.[52] This approach emphasised national control over data, treating data generated in South Africa as national property, and designating critical digital infrastructure, such as data centres, as strategic assets.[53] The draft also required that a copy of any cross-border transferred data be stored locally, positioning the government as a trustee for such data to reinforce data sovereignty.

In the final version, Sout Africa adopts a more flexible approach. While maintaining the importance of national security and sovereignty, it allows for CBDFs for most business operations, provided they comply with South African laws.[54] Data localisation is now only mandated for sensitive government data related to national security,[55] offering greater flexibility for cross-border operations and reducing regulatory burdens. The final version strikes a balance between openness and regulation, prioritising international cooperation and economic growth over strict localisation requirements for all critical data.

The policy interventions in the NCDP stress that all data collected within South Africa must comply with national data protection and security laws.[56] Government data concerning national security and sovereignty must be stored locally on infrastructure within South Africa.[57] Furthermore, cross-border data transfers and sharing agreements must promote national interests, such as socio-economic development and security, while adhering to South African laws,[58] encourage mutually beneficial cooperation and support regional initiatives, including the AfCFTA, Southern African Customs Union, Single Digital African Market and other AU/SADC protocols.[59]

These examples highlight the presence or consideration of data localisation policies among certain State Parties. However, many State Parties either lack such policies or follow divergent approaches, which may be due to limited technical capacity for implementing data localisation. As a result, the current landscape does not readily suggest convergence in this area, underscoring the potential role of the DTP in establishing a cohesive framework.

3.2.2 Arts 20 and 22: Data Transfer and Localisation

Meeting minutes reveal a spectrum of views on data localisation. Some advocate for outright bans on data localisation requirements, arguing that dictating data retention

---

[52] Draft NCDP, 9, 10.1, 10.4; 13, 17 & 25–27.

[53] *Ibid*, 10.4(4), 27–28.

[54] NCDP, 15.4.

[55] *Ibid*.

[56] NCDP, 15.4(1).

[57] NCDP, 15.4(2).

[58] NCDP, 15.4(3)(1)–(2).

[59] NCDP, 15.4(3)–(4).

or location could hinder digital trade by creating barriers to data flows and increasing costs, especially given Africa's developing digital infrastructure. Others support no restrictions on the location of data facilities, favouring state discretion. Meanwhile some argue for locating computing facilities within Africa to retain data on the continent, suggesting that this could stimulate local digital infrastructure growth, with relevant mechanisms to be developed to support implementation. Despite these diverse opinions, Arts 20 and 22 have emerged, mirroring Arts 23.2 and 3, and 24.2 and 3 of the Australia-Singapore DEA, Arts 4.3(2) and (3), and 4.4(2) and (3) of the Digital Economy Partnership Agreement (DEPA) and Arts 14.11(2) and (3), 14.13(2) and (3) of the CPTPP, favouring free data flow as the default rule.[60]

Art 20.1 specifically requires that cross-border data transfers, including personal data, be permitted only 'provided the activity is for the conduct of digital trade' by entities from State Parties.[61] This condition implies potential restrictions for non-State Party entities or transfers unrelated to digital trade, significantly narrowing the scope of required free data flow from the broader business activities outlined in the previous confidential draft of the Protocol. The focus on digital trade operations marks a departure from the general business scope of the provisions that inspired Art 20.[62]

In parallel, Art 22.1 stipulates that State Parties cannot require the localisation of computing facilities as a condition for conducting digital trade within their jurisdictions, subtly allowing localisation requirements in scenarios involving non-State Party entities or activities unrelated to digital trade. This approach aligns with Art 20.1's specific focus on digital trade and marks a shift from the broader business focus of the previous draft, reflecting a similar departure from the general business emphasis found in the provisions that inspired Art 22.[63] For instance, Rwanda's strict localisation requirements for critical government and public data, contingent on regulatory approval, are unlikely to be imposed on digital trade related operations.

The exceptions outlined in paragraphs 2 allow a State Party to adopt or maintain measures that diverge from the general rule of unrestricted data flows if such measures serve a legitimate public policy objective or protects essential security interests.[64] However, these measures must meet two conditions: they must not be applied in a manner that constitutes arbitrary or unjustifiable discrimination, or be a disguised restriction on digital trade; and they must not impose data transfer restrictions greater than required to achieve the objective. These phrases mirror the 'necessity' criterion

---

[60] While Arts 19.11(1) and 19.11(2) of the USMCA are identical regarding cross-border transfer, Art 19.12 on data localisation includes no exception. The same applies to the wording of Art 11 of the US Japan Digital Trade Agreement.

[61] The term used in the DEPA, CPTPP and USMCA is 'covered person', and in the DEA and EU-UK Trade and Cooperation Agreement (TCA) parties (Art DIGIT.6).

[62] See on general business scope, Art 23.2 DEA; Art 4.3(2) DEPA; Art 14.11(2) CPTPP; Art 19.11(1) USMCA; Art 7.4(a) ASEAN AEC; not even a restriction to business activities in Art DIGIT.6 EU-UK TCA.

[63] See Art 24.2 DEA; Art 4.4(2) DEPA; Art 14.13(2) CPTPP; Art 19.12 USMCA; Art 7.6(b) ASEAN AEC.

[64] This distinction suggests that they are considered a distinct category.

and the so-called Chapeau of the general exceptions found in both the General Agreement on Tariffs and Trade (GATT) and the General Agreement on Trade in Services (GATS),[65] suggesting that interpretations of these exceptions may be guided by established WTO panels rulings.

Broad data localisation requirements that mandate data storage and processing within a country, potentially leading to outright bans on CBDFs, are likely to conflict with the exceptions' criteria. Such measures may be considered more trade restrictive than necessary if they exceed reasonably available alternatives that equally contribute to the public policy goal or security interests, thereby failing the WTO's necessity test.[66] The Kenyan government's requirement for personal data to be processed 'exclusively through servers or data centres located in Kenya', justified by strategic or revenue protection interests,[67] illustrates this point. While such strict localisation rules are unlikely to result in discrimination between service suppliers or goods from different State Parties, if discrimination occurs, the application could be deemed arbitrary due to rigidity or unjustifiable if less restrictive yet equally effective alternatives are ignored.[68]

A regulation that requires local data storage without outright prohibiting data transfer abroad offers flexibility. Such rule might permit 1) transferring data overseas, 2) storing copies of data abroad, and 3) introducing specific compliance requirements for CBDFs and storage. This flexibility allows for varying degrees of restrictiveness in conditional data transfers, ranging from free flow to hard, intermediate, and soft conditional restrictions, depending on the regulation's design and application. Compliance regimes may span from stringent measures, such as country-specific approvals for transfers via adequacy decisions, regulatory consent, and approved contracts, to less stringent ones like obtaining user consent, adhering to notice requirements, or allowing data processors to transfer data based on self-assessment of the recipient country's data protection adequacy.

WTO Appellate Body and panel interpretations of Art XX of the GATT grant states discretion to set their desired level of protection for public policy or essential security interests.[69] If a measure aligns with these broadly defined interests, its level of protection is generally not contestable. However, the argument for the necessity of a measure is often stronger for compliance requirements than for strict localisation, depending on the regulation's specific aim. Importantly, the application of such exceptions often hinges on satisfying the third requirement, which focuses on practical implementation. For example, overly specific consent requirements for data processing, particularly when country-specific, could lead to varying degrees of discrimination. In contrast, adequacy decisions and similar compliance frameworks offering alternative methods may be considered justifiable forms of discrimination.

---

[65] Art XX of the GATT & Art XIV of the GATS.

[66] Eg EC – Asbestos (2001), p. 169; Brazil – Retreated Tyres (2007), p. 178.

[67] Sec 50 KPDA.

[68] Eg US – Shrimp (1998), p. 177; US – Gasoline (1996), pp. 28–29.

[69] Eg EC – Seal Products (2014), 5.200.

In essence, Art 20.1 and Art 22.1 promote greater convergence by establishing a general rule of unrestricted CBDFs. These provisions compel State Parties to shift from their prevailing systems – where the transfer of personal data is typically allowed after certain conditions are met, and non-personal data transfers remain largely unregulated – to a new default where the free flow of data becomes the standard, with restrictive conditions requiring justification. Similarly, they move the approach from permitting data localisation for specific purposes to treating localisation as an exceptional measure. The exceptions outlined in Art 20.2 and Art 22.2 allow deviations from the general rule of unrestricted CBDFs under specific conditions, advocating for convergence against strict localisation while enabling flexibility where less restrictive measures meet policy objectives. In other words, the framework steers toward regulatory convergence by prohibiting outright bans or unnecessary constraints on data flows, while still allowing divergent practices among State Parties regarding data transfer and localisation requirements, particularly in the application of conditional data transfer regimes. This approach, therefore, navigates between convergence and the realities of diverse regulatory environments, especially in interpreting and applying exceptions.

While not present in earlier drafts, in the final version, Art 20.3 introduces the requirement to develop an Annexure on CBDFs and specifies that it 'shall, among others, set out legitimate public policy objectives, how data may be used, restrictions on sharing of data to third parties, including data protection regulations and restrictions that may be applied by regulations'. Depending on its content, this additional clarity on interpretation could either promote convergence or allow for regulatory diversity in digital trade and data flow regulation. Importantly, the Annexure provides State Parties the opportunity to gradually clarify terms and refine the application of the DTP over time. Notably, the final version of Art 20.1 now expressly subjects the general principle of unrestricted data flow to the stipulations of the Annex, introducing a conditionality that was absent in earlier drafts.

Lastly, Art 22.3, a new addition in the final version of the Protocol, stands out as an atypical provision. It obligates State Parties to 'encourage and support the establishment and use of computing facilities' domestically 'to promote the development of local digital infrastructure and access', aligning with the DTP's objectives. While this clause may not significantly influence legal frameworks or directly drive regulatory convergence, its mandatory nature provides a valuable opportunity to enhance the development of much-needed digital infrastructure.

3.3 Towards Convergence Through Interoperability Provisions Relating to Data Flows

Provisions relating to interoperability, whether directly or indirectly connected to CBDFs, have the potential to further drive regulatory convergence. For instance, Art

2.e identifies the promotion of 'common and open standards to enable the interoperability of frameworks and systems to facilitate cross-border digital trade' as a key objective of the DTP. Moreover, Art 43.t explicitly lists interoperability and mutual recognition among the areas that require cooperation form State Parties. Art 19.3 also obliges State Parties to 'promote interoperability in technologies and applications required to facilitate digital trade' across various sectors, including cross-border data transfers, while Art 19.2 mandates the adoption of mutual recognition mechanisms. Although the proposal to establish the Pan-African Digital Trade Centre, which was intended to identify 'priorities for standards and interoperability in sectors critical to the continental digital market,' has been removed from the latest version of the DTP, the remaining provisions outline a clear strategy for enhancing interoperability and mutual recognition. This structured approach could help advance regulatory convergence in key areas critical for digital trade, including CBDFs.

4 Conclusion

This exploration of regulatory convergence in CBDF regulation across African countries has focused on three key themes: (i) the significance of such convergence for the continent, (ii) the current state of regulatory alignment, and (iii) the potential of the DTP to enhance further convergence. While we observe significant alignment, particularly in areas like data protection and cybersecurity, likely influenced by the Malabo Convention, the potential of regulatory divergence remains, especially with regard to explicit data localisation mandates and enforcement practices that may lead to de facto localisation.

The DTP presents a unique opportunity for African countries to consolidate their approaches to digital trade and data governance, which could reduce regulatory disparities, particularly in areas where clear regulations are lacking or where significant divergences are evident, such as data localisation. By fostering a Pan-African approach for coordination, the DTP may create a platform for articulating a continental digital trade agenda that responds to Africa's specific needs, while strengthening its position in international digital trade negotiations. However, the success of this effort will depend on how State Parties interpret and implement the DTP's provisions and how future developments, such as the CBDF Annexure, unfold. A critical factor will be the ability of State Parties to balance 'legitimate public policy objectives' with the principles of free data flow.

Importantly, our advocacy for regulatory convergence is not about uniformity for its own sake, but rather about balancing alignment with the need for effective, high-quality regulations, especially in areas like data protection, cybersecurity, and localisation. Regulating CBDFs requires a flexible, evidence-based, holistic approach that accommodates the diverse policy objectives of African countries. The long-term success of regulatory convergence across the continent will depend on how well State Parties adapt their national data frameworks to align with the DTP's standards. Ultimately, the framework's effectiveness will depend on the extent to which these standards are embraced and implemented, striking the right balance between regulatory alignment and the unique needs of each country.

References

Agarwal B, Mishra N (2022) Addressing the global data digital divide through digital trade law. Trade Law Dev 14(2):238–288

Alarashi AH (2021) The concept of harmonisation and unification of the law in Malaysia: an Islamic appraisal. J Integr Sci 2(1):14–26

African Convention on Cybersecurity and Personal Data Protection (Malabo Convention), adopted in 2014, entered into force June 2023

African Union (AU) (2020a) Decision on the African Continental Free Trade Area (AfCFTA). Assembly/AU/Dec.751 (XXXIII)

AU (2020b) The digital transformation strategy for Africa (2020–2030). https://au.int/sites/default/files/documents/38507-doc-dts-english.pdf. Accessed 22 Feb 2025

Banga K, Beyleveld A, Munu M (2025) Trading away tax sovereignty? How trade rules shape taxation of the digital economy in Africa. J Int Econ Law 28(1):43–62

Beyleveld A, Sucker F (2023) Regulating cross-border data flows under the AfCFTA protocol on digital trade: the what, why, how, where and when. Manchester J Int Econ Law 20(2):299–326

Beyleveld A, Sucker F (2022) Cross-border data flows in Africa: policy considerations for the AfCFTA protocol on digital trade. CSEA & Mandela Institute. https://papers.ssrn.com/sol3/papers.cfm?abstract_id=4278748. Accessed 22 Feb 2025

Bradford A (2023) Digital empires. The global battle to regulate technology. OUP, Oxford

Brown D (2020) Big tech's heavy hand around the globe. Human Rights Watch. https://www.hrw.org/news/2020/09/08/big-techs-heavy-hand-around-globe. Accessed 22 Feb 2025

Burri M, Kugler K (2024) Regulatory autonomy in digital trade agreements. J Int Econ Law 27(3):397–423

Burri M, Vasquez Callo-Müller M, Kugler K, TAPED (2022) Trade agreement provisions on electronic commerce and data. https://unilu.ch/taped. Accessed 22 Feb 2025

Chander A, Schwartz PM (2023) Privacy and/or trade. Univ Chicago Law Rev 90(1):49

Chander A, Sun H (2023) Sovereignty 2.0. Vanderbilt J Int Law 55(2):283

Data Protection Africa (2024). https://dataprotection.africa/#map. Accessed 22 Feb 2025

Henneman M, Boshe P, von Meding R (2022) African data protection laws—current regulatory approaches, policy initiatives, and the way forward. GPLR 3(2):56–88

Hlomani H, Ncube C (2023) Data regulation in Africa: free flow of data, open data regimes and cybersecurity. In: Ndemo B, Ndung'u N, Odhiambo S, Shimeles A (eds) Data governance and policy in Africa. Palgrave Macmillan, London, pp 97–130

Legal Affairs (Ministerial) 10 February 2024 Durban, South Africa; adopted by the AU Assembly at the 37th AU Summit, 18 February 2024 https://www.bilaterals.org/IMG/pdf/afcfta_digital_trade_protocol_-_9_february_2024_draft.pdf, Accessed 22 Feb 2025

National Data and Cloud Policy (NDCP) (2024) Notice 2533, Government Gazette No 50741 of 31 May 2024 120–165. https://www.gov.za/sites/default/files/gcis_document/202406/50741gen2533.pdf. Accessed 22 Feb 2025

National Data and Cloud Policy (NDCP) – Draft (2021) Government Gazette No 44389 of 21 April 2021 4–39 https://www.gov.za/sites/default/files/gcis_document/202104/44389gon206.pdf, Accessed 22 Feb 2025

Mishra N (2024) International trade law and global data governance. Hart Publishing, Oxford

Mishra N (2022) Can trade agreements narrow the global data divide? A novel agenda for digital trade. Hinrich Foundation Report. https://www.hinrichfoundation.com/research/wp/digital/trade-agreements-global-data-divide/. Accessed 22 Feb 2025

Mishra N (2020) The trade: (cyber)security dilemma and its impact on global cybersecurity governance. J World Trade 54(4):567
Protocol to the agreement establishing the African continental free trade area on digital trade, adopted 18 February 2024. https://au-afcfta.org/wp-content/uploads/2024/11/EN_-PROTOCOL-ON-DIGITAL-TRADE-clean.pdf. Accessed on 8 May 2025
Sucker F (2025) Navigating economic inequalities alongside African digital markets: the role of the AfCFTA protocol on competition policy. Legal Issues Econ Integr 52(1):5–44
Sucker F, Klaaren J (2021) Trade and competition (laws): interrelations from a southern African perspective. In: Kugler K, Sucker F (eds) International economic law: (southern) African perspectives and priorities. Juta, Chapter 14, pp 563–601
Sucker F (2020) The international trading system and market distortions. Hungar Yearbk Int Eur Law HYIEL 2019:169
Tominaga T (2020) Expert commentary: diverse meanings of regulatory "convergence." Ther Innov Regul Sci 54:1138–1140. https://doi.org/10.1007/s43441-020-00135-1
U.S.-Kenya Strategic Trade and Investment Partnership, Docket Number USTR–2022–0008, Federal Register/Vol. 87, No. 150/Friday, August 5, 2022/Notices. https://www.govinfo.gov/content/pkg/FR-2022-08-05/pdf/2022-16798.pdf. Accessed 22 Feb 2025
WTO (2024) Joint statement initiative on electronic commerce, 26 July 2024, WTO INF/ECOM/87 (AEC)
WTO (2023) Electronic commerce negotiations. Updated Consolidated Negotiating Text, 15 Nov 2023, WTO INF/ECOM/62/Rev.5. https://www.bilaterals.org/IMG/pdf/wto_jsi_ecommerce_text_rev_5.pdf. Accessed 22 Feb 2025
WTO (2019) Joint statement on electronic commerce. Communication from Côte d'Ivoire, 16 Dec 2019, WTO INF/ECOM/49
WTO AB European Communities—Measures prohibiting the importation and marketing of seal products. WT/DS/401/AB/R (18 June 2014) (EC – Seal Products)
WTO AB Brazil—Measures affecting imports of retreaded tyres. WT/DS/332/AB/R (17 December 2007) (Brazil – Retreated Tyres)
WTO AB European Communities—measures affecting asbestos and products containing asbestos. WT/DS/135/AB/R (5 April 2001) (EC – Asbestos)
WTO AB United States—import prohibition of certain shrimp and shrimp products. WT/DS58/AB/R (6 November 1998) (US – Shrimp)
WTO AB United States—standards for reformulated and conventional gasoline. WTO/DS2/AB/R (29 April 1996) (US – Gasoline)

Prof. Franziska Sucker is an Associate Professor at the School of Law and Co-Assistant Dean (Postgraduate Affairs) at the Faculty of Commerce, Law and Management (CLM), University of the Witwatersrand (WITS), Johannesburg, where she has been teaching, researching and supervising in the field of international trade law since 2011. Prior to joining WITS, Prof. Sucker held positions at the South African Institute for Advanced Constitutional, Public, Human Rights and International Law (2009–2011); as a Senior Researcher at the Max Planck Institute for Comparative Public Law and International Law in Heidelberg, Germany (2006–2010) and as a Legal Adviser for the Good Governance Programme, Revenue Mobilisation Support at the GIZ in Accra, Ghana (2006). From 2018 to 2024, Prof. Sucker served as Executive Co-Treasurer of the Society of International Economic Law (SIEL). Her research focuses on international trade law, especially digital trade law and trade linkages, with a particular emphasis on African perspectives and approaches.

Dr. Alex Beyleveld is a legal, economics and policy professional with experience in the public, international public, private, NGO and academic sectors. Dr. Beyleveld has a PhD from the Graduate School of Economic Globalisation and Integration at the World Trade Institute, University of Bern. He is also an admitted legal practitioner of the High Court of South Africa (enrolled as an attorney) and a senior researcher at the Mandela Institute (WITS Law School). Alex predominantly works on issues of economic law (international trade, competition and taxation for the most part), technology and public policy, with a particular focus on economic development, inequality and inclusion.

Unlocking Data Sharing Dilemmas: A Comparative Analysis of Business-To-Government Data Sharing Regulations

Barbara Lazarotto

Abstract The sharing of and access to privately held data by governments is a delicate topic. The idea of business-to-government (B2G) data sharing challenges big tech companies' data monopolies to redistribute the value of data to governments as a way to benefit society. In the European Union, the topic gained new nuances with the new European Data Strategy, which seeks to push for further data sharing via multiple methods. The same phenomenon can be seen in the United States, where a few regulatory measures have been recently enacted aiming to enhance business-to-government data-sharing rules between companies present in the sharing economy. However, although there are fundamental differences between the European Union and the United States' data-sharing regulations – especially due to the underlying philosophy behind the idea of data –, it is possible to observe that these manners of regulating B2G data sharing still land the same result: the resistance of privately held data monopolies. Thus, this chapter aims to explore the different forms of regulating B2G data sharing in the EU and US, the pushback from the private sector, and the main results of these methods. Through this paper, we propose not only to proceed with a comparative analysis of the structural choices of these laws but to advance on a holistic analysis of how this comparison can be beneficial to generate structural suggestions for the European Union's future regulations in the area.

Keywords Business-to-government data sharing · Regulations · European Union · United States · Data monopolies

1 Introduction

Data is one of the central aspects of our economy and society. Due to its inner characteristics of non-rivalry, non-excludability (by default), and zero-cost of reproduction, data can be considered to be an essential feature for improvements in several areas

B. Lazarotto (✉)
Vrije Universiteit Brussel, Law, Science, Technology and Society (LSTS), Brussels, Belgium
e-mail: barbara.da.rosa.lazarotto@vub.be

J. Drexl et al. (eds.), *Comparative Data Law*, MPI Studies on Intellectual Property and Competition Law 32, https://doi.org/10.1007/978-3-031-91401-0_9

such as health, well-being, transportation, environment, climate actions, and public service delivery.[1] The impact of data is visible in numbers: According to research by the Organization for Economic Cooperation and Development (OECD), data-driven innovations and data analytics are directly linked to faster productivity and growth by approximately 5% to 10%.[2] Additionally, the use of data and digital technologies in the health sector is deemed to lead to a saving of EUR 120 billion a year.[3] In the mobility sector, data promises to save more than 27 million hours of public transport users' time, benefitting the environment due to reduced CO2 emissions and air pollution.[4]

However, despite the public benefit of data, the sharing between public and private parties is a delicate topic, standing between balancing the power held by the government and the data monopolies of the private sector with the main purpose of distributing the value of data to society. In this context, multiple regulations have emerged in recent years as a tool of governmental mechanisms to achieve the balance between the economic benefits of data and its potential for public interest.[5] This dichotomy is at the center of multiple regulations that compose the European Data Strategy, a package of Regulations enacted in 2020 by the European Commission, which has the objective of enhancing the sharing of data between different parties through multiple manners.[6] This movement is grounded in the assumption that data has multiple aptitudes besides being an economic source, and due to that, its value must be reallocated to other stakeholders.[7] Meanwhile, it is possible to observe a movement in the same direction in the United States, where certain municipalities are enacting business-to-government data-sharing ordinances in a quest to fight against the effects of the sharing economy, such as Airbnb and Uber through the sharing of data to facilitate public sector overview. Nonetheless, the American conception of data is mostly focused on its economic asset angle, infiltrating governmental actions against data monopolies.

Although there are fundamental differences between the European and American business-to-government data-sharing approaches, this study will demonstrate that it is possible to observe that the results are similar on both sides of the Atlantic. Regulations are faced with strong pushback from the private sector, grounding their rejections in intellectual property rights and the protection of the privacy of data subjects to avoid sharing data with other parties, especially the public sector. The

[1] Floridi (2010), p. 30.

[2] OECD (2015).

[3] Eastburn et al. (2024).

[4] Huyer and van Knippenberg (2020).

[5] Ranchordas (2017), p. 52.

[6] This study will focus its analysis on the Data Governance Act and the Data Act, both part of the European Data Strategy.

[7] The strategy does not explicitly mention the term "reallocation"; however, it emphasizes that the concentration of data in the hands of a few players in the economy leads to market imbalances, which hinder economic development.

deepening of data monopolies at the same time exposes the continuous need to expand further business-to-government data sharing.

In this context, this research aims to explore the different conceptions of data by the European Union and the United States, proposing not only to proceed with a comparative analysis of the structural choices of these laws but to advance on a holistic analysis of how this comparison can be beneficial to generate structural suggestions for the European Union's future regulations in the area. To do so, this study is organized as follows. Following the Introduction, Sect. 2 will explore data and its value chain, focusing on its different conceptions as an economic asset with public interest. Afterward, the analysis will move to explore how data is perceived differently across the Atlantic, in the EU, and in the United States, setting the foundation for the following analysis. Section 3 dives into the general aspects of data sharing, moving to business-to-government data sharing and the different regulations in the EU and the United States on the topic which demonstrate the difference between these two legal frameworks. At last, Sect. 4 will focus its concluding remarks on the analysis of the differences between the American and the European approaches and how we can learn from them.

2 Data and Its Value Chain

In English, the word data comes from Latin datum, around the seventeenth century, used in the realm of mathematics. However, it was only in the eighteenth century that the word data was used more frequently to refer to a result of an investigation. The use of the word possibly in the eighteenth century laid the foundation for its contemporary meaning in the twenty-first century, which is a combination of information in numerical form and a premise for an argument.[8]

Despite different definitions, humanity has always collected, stored, and analyzed data for centuries as a method to record and manage their activities, such as agricultural recordings in the Nile Basin. For a long period, data did not mean a thing. In fact, it was considered to be a burden by governments and companies that had to spend energy and resources to store and keep track of it with no economic benefits, such as accounting books and paper files. Yet, the relationship between humans and data has taken a shift with the development and widespread technology, especially computers and the internet. They have allowed the creation of an interactive and responsive environment of information processes where the boundaries between the material and the immaterial are blurred.

This process has shifted the way we perceive data, transforming it into a useful resource that has multiple rationales: data as information, data as an economic asset, and data as a public good. This new reality has elevated data to a new meaning,

[8] Rosenberg (2013), p. 15–40.

creating a potential for a new revolution of the same stature as agricultural and industrial revolutions.[9] Through a process of establishing correlations between different sets of data, datasets cannot only reveal details about a single individual's behavior but also predict future occurrences, such as climate predictions and virus spreads, providing better and tailored services. With that said, considering the availability of digital information, private companies began to collect and process large amounts of data, extracting complete and accurate insights about consumer preferences and obtaining profit from this data. This movement marked a paradigm shift; whereas data was considered a burden, now it is an asset that companies and governments hold on to very dearly.[10]

Generally, data is either seen as a thing, such as a fixed object or as a wave-like fluid. It was following this logic that one of the most famous metaphors, "data is the new oil," emerged alluding to the ubiquity and the quantity of data, and its potential value as a commodity and as a social and technical asset. At the same time, data flows and can be stored in "data lakes" or "data warehouses," metaphors often adopted by the industry to explain the aggregation and management of data resources.[11] Following this logic, data has been treated as a combination of "data as form" and "data as flow," allowing private companies and individuals to profit from this amorphous asset.

This cycle of data collection, processing, and profitable inferences has led to the creation of data monopolies. This can be defined as the large amounts of siloed data held by major tech companies, which are collected from free services and processed for profit.[12] According to a report issued by the Organization for Economic Cooperation and Development (OECD) in 2019, some 1.4 trillion dollars of the combined 1.9 trillion dollars in market value of Alphabet and Facebook comes from user's data. It is due to these huge numbers that some affirm that data can now be considered a commodity, "the new oil" or "the new gold" for innovation and economic growth.[13] Different industries accumulate different kinds of data to fit their own motivations and goals. Value can also be extracted from many other kinds of data about things like machinery, transportation, and moon phases. Different types of data are valued differently by different businesses. The larger and more diverse a data silo is, the more information and uses can be derived from it. One individual's data may not be readily converted to economic capital, but the aggregated data of hundreds, thousands, and millions of individuals can be immensely valuable.[14]

In this context, data monopolies are mostly composed of companies that are reliant on a data-driven network effect, meaning that the more data the company has, the better the product due to its capacity to generate more precise data-based recommendation systems. This has two main consequences: creating high degrees

[9] Floridi (2010).

[10] De Gregorio and Ranchordás (2020), pp. 204–231.

[11] European Commission. (2011).

[12] Sadowski (2019).

[13] Apráez (2021).

[14] OECD (2019).

of dependence from businesses and end-users and lock-in effects, which eventually impact the distribution of data for the public good. Due to this data-driven relationship, it is possible to affirm that data is also a form of capital since, without it, many of these technologies and organizations would not be able to operate, let alone be able to generate value. Data capital can be described as discrete bits of information that are digitally recorded, machine-processable, easily agglomerated, and highly mobile. Like social and cultural capital, data capital is convertible to economic capital, but not only that. It is institutionalized in the information infrastructure of collecting, storing, and processing data: that is, smart devices, online platforms, data analytics, network cables, and server farms. These characteristics of data capital means it can be continually captured and circulated; thus, data collection is driven by the logic of capital accumulation as described by Karl Marx.[15]

In this context, data sharing has emerged as a suitable alternative to redistribute the benefits of data to society since once data is generated, it can be shared and used by multiple users for different purposes an unlimited number of times, both in the public and the private sector.[16] A report produced according to research by the Organization for Economic Cooperation and Development (OECD) in 2019 has pointed out several benefits that emerge from data sharing, such as enhancement of transparency, accountability and user empowerment, new business opportunities, and increased efficiency.[17] However, despite all the potential benefits that may come with the sharing of data, the road ahead is still bumpy and unsure as it will be further explored.

2.1 *How Data is Perceived: EU-US Landscape*

This logic of seeing data as "form" and "flow" was transposed to how data is perceived both in the European Union and the United States, and it is precisely the different ways data can be perceived across the Atlantic that has shaped how these two different legal systems regulate business-to-government data sharing. Although privacy policies and data regulation in Europe and the United States are a result of a combination of technological, social, and political factors, big differences still remain.[18]

It is worth noting that although the initial movements of data regulation were taken at a federal level in the United States with the Privacy Act in 1974, in the European Union this movement was initiated by the Member States with the 1973 Swedish Data Act, the 1977 West German Data Protection Act, and the 1984 British Data Protection

[15] Gunst and De Ville (2021).

[16] Purtova (2008), p. 193.

[17] Hummel (2021), p. 545–572.

[18] Hummel (2021), p. 545–572.

Act.[19] However, this paradigm was inverted afterward, with the fragmentation of the American approach which took a sectorial path to data regulation in comparison to the European cross-sectoral approach. Not to mention the privacy regulations that are located at a state level in the United States[22] in comparison to the European General Data Protection Regulation, which was intended to homogenize Europe's data protection approach, some authors argue that the heterogeneity still remains.[20]

Colin J. Bennett highlights in his seminal work on data protection in both the US and EU that the American approach to data regulation has been mainly characterized by disagreement, competition, and negotiation amongst different stakeholders and interest groups, a practice influenced by the American tradition of individualism and the emphasis on individual rights and liberties. The US has a more restrictive approach to privacy, placing commercial purposes for the use of data above data privacy in certain situations. This is in contrast with the European consensual approach to policymaking, which led to the development of common principles and objectives in the Union.[21] This movement was very influenced by the EU Charter of Fundamental Rights which established data protection as a fundamental right, causing a butterfly effect that led to the approval of the General Data Protection Regulation (GDPR) in 2016. The GDPR, following this European tradition of protection of personal data, has provided data subjects several data protection rights, while trying to balance the free flow of personal data. Hence, as a result of the Brussels Effect of the GDPR, the United States has seen a surge in data privacy regulations such as the California Consumer Privacy Act (CCPA) and the California Privacy Rights Act (CPRA) of 2020, which amends and expands the CCPA, which applies to consumers who are California residents, granting them opt-out rights and introducing changes to the privacy law.[22]

Due to the abovementioned development of data protection as a fundamental right, the dominant view in legal theory is that individual ownership of data goes in conflict with data protection frameworks that suggest that data-related rights are inalienable and unsuitable for propertization, commodification, and commercialization.[23] At the same time, regulations do not ignore the fact that despite that, there is already an ongoing phenomenon of commodification of personal data which is the core feature of big tech business models.[24] It is within this context that the topic of data sharing emerges.

---

[19] Such as the California Consumer Privacy Act and the California Privacy Rights Act. For a complete track of the US State Privacy Legislation see International Association of Privacy Professionals. US State Privacy Legislation Tracker." Last modified June 17, 2024. https://iapp.org/resources/article/us-state-privacy-legislation-tracker/. Accessed 24 February 2025.

[20] Bennett (1992).

[21] Van der Sloot (2018).

[22] Bennett (1992).

[23] Gunst and De Ville (2021).

[24] Purtova (2008), p. 193.

3 General Aspects of Data Sharing

Data sharing is a concept that refers to data being shared between two or more organizations or individuals.[25] Data sharing can take place in multiple forms, between public and private parties such as business-to-business, business-to-individual, and between business-to-public parties. It is a phenomenon that has emerged in the context of the massive collection of multiple types of data by different stakeholders, and that promises to help generate social and economic benefits between 0.1% and 1.5% of gross domestic product (GDP) in the case of public-sector data, and between 1% and 2.5% of GDP (in few other studies up to 4% of GDP) when also including private-sector data.[26] There are different rationales for the sharing of data between parties, namely necessity, asymmetry, reciprocity, efficiency, stability, and legitimacy.[27]

Data sharing in the context of efficiency, stability, and legitimacy is the sharing of data that occurs "behind the scenes" where private organizations share data for cost savings, uncertainty reduction, and reputational reasons. This includes the sharing of data in the context of donorship, where data is shared for free in the context of corporate social responsibility. However, data partnerships, such as data intermediaries, where third parties are requested to process shared data for a specific objective – are the most common method of data sharing since they offer benefits to private companies that do business with scarce data while creating a cycle of reciprocal benefits by avoiding wasting resources with duplicate data collection and maintenance.[28]

Data sharing, due to necessity, refers to mandates and authority-based requests for data sharing, such as legislation and regulation. This is present in the recent data regulations but has also been present throughout history in the context of private sector compliance with laws such as tax compliance, workers' rights, and other situations. Necessity also encompasses asymmetry in the recent regulations, especially in the European Union, where regulations demand the sharing of data in the context of power asymmetries, such as in the context of data monopolies.[29]

3.1 *Business-To-Government Data Sharing*

In the past, governments were the ones that held the biggest amount of data about an individual, for instance, ID number, social security, address, and phone number. Now, this paradigm has shifted. Private companies – often big tech companies – hold more data than any government has ever dreamed of.[30] At the same time, the

---

[25] De Gregorio and Ranchordás (2020), p. 204–231; Harvey, and Tulloch (2006), p. 743–768.

[26] Harvey and Tulloch (2006), p. 743–768.

[27] OECD (2019).

[28] Welch (2016), p. 393–403.

[29] Azad, and Wiggins (1995), p. 22–43; De Gregorio and Ranchordás (2020), p. 204–231; Welch (2016), p. 393–403.

[30] Richter (2021), p. 529–572.

sharing of data between private companies and governments is not a new concept. There is a myriad of laws and regulations that oblige companies to share information to assist governments in observing accountability by the private sector to certain laws, such as financial information for tax purposes. This type of data sharing has been effective; for instance, empirical work has shown that coercive regulations have helped implement an effective online anti-corruption system in Korea.[31]

However, it is important to point out that private companies—especially big tech companies—harvest and generate a huge amount of data that is kept under their management and access. Thus, a large amount of data is publicly relevant but not shared. In this context, business-to-government data sharing (B2G) emerges as an alternative to redistributing data from private data monopolies to the public sector.

The United States and the European Union, with their unique historical backgrounds and diverse philosophical frameworks, have adopted distinct methods of regulating the sharing of data between private and public entities. To better understand these discrepancies, the following section will delve into the nuances of each approach by analyzing different categories of B2G data sharing, with the objective of making a complete analysis of both countries.

3.2 *The EU Legal Landscape on Business-To-Government Data Sharing*

When it comes to business-to-government data sharing, the European Union has gradually built a diverse set of regulations that aims to incentivize the sharing of data between different parties. One of the most relevant examples is the EU Free Flow of Non-Personal Data Regulation,[32] which aims to remove unjustified national measures and avoid possible lock-in factors in non-personal data. Some also defend that the General Data Protection Regulation (GDPR) can be considered a regulation that incentivizes (or does not hinder) the sharing of data due to its dual aspect of protecting the right to data protection while enhancing the flow of data in the internal market.[33] Yet others might also see the GDPR as an obstacle to further data sharing due to its strict regulation on the sharing and re-use of data present in Article 6 and in the principles of purpose limitation and data minimization present in Article 5.

Nevertheless, it is the first position in which the European Commission has grounded its European Data Strategy published in 2020. A package of regulations that covers the sharing of data between different parties, such as business-to-business

[31] Seongcheol et al. (2009), p. 42–50.

[32] Regulation (EU) 2018/1807 of the European Parliament and of the Council of 14 November 2018 on a framework for the free flow of non-personal data in the European Union.

[33] Regulation (EU) 2016/679 of the European Parliament and of the Council of 27 April 2016 on the protection of natural persons with regard to the processing of personal data and on the free movement of such data, and repealing Directive 95/46/EC (General Data Protection Regulation).

and from the public sector to the private sector, with the main objective of all these proposals to create a breeding ground for a free-flowing data economy.[34]

The first regulation of the package to come into force in June 2022 was the Data Governance Act (DGA), aiming to Develop a borderless digital internal market and a human-centric, trustworthy, and secure data society and economy by creating a harmonized framework for data exchanges and laying down certain basic requirements for data governance, covering public and private non-personal data and personal data voluntarily made available by data holders. The actors that are regulated by the act are data intermediation service providers, public sector bodies, and data altruism organizations.[35]

Although the DGA mostly focuses on the re-use of public sector data for commercial and non-commercial purposes, it also creates data governance mechanisms that facilitate the sharing of data for reuse; in this context, the DGA emphasizes broader aspects of data governance, including intermediary-assisted data sharing and altruistic data practices. These efforts align with the goal of fostering common European data spaces. These data intermediary services can be later used to enhance the sharing of data between private and public institutions.[36] Data intermediation services, according to Article 2 of the DGA, are new services that have the main purpose of data sharing between an undetermined number of data subjects and data holders on the one hand and data users on the other through technical legal and other means." Thus, data intermediation services tackle one of the main obstacles of B2G data sharing, which is the protection of data throughout the sharing process, offering auxiliary functionalities such as anonymization services.[37]

The last regulation as part of the Data Strategy to enter into force in January 2024 was the Data Act, aiming to establish fair rules for data access and use in the EU, promoting innovation and protecting trade secrets, and creating a fair data economy by balancing the interests of data holders and users. It covers private sector data, personal and non-personal data, and co-generated data by establishing explicit obligations of data access and portability on connected products and services data and on data used by data processing services.[38]

When it comes to business-to-government data sharing the Data Act is innovative, dedicating Chapter V to business-to-government data sharing provisions. The chapter begins with Article 14, which establishes a general obligation to make data and relevant metadata available in exceptional circumstances where the data is needed to carry out legal responsibilities in the public interest. Article 15 outlines the specific circumstances that can be considered as constituting an Exceptional need and puts

[34] This conflict of interests that is often treated as non-contradictory is also emphasized in and van der Sloot (2023).

[35] Communication From The Commission To The European Parliament, The Council, The European Economic And Social Committee and The Committee Of The Regions, A European Strategy For Data, Com/2020/66 Final.

[36] Pathak (2024).

[37] Ruohonen and Mickelsson (2023), p. 10.

[38] Ruohonen and Mickelsson (2023), p. 10.

limitations on both the time and scope of such requests. These circumstances include when data is requested to respond to a public emergency, to prevent a public emergency, or to assist in the recovery from it. Additionally, an exceptional need exists when the lack of available data prevents a public sector body from fulfilling a specific task in the public interest that has been explicitly provided for by law. Article 15 is closely related to Recitals 56, 57, and 58, which are the guides for defining what can be considered exceptional needs and public emergencies.

The concept of Exceptional need, which was not included in the initial Proposal, has been elaborated on in Recital 56 and defined as unforeseeable and limited in time, as opposed to other circumstances that may be planned, scheduled, periodic, or frequent. Additionally, Recital 57 provides examples of public emergencies, such as public health, climate change, environmental degradation, and cybersecurity incidents. Recital 58 emphasizes that if the lack of timely access to requested data hinders fulfilling a specific task, this task should fall within the competence of the public sector body making the request and should be explicitly outlined in their mandate. It goes on to list examples of such tasks, such as local transport or city planning, as well as the enhancement of structural services such as energy, waste, and water management. This clarification with regard to "public interest" was put forward in the joint opinion by EDPB-EDPS.[39] Finally, it can be said that the Data Act opens new avenues to business-to-government data sharing in the EU data framework, although some may say they are still restricted.[40]

Lastly, the most recent approved regulation in the realm of business-to-government data sharing is the regulation on the collection and sharing of data related to short-term accommodation rental services such as Airbnb.[41] It aims to create a data-sharing framework between hosts and platforms to inform effective and proportionate local policies, reducing bureaucracy for hosts, impacting the market, and facilitating the development of urban planning plans through data harmonization. Regulating a market that has brought disruptions to European municipalities, impacting renting prices and the tourism market while causing regulatory uncertainty and data deficit for municipalities, makes public oversight even more difficult.[42] To do so, the Regulation demands the sharing of data such as the host's name, national identification number, or any other identification information, address, telephone number, and mail address. Under this Regulation, platforms must design and organize their interface in a way that makes it possible for hosts to self-declare where the rental service is located, allowing the creation of a "short-term services map", with "red zones" areas in which short-term rentals are forbidden.

[39] EDPB-EDPS Joint Opinion 2/2022 on the Proposal of the European Parliament and of the Council on harmonized rules on fair access to and use of data (Data Act).

[40] Da Rosa Lazarotto (2022); da Rosa Lazarotto (2023).

[41] Regulation (EU) 2024/1028 of the European Parliament and of the Council of 11 April 2024 on data collection and sharing relating to short-term accommodation rental services and amending Regulation (EU) 2018/1724Text with EEA relevance.

[42] Scassa (2017), p. 1017.

Following this analysis it is possible to observe that within the European Union, the B2G regulatory framework encompasses regulations that facilitate both voluntary and mandatory data sharing with the objective of allowing the flow of data to the economy but also to facilitate public policies. This is grounded on the premise of the internal market regulatory competency of the EU but also the rejection of data ownership claims by the EU's data regulatory framework. In this context, the Data Governance Act does not impose any specific data sharing requirements, but it strives to establish a reliable environment that encourages voluntary data sharing, potentially benefiting B2G data exchanges. In contrast, the Data Act enforce data sharing mandates to support public decision-making processes although it also emphasizes that other types of voluntary B2G data sharing are not forbidden, finally, the Short-Term Rental Regulation enforce data sharing mandates to support public decision-making processes, such as regulation of short-term rentals.

3.3 *The US Legal Landscape on Business-To-Government Data Sharing*

When it comes to the United States legal landscape on B2G data sharing, although the US has a more liberal history of regulatory measures, especially in the data protection realm,[43] a few business-to-government data-sharing regulations have emerged recently. They serve both as a regulatory and as a data collection function, with the main objective of correcting market defects caused by sharing platforms, emulating the initial development of regulation in the US with the Sherman Act in 1890.[44]

One of the first mandatory B2G data sharing regulations was enacted by the city of San Francisco in 2016, which required sharing platform drivers to apply for business licenses if they drive seven or more days a year; this information would then be publicly available in a database.[45]

In 2019, the Los Angeles Department of Transportation (LADOT) launched a groundbrea- king initiative by introducing the largest dockless mobility program in the United States. This program granted permission for approximately 37,000 dockless vehicles to operate on the city streets. As part of this innovative program, dockless on-demand mobility products were required to obtain a permit from the city. This permit facilitated the creation of a sophisticated mobility interface that gathered real-time data on the utilization of vehicles, as well as their pickup and drop-off locations. This data was instrumental in informing the development of public traffic

[43] Regulation (EU) (2016). It is outside of the scope of this paper to explore the differences between the EU and US conceptualizations of data protection and privacy. On this topic, See Bakare et al. (2024), p. 528–543 and Fuster (2014).

[44] Ducci and Tremblay-Huet (2018), p. 295–318.

[45] Scassa (2017), p. 1017.

management policies, allowing for more efficient and responsive urban transportation solutions.[46]

In 2018, New York City enacted Local Law 146, demanding home-sharing platforms, such as Airbnb, to share data with the city's Committee on Housing and Buildings such as the physical address of the premises; the legal name, phone number, email, address, and physical address of the host, and the URL and other identifications of the listing on the platform's website.[47]

When it comes to voluntary data sharing landscape, the American environment is quite more liberal than the European one when it comes to personal data. As Chander Kaminski and McGeveran emphasize, the new wave of privacy regulations recently enacted in the US follows the "Virginia Model of the Virginia's Consumer Data Protection Act of 2021, with a strong business friendly model which allow the voluntary B2G data sharing model, which includes personal data through private contracts and agreements.[48]

Additionally, mandatory data-sharing ordinances faced strong pushback from the industry. Amongst different arguments, the main one was that the data collected by these companies is a part of their business records, which is owned by the company, and that the company has a possessory interest. This argument is grounded in overall american legal framework which ensures companies have control and possessory interest in their records, with some regulations dictating how they manage them.[49] This essentially creates a legal and tech barrier that prevents further sharing of data.[50]

4 Concluding Remarks: Analyzing the Variances in Business-To- Government Data Sharing Regulations

The previous section explored the business-to-government data-sharing regulation landscape both in the European Union and in the United States, observing their differences and similarities both at a foundational and a basic level.

The initial analysis reveals that the landscape for sharing data between businesses and the government is significantly different in the United States compared to the EU. Firstly, the regulations mentioned earlier are implemented at a local level, reflecting the federal organizational structure of the United States, as opposed to the EU's regulatory framework which aims to be more or less homogeneous in all Member States. Additionally, data sharing regulations between businesses and the government

[46] Ranchordás (2019), p. 203–237. Arcila (2021), p. 1015.

[47] Arcila (2021), p. 1015.

[48] Chander et al. (2020); Newell et al. (2023).

[49] Such as The Securities and Exchange Commission (SEC) that has regulations that require publicly traded companies to maintain and disclose certain business records to investors, and Internal Revenue Service (IRS) regulations that require companies to maintain business records for tax purposes.

[50] Scassa (2017), p. 1017.

in the US are enacted in specific sectors, while in the EU they are more broadly applicable across multiple sectors.[51]

The second point worth noting that the perception of data differs significantly between Europe and America, leading to distinct regulatory approaches in the two regions. In Europe, while data is recognized for its economic importance, it is not considered an asset that can be owned. Additionally, the public interest aspect of data is acknowledged, resulting in the enactment of broader regulations in B2G data sharing for other purposes than public oversight. This approach is heavily influenced by the EU's view of data protection as a fundamental human right, equating it with free speech and due process and necessitating constitutional protections. Conversely, the concept of "privacy in the United States is narrower in scope, accommodating more liberal and commercial use of data in American markets. This fundamental difference in perspective on data's ownership and public interest implications has far-reaching effects on the regulatory landscape in both Europe and America.[52]

Based on the analysis, it is evident that Business-to-Government (B2G) data sharing in the United States will continue to have limitations, particularly for purposes related to policymaking, such as traffic management and the regulation of short-term rental platforms. Conversely, in the European Union (EU), B2G data sharing regulations are set to be significantly influenced by data protection laws, particularly the General Data Protection Regulation (GDPR). although they have more room to develop due to the European emphasis on data as a common good that should flow. This influence is expected to introduce potential challenges to the sharing of data for various purposes. Furthermore, in the United States, the impact of these data protection regulations is anticipated to be relatively minimal, mainly due to the already established business-friendly privacy regulatory framework.

References

Apráez BE (2021) Reconsidering the public-private data dichotomy in the European Union's data sharing policies. Eur J Law Technol 12(1):1–30

Arcila BB (2021) The case for local data sharing ordinances. Wm & Mary Bill Rts J 30:1015

Azad B, Wiggins LL (1995) Dynamics of inter-organizational geographic data sharing: a conceptual framework for research. Sharing Geogr Inf 2:22–43

Bakare SS, Adeniyi AO, Akpuokwe CU, Eneh NE (2024) Data privacy laws and compliance: a comparative review of the EU GDPR and USA regulations. Comput Sci IT Res J 5(3):528–543

Bennett CJ (1992) Regulating privacy: data protection and public policy in Europe and the United States. Cornell University Press, Ithaca

Chander A, Kaminski ME, McGeveran W (2020) Catalyzing privacy law. Minn L Rev 105:1733

Communication From The Commission To The European Parliament, The Council, The European Economic And Social Committee and The Committee Of The Regions, A European Strategy For Data, Com/2020/66 Final

[51] Mendez (2010), p. 617–645.

[52] Newell et al. (2023).

da Rosa Lazarotto B (2022) The data act: empty promises for business-to-government data sharing? A critical analysis of the Proposal on the Data Act and its implications for the redistribution of data. Privacy in Germany (PinG) Datenschutz und Compliance Journal

da Rosa Lazarotto B (2023) Business-to-government data sharing on the data act: between a rock and a hard place. EU law live

De Gregorio G, Ranchordás S (2020) Breaking down information silos with big data: a legal analysis of data sharing. In: Cannataci J, Falce V, Pollicino O (eds) Legal challenges of big data. Edward Elgar Publishing, Cheltenham, pp 204–231

Ducci F, Tremblay-Huet S (2018) CHAPTER IX Competition law and policy issues in the sharing economy. In: Law and the "Sharing Economy": Regulating Online Market Platforms, edited by Derek McKee, Finn Makela, Teresa Scassa, Harry Arthurs, Francesco Ducci, Marie-Cécile Escande-Varniol, Vincent Gautrais, Michael Geist, Eran Kaplinsky, Nofar Sheffi, Sabrina Tremblay-Huet, Eric Tucker and Mariana Valverde, Ottawa: University of Ottawa Press, 2018 pp 295–318

Eastburn J, Fowkes J, Kellner K, Swanson B (2024) Digital transformation: Health systems' investment priorities. McKinsey & Company. https://www.mckinsey.com/industries/healthcare/our-insights/digital-transformation-health-systems-investment-priorities. Accessed 24 Feb 2025

European Data Protection Board & European Data Protection Supervisor (2022) EDPB-EDPS joint opinion 2/2022 on the proposal of the European Parliament and of the Council on harmonized rules on fair access to and use of data (Data Act)

European Commission (2011) Digital agenda: turning government data into gold. Brussels, Belgium

Floridi L (2010) Information: a very short introduction. OUP, Oxford

Fuster GG (2014) The emergence of personal data protection as a fundamental right of the EU, vol 16. Springer, Berlin

Graef I, van der Sloot B (2024) The legal consistency of technology regulation in Europe, Bloomsbury Academic, 2024

Gunst S, De Ville F (2021) The Brussels effect: how the GDPR conquered Silicon Valley. Eur Foreign Affairs Rev 26(3):437–458

Harvey F, Tulloch D (2006) Local-government data sharing: evaluating the foundations of spatial data infrastructures. Int J Geogr Inf Sci 20(7):743–768

Hummel P, Braun M, Dabrock P (2021) Own data? Ethical reflections on data ownership. Philos Technol 34(3):545–572

Huyer E, van Knippenberg L (2020) The economic impact of open data: opportunities for value creation in Europe. European Commission

Kim S, Kim HJ, Lee H (2009) An institutional analysis of an e-government system for anti-corruption: the case of OPEN. Gov Inf Q 26(1):42–50

Mendez F, Mendez M (2010) Comparing privacy regimes: federal theory and the politics of privacy regulation in the European Union and the United States. Publius J Federal 40(4):617–645

Newell BC, Purtova N, Moon YE, Paterson III HJ (2023) Regulating the US consumer data market: comparing the material scope of US consumer data privacy laws and the GDPR. University of Pennsylvania Journal of International Law, Forthcoming, Utrecht University School of Law Research Paper

OECD (2019) Enhancing access to and sharing of data: Reconciling risks and benefits for data re-use across societies. OECD Publishing

OECD (2015) Data-driven innovation: big data for growth and well-being. OECD Publishing

Pathak M (2024) Data governance redefined: the evolution of EU data regulations from the GDPR to the DMA, DSA, DGA, Data Act and AI Act. DSA, DGA, Data Act and AI Act (February 6, 2024)

Purtova N (2088) Property in personal data: a European perspective on the instrumentalist theory of propertisation. Eur J Legal Stud 2:193

Ranchordas S (2015) Innovation experimentalism in the age of the sharing economy. Lewis & Clark l Rev 19:871

Ranchordas S (2017) Consultations, citizen narratives and evidence-based regulation. Eur J Law Reform 19:52

Ranchordás S (2018) On sharing and quasi-sharing: the tension between sharing-economy practices, public policy, and regulation. The rise of the sharing economy: exploring the challenges and opportunities of collaborative consumption. Greenwood Publishers, Denver, pp 263–290

Ranchordás S (2019) Public values, private regulators: between regulation and reputation in the sharing economy. Law Ethics Hum Rights 13(2):203–237

Regulation (EU) 2016/679 of the European Parliament and of the Council of 27 April 2016 on the protection of natural persons with regard to the processing of personal data and on the free movement of such data, and repealing Directive 95/46/EC (General Data Protection Regulation). (2016). Official Journal of the European Union, L 119, 1–88

Regulation (EU) 2018/1807 of the European Parliament and of the Council of 14 November 2018 on a framework for the free flow of non-personal data in the European Union. (2018). Official Journal of the European Union, L 303, 59–68

Regulation (EU) 2024/1028 of the European Parliament and of the Council of 11 April 2024 on data collection and sharing relating to short-term accommodation rental services and amending Regulation (EU) 2018/1724. (2024). Official Journal of the European Union, L 126, 34–48

Richter H (2021) The law and policy of government access to private sector data ('B2G data sharing'). In: Data access, consumer interests and public welfare. Nomos Verlagsgesellschaft mbH & Co. KG., pp 529–572

Rosenberg D (2013) Data before the fact

Ruohonen J, Mickelsson S (2023) Reflections on the data governance act. Digit Soc 2(1):10

Sadowski J (2019) When data is capital: datafication, accumulation, and extraction. Big Data Soc 6(1):2053951718820549

Scassa T (2017) Sharing data in the platform economy: a public interest argument for access to platform data. UBCL Rev 50:1017

US State Privacy Legislation Tracker (2024) US State privacy legislation tracker. International Association of Privacy Professionals. https://iapp.org/resources/article/us-state-privacy-legislation-tracker/. Accessed 24 Feb 2025

Van der Sloot B (2018) Legal consistency after the General Data Protection Regulation and the Police Directive. Eur J Law Technol 9(3):1–18

Van der Sloot B (2023) Data protection rights for legal persons. Eur Data Prot Law Rev (EDPL) 9:2

Welch EW, Feeney MK, Park CH (2016) Determinants of data sharing in US city governments. Gov Inf Q 33(3):393–403

Barbara Lazarotto is a PhD researcher at the Law, Science, Technology & Society (LSTS) Research Group at Vrije Universiteit Brussel and an executive member of the Brussels Privacy Hub. She is also a former Marie-Sklodowska-Curie fellow.

Navigating the Data Transfer Maze: Understanding Intra-African Approaches to Data Transfers

Mercy King'ori and Ridwan Oloyede

Abstract This chapter explores existing data protection laws in 40 African countries. Particularly, the chapter analyses the existing data transfer mechanisms for intra-African data transfer within these frameworks. In light of growing interest in international data transfers globally, like the rest of the world, Africa's focus has been on legal approaches to transferring data out of the continent. This outward-facing perspective on data transfers can be attributed to the need to align with international best practices, integration, and participation in the global digital economy. However, efforts to improve intra-African trade in goods and services on a continent with the lowest intra-continental trade, particularly in this digital era, appear to be redirecting the focus back to Africa, owing to continental-wide initiatives to ensure the free flow of goods and services among countries. The chapter examines intra-African approaches by identifying, categorising and analysing the tools and conditions applicable to intra-African data transfers. A cursory look at cross-border transfer provisions reveals that the laws provide mechanisms for facilitating transfers similar to those found in widely adopted laws such as the European Union General Data Protection Regulation (GDPR). However, a closer look reveals that the conditions for implementing some of the tools vary, indicating unique adaptations of data protection regulations that could impact the free flow of data within the continent. Therefore, the chapter aims to provide policymakers, lawmakers, and practitioners with a clear understanding of Africa's diverse and nuanced landscape to ground and support data protection interoperability efforts and facilitate the flow of data within the continent.

M. King'ori (✉)
Nairobi, Kenya
e-mail: mkingori@fpf.org

R. Oloyede
Lagos, Nigeria
e-mail: ro@techhiveadvisory.africa

J. Drexl et al. (eds.), *Comparative Data Law*, MPI Studies on Intellectual Property and Competition Law 32, https://doi.org/10.1007/978-3-031-91401-0_10

1 Introduction

The dynamics of cross-border data transfers (CBDT) have always been important for countries worldwide, and Africa is no exception. Since the first data protection law in Africa, in 2001, in Cabo Verde, 39 other countries have enacted comprehensive data protection laws,[1] 39 of which have specific provisions that address CBDT.[2] The emergence of the digital economy has served to amplify these discussions on CBDT as countries seek to protect the personal data of their citizens and residents as they move to other jurisdictions. Within the African context, the evolving landscape of intra-continental trade initiatives that hold profound implications for economic development, innovation, and regional collaboration has brought the importance of CBDT to the forefront.[3] Continental-wide initiatives such as the African Continental Free Trade Area Agreement (AfCFTA) seek to improve intra-continental trade on a continent with the lowest intra-continental trade in the world,[4] calling for the "elimination of the adverse effects of measures on trade in services to boost intra-African trade in services."[5] The Digital Trade Protocol under the AfCFTA Agreement provides rules on cross-border data flows.[6] Similarly, the continental strategy on data governance, the African Union Data Policy Framework, views the free flow of data as an enabler of cross-border trade and dissuades states from imposing broad data localisation provisions.[7] Particularly, it calls for states to take a cautious approach towards data localisation requirements and other restrictions on cross-border data flow as part of creating a digital single market. This means that a key aspect of the free flow of goods and services in Africa is the free flow of data among African countries.[8]

The concept of international data transfer lacks a precise and accepted definition in many African data protection laws. While these laws often outline mechanisms for data transfer, they fall short of clearly defining what constitutes an international data transfer. However, Kenya's Data Protection (General) Regulation provides a more operational definition. According to this regulation, international data transfer is the transmission of personal data from Kenya to an external entity.[9] This includes any act

[1] Algeria, Angola, Benin, Botswana, Burkina Faso, Chad, Cote d'Ivoire, Democratic Republic of Congo, Egypt, Equatorial Guinea, Eswatini, Ethiopia, Gabon, Ghana, Guinea, Kenya, Lesotho, Madagascar, Malawi, Mali, Mauritania, Mauritius, Morocco, Niger, Nigeria, Republic of Congo, Rwanda, Sao Tome & Principe, Senegal, Seychelles, Somalia, South Africa, Tanzania, Togo, Tunisia, Uganda, Zambia, and Zimbabwe.

[2] While Ghana does not have a specific provision that addresses CBDT, Seychelles', repealed data protection law does not have a clear mechanism for CBDT like other laws. Article 16 of the law envisages data transfer to other countries, but it is silent on the mechanisms to facilitate it.

[3] ElGanainy AA, et al. (2023); Ridwan O (2019).

[4] African Union (2012).

[5] Baker P, Quiles P, Bheenick S (2023).

[6] Kipkoech DA (2023).

[7] King'ori M. (2023).

[8] Salami E. (2022).

[9] Article 39 of Data Protection (General) Regulation.

of transmitting, sharing, or storing personal or sensitive data outside the country of its original collection. The definition suggests that international data transfer occurs when an entity transmits data outside Kenya to another entity. This definition aligns with the European Data Protection Board's (EDPB) 3-step criteria.[10] CBDT can occur for various reasons, including business, regulatory, or technological needs. Essentially, international data transfer involves the cross-border sharing of personal data between different entities, each functioning as a controller, joint controller, or processor.[11]

The CBDT provisions within the data protection laws are expected to play a decisive role in regulating the free flow of personal data within the continent. A key aspect of the expansive discussion on CBDT relates to the tools and accompanying mechanisms or conditions for data transfer. While Europe's data protection legal framework, which allows data to flow freely within the European Economic Area (EEA) without the need for additional safeguards, has had a major influence on the content of African data protection laws, the free flow of personal data in Africa would be elusive under the current national legal data protection frameworks. Indeed, a cursory look at the CBDT provisions of African laws reveals the heavy influence of European data protection legal frameworks such as the GDPR, its predecessor, and the OECD Guidelines on the Protection of Privacy and Transborder Flows of Personal Data.[12] Broadly, numerous commentators on the state of data protection laws on the continent have posited that the text of African data protection laws resembles that of internationally accepted legal frameworks such as the OECD Guidelines on Cross-Border Data Flow, the GDPR and its predecessor.[13]

However, existing literature overlooks the intricacies and unique adaptations present in CBDT provisions across diverse African jurisdictions. Scholarly literature on CBDT in Africa has dwelt heavily on the overarching principles and general compliance requirements.[14] It acknowledges the presence of standard data transfer tools in these legal frameworks, such as adequacy decisions, Standard Contractual Rules (SCC) and Binding Corporate Rules (BCR), as presenting conflicting standards without further analysis of the differences.[15] This chapter contends that data transfer requirements in Africa vary, contrary to the common assumption of uniformity or similarity in the CBDT provisions across African countries. A closer inspection reveals intricate variations and unique contextual considerations that impact the free data flow among African countries. There is scant literature dissecting the specific adaptations embedded within these provisions across the different African jurisdictions and their impact on the free flow of data from one African country to another.

---

[10] Guidelines 05/2021 on the Interplay between the application of Article 3 and the provisions on international transfers as per Chapter V of the GDPR.

[11] Adesokan B, Uzor D, (2023).

[12] Organisation for Economic Co-operation and Development, OECD Guidelines on the Protection of Privacy and Transborder Flows of Personal Data (1980).

[13] Greenleaf G, Cottier C (2022).

[14] Daigle B, (2021).

[15] Kipkoech DA (2023).

Some publications have briefly acknowledged the presence of these different provisions.[16] However, they fall short of delving into the granular details and nuanced adaptations present within the legal texts. To substantiate the claim of nuance, the first part of this chapter begins by providing a brief background on the circumstances that generally contributed to varying national data protection laws. It does this by looking into various initiatives that led to the enactment of varying national data protection laws and the enabling factors that will lay the foundation for understanding the variations in data protection frameworks generally and CBDT provisions.

The second part provides a comparative analysis of the differences in the data transfer tools, highlighting notable differences and providing examples of the varying provisions on data transfers in various countries that focus on approaches to intra-African data transfer. It accomplishes this by categorising the CBDT regimes while explaining the impact of the data transfer regimes under each category on intra-African free data flow. The third section explores emerging CBDT trends in Africa. The fourth section examines challenges hindering intra-African CBDT and their impact on successful implementation, while the fifth provides recommendations for improving the landscape. The final section of the chapter offers a conclusion.

A granular view of these specificities aims to fill this gap through an in-depth comparative analysis of the diverse and often underrepresented provisions related to CBDT in Africa that demonstrates the contextual complexities shaping data transfer mechanisms in these laws. Highlighting these variations and the factors influencing the nuances aims to contribute to comprehending African data protection regulations. This will provide a good understanding of the nuanced adaptation and contextual factors shaping CBDT mechanisms in various African jurisdictions and the different approaches to data flows for policymakers, lawmakers, and other relevant stakeholders.

The chapter finds that while the influence of global frameworks on CBDT is clear, variations exist in the laws, some introducing more stringent provisions to intra-Africa data transfer and others omitting certain CBDT tools. The fewest intricacies in CBDT provisions relate to derogations. The least commonly provided CBDT tool is certification mechanisms, which are more common with post-GDPR laws. Lastly, it finds that more recent laws have a wider range of tools for CBDT.

2 A Brief Analysis of the Basis for Variations in National Data Protection Frameworks

With the emergence of data protection frameworks in Africa, comparing them with internationally recognised frameworks such as the GDPR and its predecessor is common. Indeed, these frameworks have influenced the scope and provisions for

[16] Boshe P, Hennemann M and von Meding R (2022).

African legislation on data protection, resulting in comparisons that focus on similarities and omit the variations within these African laws. This section delves into some influencing factors leading to variations in national data protection frameworks.

2.1 Absence and Subsequent Weaknesses in the Continental Framework to Govern Data Protection

For over two decades, since the first data protection law on the continent in 2001, Africa did not have a single authoritative framework by which countries could align their national laws until recently when the African Union Convention on Cybersecurity and Protection of Personal Data (Malabo Convention) that came into force in 2023.[17] Although not entirely similar, this can be narrowly contrasted with the European Union, which has had a single overarching data protection framework that countries have adopted with varying modifications allowed with the creation of the 1995 Directive and its successor, the GDPR.[18] Notwithstanding the absence of an enforceable continental instrument, African data protection frameworks developed at different times and were influenced by varying issues, such as differing national priorities. Therefore, early adopters of data protection laws, such as Cabo Verde and Cote d'Ivoire, did not have a regional treaty on personal data protection on which they would have relied.

In 2014, the Malabo Convention was adopted, a culmination of a three-year process of developing the treaty.[19] The Convention was described as "potentially the most important data protection development in Africa".[20] The treaty required accession by 15 countries before it would come into force. This was a slow process. The treaty was also passed in an environment of ongoing national legislative efforts. There were also some ambiguous provisions in the Convention, such as a proposal to conduct certain formalities before processing personal data without describing the formalities.[21] Nonetheless, for countries without ongoing legislative efforts on data protection, the numerous ambiguities within the Malabo Convention may have dissuaded them from acceding to it or using the Convention as a minimum standard in enacting data protection legislation.

The Convention finally came into force in June 2023, when more than 30 countries had enacted their laws (based on the differing national priorities and circumstances that influenced law-making).[22] The coming into force of the Malabo Convention aligned with the creation of national data protection laws in some countries that

[17] Team, A. L. T. (2023).

[18] The rule making process in the EU and the AU are different and do not have similar effects.

[19] Greenleaf G, Cottier B (2022).

[20] Graham Gand Marie G (2014), p. 18–21.

[21] Abdulrauf LA, Fombad CM (2016), p. 67–97.

[22] Carnegie Endowment for International Peace (2023).

currently have pending bills.[23] However, it is unclear what influence the Convention will have, given that it is currently under review for amendments. A major weakness in the treaty's provisions is the omission of sanctions following non-compliance. While compliance with international treaties is a major function of norm acceptance rather than the presence of sanctions, the absence of sanctions for failure to establish a national framework as per the Malabo Convention may have influenced disregard for the Convention.[24]

2.2 Regional Initiatives Aimed at Harmonisation of ICT-Related Laws

Another notable influence on the variations in national data protection frameworks is the Harmonisation of ICT Policies in Sub-Saharan Africa (HIPSSA) project of 2008, which started before the adoption of the Malabo Convention.[25] This was a continental initiative aimed at harmonising ICT legislative developments, including data protection frameworks. Like the development of the Malabo Convention, the HIPSSA project was also implemented in an environment of ongoing legislative efforts in various countries, and the harmonisation process was designed considering these.

However, the approach taken by the HIPSSA project implementers had the opposite effect of creating a harmonious legal landscape, exacerbating the fragmentation of the data protection ecosystem in the continent. The HIPSSA project used the different sub-regions created under the Abuja Treaty to guide the implementation of the data protection frameworks. HIPSSA demarcated regions considered prepared or close to having sub-regional data protection frameworks by leveraging the Regional Economic Communities (RECs).[26] The implementers developed a methodology that moved away from a one-size-fits-all approach by considering regional specificities.[27] Therefore, a key step was to conduct situational assessments of each beneficiary country. The outcomes of these assessments were then used to develop draft regional model policy guidelines for each identified priority area.[28]

Subsequently, 4 of the 8 RECs adopted model data protection frameworks that vary in scope, applicability, and language. The following section shows how using RECs as vehicles for harmonisation may have led to further deviation from a single standard of data protection on the continent.

---

[23] Cameroon, Djibouti, Gambia, Namibia, Sierra Leone, and South Sudan all have draft laws at different stages.

[24] Ibid.

[25] HIPSSA Project (*ITU*) (2008).

[26] ITU-EC-ACP PROJECT. In: ITU.

[27] Methodology: ITU.

[28] Ibid.

2.2.1 Data Protection Frameworks in Regional Economic Communities

Following the subregional policy development process, the ECOWAS region was the first to develop a regional data protection framework. In 2010, the ECOWAS Supplementary Act was adopted. The ECOWAS Act is the only legally binding framework of all four subregional harmonisation frameworks since it is part of the ECOWAS Treaty.

The Southern African Development Community (SADC) Model Law[29] and the Draft East African Community (EAC) Legal Framework for Cyber Law[30] deviated greatly from the ECOWAS Supplementary Act by being voluntary frameworks for their respective member states. Beyond being voluntary frameworks, for example, the EAC Legal Framework for Cyber Law further allowed member states to adopt varying models of data protection enforcement.[31] The Framework allows member states to adopt varying data protection authority models depending on the available resources.[32] This could explain the two models of data protection authorities visible in the sub-region; some have created a standalone authority, while others have delegated the data protection function to an existing regulator. The circumstances were similar in West Africa, where the ECOWAS Supplementary Act was enacted while countries were at different stages of developing their national ICT-related legal frameworks. Three out of the five EAC member states had drafted bills, including Kenya, Uganda and Rwanda. Burundi and Tanzania did not have any drafts.[33]

3 Emerging Trends in Africa's CBDT Landscape

Since the first data protection law was enacted in 2001, the continent's CBDT landscape has evolved significantly. This evolution is characterised by a dynamic progression, with countries enacting and updating data protection laws and engaging in international cooperation and frameworks to enhance their data governance capabilities. The trends highlight a multifaceted approach to CBDT, ranging from efforts to secure the European Commission's adequacy decision to the reciprocal recognition of data protection adequacy among African countries and the acknowledgement of some African countries by countries outside the continent.

These developments are further complemented by the influence of the digital trade protocol under the African Continental Free Trade Agreement and the slowly growing influence and alignment with global Cross-Border Privacy Rules (CBPR). Collectively, these trends underscore a maturing CBDT ecosystem in Africa, reflecting both

---

[29] Southern African Development Community (SADC) Model Law.

[30] Draft East African Community (EAC) Legal Framework for Cyber Law.

[31] Article 2 of the EAC Legal Framework for Cyber Law.

[32] Ibid.

[33] International Telecommunication Union (ITU) (2009).

the growing sophistication of national data protection regimes and the continent's proactive stance in engaging with global data transfer mechanisms.

3.1 Recognition of African Countries by Non-African Countries

A significant trend in international data transfer in Africa involves the mutual recognition of data protection adequacy among African countries and recognition by non-African nations. This trend is marked by countries like Bahrain,[34] Russia,[35] and Serbia[36] granting adequacy status to select African countries, acknowledging that they have comparable data protection standards. Bahrain recognises Egypt, Morocco, and Nigeria; Russia acknowledges Angola, Benin, Chad, Gabon, Niger, Nigeria, South Africa, Togo, and Zambia; and Serbia acknowledges Cabo Verde, Mauritius, Morocco, Senegal, and Tunisia. Despite surprises such as Egypt's recognition by Bahrain[37] and Togo's by Russia, despite the two countries lacking a data protection authority, these acknowledgements signal a move towards global cooperation beyond the strict confines of EU standards.

Additionally, the Data Protection Office of the Dubai International Finance Center (DIFC) has developed the Ethical Data Management Risk Index, which includes an assessment of some African countries. However, no African country is on the DIFC's adequacy list.[38] This index provides a risk-rating framework where countries, including some in Africa, are evaluated based on their legal and institutional frameworks for data protection. The assessment categorises countries into various risk severity levels, offering a nuanced view of their data protection capabilities.[39] In 2021, as a wider part of reform to its CBDT rules, the United Kingdom government announced that Kenya is considered a priority country for an adequate decision.[40] Other non-European countries include Australia, Brazil, Colombia, India, and Singapore. Similarly, the European Union indicated that it is considering Kenya for an adequacy decision, which will make it the first African country to get such status.[41]

---

[34] Bahrain Adequacy List (2022).

[35] Russia's Adequacy List (2021).

[36] Serbia's Adequacy List (2019).

[37] Musa S, Oloyede R, et al. (2022), p. 6.

[38] Data Export & Sharing.

[39] The April 2023 version of the Index include the assessment of African countries like Egypt, Ethiopia, Gambia, Kenya, Morocco, Nigeria, Rwanda, South Africa, Tanzania, and Uganda, with South Africa ranking the highest with the low/meidum risk.

[40] Gov.UK (2021).

[41] Delegation of the European Union to Kenya (2024).

The recognition and reciprocity between African and non-African countries can enhance trust, facilitating smoother and more secure global cross-border data transfers. The recognition by non-African countries like Bahrain, Russia, and Serbia indicates an endorsement of the data protection frameworks in these African countries, which can facilitate smoother data flows between African countries and international partners, promoting cross-border cooperation. It indicates a growing alignment with global data protection standards, enhancing the international reputation of African data protection laws.

These developments could influence regional data transfer policies within Africa, encouraging countries with less robust data protection laws to strengthen their frameworks. This, in turn, could lead to more uniform and stringent data protection across the continent. As African countries gain recognition for data protection standards, it can boost intra-continental digital trade and facilitate better participation in global digital trade. Companies and investors are more likely to engage in digital activities within a region where data protection is taken seriously and is in line with international norms.

However, while this trend is positive, it also underscores the challenge of achieving harmonised data protection standards across all African countries. The varying levels of recognition and adequacy can create disparities in how data is treated across different jurisdictions within the continent. Also, it presents challenges in maintaining and continuously improving their data protection standards to retain their adequacy status.

3.2 *Impact and Implications of the AfCFTA and AU's Data Policy Framework on Cross-Border Data Transfer in Africa*

The African Continental Free Trade Agreement (AfCFTA) and the African Union's Data Policy Framework (DPF) represent transformative steps towards enhancing digital trade and data governance across Africa. The AfCFTA's digital trade protocol aims to significantly improve Africa's digital landscape by facilitating the flow of digital goods, services, and data across borders.[42] This is critical for a continent that has historically seen low volumes of intra-continental trade.[43] With a mandate to create a single market of approximately 1.3 billion people and a combined GDP of around US$ 3.4 trillion,[44] the protocol addresses key areas such as e-commerce, cross-border data flows, digital identity, and privacy, aiming to stimulate economic growth and innovation.

[42] AfCFTA (2021a, b) Digital Trade.

[43] UNCTAD (2019) Facts & Figures.

[44] AfCFTA (2021a, b) About the AfCFTA.

Key provisions in the protocol encourage cooperation and collaboration in data protection and cross-border data flow, aiming to strengthen existing harmonisation efforts. Notably, 40 of the 54 AfCFTA signatories have enacted data protection laws,[45] with 31 establishing data protection authorities, indicating significant progress towards harmonised data governance on the continent. The protocol also promotes the development of cross-border complaint mechanisms and co-regulatory investigation and enforcement actions, further enhancing the legal framework for data protection.

However, the protocol addresses complex issues like computing facility localisation and cross-border data transfer rules. While it generally promotes the liberalisation of data transfers and discourages mandatory localisation, broad exceptions for public policy and national security could potentially limit the free flow of data. These provisions reflect a delicate balance between fostering digital trade and respecting national sovereignty and public interest.

The Africa's Data Policy Framework (DPF), adopted in February 2022, complements the AfCFTA by aiming to create a unified data market and harmonised data governance across Africa.[46] It seeks to secure inclusive data handling, with the Data Governance and Innovation Forum for Africa (DGIFA) playing a pivotal role in its rollout.[47] DGIFA's collaborative platform is crucial for engaging stakeholders, developing policies, and driving the framework's adoption by Member States.

Collectively, these initiatives mark a shift towards more integrated and coordinated data governance and digital trade practices in Africa. They promise to streamline digital transactions, reduce cross-border trade obstacles, and promote a secure, efficient digital economy. Implementing the AfCFTA's digital trade protocol and the DPF is expected to have far-reaching implications for intra-African cross-border data transfers, enhance Africa's position in the global digital economy, and facilitate economic integration and development.

3.3 *Pursuit of EU Adequacy Decision*

A notable trend in the African cross-border data transfer landscape involves the strategic moves by some African countries to earn the EU adequacy badge. Earning this decision may be crucial, as it could signify that an African country has data protection laws comparable to the EU's stringent standards, facilitating smoother data transfers between the EU and the African country. Kenya, Mauritius, and Morocco have either attempted or are considering applying to the EU for its recognition of adequacy decision.

[45] TRALAC (2024) AfCFTA Which Countries Have Ratified the AfCFTA Agreement? Instrument of Ratification Deposited AfCFTA Agreement Signed AfCFTA Agreement Not Signed.

[46] African Union (2022).

[47] African Union (2023).

Mauritius and Morocco have previously applied for the EU adequacy decision but did not succeed.[48] Morocco applied for an EU adequacy decision on data flow with the European Commission in 2009, but it was not granted.[49] In 2010, Mauritius also sought an EU adequacy decision from the European Commission but was unsuccessful.[50] Mauritius also indicated in its 2022 annual report of the ongoing efforts to align more closely with EU standards and actively engage with the European Union Commission to achieve this objective.[51] Similarly, Kenya has been making concerted efforts in this direction. In 2023, the Office of the Data Protection Commissioner announced initiatives to work with the EU towards an adequacy decision.[52] The high-level engagements between Kenyan officials and the EU, including discussions with the Directorate-General for Justice and Consumers, signify a deepening partnership in data protection and the digital economy. Given the similarities in data protection laws between Kenya and the EU, these discussions have explored the potential for a mutual adequacy decision. These efforts reflect a broader regional trend where African countries increasingly align their data protection laws with global standards to facilitate international data transfers.

These countries' pursuit of EU adequacy decisions underscores their commitment to meeting international data protection standards, potentially positioning them as African data governance leaders. While these efforts could enhance intra-African data transfers and shape regional practices, achieving adequacy has proven elusive and challenging.

The EU's adequacy decision, often pursued as a benchmark for international data transfer, warrants critical examination. Despite its prestigious status, its process appears to be partly hinged on economic and political interests rather than strict legal compliance and human rights considerations, presenting a skewed playing field for African countries. This is evident in the EU's repeated efforts to accommodate the United States in the data transfer regime, overlooking substantial legal gaps such as the persistent surveillance regime, the absence of a federal data protection law, and a dedicated data protection authority—issues that have led to challenges before the Court of Justice of the European Union (CJEU).[53] Similarly, Canada's ombudsman model has come under scrutiny for enforcement inefficiencies. Also, the law has been criticised for not being modern enough to address emerging challenges,[54] leading to the Privacy Commissioner's asking for reform in the legal framework to grant real enforcement powers.[55] For context, the EU has recently revalidated Canada's commercial sector adequacy decision despite its legal framework's known flaws

[48] Boshe P, Hennemann M, and von Meding R (2022).

[49] Chenaoui H (2018).

[50] Data Guidance, (2022).

[51] Mauritius Data Protection Commission (2022), p. 11.

[52] Comments on the Engagement with the EU by Kenya's Data Protection Commissioner.

[53] Case C-311/18 - Facebook Ireland and Schrems, ECLI:EU:C:2020:559.

[54] Office of the Privacy Commissioner of Canada (2016).
Office of the Privacy Commissioner of Canada (2017).

[55] Government of Canada (2019).

and inadequacies.[56] These examples suggest that factors beyond the stringent legal criteria it upholds may influence the adequacy decision.

3.4 *Adoption of the Global Cross-Border Privacy Rules as an Alternative Framework*

The growing interest in the Global Cross-Border Privacy Rules (CBPR)[57] Forum is emerging as a significant trend in African data governance. This interest is likely fuelled by African countries' challenges in securing the European Union's (EU's) adequacy decision for data transfers. The Global CBPR presents a viable and less stringent alternative, offering a framework that potentially eases cross-border data transfer while ensuring robust data protection. The CBPR membership comprises countries of significant economic importance, such as Australia, Canada, Japan, Mexico, Singapore, South Korea, and the United States of America, among others.[58] The United Kingdom has also expressed its intention to join the CBPR and currently enjoys associate membership status.[59]

Some African countries have shown considerable interest in the CBPR. In Nigeria, notable engagements have occurred, including discussions between the Nigeria Data Protection Commission (NDPC)[60] and United States Department of Commerce Officials[61] and the NDPC's participation in the London Cross-Border Privacy Rules Forum.[62] Nigeria's recent Code of Conduct for Data Protection Compliance Organisations (DPCO) also provides that the Nigeria Data Protection Commission can develop an approval system aligned with the CBPR.[63] Moreover, the recently amended Seychelles' data protection law includes specific provisions for international data transfer under the CBPR framework.[64] It is the first law on the continent with clear provisions for the CBPR. This inclusion signifies a strategic move towards adopting global data governance standards that facilitate cross-border data flows while maintaining accountability. African countries with certification mechanisms in their laws could integrate the CBPR framework. In addition, the United States

[56] Torkin Manes LLP (2024) European Commission Approves of Canada's Data Protection Regime (Again).

[57] AfCFTA, About The AfCFTA.

[58] Global CBPR Forum, Members of the Global CBPR Forum.

[59] International Association of Privacy Professionals (IAPP) (2023).

[60] The NDPB has been renamed to Nigeria Data Protection Commission in June 2023 after the enactment of the Nigeria Data Protection Act.

[61] Essien P (2023).

[62] NDPC Nigeria (2023).

[63] Code of Conduct for Data Protection Compliance Orgabisations, Article 3(2)(g).

[64] Syechelles Data Protction Act 2023, Article 47 (2) (d) and (5).

Department of Commerce issued joint statements with the governments of Kenya[65] and Nigeria[66] to encourage the adoption and participation in the CBPR to encourage cross-border data transfer.

The CBPR is not just limited to facilitating data transfers; it also introduces the Global Cooperation Arrangement for Privacy Enforcement (GlobaCAPE), providing essential cross-border enforcement capabilities.[67] This system promotes compliance and security in international data transfers, potentially reducing transfer barriers and broadening global reach, boosting Africa's digital trade. For instance, the Dubai International Financial Centre (DIFC) recognises CBPR adherence in its adequacy assessments, opening up opportunities for Africa's integration into the CBPR network.[68] Africa's engagement with the CBPR signals a shift towards an adaptable CBDT mechanism, positioning the continent for active participation in the global digital economy and streamlining secure, compliant intra-African data exchange practices. As African countries continue to explore and adopt the CBPR, it will likely shape the future of intra-African cross-border data transfers, offering a pathway to more streamlined, secure, and compliant data exchange practices across the continent.[69]

3.5 *The Wave of New and Amended Data Protection Laws in Africa*

The wave of new and proposed laws in Africa can alter the CBDT landscape. Countries such as Djibouti, Ethiopia, Gambia, Libya, Malawi, Namibia, Sierra Leone, and South Sudan are at various stages of proposing or enacting new data protection legislation. These proposals include varying provisions on CBDT. Concurrently, there is a move in countries with pre-existing data protection laws to amend these laws. Countries like Botswana,[70] Angola,[71] and Tunisia[72] are in the process of updating their laws. These amendments are expected to address contemporary challenges in data protection, considering the rapid advancements in technology and changes in

---

[65] U.S. Department of Commerce (2024) Joint Statement on Harnessing Artificial Intelligence, Facilitating Data.

Flows and Empowering Digital Upskilling Between the United States Department of Commerce and the Kenyan Ministry of Information, Communication and the Digital Economy.

[66] U.S. Department of Commerce (2024) Joint Statement on Harnessing Artificial Intelligence, Facilitating Data Flows and Empowering Digital Upskilling Between the United States Department of Commerce and the Nigerian Ministry of Communications, Innovation and Digital Economy. https://www.commerce.gov/news/press-releases/2024/07/joint-statement-harnessing-artificial-intelligence-facilitating-data. Accessed 22 February 2025.

[67] Global Cooperation Arrangement for Privacy Enforcement (2023).

[68] Data sharing & export.

[69] Vasquez-Callo-Müller (2023).

[70] Maramwidze A (2022).

[71] AGÊNCIA DE PROTECÇÃO DE DADOS (2023).

[72] Instance Nationale de Protection des Données Personnelles (INPDP) (2022).

the global data privacy landscape. For example, Seychelles recently amended law includes innovative alternative models, like the CBPR. Also, the proposed amendment in Ghana is expected to address the gap in CBDT rules. This surge in legislative activity reflects a growing awareness of the importance of data protection in the digital age and a concerted effort to align with global data protection standards.

The introduction of new laws and the amendment of existing ones are poised to usher in a new era of digital interconnectivity within Africa. These developments signify a move towards more standardised and robust data protection regimes across the continent. As these laws become more harmonised with international standards, they will likely facilitate smoother cross-border data transfers, fostering trust and cooperation among African nations.

The evolving legal landscape will require businesses and organisations across Africa to stay abreast of these changes and ensure compliance with diverse data protection laws. This trend towards enhanced data protection is also expected to bolster the overall security of personal data within the continent, providing a more stable and secure environment for digital trade and information exchange.

3.6 Increased Regulatory Actions on International Data Transfer Compliance in Africa and Growing Scrutiny by DPAs, and High Courts

African Data Protection Authorities (DPAs) are exhibiting greater vigilance and taking decisive action against non-compliance with international data transfer provisions, indicative of a maturing data protection environment on the continent. In 2023, Morocco's DPA launched an investigation against TLS Contact for failing to notify it of data transfers.[73] One of the mechanisms for data transfer under the Morrocan law is seeking authorisation from the authority.[74] Also, in 2022, Tunisia's DPA warned against unsafe data transfers to the United States, highlighting the rigorous standards expected for data protection adequacy.[75] Similarly, Côte d'Ivoire's DPA expressed reservations about transferring data to the United States[76] after a company's authorisation request to transfer data. According to the Ivorian DPA, "the USA is a country that does not guarantee an adequate level of protection." It has also prohibited a telecommunications company from transferring data to countries that do not

[73] Sahnouni M (2023).

[74] Morocco's Data Protection Law, Article 44 (3).

[75] Instance Nationale de Protection des Données Personnelles (INPDP) (2022).

[76] Telecommunications Regulatory Authority/ICT of Ivory Coast, Protection Authority (ARTCI) (2022).

offer adequate data protection.[77] These efforts point to a shift towards more consistent enforcement of data transfer, requiring greater diligence to align with these regulations.

Apart from interventions by the DPAs, the court also plays a role in international data transfer. A recent Federal High Court ruling in Nigeria invalidated a DPA-created adequacy list, citing the inclusion of countries that failed to meet the mandated protection levels.[78] This decision underscores the imperative for DPAs to comply with their law and necessitates a thorough country-specific assessment for data transfer adequacy. The judgment could precipitate other African countries' reassessment of adequacy lists, ensuring they reflect a genuine and robust data protection assessment rooted in evidence. The move towards stringent evaluations and compliance with data protection laws can improve the compliance of Africa's CBDT practices, thereby building trust and reliability in the region's digital economy. Adequacy decisions must be merited, not given lightly.

As we look forward, these trends illuminate the current state of CBDT in Africa and chart a course towards a future marked by more integrated, secure, and globally recognised data protection standards. This ongoing evolution highlights Africa's increasing significance in the global digital economy and its commitment to developing a secure, efficient, and compliant environment for data transfers.

4 Similar but Different: Classification and Analysis of CBDT Regimes on the Continent

Cross-border data transfer provisions are one aspect of data protection frameworks that vary in scope and application and impact intra-African cross-border data transfers. To this end, this chapter classifies intra-African approaches to data transfer in Africa into two categories that represent the diverse regulatory landscape. These categories aim to capture the nuances of how countries regulate personal data transfers from one African country to another. The first category encompasses countries with no CBDT provisions because such provisions are omitted from the law or countries that lack comprehensive data protection laws. The second category includes countries with restrictions based on conditional transfer requirements. The chapter limits its analysis to conditions that impact intra-African data transfer within this second category. These categories highlight the challenges to the free flow of data within the continent.

---

[77] Telecommunications Regulatory Authority/ICT of Ivory Coast, Protection Authority (ARTCI) (2022).

[78] Adegoroye A, Tsebee D, and Bashir R (2023) (n 43).

4.1 The Absence of CBDT Provisions

This classification considers countries with data protection laws but no provisions on data transfers and countries without comprehensive data protection laws. Countries in this last sub-category have no overarching framework for CBDT. Still, they could have sectoral laws that may include provisions on how data from a particular industry, such as the finance sector, may be transferred out of a country. The lack of enforceable general data transfer provisions in these countries means no comprehensive regulations to oversee data transfer across borders. In unregulated industries, this could result in data being sent to jurisdictions with inadequate data protection standards or countries deemed unsafe or at high risk for data transfer. Furthermore, these countries might be perceived as high-risk due to their minimal safeguards, potentially limiting reciprocal data transfer agreements with countries that have established data protection provisions.

One example of a country with a comprehensive law but without provisions for international data transfer is Ghana.[79] Under the 2012 Data Protection Act, there is no clear mechanism to facilitate international data transfers. Although this provision has been argued to mean no restrictions on CBDTs.[80] However, the absence of any clear mechanism to facilitate this creates uncertainty and no oversight, which creates loopholes. Although other provisions of the law, like the prohibition on the sale and purchase of data,[81] have often been stretched to address CBDT,[82] these measures are inadequate to address CBDT risks comprehensively. Comparably, CBDT provisions under the old Seychelles law envisage data transmission outside the country[83] but fall short of providing mechanisms for such transfer. The lack of clear provisions for international data transfer is cited as one of the reasons for the amendment of the law.[84]

Furthermore, there are countries without comprehensive data protection laws; consequently, there is no provision to address CBDT. Several countries, including Libya, Sierra Leone, Gambia, Djibouti and Ethiopia, lack data protection laws and have no comprehensive CBDT provisions. This absence jeopardises the privacy of data subjects and elevates compliance risks. While there are no data protection laws and, therefore, no overarching transfer provisions in these countries, certain regulated sectors, such as those in finance, may have sectoral laws regulating data flow out of the country. However, data transfer gaps exist for exporters and recipients without sector-specific regulations on data transfers.

Without regulatory oversight, there is an increased risk of data misuse as information can be transferred to entities in countries with insufficient data protection

[79] Hoffmann T, (2022).

[80] Bowmans, (2022).

[81] Ghana Data Protection Act, Sect. 89.

[82] Transfer in Ghana - DLA Piper Global Data Protection Laws of the World.

[83] Seychelles Data Protection Act 2003, Article 16.

[84] Tsebee D, Owoyemi O and Nwadike P (2024).

standards.[85] This situation threatens the security and privacy of personal data, limits legal recourse for individuals in cases of violation, and undermines trust in digital services. The unregulated data flow across borders, often to jurisdictions with lower data protection standards, compounds these risks.[86] Furthermore, the absence creates a challenging environment for international businesses and hinders the growth of digital economies.[87] Data controllers and processors in these countries face complex legal landscapes, navigating varying and sometimes non-existent data protection regulations and CBDT mechanisms. This uncertainty can deter investments in these markets.[88] Additionally, the absence of data protection laws undermines consumer trust in digital services and impedes cross-border digital collaboration, posing broader socio-economic challenges.[89]

4.2 Restrictions Based on Conditional Transfer Requirements

This category encompasses countries whose laws feature commonly known data transfer tools, such as adequacy decisions and the implementation of appropriate safeguards and derogations. A common denominator for countries under this category is that they have varying requirements for data exporters intending to use these tools for intra-African data transfers.

4.2.1 Adequacy Decisions as Tools for Intra-African Data Transfers

Article 45 of the GDPR provides for adequacy decisions as one of the mechanisms for transferring personal data from the EU to a third country or international organisation that ensures adequate protection as the GDPR. However, there are no restrictions to data flow within the European Economic Area. This is a sharp contrast to the state of data flow in Africa despite transplanting adequacy decisions as a tool for data transfer from the GDPR and its predecessor. Differences in how adequacy decisions are implemented indicate the nuanced approach to CBDT regulation that countries in the continent have taken. This fragmentation has resulted in varying approaches to adequacy decisions, with African countries considering each other inadequate. This inevitably poses challenges for intra-African data transfers, with countries subjecting each other to adequacy assessments.

The fragmentation in adequacy procedures is seen in African countries, which issue lists of countries they consider adequate. Other than Nigeria's list, which was nullified and contained numerous African countries, adequacy lists by other

---

[85] World Bank data protection and privacy laws.

[86] Meltzer JM, Lovelock P (2018).

[87] Cory N, (2017).

[88] Meltzer JM, Lovelock P (2018).

[89] Digwatch (2023).

African countries have historically included few African countries.[90] For example, Botswana's list contained two African countries - Kenya and South Africa.[91] Also, in 2018, Tunisia published its list of adequate countries, and it recognised Algeria, Mauritius, Senegal, Morocco, and Mauritania as having adequate data protection standards.[92] In contrast, Morocco's list published in 2015 does not include any African country.[93] The fact that most African countries consider their African counterparts inadequate creates legal complexity and an increased compliance burden. This suggests that a country without an adequate framework would have to implement additional safeguards and mechanisms to allow data flow between respective African countries. Restrictive regulations on data transfers between African countries could potentially stifle innovation and collaboration, while a lax framework also poses a risk. Mauritania is an example of an African country with legal restrictions on data transfer based on adequacy protection. Its Data Protection Law defines a third country as "any state/country other than the Islamic Republic of Mauritania".[94]

Further fragmentation is seen in the responsibility to conduct adequacy assessments. Under the GDPR, the European Commission is mandated to conduct these assessments. The mandate to conduct an adequacy assessment in countries like Nigeria can be the national data protection authority or the data controller. Yet, the Information Regulator does not have an express mandate to conduct adequacy assessments in South Africa. Therefore, data controllers would be required to conduct their assessments. Furthermore, unlike under the GDPR framework, where once an adequacy assessment has been made in favour of a country, there is no need for additional safeguards. In some African countries, this is not the case. For example, in Cote d'Ivoire, adequacy does not preclude a data exporter from obtaining authorisation from the data protection authority to transfer data outside the country.[95]

The varying conditions for adequacy decisions bring to the fore two other notable requirements that stand out in this regard. Some countries require ratification of the Malabo Convention as part of the conditions for assessing the adequacy of the legal framework. Some countries consider countries outside their REC third countries for CBDT purposes.

4.2.2 Restrictions Based on the Adoption of the Malabo Convention

The reliance on the Malabo Convention as a benchmark for data protection sufficiency is emerging in some countries. Some countries on the continent are using the signature or ratification of this Convention as a criterion to evaluate and recognise the adequacy

[90] Adegoroye A, Tsebee D, and Bashir R (2023).

[91] Musa S, Oloyede R, et al. (2022), p. 5.

[92] Tunisia list of adequate countries.

[93] Commission for the Protection of Personal Data (CNDP) Morocco, Deliberation n°236-2015 (2018).

[94] Mauritania's Data Protection Law, Article 2.

[95] Cote d'Ivoire's Personal data Protection Law, Article 26.

of other countries' data protection laws. These harmonisation efforts are particularly evident in countries like Kenya, which acknowledges ratification as a basis for data protection adequacy,[96] and Nigeria, which recognises the Malabo Convention signatories.[97] In the case of the latter, a recent Federal High Court decision brought controversy when it invalidated Nigeria's adequacy list for not complying with Article 2.11 of the Nigeria Data Protection Regulation by including countries that either lack data protection laws or have not established data protection authorities, which contradicts the required compliance metrics.[98] Among these, signatories to the Convention, such as Cameroon, Comoros, Djibouti, Gambia, Guinea-Bissau, Mozambique, Sierra Leone, and Sudan, have no laws in place. Despite having laws, Congo and Togo have yet to establish their Data Protection Authorities.[99]

4.2.3 Restrictions Based on REC Membership

Countries in this category have provisions that restrict data flow out of their respective RECs. Under such a regime, countries outside a particular REC are considered third countries with regard to CBDT. Part V of the Eswatini Data Protection Act considers CBDT within SADC and non-SADC countries. Section 32 of the Act provides that data may be transferred to countries that have transposed the SADC data protection requirements after evaluating the necessity for transfer. The law permits transferring personal data to non-SADC countries if the recipient maintains adequate protection for the personal data. Other countries with similar provisions restricting the transfer of data to other African countries not within their REC include Benin, Côte d'Ivoire, Chad, Guinea, Lesotho, Chad and Niger.

4.2.4 Appropriate Safeguards

In the absence of an adequacy determination, data protection frameworks in most African countries provide data controllers with the ability to implement appropriate safeguards for CBDT. As with other CBDT mechanisms, variations exist. Countries that provide for CBDT provisions but omit certain tools for transfer are also included here, such as Rwanda and Uganda, which omit BCRs as a tool for transfer. Uganda's DPA proposes "appropriate measures". Another distinctive mechanism is obtaining

[96] Kenya's Data Protection (general) Regulation, Article 42(a).

[97] Annexure C of the Nigeria Data Protection Regulation Implementation Framework.

[98] Before a regulator can designate a country as adequate for personal data transfer, the country must ensure an adequate level of protection, demonstrated through its legal system, including respect for human rights and data protection laws, effective data protection implementation and enforcement, independent supervisory authorities for data protection, and international commitments to personal data protection.

[99] Musa S, Oloyede R, et al. (2022) and Adegoroye A, Tsebee D, and Bashir R (2023).

prior authorisation or permission from the data protection authority before transferring data internationally, as observed in Rwanda,[100] Egypt, Morocco, and Cote d'Ivoire. Also, some countries have gone ahead and provided clarity on these safeguards. For example, Rwanda is the first African country to publish an SCC module, among other countries adopting SCC as a data transfer mechanism.[101] While there are variations in CBDT mechanisms across the continent, the emphasis on appropriate safeguards remains a common requirement.

5 Challenges to Intra-African CBDT

The vision of a more integrated intra-African CBDT is promising. Yet, it demands cautious optimism to prevent undermining the foundational principles of why the rules exist in the first place. The diversity of countries and varying maturity levels of data protection laws pose significant barriers to achieving a continental framework for free data flow across Africa. This concern is similar to those raised by the Deputy Commissioner of Singapore's Data Protection Commission on the limitation of CBDT among Asia Pacific Economic Countries.[102] Other challenges include differing legal strengths and the autonomy and capability of data protection authorities. Some African countries still do not have specific data protection legislation. This absence of a legal framework poses a challenge to intra-African CBDT, as there are no guarantees for the protection of transferred data. The lack of laws in countries such as Libya and Sudan will make engaging in secure and regulated data exchanges difficult. This section identifies some of the challenges to achieving seamless intra-African CBDT.

5.1 Diverse Data Protection Regimes

The varying degrees of data protection laws across African countries present a significant challenge to harmonising CBDT. For example, while most laws include mechanisms for international data transfer, the absence of these under Ghanaian law creates a disparity. Also, other countries may have less stringent or no data protection laws with no real guarantees. These disparities complicate the establishment of a unified standard for data transfers across the continent.

[100] Rwandan Data Protection and Privacy Law, Article 48 (1).

[101] Standard Contractual Clauses for Personal Data Transfer Outside Rwanda under the Law N° 058/2021 of 13/10/2021 Relating to the Protection of Personal Data and Privacy, (NCSA) (2024).

[102] Duball J (2022).

5.2 *Independence and Competence of Data Protection Authorities (DPAs)*

The effectiveness of DPAs varies widely across Africa, with some countries boasting well-established, independent authorities,[103] while others lack the independence or resources to enforce data protection laws effectively.[104] Differing capabilities and capacity of DPAs across the continent can hinder the enforcement of cross-border data transfer regulations and undermine trust in the system.

5.3 *Implementation of the AfCFTA Digital Trade Protocol*

The African Continental Free Trade Agreement (AfCFTA) and its digital trade protocol aim to boost digital trade across the continent and emphasise the importance of data flow. However, the practical implementation of the digital trade protocol faces obstacles in the face of the fragmented legal regime of CBDT across the Continent owing to differing national priorities, infrastructure gaps, and the slow pace of legal harmonisation, which could impede the effective realisation of a continent-wide digital market.

5.4 *Cross-Border Enforcement and Legal Option*

The increasing interconnectedness of the digital world contrasts sharply with Africa's fragmented regulatory landscape for data protection. The absence of a continent-wide cooperation framework significantly hampers DPAs' ability to conduct effective cross-border investigations and joint enforcement actions. Jurisdictional limitations, such as conflicts of law and challenges in evidence gathering, further exacerbate these difficulties. This issue is further exemplified by the difficulty in ensuring legal recourse for violations that span multiple countries, complicating the protection of individual rights and the imposition of penalties on violators. However, it is hoped that the increasing wave of cooperation among DPAs[105] on the Continent or addressing this issue under the Network of African Data Protection Authorities could offer solutions.

---

[103] Thirty countries have established data protection authorities. These include Algeria, Angola, Benin, Botswana, Burkina Faso, Cabo Verde, Chad, Cote d'Ivoire, Eswatini, Gabon, Ghana, Kenya, Mali, Malawi, Mauritania, Mauritius, Morocco, Niger, Nigeria, Rwanda, São Tomé and Príncipe, Seychelles, Senegal, Somalia, South Africa, Tanzania, Tunisia, Uganda, Zambia, and Zimbabwe.

[104] For example, Kenya, Nigeria, and South Africa, among others.

[105] Adegoroye A, Monyango F, Odeshina N, et al. (2021), p. 7.

These challenges underscore the complexity of achieving a seamless intra-African CBDT framework. Overcoming them requires concerted efforts toward legal harmonisation, capacity building for DPAs, and establishing comprehensive, continent-wide data protection standards that align with global best practices.

6 Recommendations

6.1 *Leveraging the Digital Trade Protocol*

To bolster digital trade, it is recommended that African countries actively leverage the digital trade protocol within the African Continental Free Trade Agreement (AfCFTA). By doing so, they can promote a more liberal and streamlined data flow across borders. This approach will facilitate digital trade and encourage technological advancements and integration across the continent.

6.2 *Adopting an Intra-African Reciprocity Model*

More African countries need to adopt a reciprocity model to recognise data protection adequacy without compromising standards. This model would involve reciprocal recognition of countries with robust data protection standards. Such mutual recognition would foster trust, ease data flow across borders, and encourage countries to uphold high data protection standards.

6.3 *Enhancing the Capacity of Data Protection Authorities (DPAs)*

Strengthening the capacity of DPAs is crucial. Enhanced capacity will empower authorities to make informed decisions regarding data protection adequacy and enforcement. For instance, with increased capacity, incidents like the Nigerian authority granting adequacy to countries without established data protection laws or authorities might be avoided. Building capacity involves providing adequate training, resources, and technological support to DPAs. Also, none of the African countries that have published an adequate list of countries publicly published its country-by-country assessment. African countries can take a cue from the Ethical Data Management Risk Index published by the DIFC, which can be an empirical critical tool to assess and manage risks associated with importing data from different countries. This helps in making informed decisions regarding international data transfers. Also, one of the critical outcomes of the decision of the Nigerian judgment is that it directed the DPA to review the list and publish a country-by-country assessment to revise it.

6.4 *Aligning National Laws with Regional and International Standards*

A key recommendation is aligning national data protection laws with regional and international standards. Such alignment will ensure a harmonised approach to data protection across the continent, facilitating easier data transfers and compliance with global data protection norms.

6.5 *Exploring Alternatives to EU Adequacy Decision*

Given the challenges in obtaining the European Union (EU) adequacy decision, African countries should consider alternative models like the Global Cross-Border Privacy Rules (CBPR) Forum, which offers a less stringent, transparent and accountable data transfer framework than the EU's. This approach should be complemented by forming regional data transfer agreements, leveraging economic partnerships, and establishing bilateral agreements beyond the continent for secure and efficient data transfers amidst geopolitical or legal constraints. Additionally, Africa should balance the pursuit of EU adequacy with opportunities in other markets, recognising that the EU's standards may sometimes prioritise its economic interests, potentially misaligning with Africa's digital trade goals and emerging data protection framework. African nations must assess their unique economic and legal situations, aiming to craft data transfer policies and partnerships that bolster their development and digital sovereignty.

6.6 *Establishing Comprehensive Political and Legal Frameworks*

Countries must establish robust political and legal conditions beyond writing "independence" of Data Protection Authorities (DPAs) into their laws. This involves creating environments that meet all essential metrics for genuine independence within the context of each country. A critical aspect is ensuring the existence and adherence to the rule of law. Political stability is fundamental; for instance, occurrences like coups can significantly impede the possibility of DPAs functioning independently and efficiently. They could also be a casualty of human rights repression as they undermine legal stability and predictability.

6.7 Ensuring an Independent Judiciary

An independent judiciary is another vital metric for achieving an efficient data protection regime. This independence is paramount for ensuring fair and unbiased enforcement of data protection laws and for building international trust in a country's data governance framework. While some African countries have made strides in this area, there must be more consistency across the continent. Strengthening judicial independence should be a priority to enhance the overall efficacy of CBDT frameworks.

6.8 Participation in International Data Protection Initiatives

Furthermore, countries should strive to accede to and participate in international data protection initiatives. This involvement enhances their global standing regarding data protection and aligns their practices with international standards, facilitating smoother CBDT. Engagement with global data protection frameworks can provide valuable guidelines and benchmarks for domestic legislation and practices.

7 Conclusion

In conclusion, this chapter has explored the dynamic landscape of CBDT within Africa, highlighting the evolving regulatory frameworks, challenges, and emerging trends. From the pursuit of European Union adequacy decisions to the adoption of the Global Cross-Border Privacy Rules (CBPR) Forum and the critical role of the African Continental Free Trade Agreement (AfCFTA), it is clear that Africa is on a path toward enhancing its data protection and CBDT mechanisms. Despite the hurdles, such as diverse data protection maturity levels among countries, the lack of clear international transfer mechanisms in some jurisdictions, and the need for stronger DPAs, there is a growing concerted effort across the continent to address these challenges.

Enhancing CBDT in Africa requires a multifaceted approach. Recommendations for improving the CBDT landscape emphasise enhancing the independence and capacity of DPAs and exploring alternative models for data transfer that do not solely rely on EU adequacy decisions. It involves establishing stable political conditions, ensuring judicial independence, participating in international data protection instruments and cooperation, and exploring broader mechanisms for data transfer. African countries can create a more conducive environment for CBDT, fostering regional integration and global participation in the digital economy. These strategies can help African countries foster a more integrated, secure, and prosperous digital economy.

As Africa continues to navigate these complex issues, the future of intra-African CBDT looks promising. The ongoing efforts to amend existing laws, the proactive stance of some countries in enforcing the CBDT requirements, establishing and potentially revising adequacy lists, and the growing cooperation among African nations signal a strong move towards a more integrated and robust data transfer framework. This evolution supports the continent's digital economy growth. It enhances its standing in the global digital ecosystem, marking an important step towards realising Africa's digital trade aspirations and strengthening its digital sovereignty.

References

Abdulrauf LA, Fombad CM (2016) The African Union's data protection Convention 2014: a possible cause for the celebration of human rights in Africa? J Media Law 8(1):67–97

Adegoroye A, Tsebee D, Bashir R (2023) Changing trend in international data transfer in Nigeria: reassessing the "adequacy of the Whitelist" and the Implications for Businesses Available via Tech Hive Advisory. https://www.techhiveadvisory.africa/insights/changing-trend-in-international-data-transfer-in-nigeria-reassessing-the-adequacy-of-the-whitelist-and-the-implications-for-businesses. Accessed 22 Feb 2025

Adegoroye A, Monyango F,, Odeshina N et al (2021) Roundup on Data Protection in Africa. Available via Tech HiveAdvisory. https://assets-global.website-files.com/641a2c1dcea0041f8d407596/644c66b9fcacf7acd18b074d_Africa_DP_Roundup_2021_Reportnew.pdf Page 7. Accessed 11 Feb 2024

Adesokan B, Uzor D (2023) Operationalising the NDPA: bridging digital boundaries with cross-border data rules. https://www.techhiveadvisory.africa/insights/operationalising-the-ndpa-bridging-digital-boundaries-with-cross-border-data-rules. Accessed 22 Feb 2025

AfCFTA (2021) About the AfCFTA. https://au-afcfta.org/about/. Accessed 22 Feb 2025

AfCFTA, About The AfCFTA https://au-afcfta.org/about/. Accessed 22 Feb 2025

AfCFTA (2021) Digital Trade. https://au-afcfta.org/trade-areas/digital-trade/. Accessed 22 Feb 2025

African Union, Action Plan For Boosting Intra-African Trade https://au.int/web/sites/default/files/newsevents/pressreleases/26498-pr-action_plan_for_boosting_intra-african_trade_f-english.pdf. Page 2. Accessed 22 Feb 2025

African Union (2022) AU data policy framework. https://au.int/sites/default/files/documents/42078-doc-AU-DATA-POLICY-FRAMEWORK-ENG1.pdf. Accessed 22 Feb 2025

African Union (2023) Unlocking Africa's data potential: data governance and innovation forum kicks off focused on continental digital transformation. https://au.int/en/pressreleases/20231117/unlocking-africas-data-potential-data-governance-and-innovation-forum-kicks. Accessed 22 Feb 2025

AGÊNCIA DE PROTECÇÃO DE DADOS - Notícias - APD aprimora estratégia de actuação para 2023. In: APD - AGÊNCIA DE PROTECÇÃO DE DADOS. https://www.apd.ao. Accessed 22 Feb 2025

Annexure C of the Nigeria Data Protection Regulation Implementation Framework. https://nitda.gov.ng/wp-content/uploads/2021/01/NDPR-Implementation-Framework.pdf

Article 39 of Data Protection (General) Regulation. https://www.odpc.go.ke/download/the-data-protection-general-regulations-2021-2/?wpdmdl=8946&refresh=65b7a525b31661706534181.

Bahrain Adequacy List (2022) Available via http://www.pdp.gov.bh/en/assets/pdf/executive-decisions/eng/trans-order-countries-and-territories-with-adequate-protection-en.pdf. Accessed 22 Feb 2025

Baker P, Quiles P, Bheenick S (2023) Mauritius and the AfCFTA Part 2: Trade in Services - International Economics https://tradeeconomics.com/mauritius-and-the-afcfta-part-2-trade-in-services/. Accessed 22 Feb 2025

Boshe P, Hennemann M and von Meding R (2022) African Data Protection Laws—current regulatory approaches, policy initiatives, and the way forward. Available via SSRN https://papers.ssrn.com/abstract=3947664. Accessed 22 Feb 2025

Bowmans, (2022) Africa guide to data protection. https://bowmanslaw.com/wp-content/uploads/2022/06/Data-Protection_01.06.2022.pdf. Accessed 22 Feb 2025

Carnegie Endowment for International Peace (2023) Continental cyber security policymaking: implications of the entry into force of the Malabo Convention for digital financial systems in Africa. https://carnegieendowment.org/events/2023/07/continental-cyber-security-policymaking-implications-of-the-entry-into-force-of-the-malabo-convention-for-digital-financial-systems-in-africa?lang=en&center=global. Accessed 22 Feb 2025

Chenaoui H, (2018) Moroccan Data Protection Law: moving to align with EU data protection? Available via IAPP https://iapp.org/news/a/moroccan-data-protection-law-moving-to-align-with-eu-data-protection/. Accessed 22 Feb 2025

Code of Conduct for Data Protection Compliance Organisations, Article 3(2)(g) https://ndpc.gov.ng/Files/coc.pdf. Accessed 22 Feb 2025

Commission for the Protection of Personal Data (CNDP) Morocco, Deliberation n°236–2015 (2018) https://www.cndp.ma/wp-content/uploads/2023/01/deliberation-n-236-2015-18-12-2015.pdf. Accessed 22 Feb 2025

Comments on the Engagement with the EU by Kenya's Data Protection Commissioner'. https://www.linkedin.com/signup/cold-join?session_redirect=https%3A%2F%2Fwww%2Elinkedin%2Ecom%2Ffeed%2Fupdate%2Furn%3Ali%3Aactivity%3A7074615439930081280%3Futm_source%3Dshare%26utm_medium%3Dmember_desktop. Accessed 22 Feb 2025

Cory N (2017) Cross-border data flows: where are the barriers, and what do they cost? https://itif.org/publications/2017/05/01/cross-border-data-flows-where-are-barriers-and-what-do-they-cost/. Accessed 22 Feb 2025

Daigle B (2021) Data protection laws in Africa: a Pan-African Survey and noted trends. Available via Journal of International Commerce and Economics. https://www.usitc.gov/staff_publications/jice/data_protection_laws_africa_pan_african_survey_and. Accessed 22 Feb 2025

Data protection and privacy laws Identification for Development. https://id4d.worldbank.org/guide/data-protection-and-privacy-laws. Accessed 22 Feb 2025

Data Export & Sharing. Available via Dubai International Financial Centre. https://www.difc.ae/business/registrars-and-commissioners/commissioner-of-data-protection/data-export-and-sharing. Accessed 22 Feb 2025

Data Guidance (2022) Mauritius: data protection in the financial sector Available via Data Guidance. www.dataguidance.com/opinion/mauritius-data-protection-financial-sector. Accessed 22 Feb 2025

Decision of the ARTCI (2022a) https://www.autoritedeprotection.ci/decision-n-2022-0737-sania-cie-transfert-vers-les-usa/. Accessed 22 Feb 2025

Decision of the ARTCI (2022b) https://www.artci.ci/images/stories/pdf/decisions_conseil_reg/decision_2022_0746_conseil_regulation.pdf. Accessed 22 Feb 2025

Delegation of the European Union to Kenya (2024) 'Data Protection: Kenya and the EU Launch Very FirstAdequacy Dialogue on the African Continent | EEAS. https://www.eeas.europa.eu/delegations/kenya/data-protection-kenya-and-eu-launch-very-first-adequacy-dialogue-african-continent_en?s=352. Accessed 22 Feb 2025

Digwatch (2023) 'Opportunities of cross-border data flow-DFFT for development | IGF 2023 WS #224 | Digital Watch Observatory https://dig.watch/event/internet-governance-forum-2023/opportunities-of-cross-border-data-flow-dfft-for-development-igf-2023-ws-224. Accessed 22 Feb 2025

Duball J (2022) State of the transfer: global data flows in focus. Available via International Association of Privacy Professionals (IAPP) https://iapp.org/news/a/state-of-the-transfer-global-data-flows-in-focus/. Accessed 22 Feb 2025

ElGanainy AA et al (2023) Trade integration in Africa: unleashing the continent's potential in a changing world available via departmental papers. https://www.elibrary.imf.org/view/journals/087/2023/003/article-A001-en.xml. Accessed 22 Feb 2025

Essien P. The National Commissioner/CEO of NDPB, Dr Vincent Olatunji received in audience https://www.linkedin.com/posts/technicallead-senatecommitteeonictandcybercrime_the-national-commissionerceo-of-ndpb-dr-activity-7014980453723987968-i6Jd. Accessed 22 Feb 2025

Facebook. https://www.facebook.com/880566588679630/posts/5416475468422030/. Accessed 22 Feb 2025

Facebook. https://www.facebook.com/100080697572218/posts/175273675172551/?mibextid=Nif5oz. Accessed 22 Feb 2025

Global Cooperation Arrangement for Privacy Enforcement (2023). https://www.globalcbpr.org/wp-content/uploads/Global-CAPE-2023.pdf. Accessed 22 Feb 2025

Global CBPR Forum, Members of the Global CBPR Forum https://www.globalcbpr.org/membership/. Accessed 22 Feb 2025

Global Freedom of Expression (2015) Schrems v. Data Protection Commissioner. In: https://globalfreedomofexpression.columbia.edu/cases/schrems-v-data-protection-commissioner/. Accessed 22 Feb 2025

Gov.UK (2021) International data transfers: building trust, delivering growth and firing up innovation. In: GOV.UK. https://www.gov.uk/government/publications/uk-approach-to-international-data-transfers/international-data-transfers-building-trust-delivering-growth-and-firing-up-innovation. Accessed 22 Feb 2025

Government of Canada (2019) Strengthening privacy for the digital age. https://ised-isde.canada.ca/site/innovation-better-canada/en/canadas-digital-charter/strengthening-privacy-digital-age. Accessed 22 Feb 2025

Greenleaf G, Cottier B (2022) International and regional commitments in African data privacy laws: a comparative analysis. Comput Law Secur Rev. https://doi.org/10.1016/j.clsr.2021.105638

Graham Gand Marie G (2014) The African Union's data protection convention: a major step toward global consistency? Available via Privacy Laws & Business International Report 18–21

HIPSSA Project (ITU) (2008). https://www.itu.int:443/en/ITU-D/Projects/ITU-EC-ACP/HIPSSA/Pages/default.aspx. Accessed 22 Feb 2025

Hoffmann T (2022) Data Protection Act(ion) – Report on the Law of Data Disclosure in Ghana https://papers.ssrn.com/sol3/papers.cfm?abstract_id=4037928. Accessed 7 Aug 2024

International Telecommunication Union (ITU) (2009) ICT regulatory harmonization: a comparative study of regional initiatives. https://www.itu.int/ITU-D/projects/ITU_EC_ACP/hipssa/docs/D_REG_HIPSSA_2010_PDF_E.pdf. Accessed 22 Feb 2025

International data transfers: building trust, delivering growth and firing up innovation. In: GOV.UK. https://www.gov.uk/government/publications/uk-approach-to-international-data-transfers/international-data-transfers-building-trust-delivering-growth-and-firing-up-innovation. Accessed 22 Feb 2025

International Association of Privacy Professionals (IAPP) UK gets Global CBPR Forum's first "associate" distinction. https://iapp.org/news/a/uk-gets-global-cbpr-forums-first-associate-distinction/. Accessed 16 Feb 2024

ITU-EC-ACP PROJECT. In: ITU. https://www.itu.int:443/en/ITU-D/Projects/ITU-EC-ACP/Pages/default.aspx. Accessed 22 Feb 2025

Kenya's Data Protection (General) Regulation, Article 42(a). https://www.odpc.go.ke/download/the-data-protection-general-regulations-2021-2/?wpdmdl=8946&refresh=65b7a525b31661706534181

King'ori M (2023) The African Union's data policy framework: context, key takeaways, and implications for data protection on the continent - future of privacy forum. https://fpf.org/blog/the-african-unions-data-policy-framework-context-key-takeaways-and-implications-for-data-protection-on-the-continent/. Accessed 22 Feb 2025

Kipkoech DA (2023) Africa's digital economy: cross-border data flows under the African Continental Free Trade Area - Centre for Intellectual Property and Information Technology Law. https://cipit.strathmore.edu/africas-digital-economy-cross-border-data-flows-under-the-african-continental-free-trade-area/. Accessed 22 Feb 2025

Maramwidze A (2022) Back to the drawing board: glaring gaps in Botswana's data protection act. https://itweb.africa/content/LPp6V7rB1Kg7DKQz. Accessed 22 Feb 2025

Mauritius Data Protection Commission (2022) Annual Report 2022. https://dataprotection.govmu.org/Documents/AR22%20DPO.pdf Page 11. Accessed 22 Feb 2025

Meltzer JM, Lovelock P (2018) 'Regulating for a digital economy: understanding the importance of cross-border data flows in Asia. In: Brookings'. https://www.brookings.edu/articles/regulating-for-a-digital-economy-understanding-the-importance-of-cross-border-data-flows-in-asia/. Accessed 22 Feb 2025

Methodology: ITU. https://www.itu.int:443/en/ITU-D/Projects/ITU-EC-ACP/Pages/unique_methodology.aspx. Accessed 22 Feb 2025

Musa S, Oloyede R et al (2022) Roundup on data protection in Africa. https://assets-global.website-files.com/641a2c1dcea0041f8d407596/644d2c11739815a42ff6bd88_Round-up-of-data-protection-Africa-2022.pdf Page 5. Accessed 22 Feb 2025

NDPC Nigeria (2023) The National Commissioner/CEO, Nigeria Data Protection Bureau attends Cross Border Privacy Rules (CBPR) forum in London, United Kingdom. https://twitter.com/ndpbngr1/status/1648309852869885952?t=W0Yr9kcVuG1v4hoRjo_DqQ&s=19. Accessed 22 Feb 2025

No transfer, no trade -the importance of cross-border data transfers for companies based in Sweden. https://unctad.org/system/files/non-official-document/dtl_ict4d2016c01_Kommerskollegium_en.pdf. Page 22

Office of the Privacy Commissioner of Canada (2016) Consent and Privacy - A Discussion Paper Exploring Potential Enhancements to Consent under the Personal Information Protection and Electronic Documents Act. https://www.priv.gc.ca/en/opc-actions-and-decisions/research/explore-privacy-research/2016/consent_201605/. Accessed 10 Feb 2024.

Office of the Privacy Commissioner of Canada (2017) News Release: Commissioner: Digital Revolution and Canadians' Privacy Fears Demand Real Solutions. https://www.priv.gc.ca/en/opc-news/news-and-announcements/2017/nr-c_170921/. Accessed 10 Feb 2024.

Oloyede R (2019) The Africa continental free trade agreement and cross-border data transfer: maximising the trade deal in the age of digital economy. Available via African Academic Network on Internet Policy - AANoIP'. https://aanoip.org/the-africa-continental-free-trade-agreement-and-cross-border-data-transfer-maximising-the-trade-deal-in-the-age-of-digital-economy/. Accessed 22 Feb 2025

Organisation for Economic Co-operation and Development, OECD Guidelines on the Protection of Privacy and Transborder Flows of Personal Data. https://www.oecd-ilibrary.org/science-and-technology/oecd-guidelines-on-the-protection-of-privacy-and-transborder-flows-of-personal-data_9789264196391-en. Accessed 22 Feb 2025

Russia's Adequacy List (2021) Available via https://rkn.gov.ru/docs/Perechen6_inostrannykh_gosudarstv.pdf. Accessed 22 Feb 2025

Salami E (2022) Implementing the AfCFTA agreement: a case for the harmonisation of data protection law in Africa Available via Journal of African Law. https://www.cambridge.org/core/journals/journal-of-african-law/article/abs/implementing-the-afcfta-agreement-a-case-for-the-harmonization-of-data-protection-law-in-africa/29DD231B417FFA84110030B9D03A2005. Accessed 22 Feb 2025

Sahnouni M (2023), TLS Contact Under Scrutiny in Morocco For Data Misuse https://www.moroccoworldnews.com/2023/01/353479/tls-contact-under-scrutiny-in-morocco-for-data-misuse. Accessed 22 Feb 2025

Serbia's Adequacy List (2019). https://www.poverenik.rs/images/stories/dokumentacija-nova/podzakonski-akti/Listadrzava.docx. Accessed 22 Feb 2025

Team ALT (2023) Africa: AU's Malabo Convention set to enter force after nine years. Data Protection Africa | ALT Advisory. https://dataprotection.africa/malabo-convention-set-to-enter-force/. Accessed 22 Feb 2025

Torkin Manes LLP (2024) European Commission Approves of Canada's Data Protection Regime (Again). https://www.torkin.com/insights/publication/european-commission-approves-of-canada-s-data-protection-regime-(again). Accessed 22 Feb 2025

TRALAC (2024) AfCFTA which countries have ratified the AfCFTA agreement? Instrument of Ratification Deposited AfCFTA Agreement Signed AfCFTA Agreement Not Signed. https://www.tralac.org/documents/resources/infographics/2605-status-of-afcfta-ratification/file.html. Accessed 22 Feb 2025

Transfer in Ghana - DLA Piper Global Data Protection Laws of the World. https://www.dlapiperdataprotection.com/index.html?t=transfer&c=GH. Accessed 22 Feb 2025

Tsebee D, Owoyemi O, Nwadike P. Review of Seychelles data protection act. https://www.linkedin.com/pulse/review-seychelles-dpa-tech-hive-advisory-africa-7pgzf. Accessed 22 Feb 2025

Tunisia list of adequate countries. Available via http://www.inpdp.nat.tn/3_protection_adequate.pdf. Accessed 22 Feb 2025

UNCTAD (2019) Facts & figures. https://unctad.org/press-material/facts-figures-0. Accessed 22 Feb 2025

US Department of Commerce (2024) Joint Statement on Harnessing Artificial Intelligence, Facilitating Data Flows and Empowering Digital Upskilling Between the United States Department of Commerce and the Kenyan Ministry of Information, Communication and the Digital Economy. https://www.commerce.gov/news/press-releases/2024/04/joint-statement-harnessing-artificial-intelligence-facilitating-data. Accessed 22 Feb 2025

US Department of Commerce (2024) Joint statement on harnessing artificial intelligence, facilitating data flows and empowering digital upskilling between the United States Department of Commerce and the Nigerian Ministry of Communications, Innovation and Digital Economy. https://www.commerce.gov/news/press-releases/2024/07/joint-statement-harnessing-artificial-intelligence-facilitating-data. Accessed 22 Feb 2025

Vasquez-Callo-Müller (2023) The making of the global CBPR forum. Global data law conference series: comparative data law

Mercy King'ori is a technology policy researcher with a keen focus on privacy and data protection in Africa. Mercy is currently working as a Policy Manager for Africa at the Future of Privacy Forum where she follows and analyzes privacy and data protection developments in Africa.

Ridwan Oloyede is the Co-Founder of Tech Hive Advisory, where he steers the technology policy team. He supports global businesses by advising on data protection laws and strategies, privacy program implementation, and monitoring. Ridwan is also the Co-Founder of PrivacyLensAfrica and Privacy Bar & Bants, where he uses visualisation and podcasting to draw attention to data protection in Africa. He is also a researcher having published widely on the nexus between technology and the law.

The Way Forward

Towards Fairer Norm Development for Digital-Rulemaking in the 21st Century

Lessons from the Global South: Africa and Latin America

Nelson Otieno Okeyo and Gabriel Zanatta Tocchetto

Abstract This chapter uses literature review through legal, historical and economic analysis and the hypothetical deductive method of building arguments. It highlights key issues that historical hindsight of colonial experience could mean for thinking and rethinking the current *status quo* of digital-rulemaking in Africa and Latin America. The chapter deepens the understanding of the matter by identifying critical themes for understanding the *status quo*, rationalizing and making recommendations aimed at promoting a fairer process of extraterritorial rulemaking by the EU.

Keywords Data governance · Data sharing models · Regulation · Data protection · Personal data · Data subject · Empowerment · Control · Individual control

1 Introduction

African and Latin American contexts for implementing the digital transformation are more or less similar when the two regions are compared with the EU, the current leading norm developer on digital regulation. Existing literature recognizes that geopolitics produce power imbalances that are, as is argued here, preserved in digital laws adopted across the world. This chapter uses data regulation standard setting (which has as representative the European General Data Protection Regulation - GDPR) and its influence in the Global South as a case study towards the contexts of Africa and Latin America both to confirm the current scholarly views and to further

N. O. Okeyo (✉) · G. Z. Tocchetto
Friedrich-Alexander-University of Erlangen-Nürnberg, Erlangen, Germany
e-mail: nelson.okeyo@fau.de

G. Z. Tocchetto
e-mail: gztocchetto@gmail.com

G. Z. Tocchetto
PUCPR, Curitiba, Brazil

J. Drexl et al. (eds.), *Comparative Data Law*, MPI Studies on Intellectual Property and Competition Law 32, https://doi.org/10.1007/978-3-031-91401-0_11

analyze key themes around which possible data injustices from digital innovations emerge and manifest themselves. It then uses the post-colonial experiences of the two regions to showcase how the development of standardizing laws, even if well-intended, may reincarnate and embolden historical data injustices in Africa and Latin America.

Using the hypothetical deductive method, it tests the hypothesis that EU's approaches to digital regulation, especially but not exclusively as seen with the GDPR, have consequences similar to those brought by colonialism. That is, they exert pressure for compliance in countries outside of the European block. The chapter is divided in three sections, starting with an overview of regulations in the twenty-first century, going through an historical and economic analysis of Latin America's history and a cultural structural analysis of the continent of Africa.

The chapter finds that the zeal for standardization of digital laws – in an environment of regional disparity in economic status – requires honest and collaborative interrogation. To support action-oriented discourse, the chapter highlights the issue of transplanting standards, development of curriculum, State-business divide, and public engagement as some of the specific themes of the interrogation. Finally, the chapter recommends policy dialogues on how to address these thematic issues towards balancing the needs for global standardization and respect for self-determination of the peoples in the Global South.

2 From Metals to Markets and Royalties: How Regulation Means Profit for the EU in the 21st Century

Far from the reality seen 500 years prior to it, the end of the Second World War gave rise to a very different world than the one humanity was accustomed to. Not only Europe was entering a locally peaceful series of decades,[1] but also some very important problems concerning, for example, nitrogen for food production were a thing of the past.[2] In this new era, technology not only became more important for the market, but the reality under which the market started existing, the digital world. As soon as 1945, inventions like the calculating machine called ENIAC[3] made permanent changes to approaches to solving problems which the best mathematical human minds could not tackle directly. And military demands didn't really end there. The second half of the 20th Century was the stage for the never-ending Space Race[4] and the military challenges of the cold war. Such events culminated in important technological advances that changed how both the market and the world work.[5]

[1] Aylwin et al. (2006), p. 2219.

[2] Ribeiro (2013) p. 1.

[3] Hartree (1946), p. 527.

[4] Pekkanen (2019), p. 92.

[5] Markusen (1992), p. 395.

Some of the big characteristics of the growing market in the twenty-first century come from the concept of ownership of immaterial goods, which derive from some concepts in law predating the First World War. One of the challenges that the industrial age put upon businesses was the need to innovate. This entails the ability to come up with techniques and methods that make production of products better and cheaper. The challenge for law was the need to protect intangible knowledge as a right, because of how valuable it became.

In the nineteenth century, Charles Woodbury, an American judge, appears as one of the important developers of concepts innate important for Intellectual Property. In one of his decisions from 1845, in the Circuit Court, D. Massachusetts. DAVOLL *et. al.* v. BROWN,[6] he sets some standards for the definition and tailoring of the protection given through Intellectual Property, a concept that is part of the basis for the big field of Immaterial Property. These concepts allow for the appropriation of knowledge and information through institutions of Intellectual Property, such as registries and patents. Such institutions enable not only creation of innovation, but differentiate what may or may not be called such for the purposes of withholding legal protection. In the twenty-first century, Immaterial Property, in the form of Intellectual Property, represents over a third of the GDP of the world's wealthiest nation, the United States of America in 2019. Out of the 21.73 trillion dollars of GDP,[7] 7.8 trillion dollars come from IP-intensive industries.[8]

Data protection and regulation is in itself a subject of Immaterial Property norms especially because both are protected by institutes of Intellectual Property. Even considering that datasets are more commonly protected through trade secrets than straight up registration under such institutes. As trade secrets they still fall under a category protected by such structures, as secrets that must be protected from the public even when best practices (for protecting consumers, for example) would advise the opposite. Such secrecy comes at a practical price, as not knowing what, when and how they are kept, results in "one of the strongest and most anti-competitive intellectual property rights ever conceived to the elementary particles and building blocks of knowledge."[9]

The big element about databases is that they do not only exist through the protection of state-enabled measures, such as laws, but also (and most importantly) through the enactment of secrecy, which is enacted by companies themselves. It is in this context that the era of Big Tech starts, with software that is protected and unavailable to the public, and datasets that are basically the building blocks of the AI that "make our lives more convenient".[10] By 2011, Neelie Kroes, one of the vice-presidents of the European Commission, who was responsible at the time for the ICT and Telecom

---

[6] Woodbury (1845). This note on Woodbury's role is taking into account the juridical answer to it, after the developments made by John Locke, Adam Smith and especially Jeremy Bentham on the matter.

[7] Bureau of Economic Analysis (2020).

[8] USPTO (2020), p. 3.

[9] Reichman/Samuelson (1997), p. 49.

[10] Kroes (2011), p. 2.

post, asked people and business to start giving up the gold they had for mining, in her speech entitled "Data is the new gold".[11] One may note that if data is the new gold, personal data comes in a format that is especially tailored for social utility, and one which is protected by a special kind of right, the right to privacy.

It is clear that Europe had intentions of leading this new way of mining and that it was aiming towards the regulation of an open approach to it, an approach which would try to influence the market towards open data sets as a public way of dealing with this new asset. This project definitely failed the test of time, as not only in the same year a scandal started forming an important critique for the concerns of privacy. The first Max Schrems case (C- 498/16[12]), showed the world that the efforts by the EU so far weren't enough for dealing with the problem. The reality of the importance of dealing with personal data as a serious matter became even more latent when Snowden released the NSA files,[13] and later with the Cambridge Analytica scandal.[14] The latter actually happened after the GDPR was already in effect.

The 2010s made it clear that a restrictive regulation was called for, and the EU had to react to the expectations left from the big events of the decade. Nevertheless, there is an innate cost to regulation that becomes obvious once the "Data is the new gold" speech is analyzed, and that its cost is hindering the possibility of mining such gold. The estimated cost of maintenance for GDPR complance to small and medium-sized companies is around 8% reduction in profits and 2% reduction in sales.[15]

It is because of operational cost that international influence is a great convenience for the EU, when it comes to personal data regulations. EU organizations have the advantage of a generally more stable currency, more available money and government protection from competition. They get a headstart on the act of compliance, because every legislation derived from the GDPR is, logically, written after its enactment. There are more local tools for enacting technical compliance, given that the European Union is not only a capable ICT developer, but a pivotal player in this area.[16] It is under these differences that the market is forcefully leveled through legal pressure of compliance, imposed without any consideration of whether this kind of regulation is a good idea for the third-party countries in question. Such are the required regulations put on as a requisite for accessing the European market.

---

[11] Kroes (2011), p. 3.
[12] Requejo (2018), p. 5.
[13] Bauman et al. (2014).
[14] Berghel (2018), p. 87.
[15] Presidente/Frey (2022).
[16] Bauer et al. (2024), p. 2.

2.1 The Social and Economic Position of the EU Against Latin America and Africa

When arranged in terms of continents or regions,, the data shown by the International Monetary Fund[17] reveals a very important reality in contexts of Latin America and Africa.In terms of markets, the whole GDP figures for Latin American countries (as described here), added up, amount for 6.373 trillion dollars while the African continent has the 2.995 trillion dollar figure. The North American market (excluding here Latin America) amounts to 29.014 trillion dollars and the European one for 24.881 trillion dollars.

Of course there are important things to be noted about inequalities, populations and quality of life between regions that cannot be noted by exclusively looking at GDP figures. Aside from that, there's a clear cut on what are generically the big markets of the world and which are the "emerging" markets in the level of continental regions. In a globalized market, economies search for beneficial integration, with the purpose of doing business and growing. Growth possibilities depend on how big a market is and whether it can be accessed, because you can't make money without trade, and you can't trade without money. That's especially the reason why accessing such a huge market as the EU has a huge impact for the Latin American and African markets.

With the EU as a great example of it[18] integration is an important tool for enhancing the competitiveness of markets. Integration is also an important tool for dealing with research and development investments and foreign direct investments.[19] This kind of integration, when worked by the EU and focused outwards, is done, among other tools, through the OECD.[20] One of the important hurdles put in place by the OECD for accession to it happens to be GDPR compliant norms, under the definition of "Interoperability of privacy and data protection frameworks".[21]

Of the single administered markets in the world, very few are bigger than the EU (with a GDP of 17.82 trillion dollars), those markets being the US (with a GDP of 26.85 trillion dollars) and China (with a GDP of 19.37 trillion dollars).[22] Understanding the fact that the EU is a trendsetter, especially for western markets, is important to make sense of why the GDPR, through the OECD also create restrictions for US trade deals, especially considering that their structure has already started adopting similar data protection frameworks as the GDPR since 2018, the same year

[17] IMF (2023).

[18] Campos et al. (2019).

[19] Ehigiamusoe/Lean (2019), p. 6.

[20] This relationship between the EU and the OECD dates back as far as the Marshall Plan. A description is laid down by the EU Delegation to the OECD and UNESCO and can be accessed at https://www.eeas.europa.eu/paris-oecd-unesco/relations-oecd-and-unesco_en?s=64.

[21] Robinson et al. (2021), p. 9.

[22] IMF (2023).

of Brazil's personal data protection law, the LGPD,[23] with the California Consumer Privacy Act (CCPA).[24]

In a nutshell, the position held by the EU is one of power towards the developing regions of Latin America and Africa, and one that can make it way harder for both the regions to ascend through integration and market deals to a position of economical parity with the developed world. With that in mind, the text of the GDPR and the creation of such hurdles for international trade deals is essentially forcing countries in the Global South to adopt european standards and views on data subjects regardless of what their internal democratic and legislative process may conclude of such subjects, under the threat of market exclusion and blockades for dealing with the world's biggest markets.

In treating the developing world through conditioning their participation in trade deals through the GDPR, not only does the EU directly undermine their democratic process, but it blocks the possibilities of structures for dealing with the same problem in different ways, essentially setting hurdles not only for the exercise of national sovereignty, but also for the development of local means of bureaucracy and law.

3 Latin American and Europe's Influence After the Loss of Military Dominance

The concept of globalization came through with a very different paradigm than the one colonialism had. A new way of putting a similar situation under very different lenses: instead of colonies, we are now talking about markets and supply chains. Instead of the exercise of political power through force, what is exercised is economical power through interests. Such exercise still comes from the "global center" (Global North) towards the "global periphery" (Global South). Inequality between countries became the engine for influence, and it also became the sphere through which this new form of exercising influence happens.[25] Instead of state military action, it became much more a process enacted through the globalized market and the ex-colonized peoples own needs for economic integration.

A good example of such a process and its mechanisms in Latin America is seen on the matter of personal data and how the EU's legal framework on it influenced the enactment of national legislations. As a block, the enactment of some provisions inside the EU started aiming at third countries for the sight of compliance as a means of accessing their own markets. Such a provision granted not only the players from inside the block the certainty that their peers from outside would have the same expenses with compliances, but also granted the EU with powers which, in practice, are equivalent to legislating in states outside of itself.

[23] Brazil (2018).

[24] California (2018).

[25] Bourguignon (2015), p. 38.

This story of extra-block legislating in the data protection sphere begins in 1995, when the Directive 95/46/EC of the European Parliament and of the Council[26] came to be. As a Directive, it started a movement of data protection inside the EU without the status that would be given later on under "regulation", but already with a provision for third country compliances and even a process for such recognition inside its text.

After the enactment of this Directive, countries in Latin America started focusing on data privacy with the direct goal of complying with article 25 (6) from Directive 95/46/EC.[27] Inside the same article, but under paragraph 4, was the dreaded provision that would exclude countries from dealing with data from the EU in case of not complying with the proper and certified security adequacies, saying if "a third country does not ensure an adequate level of protection [...] Member States shall take the measures necessary to prevent any transfer of data of the same type to the third country in question."[28] This provision was an obvious red-alert for a world that has seen the rise of the tech industry and that was just about to bear witness to the dotcom bubble burst in the year 2000.[29]

By the year 2000, Argentina already had Law No. 25.326 and by 2008,[30] Uruguay did it through Law No. 18331,[31] and both of them were "recognized by the European Commission in 2012 as a country that ensures an adequate level of protection for personal data transferred from the EU",[32] under the article of 95/46/ECc mentioned above. Even Mexico, which holds data protection as a constitutional provision since 1917 updated its standards in 2010 by law, and 2011 through regulation.[33]

3.1 *When Data Became a Problem and the EU Had the Solution*

In the 2010s it became obvious that data was very much an important asset for the evermore connected society. Personal data became central in the public debate in the EU from the case of Max Schrems, which culminated in case C-362/14,[34] and around the world because of the NSA leaks[35] and the Cambridge Analytica scandal,[36] which were among the many cases in which personal data protection was the subject

---

[26] European Union (2016).

[27] European Union (2016).

[28] European Union (2016).

[29] Panko (2008), p. 182.

[30] Argentina (2000).

[31] Uruguay (2008).

[32] Pehlivan (2021), p. 102.

[33] Pehlivan (2021), p. 105.

[34] Court of Justice Of The European Union (2014).

[35] Bauman et al. (2014).

[36] Berghel (2018), p. 84.

of concern.[37] Even before the Cambridge Analytica scandal, the case was made for the EU to set up something more strict than a Directive to deal with personal data not only of its citizens, but as a way to set it as a standard for the world.

By 2016, the EU had its new standard legislation for personal data protection, and now with a regulation, which means it is written to be held up as law in its member states. The GDPR[38] became a tool for the definition of a standard, which was quickly made to be understood and internalized by markets (the ones which held OECD partnerships valuable) aware of the need for new regulations about the matter. In 2018 Brazil, Latin America's largest global player by most standards, adopted its version of the GDPR through Law No. 13.709, called LGPD, for the portuguese acronym of General Data Protection Law,[39] containing a great number of similarities with its European counterpart,[40] in the year that Bauman followed the beginning of its process to join the OECD.[41]

Of course, the GDPR's success in Latin America does not end with Brazil, as it influenced legislation in Uruguay, Mexico and Argentina,[42] which actually allowed for the two countries to accede to Convention 108.[43] For all ends and purposes, it is necessary to consider that new regulations present a higher cost for operating in the market, and also important to notice that the playing field is hardly leveled when comparing Latin America to Europe. Such hurdles are already hard for innovating performance in the regulated markets,[44] but especially so when the field is not leveled.

This is where a question still remains, for not asking it would be equivalent to believing in the benevolence of states in the international scenario. What is in it for the EU to play the role of world regulation implementor besides the supposed role of improving countries' bureaucracies through its influence? Aside from market protection, which grants EU companies a horizontalization of some legal hurdles and costs (without granting companies outside of the EU the same access to its markets and money), it grants EU citizens the position of being the ones kept in mind for the drafting of such policies, meaning elements such as culture, average digital literacy and economic access are considered from a European standpoint for structural legislations such as the GDPR.

---

37 O'Neil (2017), p. 82.

38 European Union (2016).

39 Brazil (2018).

40 Lorenzon (2021), p. 50.

41 Zanetoni (2020), p. 38.

42 Pehlivan (2021), p. 105.

43 Council of Europe (1981).

44 Blind (2012), p. 393.

4 Coloniality of Data in the African Continent

The colonial era in Africa spans from the 18 th to the twentieth century. It was marked with aggressive colonial concession agreements, invasions, conquests, genocide, and expeditions in Africa. So deep and intense were the colonial conquests that by the 1900s, the colonizing powers had occupied almost 90% of the African continent.[45] This continued during the formation of the League of Nations, the United Nations and even during the first phase of the Cold War. The twentieth century phase – before the Berlin Conference on the partition of Africa –coincided with the industrial revolution that necessitated capitalistic tendencies of overexploitation of African resources, more especially raw materials such as rubber, tea, gold, copper among others.[46] Besides rich natural resources, provision of manpower during the first and second World Wars, and vantage points for military operations,[47] and implications of selective infrastructural investments in African States,[48] the scramble and partition of Africa was informed by certain motivations from which nature, traces and implications still persist in the digital age. Four are the motivations and approaches used by colonizers in the process, as is discussed below.

First, colonization of Africa was marked with cultural arrogance and related European ethnocentrism and international prestige or bragging rights for dominating a country overseas, and imperialism.[49] Coleman, who quotes Tanabe[50] in part, explains cultural arrogance as the 'White imagination that the African peoples were backward and undeveloped and that European were going to be their trustees of their affairs until they are mature enough to take over'.[51] This arrogance played out indirectly through use of agents, some of whom doubled as religious missionaries or explorers.[52] In some instances, where negotiations with leaders or works of missionaries and explorers failed, colonizers deployed force to promote such arrogance.[53]

Second, the phase was marked with an unholy union between the colonizing State and the businesses' interests. The colonialist governments granted monopolies to several trading companies who acted as agents of colonial expansionism and profit maximization. Britain, for example, used chartered companies such as the Imperial British East Africa Company (IBEACO) to initiate, manage and coordinate

---

[45] Coleman (2018), p. 418.

[46] Coleman (2018), p. 419.

[47] For example, the British Occupation of the Cape of Good Hope.

[48] Coleman (2018), p. 419.

[49] Khapoya (2015), p 101.

[50] Tanabe (2015).

[51] Coleman (2018), p. 417.

[52] The European States often subsidized exploratory trips to Africa. See Khapoya (2015), p 102. In the case of King Leopold II's expedition in Congo, he used Morton Stanley as an agent both for exploration and entering secretive cession agreements with leaders of communities that surrounded the Congo River. The use of agents was also present in the power structures that Britain, France, Germany and Portugal applied in their direct and indirect rule strategies.

[53] Coleman (2018), p. 420.

its acquisition of territories and protectorates in East Africa. Such companies, as Coleman notes, are taking a dominant role in the second wave of colonialism[54] while operating as trade monopolies and as 'legal extension of the crown' with power to exert sovereignty and exercise authority over the subjects and its resources.[55]

Third, the colonization phase witnessed dominant deployment of top-down structures and approaches for administration. The decisions including drawing boundaries during Conferences in Berlin were based on the convenience of the colonizing powers and were subsequently implemented at the community levels. Consequently, colonial administration reflected orders from the colonial powers and not based on the consensus of members of communities. Even at these community levels, colonial powers often engaged in 'high-level' discussions with the Chiefs and leaders who were mostly the collaborative agents of the colonial powers.

Fourth, the education and education styles were used as a tool of advancing the colonial agenda. Colonial powers, working in cahoots with missionaries, banned African indigenous languages and African heritage and identity and instead tailor-made the education curriculum to implement indirect rule. The replacement science-core curriculum introduced the so-called 'international trends' through a 'progressive' pedagogy.[56] Some education policies such as those of 'Britain's adapted education'[57] also played a key part. In the same vein, the structure of the replacement education curriculum was limited only to the extent that it served as a colonial tool of countering the African social and cultural beliefs which were the center of traditional learning. For example, science curriculum was not offered at the highest level making it largely non-academic with low career expectations for the African youth who were to serve as cheap labor.[58] So engrained was the problem that students in countries like Tanzania (now United Republic of Tanzania) publicly resigned from engineering schools complaining that the design of the education and curriculum aimed at making them junior engineers serving as cheap labor for senior engineers all of whom were non-Africans.[59]

The implication of the so called colonial aggression in teh scramble for Africa[60] in this phase both resulted into a blatant disregard to legitimate cultural, economic and political interests and concerns of African peoples. This too occurred whenever there was cultural or religious resistance against colonialism[61] or colonial expeditions'.[62] In the top-down administrative structure, feelings and input of the everyday

[54] Coleman (2018), p. 420.

[55] Coleman (2018), p. 422.

[56] See for instance the discussion in British Social Hygiene Council (BSHC) Memo on Biology and its place in Native Education in East Africa in Kallaway (2020).

[57] Kallaway (2020).

[58] Burton (2020), p. 211.

[59] Burton (2020), p. 210–211.

[60] Dimkpa (2015), p. 7.

[61] Refer to the killing of Bishop Hannington in Uganda. The bishop mounted religious resistance against British Rule.

[62] Khapoya (2015), p. 102.

community members, who were most affected by their decisions and laws, were disregarded. The motivations and approaches also disrupted the African peoples' socio-economic and political arrangements in the continent.[63]

4.1 *Relational Renaissance and Digital Rule-Making*

Between 1957 when Ghana first gained independence and shortly after South Africa gained independence in 1990, African governments sought to re-establish the relationship with the former colonial governments. This was done through foreign aid and donor funding agreements.[64] The former colonial powers also maintained foreign policies in Africa for restoration of trade partnerships and arrangements for restoration of companies from former colonizing States. Though it spanned over a long period of time, it was mainly concentrated during the period of so-called Third-Worldism commercial and political partnerships from the 1970s onwards.[65]

Also, as the African States were enjoying their new independence, the second phase of the Cold War presented them with an opportunity to strike global relationships with powers other than their former colonial masters[66] and navigate the field of global politics. Both phenomena birthed instances of transplant of industry standards which birthed technological dependence on the former colonies. Relational renaissance phase produced diversified interest of foreign powers in African States.[67] This phenomenon hindered the newly independent African States from making meaningful progress in implementing their regional good governance goals of the Organization of the African Unity.[68]

The impact of the renaissance period lived on until the era of development of digital regulations. Owing to the significant developments of the data protection laws in other regions, the data protection laws have been mostly inspired by foreign laws. The influence grew more prominently after the EU adopted its GDPR in 2016 effectively replacing the EU Data Protection Directive 1995. This played, and still continues to play, out as part of the 'Brussels effect',[69] a phenomenon which described the unilateral application of European regulatory frameworks and their externalization beyond their EU borders..[70] This effect caused states with data protection legislation

---

63 Coleman (2018), p. 418.

64 Burton (2020), p. 212–213. The Author quotes the Late Tanzanian President Nyerere saying that the Federal Republic was his preferred donor for the engineering faculty because of its financial power and the excellent reputation of German technology.

65 Calzati (2022), p. 273.

66 Onwaniban (2021), p. 284.

67 Onwaniban (2021), p. 287.

68 Fofack (2022).

69 Bradford (2020), p. 25.

70 This phenomenon is partly attributed to the more than other equally critical issues such as transnational waste dumping in Africa.

in Africa to increase even as most African states shun the AU's encouragement to ratify the African Convention on Cyber Security and Personal Data Protection 2014.[71] Besides general legislative developments, the GDPR also influenced some AU states to cause immediate reform on their data protection law to ensure it is aligned to the instrument. As a result, the period of proliferation has been marked with an unchecked transplant of regulatory standards to Africa. In some cases, it resulted in a rather curious affinity of African Member States to the Council of Europe's Cybercrime Conventions more than to the regional Malabo Convention.[72]

In the African context, Makulilo, a Professor of privacy law, notes that the influence of the instrument has led to a phenomenon where he describes the Brussels effect phenomenon as 'long arm of GDPR in Africa'.[73] Unlike a former Director General of the Council of Europe who thinks adopting the European standards is for the good of African societies,[74] Makulilo is of a more considered view that the adoption of the standards of the western "powers" during this era of proliferation is mainly motivated by the fear of loss of foreign investment in African States[75] and is done in defense of economic interests in the long-term. Makulilo' s verdict points to possibilities that an unchecked borrowing of best practices tends to lead to sidestepping of the realities, culture and social values of some sections of African societies in a fashion that follows the colonial footprints. The view shows how legal development could be which side step the perception of the people could be counterproductive either due to lack of legitimacy of data protection laws adopted by African States. Besides lack of legitimacy, the unchecked adoption of regulatory standards could lead to inheriting legal and legitimacy gaps in foreign laws. The legitimacy issues affect law's implementation and enforcement.

4.2 *Major ReThink: Beyond 'Honeymoon'*

Since 2018, there has been an emerging scholarly contribution that questions the motivations for the phenomena witnessed in the proliferation era. Coming against the backdrop of realization of data as the 'new oil or gold' or 'most valuable resource',[76] scholars are increasingly skeptical about the lack of effective protection of rights and fundamental freedoms for 'data mining' activities[77] and exploitation in Africa. The African continent still attracts major players in the field of technology as 'testing

[71] For instance, the GDPR and the Budapest Convention; See also Daigle (2021).

[72] Mbuvi (2011).

[73] Makulilo (2021), p 121.

[74] Mbuvi (2011).

[75] Makulilo (2021), pp. 117–146.

[76] Bhageshpur (2019); Coleman (2018), p. 424, also explains that data as a resource and access to data as the most valuable asset available both to States and corporations.

[77] Gwagwa/Kazim/Hiliard (2022), p 3.

grounds for their new technologies'[78]. Coleman faults the unchecked regulation and adoption of standards as reflecting digital colonialism, modern day scramble for Africa motivated by the resource in Africa, save this time, it is data which serves as a raw material whose harvesting and use yields profit.[79] The sentiments of Coleman are supported by the recent tussle between the US and Chinese model of digital investment in Africa which confirms, at least in the eyes of major world powers, that Africa is still a pawn of technological geopolitics and without a firm regulatory approach of its own.

For these reasons, Couldry and Ali made a note in 2021, that Africa has 'reached the breaking point' noting that the honeymoon of celebrating innovative technologies in Africa may well be 'thankfully' over. The authors' reference to a breaking point is the antithetical impact of discrimination exclusion and inequalities on various fronts such as gender, race and ethnicity that has resulted from the design, roll-out, and implementation of digital technologies in Africa. Couldry and Ali are of the view that law and practice has not addressed these impacts especially those from emerging technologies which result in mining of African data and dictation of algorithmic coding by the ideology of privileged whiteness,[80] itself a reflection of imperial and colonialist tendencies. Gwagwa, Kazim and Hilliard also share the concern of exclusion of African societies resulting from the design of emerging technologies such as artificial intelligence and algorithmic decision making[81].

The reality of globalization places African States at crossroads. They find themselves in a structure where they should be friends of the United States, cooperate with the European Union, trade with China while entertaining Russian interests.[82] This position, even with its potential for diversified growth, weakens the regulatory stance of the African states. It shifts the focus from having a harmonized approach to data protection and instead reduces them to pawns in geopolitics. As pawns of geopolitics, the State power to use legitimate, proper and effective data protection regulations have been reduced.[83]

Furthermore, just like the trading companies in the second wave of colonialism, the big technology companies wield immense powers due to their access to enormous amounts of data and their ability to 'leverage' their state linkages to pursue economic interests under the mantra of 'saving African peoples'. This motivation is strikingly similar, or at least comparable, to that of the colonial project. Also, the experiences of affected communities and individuals have 'peeled back the sugarcoat' and come to the inevitable realization of the realities of global digital geopolitics.

---

[78] Munya (2021).

[79] Coleman (2018), p. 417.

[80] Couldry/Ali Mejias (2021).

[81] Gwagwa/Kazim/Hilliard (2022), p. 3.

[82] Kohnert (2022). This article explains the Kremlin approach to access African elites, authoritarians and target the largely non-aligned States.

[83] Teevan/Tadesse (2022).

5 Conclusion

Not only in a historical perspective, but also considering a contemporaneous one, it is important to notice how the European region, especially under what is now the EU, provides an array of examples of successful attempts on exercising its will on other parts of the world. With time, the ones exercising such power and how it is exercised changes, but there has been a constant in the position of being controlled in such ways by the African and Latin American continental regions. Of course these controls are exercised with different degrees of success and of subjugation of the regions inside these contexts, but inside both of them it is possible to note similar characteristics in this specific position towards Europe.

It is not by accident that the organization of the EU accounts for the better-off countries in the region, which have important similarities that allow for the formation of such an union, and accounts for the countries that were most successful in their colonial sagas around the globe. As much as that is true, it should be realized that this position of power, when recognized in its problematic origins and position, should take care not to repeat the same mistakes (which are openly considered as such) with different kinds of acts of power.

When the data that compels the world and especially the African and Latin American contexts to follow the European Union show an uneven field for setting such standards, which ignore not only sovereignty, but the democratic interests of the states which end up regulated, a red alert should make the procedure one that is characterized by attention, and maybe even participation of stakeholders (states) which may undergo such standardization. Without taking this into account, this is a scenario where market inequality is the new powder and the legislation the new gun, which is once again aimed towards the old colonized players.

The clear character that plays the gold in this updated theater of horrors is partly played by money in itself and data privacy, the latter because it comes as a *sine qua non* condition for the compliance with the new regulations and the first because creating hurdles for the development of technologies abroad makes developing them in the EU more cost-effective. Without a choice on standards and with companies bleeding royalties money towards the first world just for operating, it becomes growingly hard for states to choose regulations which their markets may or may not respond to, which in turn is a condition that has to be weighed against the exclusion of participation in such markets in the first place.

In that process, the GDPR is not the first, but insofar one that really hits the target for the structure proposed within this article, being enough for the confirmation of the raised hypothesis of the similarities between the GDPR's consequences and the consequences of colonialism. It is important to notice that there are some overarching texts from the EU that raise similar colonial concerns in the case of extraterritoriality, under the scope of due diligence and corporate accountability[84], but this is a subject for future research.

[84] European Parliament (2020).

References

Argentina (2000) Ley 25.326 desde Octubre 4 de 2000. https://oas.org/juridico/PDFs/arg_ley25326.pdf. Accessed 24 Feb 2025

Aylwin CJ, König TC et al (2006) Reduction in critical mortality in urban mass casualty incidents: analysis of triage, surge, and resource use after the London bombings on July 7, 2005. The Lancet 368(9554):2219–2225

Bauer M, Pandya D, du Roy O (2024) Openness as strength: the win-win in EU-US digital services trade (No. 05/2024). ECIPE Policy Brief. https://www.econstor.eu/handle/10419/299180. Accessed 24 Feb 2025

Bauman Z, Bigo D et al (2014) After Snowden: Rethinking the impact of surveillance. Int Polit Sociol 8(2):121–144

Berghel H (2018) Malice domestic: the Cambridge analytica dystopia. Computer 51(05):84–89

Bhageshpur K (2019) Data is the new oil--and that's a good thing. Diakses di https://www.forbes.com/sites/forbestechcouncil/2019/11/15/data-is-the-new-oil-and-thats-a-good-thing. Accessed 24 Feb 2025

Blind K (2012) The influence of regulations on innovation: a quantitative assessment for OECD countries. Res Policy 41(2):391–400

Bourguignon F (2015) The globalization of inequality. Princeton University Press, Princeton

Bradford A (2020) The Brussels effect: how the European Union rules the world. Oxford University Press, Oxford

Brazil (2018) Law n. 13.709 from August 14th of 2018. http://www.planalto.gov.br/ccivil_03/_ato2015-2018/2018/lei/l13709.htm. Accessed 24 Feb 2025

Bureau of Economic Analysis (2020) Gross domestic product, fourth quarter and year 2019. Cit, 2(5). https://www.bea.gov/news/2020/gross-domestic-product-fourth-quarter-and-year-2019-advance-estimate. Accessed 24 Feb 2025

Burton E (2020) Engineering socialism: the faculty of engineering at the University of Dar es Salaam (Tanzania) in the 1970s and 1980s. In: Education and development in colonial and postcolonial Africa: policies, paradigms, and entanglements, 1890s–1980s. Springer International Publishing, Cham, pp 205–233. https://library.oapen.org/bitstream/handle/20.500.12657/23014/1007147.pdf?sequen#page=217. Accessed 24 Feb 2025

California (2018) California Consumer Privacy Act (CCPA). https://oag.ca.gov/privacy/ccpa. Accessed 24 Feb 2025

Calzati S (2022) 'Data sovereignty'or 'Data colonialism'? Exploring the Chinese involvement in Africa's ICTs: a document review on Kenya. J Contemp Afr Stud 40(2):270–285. https://doi.org/10.1080/02589001.2022.2027351

Campos NF, Coricelli F, Moretti L (2019) Institutional integration and economic growth in Europe. J Monet Econ 103:88–104

Coleman D (2018) Digital colonialism: The 21st century scramble for Africa through the extraction and control of user data and the limitations of data protection laws. Mich J Race Law 24:417

Couldry N, Mejias UA (2021) The decolonial turn in data and technology research: what is at stake and where is it heading? Inf Commun Soc 26:786–802

Council of Europe (1981) Convention 108 - Parties. https://www.coe.int/en/web/data-protection/convention108/parties. Accessed 24 Feb 2025

Court of Justice Of The European Union. Maximillian Schrems v Data Protection Commissioner, C-362/14. https://curia.europa.eu/juris/liste.jsf?num=C-362/14. Accessed 24 Feb 2025

Daigle B (2021) Data protection laws in Africa: a pan-African survey and noted trends. J Int Comput Econ 1. https://heinonline.org/HOL/LandingPage?handle=hein.journals/jice2021&div=2&id=&page=. Accessed 24 Feb 2025

Dimkpa P (2015) Colonialism, independence and underdevelopment in Africa: the pre-eminence and blame game. https://www.diva-portal.org/smash/get/diva2:1386410/FULLTEXT01.pdf. Accessed 30 May 2025

Ehigiamusoe KU, Lean HH (2019) Do economic and financial integration stimulate economic growth? A critical survey. Economics 13(1):20190004. https://doi.org/10.5018/economics-ejournal.ja.2019-4/html

European Parliament (2020) 2020/2129(INL) Corporate due diligence and corporate accountability. https://oeil.secure.europarl.europa.eu/oeil/popups/ficheprocedure.do?lang=en&reference=2020/2129(INL). Accessed 24 Feb 2025

European Union Directive 95/46/ECc of the European Parliament and of the Council. https://eur-lex.europa.eu/legal-content/EN/TXT/PDF/?uri=CELEX:31995L0046&from=EN. Accessed 24 Feb 2025

European Union (2016) General data protection regulation. https://eur-lex.europa.eu/legal-content/EN/TXT/PDF/?uri=CELEX:32016R0679. Accessed 24 Feb 2025

Fofack H (2022) Africa and the new Cold War: Africa's development depends on regional ownership of its security. https://www.brookings.edu/blog/africa-in-focus/2022/05/19/africa-and-the-new-cold-war-africas-development-depends-on-regional-ownership-of-its-security/. Accessed 24 Feb 2025

Gwagwa A, Kazim E, Hilliard A (2022) The role of the African value of Ubuntu in global AI inclusion discourse: a normative ethics perspective. Patterns 3(4):100462

Hartree DR (1946) The ENIAC, an electronic calculating machine. Nature 157(3990):527

International Monetary Fund - IMF GDP, current prices. https://www.imf.org/external/datamapper/NGDPD@WEO/OEMDC/ADVEC/WEOWORLD. Accessed 24 Feb 2025

Kallaway P (2020) Welfare and education in British Colonial Africa, 1918–1945. Education and development in colonial and postcolonial Africa: policies, paradigms, and entanglements, 1890s–1980s:31–54. https://library.oapen.org/bitstream/handle/20.500.12657/23014/1007147.pdf?sequen#page=46. Accessed 24 Feb 2025

Khapoya V (2015) The African experience. Routledge

Kohnert D (2022) The impact of Russian presence in Africa. https://papers.ssrn.com/sol3/papers.cfm?abstract_id=4067193. Accessed 24 Feb 2025

Kroes N (2011) Data is the new gold, Opening Remarks, Press Conference on Open Data Strategy. https://ec.europa.eu/commission/presscorner/api/files/document/print/en/speech_11_872/SPEECH_11_872_EN.pdf. Accessed 24 Feb 2025

Lorenzon LN (2021) Análise comparada entre regulamentações de dados pessoais no Brasil e na União Europeia (LGPD e GDPR) e seus respectivos instrumentos de enforcement. Revista Do Programa De Direito Da União Europeia 1:39–52

Makulilo AB (2021) The long arm of GDPR in Africa: reflection on data privacy law reform and practice in Mauritius. Int J Hum Rights 25(1):117–146. https://doi.org/10.1080/13642987.2020.1783532

Markusen A (1992) Dismantling the cold war economy. World Policy J 9(3):389–399

Mbuvi D (2011) African states urged to ratify Budapest Cybercrime Convention. In: African States Urged to Ratify Budapest Cybercrime Convention| CSO Online. https://www.csoonline.com/article/532916/data-protection-african-states-urged-to-ratify-budapest-cybercrime-convention.html. Accessed 24 Feb 2025

Munya A (2021) Five issues shaping data, tech and privacy in the African region in 2021. https://blog.mozilla.org/netpolicy/2021/01/27/five-issues-shaping-data-tech-and-privacy-in-the-african-region-in-2021/ Accessed 24 Feb 2025

O'Neil C (2017) Weapons of math destruction: how big data increases inequality and threatens democracy. Crown

Onwaniban E (2021) 281–296. In: Falol T, Salau MB (eds) (2021) Africa in global history: a handbook. Walter de Gruyter GmbH & Co KG. https://books.google.com.br/books?hl=pt-BR&lr=&id=Nw5QEAAAQBAJ&oi=fnd&pg=PP5&dq='Africa+and+the+Cold+War'+In+Falola,+Toyin,+and+Mohammed+Bashir+Salau,+eds.+Africa+in+Global+History:+A+Handbook+&ots=sBKp74BX55&sig=O5Ne3gD6DNrF8nyk5yu3sq6Gr6U#v=onepage&q='Africa%20and%20the%20Cold%20War'%20In%20Falola%2C%20Toyin%2C%20and%20Mohammed%20Bashir%20Salau%2C%20eds.%20Africa%20in%20Global%20History%3A%20A%20Handbook&f=false. Accessed 24 Feb 2025

Panko RR (2008) IT employment prospects: beyond the dotcom bubble. Eur J Inf Syst 17(3):182–197. https://doi.org/10.1057/ejis.2008.19

Pehlivan CN (2021) Data protection in Latin America: an overview. Global Priv Law Rev 2(2). https://web.archive.org/web/20220329093317id_/https:/kluwerlawonline.com/api/Product/CitationPDFURL?file=Journals%5CGPLR%5CGPLR2021010.pdf. Accessed 24 Feb 2025

Pekkanen SM (2019) Governing the new space race. Am J Int Law 113:92–97

Presidente G, Frey CB (2022) The GDPR effect: how data privacy regulation shaped firm performance globally. https://cepr.org/voxeu/columns/gdpr-effect-how-data-privacy-regulation-shaped-firm-performance-globally. Accessed 24 Feb 2025

Reichman JH, Samuelson P (1997) Intellectual property rights in data. Vand L Rev 50:49

Requejo M (2018) Max Schrems against Facebook. Max Planck Institute Luxembourg Working Paper, (2018-4). https://papers.ssrn.com/sol3/papers.cfm?abstract_id=3206707. Accessed 24 Feb 2025

Ribeiro D (2013) Processo de Haber-Bosch. Revista de Ciência Elementar, 1:1–2. https://rce.casadasciencias.org/rceapp/art/2013/031/. Accessed 24 Feb 2025

Robinson L, Kizawa K, Ronchi E (2021) Interoperability of privacy and data protection frameworks. Going Digital Toolkit Note, No. 21. https://goingdigital.oecd.org/data/notes/No21_ToolkitNote_PrivacyDataInteroperability.pdf. Accessed 24 Feb 2025

Tanabe J (2015) Scramble for Africa. New World Encyclopaedia. https://www.newworldencyclopedia.org/p/index.php?title=Scramble_for_Africa&oldid. Accessed 24 Feb 2025

Teevan C, Tadesse L (2021) Digital geopolitics in Africa: moving from strategy to action. https://ecdpm.org/application/files/7816/7578/1436/Digital-Geopolitics-Africa-Moving-Strategy-Action-ECDPM-Briefing-Note-150-2022.pdf. Accessed 24 Feb 2025

United States Patent and Trademark Office - USPTO (2020) Intellectual property and the U.S. economy: Third edition. 2020. https://www.uspto.gov/ip-policy/economic-research/intellectual-property-and-us-economy. Accessed 24 Feb 2025

Uruguay (2008) Ley N° 18331, desde 11 de Agosto de 2008, Ley de Protección de Datos Personales. https://www.impo.com.uy/bases/leyes/18331-2008. Accessed 24 Feb 2025

Woodbury CJH (1845) Circuit Court, D. Massachusetts. DAVOLL et al. v. BROWN. https://law.resource.org/pub/us/case/reporter/F.Cas/0007.f.cas/0007.f.cas.0197.pdf. Accessed 24 Feb 2025

Zanetoni JDPL (2020) PERSPECTIVAS PARA A ACESSÃO DO BRASIL JUNTO À OCDE: PASSADO, PRESENTE E FUTURO. Revista Brasileira De Direito Internacional 6(1):36–56

Nelson Otieno Okeyo is digital rights advocate with a keen interest in data protection. He is an active legal practitioner and currently the team leader for the data protection practice at MMK Advocates, Nairobi. He is a doctoral researcher in the field of business and human rights at the Friedrich-Alexander University of Erlangen-Nuremberg, Germany. Nelson is also a teaching assistant at the Chair of African Legal Studies at the University of Bayreuth, Germany, where he is also completing PhD on data protection impact assessments.

Gabriel Zanatta Tocchetto is a PhD candidate in Law in the field technology regulations and Law at PUCPR with CAPES/PROEX scholarship (2021) and PhD Candidate in Law at Friedrich-Alexander-Universität Erlangen-Nürnberg, under a cotutelle agreement. He also worked as a guest researcher at Friedrich-Alexander-Universität Erlangen-Nürnberg with a DAAD/CAPES scholarship (2022/2023). Gabriel has a Masters in Law from Faculdade Meridional with CAPES/FAPERGS scholarship (2018/2020) and holds a postgraduate degree in Business Law from Faculdade Estácio (2020/2021). He is a licensed attorney and holds a Bachelor degree in Law from Faculdade Meridional Imed (2013/2017).

Data Localization, Hegemony, and the Popular Will: A View from Canada

Matt Malone

Abstract Data localization, the practice of keeping data within the region it originated from, is a persistent demand in many parts of the world – and calls for data localization are not going away. Many citizens are beginning to express concerns about the dangers of data that is not localized; at the same time, they are often making countervailing demands on their governments for more unrestricted access to data, facilitated by new information communication technology services. This chapter examines the tensions imminent to the free movement of data while respecting the power of states to guarantee essential rights and freedoms of data subjects. It suggests an underlying tension between hegemonic power (state and non-state, often corporate) and the popular will is a defining feature of the legal and regulatory landscape. Using a Canadian example, this article examines how citizens often support data localization as a concept, until it interrupts their digital landscape. The adverse interests of government actors, corporate entities, and the popular will have given rise to conflicts marked by questions about the nature of where power truly resides in this online sphere.

Keywords Data localization · Popular will · National security · Cross-border data flows · Jurisdiction · Data harvesting · Social media · Data protection · Data protectionism

1 Introduction

In a paradigm where technology is driving much of contemporary social, cultural, and technological innovation, data has become the oil of the digital economy; and cross-border data flows are its combustion. As sites where collective and individual actors assert often dueling interests and values, cross-border data flows have become

M. Malone (✉)
Faculty of Law, University of Ottawa, Ottawa, ON, Canada
e-mail: matt.malone@uottawa.ca

J. Drexl et al. (eds.), *Comparative Data Law*, MPI Studies on Intellectual Property and Competition Law 32, https://doi.org/10.1007/978-3-031-91401-0_12

a key vector reflecting and channeling power dynamics in the early 21st Century.[1] Against this backdrop, calls for data localization manifest how state and non-state entities seek to assert or thwart jurisdiction, protect or erode national security, elevate or diminish economic and social development, and achieve other ends. Erecting or evading legal, administrative, and technical barriers to facilitate the flow of data across borders is a signature conflict in today's interconnected and digital world.

In this context, calls for data localization are not going away any time soon.[2] As McKinsey notes, there has been a wave of legislative and policy efforts to enshrine data localization around the world – 75 percent of all countries have "implemented some level of data localization rules" in recent years.[3] Such calls are far from merely technical in nature; they are expressions of power that speak to the urgency of addressing the challenges of applying jurisdiction to digital activity. These battles are largely being fought by powers like states (e.g., the United States, China, and the European Union) and non-state multinational corporations (e.g., Alphabet, Meta, TikTok). But these battles over data localization fought by state and non-state hegemonic powers involve another actor: the popular will, the aggregate of data subjects that exist in these actors' respective spheres of influence and control. The popular will serves to constrain both sets of powers, although it makes often contradicting demands of its own for more permissive *and* more restrictive data governance.

Myriad questions face governments, public citizens, and lobbyists alike when it comes to data localization, which this chapter will explore as its main research subjects and questions. How can personal data move freely while respecting the power of states to guarantee essential rights and freedoms of data subjects? To what extent are those data subjects better considered users of services instead of citizens of countries? And to what degree should they be concerned about the discourse to power by both state and non-state actors? How do the different approaches impact them? What responsibilities for all should exist as a baseline? This chapter seeks to answer, or at minimum address, these questions, through careful consideration of several international perspectives on data localization, as well as examine the tension between hegemonic power and the will of the populous.

For example, in Canada, polls show data localization measures are very popular with Canadians.[4] Recent parliamentary hearings into the use of social media platforms for data harvesting and unethical or illicit sharing of data with foreign entities reflected this popularity, with politicians expressing reflexive support for data localization. Questions during the committee hearings lobbed by politicians at representatives from social media companies frequently channeled concerns about the physical location of data. "How does that protection of data play out when we see that a company like TikTok is storing data in the U.S., in Singapore, in Malaysia and not in Canada?" one politician asked. "How do we control the servers or the access to

---

[1] Meltzer et al. (2018).

[2] Corey et al. (2021).

[3] McKinsey (2022), p. 2.

[4] BC Freedom of Information and Privacy Association (2021).

Canadian data when it's physically not present in Canada?" asked another.[5] These questions tap into a discourse of a population that is strongly supportive of data localization measures.

Many of the questions posed in the introduction to this chapter are answered as a matter of course by state/bloc and corporate conduct. Small states like Canada are frequently caught in a bind. Not only do such states often lack expertise or capacity to implement and enforce effective data governance regimes, but they also face pressure from larger actors to adopt their standards or risk losing access to their markets. In Canada, British Columbia's decision-makers have, for some time, had to reckon with provisions in the Canada-United States-Mexico free trade agreement, which requires that no party country restrict cross-border data flows.[6] In 2021, a superior court in the province addressing a question of Twitter's exposure to liability for defamatory comments posted on its platform saw the social media company invoke this treaty in its defense from liability.[7] The Comprehensive and Progressive Agreement for Trans-Pacific Partnership imposes similar obligations on Canada.[8] Proposed privacy and data protection legislation for the private sector currently before federal Parliament omits any mention of cross border data flows specifically out of deference to these treaties, eschewing any new or European-style restrictions on the flow of personal information across borders.[9] Meanwhile, efforts to constrain Meta and Alphabet have been met with threats of embargoes (or actual embargoes) by those entities on services in the country (e.g., news sharing and new generative AI services).[10]***Hypothesis.***

This chapter stakes two essential claims. First, it argues the popular will is often confused and contradictory with respect to data governance, in ways where hegemonic powers operating in this world – with clearer goals like increased control or surveillance power – are rarely similarly disarrayed. Second, it argues that while calls for data localization are unquestionably popular when data subjects are surveyed, such polls often take a simplistic measure of support.

2 The Canadian Perspective

Canada has already established limited data localization requirements for certain types of data, based on sensitivity. For example, the Canadian federal government's standards on online public opinion research surveys require researchers to ensure "that all databases containing any information related to the [public] survey be stored on servers and back-up servers located solely in Canada."[11] There is little mystery as

[5] Standing Committee on Access to Information, Privacy and Ethics (2023).

[6] CUSMA (2018), Chapter 19.

[7] Giustra v Twitter Inc (2021) BCSC 54.

[8] CPTPPA (2018), Chapter 14.

[9] A-2023–00132 (2023).

[10] Bloomberg News (2023); CBC News (2024).

[11] Public Services and Procurement Canada. Government of Canada (2020), p. 41.

to why such protocols are in place: they enjoy widespread popular support. A survey recently noted 75% of Canadians have concerns about an organization transferring their personal information outside of Canada.[12] Many sub-state actors in Canada have also made calls for better control of their data. For example, data sovereignty is seen as an important way for Indigenous peoples within Canadian territories to create, collect, and make use of culturally relevant information that reflects their unique worldviews, needs, and priorities, which may not align with the Canadian state.[13] The passage of the United Nations Declaration on the Rights of Indigenous People, which has been incorporated into Canadian law, affirms such rights.

And yet while data localization is popular in Canada, Canadians are often quick to lament when digital services from companies such as TikTok, Meta, and Alphabet are not unrolled in their jurisdiction when they are available elsewhere – even when the reason traces back to data governance initiatives imposed by the government in response to expressions of the popular will. This sentiment was displayed recently in the popular Canadian uproar over Meta's decision to block news in the country and Alphabet's failure to implement its Gemini project in Canada. These companies took such measures on account of restrictive data governance policies and laws imposed by the federal government in response to demands of the popular will.[14] This inconsistent set of demands is emblematic of the contradictory impulses that underlie calls for data localization. Despite the popularity of data localization measures, they can have adverse effects that are rarely contemplated in the same polls that measure their popularity – such as increased costs; downward pressure on economic forces; performance inefficiencies (e.g., increased latency); greater friction for users; and even cybersecurity vulnerabilities.[15] Where the popular will with respect to data flows is confused and prone to making contradictory demands, hegemonic forces have clearer, targeted objectives which they are often more successful in pursuing. Their calls for and against data localization favour more direct and self-serving objectives that do not reflect or channel these conflicting interests. The public is caught in-between.

No example better illustrates these dynamics than the recent dismantling of a signature data localization measure in British Columbia. In 2004, British Columbia amended its de facto privacy and data protection legislation to require data localization for certain public sector organizations collecting personal information, such as hospitals, schools, and policing bodies.[16] That data localization provision created many administrative and technical challenges, which were heavily criticized and targeted by lobbyists.[17] The province's Office of the Information and Privacy Commissioner – the equivalent of a regulatory privacy and data protection body in

[12] BC Freedom of Information and Privacy Association (2021).

[13] Access to Information Review (2023).

[14] Lee (2023).

[15] Carr (2020) and ECIPE (2023); Christakis (2020b); Swire et al. (2022, 2023); Huddleston et al. (2020).

[16] Miscellaneous Statutes (Minor Corrections) Amendment Act (2021).

[17] BCNET, 2016.

the province, albeit with restrained powers compared to a European data protection authority – strongly defended the maintenance of the law against these actors' calls to dismantle it. A review by a special committee of the B.C. provincial legislature ultimately concluded that the requirement should be preserved due to its importance in protecting personal information. However, at the continued pressure of lobbyists, the provincial government scrapped the data localization requirement, even as it was promising to clamp down on online injustices by introducing legislation pertaining to greater assignment of liability to social media companies for their processing of user data.[18]

One notable exception to the embargoes mentioned above has been the posturing around TikTok, which the Canadian federal government banned on government-issued devices in early 2023. Modeled after a similar American move that was taken in December 2022, the federal government's decision to ban TikTok came in the aftermath of embarrassing allegations of Chinese foreign interference in the 2019 and 2021 Canadian federal elections.[19] Citing "privacy and security" risks, the federal government's move to ban the specific app on government-issued devices was intended to address threats identified in underlying intelligence briefs by imposing a hard block on any data flows.[20] Here, the government's stated concerns focused on the physical location of data, either in China or with potential access by China. While these fears have been stoked by politicians, they have not been accompanied with any awareness of the fact that Canadian data law is the main culprit for these practices, given it embraces a nearly fully unregulated approach to cross-border data flows.

Other inconsistencies arose from the federal government's targeted ban on TikTok. The intelligence brief that warned about the data harvesting practices was five months old by the time the selective ban was implemented; and even after the selective ban was implemented, the Canadian government continued to buy social media advertising on TikTok – spending almost $2 million last year on the app, despite its stated concerns.[21] Moreover, the federal government did not take any measures to ban other social media apps on government-issued devices, such as VKontakte, Facebook, Tinder, Grindr, Gab, Truth Social, or Discord. All of these remained accessible on government devices. To be sure, TikTok deserved opprobrium for its privacy violations, data harvesting, and narrative control practices, as well as for granting access to data despite assurances otherwise.[22] Like other social media apps, it has been a vector for online harm, with a business model focused on privacy-invasive targeted advertising. The app's safety features for children have also been easy to bypass. But the federal government's outrage ignored the fact that these harms were occurring on other social media services, too – and that reforms to privacy and

[18] Amendment Act (2021).

[19] Fife et al. (2023).

[20] Treasury Board Secretariat (2023).

[21] Patel (2023); Public Services and Procurement Canada (2023).

[22] Baker-White (2022); Fürst Haugen (2022); Reuters (2022); Goujard (2023).

data protection laws would not only have addressed the problems with TikTok, but with *all* social media companies.

Simplistic moves, like the one to ban TikTok on government-issued devices – the Canadian federal government ban was mirrored in most of the provinces afterwards, as well as in many peer jurisdictions – have been very popular with liberal democratic governments invoking discourses of "privacy and security." These discourses inform similar but more widespread calls for restrictions on cross-border flows, up to and including calls for data localization. But they exhibit many inconsistencies. And they have not always been popular with people when it comes time to pay the bill for their real costs, suggesting that such calls remain poorly understood. While such moves are a blunt example of attempts to restrict data flows, they are also an example of a more complex battle that is, principally, fought between differing sets of hegemonic actors fighting to control the movement of data. The popular will is often ignored in these battles. As the case of TikTok shows, many of these disputes between hegemonic actors neglect certain demographics. In the case of TikTok, the most important demographic backdrop has remained generational. Internal federal Canadian government surveys showed that about 10% of people below the age of 35 use the app for "several hours a day."[23] Likewise, while American politicians have uniformly clamoured to ban the app, two-thirds of teens are on it, and 30% of people below the age of 29 regularly get their news from it.[24] Yet one American state has already taken measures to ban it, albeit unsuccessfully so far.[25] Overall, this context suggests that efforts to control how, what, and where data is collected by this private app are out of alignment with segments of the popular will, insofar as it is expressed through actual use of the app.

3 The European Perspective

The implicit tension between increasing data flow in the digital economy and imposing restraint on data flow with measures like localization has already become a frequent site of strain, notably with the longstanding European Union-United States cross-border data flows dispute. As sovereign actors engage with their responsibilities around issues like privacy and security, private corporate actors focus on increasing data flow to achieve profit objectives. These countervailing interests have given rise to conflicts marked by difficult questions about the nature of where power truly resides in the online sphere.

The TikTok example above is an a relatively recent case study. In the European Union, the restrictive approaches to privacy and data protection undertaken since the passage and implementation of the General Data Protection Regulations (GDPR) have offered a strong indication of a preference for restrictive approaches to data

[23] A-2023–00007 (2023).

[24] Eva Matsa (2023); Paz (2022).

[25] Vanian (2023).

governance. The recently proposed European Cybersecurity Certification Scheme for Cloud Services has promised to take these even further – hinting at the establishment of certifications promising varying levels of assurance, with the highest-level requiring data localization.[26] These trendlines mirror other recent moves. Following the *Schrems II* decision, wherein the Court of Justice of the European Union invalidated the Privacy Shield adequacy agreement sanctioning cross-border flows of European personal information to the United States; at the time, many European politicians and administrators made coded calls for data localization through digital independence.[27] Subsequently, guidelines from the European Data Protection Board were understood by data law experts as moving towards harder data localization requirements.[28] Of course, many corporate actors have proven to be nimble at responding to data localization requirements by investing in the type of digital infrastructure that suits these localization mandates. Many cloud servers have responded to the European initiatives by unveiling locally tailored options. One start-up, InCountry, was created in direct response to the obligation to meet data residency requirements.[29] These business tactics are mirrored in Canada, too: after data localization efforts were introduced in British Columbia, several cloud computing companies began opening data centers in that jurisdiction.[30]

4 The Broader Perspective

Of course, countries in the liberal democratic world are not the only ones embracing stricter data governance. As McKinsey notes, "75 percent of all countries have implemented some level of data localization rules" in recent years.[31] Several countries with varying commitments to democracy and the rule of law are enforcing such measures. In 2014 and 2015, Russia introduced Federal Law No. 97-FZ (amending Federal Law No. 149 FZ) and Federal Law No. 242-FZ, which require the storage of personal information concerning Russians on Russian servers (initially only copies – then expanded to a stricter requirement to record, store, and process data in Russia). Most recently, in July 2022, Federal Law No. 266-FZ (amending Federal Law No. 152-FZ) implemented sweeping measures for the extraterritorial application of the law, along with other stricter provisions. Since 2016, when China passed the Cyber Security Law, which enables regulators to impose localization requirements (i.e., art. 37: "Critical information infrastructure operators that gather or produce personal

---

[26] Yun Chee (2023).

[27] *Data Protection Commissioner v Facebook Ireland Limited, Maximillian Schrems* (2020) CJEU C-311/18; Berliner Beauftragte für Datenschutz und Informationsfreiheit (2020); Christakis (2020a).

[28] Recommendations 01/2020 (2020); Christakis (2020a).

[29] Sawers (2019).

[30] Amazon will open its first Canadian data centre in Montreal (2016); Sverdlik (2015).

[31] McKinsey (2022), p. 2.

information or important data during operations within the mainland territory of the People's Republic of China, shall store it within mainland China"), the country has undergone a strong push towards localization with supplementary provisions in the Data Security Law (2021) and Personal Information Protection Law (2021). And in various other countries, similar moves are afoot. In October 2018, India implemented a requirement that payment data on domestic transactions be stored in India (this was subsequently scrapped following American pressure). In October 2021, Indonesia implemented data localization requirements for the processing of certain personal data. In August 2022, Vietnam imposed localization requirements for nearly all personal information, including biometric and financial data.

Although these state actors have operated under putatively desirable rationales to justify their actions, like security and privacy, they indicate an interest in data localization in non-democratic states, too. The invocation of digital sovereignty and calls for data localization by democratic and authoritarian regimes alike has revealed the difficulty, as Prof. Theodore Christakis has noted, of distinguishing "between data *protection* and data *protectionism*."[32] (Original emphasis). These observations have helped create the case for (re)assessing risks with respect to the increasing calls for data localization, as they concern economic costs, cybersecurity disadvantages, and potential infringements on human rights.[33]

5 The American Perspective

To account for these trends, history should not be forgotten. Unquestionably, American activities have provided an important catalyst for Canadian, European, and others' actions with respect to more restrictive data governance. For example, the passage of the *Patriot Act* explicitly motivated Canadian administrators to require that all public opinion research conducted for the government remain localized in Canada.[34] The trauma of the Snowden revelations has motivated an unprecedented push back against American approaches to data governance by Europeans, which many Americans still struggle to comprehend. The fact that Snowden has still not received a pardon for his activities shows that the "traitor or whistleblower" discussion, that has long been answered by other countries, remains unsettled in the United States. Further, the United States seems to put little effort into assuaging broader concerns by implementing uniform privacy or data protection law. The United States has also demonstrated strong resistance to sovereign-centered data governance in global fora. For example, in 2019 the Trump Administration introduced demands at the World Trade Organization (WTO) e-commerce negotiations that would require strong mandates for cross-border data flows and prohibitions on data localization. While the Biden administration retracted these demands in October 2023, the United

[32] Christakis (2020b).

[33] Christakis (2020b).

[34] Public Services and Procurement Canada. Government of Canada (2020).

States has a long history of exporting legal norms and requirements through trade fora like the WTO.

6 Bringing It Together

Ultimately, the question of who will determine the normative order of data flows is an unsettled question, to be answered by the degree to which hegemonic actors successfully navigate the inconsistent demands of the public will. In the absence of citizens taking control of data for themselves – a phenomenon no one expects on a widespread basis soon – a state or private-sector order seems likely to prevail. For now, this question remains unresolved in the democratic world. European authorities show an eagerness and creativity in developing new regulations and imposing fines on powerful American corporate actors, while the United States avoids this approach. American private actors show a willingness to absorb such fines as a cost of doing business – moving fast and breaking things – while European companies remain, by comparison, largely non-competitive. Attempts to draw closer to one another seem, inherently, to result in conflict, only highlighting differences in norms and values.

7 Contemporary Movements

It is plausible that the character of these disputes has been crystalized from their beginnings by misperceptions about each side's ability to grasp the others' concerns. Max Schrems's own legal activism originated following an educational exchange at Santa Clara University in Silicon Valley, when a guest to his course, a Facebook-employed privacy lawyer, showed "limited grasp of the severity of data protection laws in Europe."[35] As Schrems stated in May 2023, after Meta had been recently fined over $1 billion for illegal data transfers: "Meta has not even given [European data law] a try. They basically said, 'We don't care what European law is, and what the Court of Justice says in the European Union,' and [so they] just continued with [illegal transfers] anyways for 10 years."[36] However, Schrems has noted that he believes there are solutions to the cross-border transfers dispute – starting with a more nuanced version of Sect. 702 of the Foreign Intelligence Surveillance Act, which has underpinned the National Security Agency's sweeping signals intelligence operations. Currently, a warrant is needed to spy on Americans, but not foreigners, so long as there is a "significant purpose" for the collection.[37]

---

[35] Hill (2012).

[36] CGTN (2023).

[37] Foreign Intelligence Surveillance Act, 50 U.S.C. § 702 (1978).

Schrems has also advocated for a "No Spy Agreement" that would help facilitate cross-border data flows and obviate the need for data localization measures.[38] Peter Swire has defended different normative frameworks for surveillance of domestic and foreign nationals, and argues the American framework meets the requirement in the GDPR for an "independent and impartial tribunal" to seek recourse against government practices concerning privacy and data security.[39] However, one persistent area of concern is Executive Order 12,333, which extends the information-gathering powers of the Central Intelligence Agency – an order unlikely to disappear anytime soon.

As that dispute drags on, authoritarian regimes are undergoing their own hardening. The European-or-American approach to data governance question may be resolved by externalities, such as non-democratic, authoritarian states enforcing their own normative orders of data localization in periods of unprecedented economic and military ascendence. As the longstanding data transfer dispute between the European Union and the United States best demonstrates, these nations have different laws and systems for data protection. And yet, as we can see from the data above, they are closer than the approaches of non-democratic states like Russia and China. This divergent set of values and norms has imposed a significant divide between the Americans and Europeans at precisely a moment when non-democratic powers are rising. What makes the dispute so striking – apart from its longevity, economic impact, and legal uncertainty – is the degree to which disagreement in the democratic bloc enables the authoritarian regimes to advance their own normative positions. Likewise, the effort to "find practicable ways for data to flow in a manner that protects privacy and other fundamental rights" among democratic states, such as through venues like the G7, where the late Japanese Prime Minister Shinzo Abe spearheaded the Data Free Flow with Trust initiative, have been repeatedly affirmed in light of the novel security landscape that includes a more aggressive Russia.[40] But they are dead on arrival.[41]

8 The "NATO" of It All

The irony of this dispute is that most members of the European Union and the United States itself already belong to a security alliance where they have mutually agreed to defend one another and come to each other's aid in the event of attack. By moving discussions around data flows to a forum where members share security interests, such as NATO, the United States and most European countries may be able to move past their narrow conceptions of security. NATO could take an even more pronounced role here, by creating a zone for the free flow of personal data. As the present author

[38] CGTN (2023).

[39] Swire (2019).

[40] G7 Hiroshima Leaders' Communique (2017).

[41] Joel (2023).

recently argued in a paper at the CyCon, NATO has the legitimacy and authority to act in this respect. NATO's governing body, the North Atlantic Council, is empowered by Article 9 of the North Atlantic Treaty to settle any disputes involving its members by any peaceful means. In effect, Article 9 gives the Council power to implement the Treaty's provisions, including Article 2's commitment to "promoting conditions of stability and well-being" through the elimination of "conflict in [members'] international economic policies" and "encourag[ing] economic collaboration between any or all [members]." Article 9 allows the Council to create "subsidiary bodies as may be necessary" to achieve the goals of the alliance. NATO has already set up multiple committees under this power (most famously, its Military Committee).

There is nothing to prevent NATO from setting up a committee laying out a personal consumer data flow framework for its members, with a Safe Harbour Principles or Privacy Shield-style framework of its own. As the GDPR notes in Article 2, its provisions do not apply to activities that "fall outside the scope of [European Union] law," as NATO does. The founding treaties of the European Union establish a particularly strong exemption to NATO from European Union law, with the Treaty of the European Union stating European Union law "shall not prejudice the specific character of the security and defence policy of certain Member States."[42] They also set forth that European Union law "shall respect the obligations of certain Member States, which see their common defence realised in the North Atlantic Treaty Organisation (NATO), under the North Atlantic Treaty and be compatible with the common security and defence policy established within that framework." The GDPR also explicitly states that its provisions do not apply to data processing when European Union member states are carrying out activities which fall within the scope of their obligations on common foreign and security. However, this solution shows no likelihood of coming to fruition, given the seemingly irreconcilable divergence between the two democratic blocs.

For now, such solutions sound fanciful. And harder localization keeps coming. Since 2015, trendlines in the European Union are shifting towards a more restrictive privacy and data protection policy and have decisively reshaped global directions in data governance. After the European Union Commission's adequacy decision on the Safe Harbour Principles was toppled by the Court of Justice for European Union in October 2015, the introduction of the GDPR represented the most significant change in information law in perhaps two decades. With its rules around the right to be forgotten (Art. 17), data transfers to foreign jurisdictions (Art. 45), and the creation of the European Data Protection Board (Arts. 68–84), the subsequent invalidation of the Privacy Shield ushered in an uncertain era of data governance. In November 2020, the introduction of the draft Data Governance Act[43] – extending the GDPR protections for personal data to non-personal data transfers – accelerated this trend. A confusing raft of other European acts and regulations have continued this trend, despite some

[42] Treaty on the European Union (2012), Article 42§7, "Mutual Defence Clause.".

[43] *European Data Governance Act*, Regulation (2022)/868 of the European Parliament, in force 23 June 2022.

recent appeasement with the announcement of the European Union-United States Data Privacy Framework.

9 Conclusion

The contemporary paradigm is accompanied with some important questions of enforceability that we also cannot ignore. The fact that data transfers by large technology companies in the United States continued unabated following the invalidation of the Privacy Shield – and in the absence of nothing but standard contractual clauses or binding corporate rules – leaves important doubts about the European Union's powers of enforceability. Shifting from the regulation of cross-border data flows to data localization requirements may obviate the shortcomings of such enforcement. As Reuters reported in May 2023, the proposed European Union Cloud Services scheme requirements, in place for cloud service providers to operate in the European Union, would require "no entity from outside the European Union having effective control over the CSP (cloud service provider), to mitigate the risk of non-European Union interfering powers undermining European Union regulations, norms and values."[44] This type of hard data localization can be seen as a form of hegemony that the cross-border data flows dispute never managed to realize, due to the enforceability challenges. As a tool of political or economic domination, protectionism, or surveillance, data localization requirements *ad ante* may be more effective ways to restrict the free flow of information, gain access to sensitive data, or create barriers for foreign competitors than attempting to police data transfers post hoc. As Max Schrems noted, following a fine on Meta for violating cross-border transfers of personal data, the failure among democratic countries to establish "a common set of rules to say there has to be probable cause [for surveillance]" likely signifies "in the short run, we will probably have more data localization, […] which is not ideal. But it is a reality of how the laws work together right now."[45]

Countries using data localization to assert their sovereignty and control over their citizens' data – and to prevent foreign surveillance through such data transfers – are also masking their attempt to gain objectives through these moves. Such calls may serve as attempts to immunize domestic markets from global competition or to create incentives for foreign companies to invest locally. Yet the impacts on openness, interoperability, collaboration, and multistakeholderism will certainly impact the openness of the internet by creating greater fragmentation. In turn, this will limit the access to and availability of information across borders, thus risking outcomes that are hostile to basic rights and freedoms in certain societies. Data localization itself may not necessarily guarantee the privacy and security of data subjects if certain governments or actors have weak or abusive data protection laws and practices. It may also limit the cultural and linguistic diversity of data subjects, especially if the local

[44] Yun Chee (2023).

[45] CGTN (2023).

or national governments or actors have or put in place restrictive or discriminatory policies or practices, and they may reduce access to global digital communities. Calls for data localization channel power in ways that can serve authoritarian tendencies.

Adding to the foregoing, these disputes between state and non-state hegemonic actors occur divorced from the demands of the popular will. Indeed, popular attitudes regarding data localization are often contradictory and conflictual, creating opportunities for hegemonic actors to seek power in self-serving ways that do not align with or reflect the popular will. These hegemonic orders have differing sets of values, which, in their own right, are power-seeking. To be sure, there is further research necessary regarding the role of data localization in fostering or hindering innovation and development; the ethical and legal challenges of data localization in relation to privacy, security, and sovereignty; and the potential of data localization to create alternative and emancipatory models of data governance and citizenship. But the reality is now clear. Data localization is not only a technical or regulatory matter. It is also a contestation between hegemonic and popular forces, with significant implications for the future of democracy and human rights in the digital age.

References

A-2023-00007 (2023) Treasury Board Secretariat. Access to Information Act.

A-2023-00132 (2023) Innovation, science and economic development. Access to Information Act.

Baker-White E (2022) Leaked audio from 80 internal TikTok meetings shows that US user data has been repeatedly accessed from China. BuzzFeed News. https://www.buzzfeednews.com/article/emilybakerwhite/tiktok-tapes-us-user-data-china-bytedance-access. Accessed 22 Feb 2025

BC Freedom of Information and Privacy Association (2021) Various polls. https://www.ipsos.com/sites/default/files/ct/news/documents/2021-11/FIPA%20Tables-2021-11-15_0.pdf. Accessed 22 Feb 2025

BCNET (2016) BCNET submission to the special committee to review the freedom of information and protection of privacy act. https://www.leg.bc.ca/content/CommitteeDocuments/40th-parliament/4th-session/foi/WrittenSubmissions/Organizations/FIPPA_40-4_BCNET.pdf. Accessed 22 Feb 2025

Berliner Beauftragte für Datenschutz und Informationsfreiheit (2020). https://www.datenschutzberlin.de/fileadmin/user_upload/pdf/pressemitteilungen/2020/20200717-PM-Nach_SchremsII_Digitale_Eigenstaendigkeit.pdf. Accessed 22 Feb 2025

Meta to block news on Facebook, Instagram in Canada over new law (2023) Bloomberg. https://www.bloomberg.com/news/articles/2023-06-22/canada-passes-law-forcing-meta-alphabet-to-pay-news-publishers?embedded-checkout=true. Accessed 22 Feb 2025

Broadbent M (2023) The European Cybersecurity Certification Scheme for cloud services. Center for Strategic and International Studies. https://www.csis.org/analysis/european-cybersecurity-certification-scheme-cloud-services. Accessed 22 Feb 2025

Carr B (2020) Data localization: costs, tradeoffs, and impacts across the economy. IIF. https://www.iif.com/Publications/ID/4225/Data-Localization-Costs-Tradeoffs-and-Impacts-Across-the-Economy. Accessed 22 Feb 2025

Amazon will open its first Canadian data centre in Montreal (15 January 2016) CBC. https://www.cbc.ca/news/canada/montreal/amazon-aws-montral-data-center-1.3405616. Accessed 22 Feb 2025

Meta's news ban changed how people share political info – for the worse, studies show (2024) CBC. https://www.cbc.ca/news/business/meta-block-news-1.7174031. Accessed 22 Feb 2025

Christakis T (2020) 'Schrems III'? First thoughts on the EDPB post-Schrems II recommendations on international data transfers (Part 3). European Law Blog. https://europeanlawblog.eu/2020/11/17/schrems-iii-first-thoughts-on-the-edpb-post-schrems-ii-recommendations-on-international-data-transfers-part-3/. Accessed 22 Feb 2025 [Christakis(a)]

Christakis T (2020) 'European Digital Sovereignty': successfully navigating between the 'Brussels Effect' and Europe's quest for strategy autonomy. https://papers.ssrn.com/sol3/papers.cfm?abstract_id=3748098. Accessed 22 Feb 2025 [Christakis(b)]

Corey N (2021) How barriers to cross-border data flows are spreading globally, what they cost, and how to address them. ITIF. https://itif.org/publications/2021/07/19/how-barriers-cross-border-data-flows-are-spreading-globally-what-they-cost/. Accessed 22 Feb 2025

CGTN Europe (2023) Privacy campaigner Max Scherems [sic] on Meta fined €1.2bn over EU-US data transfers. https://www.youtube.com/watch?v=t3VF21J8obo. Accessed 22 Feb 2025

CPTPPA (2018) Chapter 14. https://www.international.gc.ca/trade-commerce/trade-agreements-accords-commerciaux/agr-acc/tpp-ptp/text-texte/14.aspx?lang=eng. Accessed 22 Feb 2025

CUSMA (2018) Chapter 19. https://www.international.gc.ca/trade-commerce/trade-agreements-accords-commerciaux/agr-acc/cusma-aceum/text-texte/19.aspx?lang=eng. Accessed 22 Feb 2025

Data Protection Commissioner v Facebook Ireland Limited, Maximillian Schrems, 2020 CJEU C-311/18

ECIPE (2013) The economic importance of getting data protection right: protecting privacy, transmitting data, moving commerce. https://www.uschamber.com/assets/archived/images/documents/files/020508_EconomicImportance_Final_Revised_lr.pdf. Accessed 22 Feb 2025

G7 Hiroshima Leaders' Communiqué (2023) The White House. https://www.whitehouse.gov/briefing-room/statements-releases/2023/05/20/g7-hiroshima-leaders-communique/. Accessed 22 Feb 2025

Giustra v Twitter, Inc, 2021 BCSC 54

Eva Matsa K (2023) More Americans are getting news on TikTok, bucking the trend seen on most other social media sites. Pew Research Center. https://www.pewresearch.org/short-reads/2023/11/15/more-americans-are-getting-news-on-tiktok-bucking-the-trend-seen-on-most-other-social-media-sites/. Accessed 22 Feb 2025

Fife R et al (2023) CSIS documents reveal Chinese strategy to influence Canada's 2021 election. The Globe and Mail. https://www.theglobeandmail.com/politics/article-china-influence-2021-federal-election-csis-documents/. Accessed 22 Feb 2025

Foreign Intelligence Surveillance Act, 50 U.S.C. § 702, 1978.

Fürst Haugen V (2022) NRK. https://www.nrk.no/osloogviken/xl/tiktok-doesn_t-show-the-war-in-ukraine-to-russian-users-1.15921522. Accessed 22 Feb 2025

Goujard C (2023) TikTok hit with €345M fine for violating children's privacy. Politico. https://www.politico.eu/article/tiktok-fine-social-media-china-violate-children-privacy/. Accessed 22 Feb 2025

Huddleston J et al (2020) Impact of data localization requirements on commerce and innovation. American Action Forum. https://www.americanactionforum.org/insight/impact-of-data-localization-requirements-on-commerce-and-innovation/. Accessed 22 Feb 2025

Joel A (2023) Trusted cross-border data flows: a national security priority. Lawfare. https://www.lawfaremedia.org/article/trusted-cross-border-data-flows-a-national-security-priority. Accessed 22 Feb 2025

Lee M (2023) Canada excluded from Google's expansion of AI chatbot Bard. CTV. https://www.ctvnews.ca/sci-tech/canada-excluded-from-google-s-expansion-of-ai-chatbot-bard-1.6480392. Accessed 22 Feb 2025

Hill K (2012) Max Schrems: The Austrian Thorn in Facebook's Side. Forbes. https://www.forbes.com/sites/kashmirhill/2012/02/07/the-austrian-thorn-in-facebooks-side/?sh=697c82357b0b. Accessed 22 Feb 2025

McKinsey (2022) Localization of data privacy regulations creates competitive opportunities. p. 2. https://www.mckinsey.com/capabilities/risk-and-resilience/our-insights/localization-of-data-privacy-regulations-creates-competitive-opportunities. Accessed 22 Feb 2025

Meltzer J et al (2018) Regulating for a digital economy: understanding the importance for cross-border data flows in Asia. https://www.brookings.edu/articles/regulating-for-a-digital-economy-understanding-the-importance-of-cross-border-data-flows-in-asia/. Accessed 22 Feb 2025

Miscellaneous Statutes (Minor Corrections) Amendment Act (2021) BC Legislature. https://www.canlii.org/en/bc/laws/astat/sbc-2021-c-3/latest/sbc-2021-c-3.html. Accessed 22 Feb 2025

Patel R (2023) Reveal: intelligence warned that TikTok gave governments 'false' reassurances about its data collection. Toronto Star. https://www.thestar.com/politics/federal/revealed-intelligence-warned-that-tiktok-gave-governments-false-reassurances-about-its-data-collection/article_fd9b0f96-a771-5e94-945e-7fd232368de3.html. Accessed 22 Feb 2025

Paz C (2022) Good luck explaining a TikTok ban to young people. Vox. https://www.vox.com/policy-and-politics/23523287/tiktok-ban-young-people-gen-z-campaign-outreach. Accessed 22 Feb 2025

Public Services and Procurement Canada. Government of Canada (2023) Annual report on Government of Canada Advertising Activities 2021 to 2022. https://www.tpsgc-pwgsc.gc.ca/pub-adv/rapports-reports/2021-2022/tdm-toc-eng.html. Accessed 22 Feb 2025

Public Services and Procurement Canada. Government of Canada (2020) Standards for the Conduct of Government of Canada Public Opinion Research—Online Surveys. https://www.canada.ca/content/dam/pspc-spac/documents/services/communication/enligne-online-eng.pdf. Accessed 22 Feb 2025

Recommendations 01/2020 on measures that supplement transfer tools to ensure compliance with the EU level of protection of personal data (21 December 2020) European Data Protection Board. https://edpb.europa.eu/our-work-tools/documents/public-consultations/2020/recommendations-012020-measures-supplement_en. Accessed 22 Feb 2025

Reuters (2022) TikTok admits using its app to spy on reporters in effort to track leaks. The Guardian. https://www.theguardian.com/technology/2022/dec/22/tiktok-bytedance-workers-fired-data-access-journalists. Accessed 22 Feb 2025

Sawers P (2019) InCountry raises $15 million to help multinational companies comply with data residency regulations. VentureBeat. https://venturebeat.com/business/incountry-raises-15-million-to-help-multinational-companies-comply-with-data-residency-regulations/. Accessed 22 Feb 2025

Standing Committee on Access to Information, Privacy and Ethics (2023) Use of social media platforms for data harvesting and unethical or illicit sharing of personal information with foreign entities. https://www.ourcommons.ca/committees/en/ETHI/StudyActivity?studyActivityId=12329142. Accessed 22 Feb 2025

Sverdlik Y (2015) First two microsoft data centers coming to Canada in 2016. DataCenter Knowledge. https://www.datacenterknowledge.com/archives/2015/06/03/first-two-microsoft-data-centers-coming-to-canada-in-2016. Accessed 22 Feb 2025

Swire P et al (2019) The important, justifiable, and constrained role of nationality in foreign intelligence surveillance. Hoover Institution. https://www.hoover.org/research/important-justifiable-and-constrained-role-nationality-foreign-intelligence-surveillance. Accessed 22 Feb 2025

Swire P et al (2022) The effects of data localization on cybersecurity – organizational effects. https://papers.ssrn.com/sol3/papers.cfm?abstract_id=4030905. Accessed 22 Feb 2025

Swire P et al (2023) Risks to cybersecurity from data localization, organized by techniques, tactics, and procedures. https://papers.ssrn.com/sol3/papers.cfm?abstract_id=4466479. Accessed 22 Feb 2025

Treasury Board Secretariat. Government of Canada (2023) Access to information review indigenous-specific what we heard report. https://www.canada.ca/en/treasury-board-secretariat/services/access-information-privacy/reviewing-access-information/the-review-process/indigenous-specific.html. Accessed 22 Feb 2025

Treasury Board Secretariat. Government of Canada (2023) Statement by Minister Fortier announcing a ban on the use of TikTok on government mobile devices. https://www.canada.ca/en/treasury-board-secretariat/news/2023/02/statement-by-minister-fortier-announcing-a-ban-on-the-use-of-tiktok-on-government-mobile-devices.html. Accessed 22 Feb 2025
Vanian J (2023) Federal judge blocks Montana's TikTok ban, which would have been the first of its kind. CNBC. https://www.cnbc.com/2023/12/01/federal-judge-blocks-montanas-tiktok-ban-which-would-have-been-the-first-of-its-kind.html. Accessed 22 Feb 2025
Yun Chee F (2023) EU draft rules propose tougher cybersecurity labelling rules for Amazon, Google, Microsoft. Reuters. https://www.reuters.com/technology/eu-draft-rules-propose-tougher-cybersecurity-labelling-rules-amazon-google-2023-05-09/. Accessed 22 Feb 2025

Prof. Matt Malone is an Assistant Professor in the University of Ottawa Faculty of Law and Director of the Canadian Internet Policy and Public Interest Clinic. He is also a Balsillie Fellow at the Balsillie School of International Affairs. His main research interest pertains to the various ways law protects secret information, especially in the context of trade secrecy, confidential information, access to information, privacy, data protection, and cybersecurity. He also maintains a broad interest in legal issues pertinent to modern workplaces, in particular workplace investigations. Prior to joining the Faculty, Matt practiced law full-time in California. He is called to the bar in British Columbia, California, and New York.

The Need for Emphasis on "Fair Terms" in Data Contracts on a Global Level

Zeynep Ülkü Kahveci

Abstract Data contracts deal with the provision or processing of data. As there is not a balanced distribution of power in the data market, players who hold vast amounts of data and whose volume of data keeps increasing exponentially, have a very strong bargaining power in data contracts. Just like in the Industrial Revolution, we are witnessing a change in powerful players in a newly emerging market (i.e. the data market) and those that were not fast enough to accumulate power in this market have no other choice than submitting to the requests of powerful players. Contractual justice has been widely accepted in the context of consumer contracts. Statutory limitations aiming for contractual justice regarding B2B contracts also exist in some jurisdictions. In the data economy, enterprises that are not powerful in the market can be as vulnerable as consumers are in other contexts. For this reason, protections against unfair terms, which is a result of contractual justice, was introduced for B2B data contracts in the EU's Data Act. This chapter argues that if implementation of unfair contract terms protections in B2B data contracts is accepted as a necessity, it will only make sense to implement it on a global level.

1 Introduction

Data markets and the data economy are rapidly growing. Yet, studies show that most of the data is not reused as data holders refrain from sharing their data.[1] As it is difficult to incentivize parties to voluntarily share their data, a new regulation on individuals' right to access data and therefore data holders' obligation to share data was created and introduced in the EU. The legislature believed that a simple right to access data is incomplete without ensuring that it is done under fair terms. Otherwise, unrealistic access terms and conditions make data access existent in theory but impossible in practice.

[1] Commission Staff Working Document (2022), p. 7.

Z. Ü. Kahveci (✉)
Istanbul Bilgi University, Istanbul, Turkey
e-mail: zeynep.kahveci@bilgi.edu.tr

J. Drexl et al. (eds.), *Comparative Data Law*, MPI Studies on Intellectual Property and Competition Law 32, https://doi.org/10.1007/978-3-031-91401-0_13

In that vein, the EU Data Act brought emphasis to fair terms for data access under its Chapter III which required data to be made available under FRAND terms and under Chapter IV which required standard terms used between the data holder and the data recipient to be fair.[2] Chapter IV is especially a striking set of rules as it brought a standard terms validity tests for B2B data contracts based on their fairness. Standard terms validity test for B2B contracts have traditionally been refused by most jurisdictions based on the ground that it is a too far-fetched limitation to freedom of contract. The characteristics of the data economy and data markets may legitimize such intervention to B2B contracts. However, protections that are limited to the EU data market are not sufficient to address the existing problems on the global level.

2 Data Contracts

To start with, it should be underlined that terminology in data law is not yet wholly established. There is a lack of uniformity in terms of terminology related to different aspects of data law. Data contracts is one example. There is not a universally accepted definition for data contracts and so far, several institutions created their own definitions. Although their definitions are different, there are overlapping parts of these definitions.

In 2018, the Ministry of Economy, Trade and Industry of Japan published its Contract Guidelines on Utilization of AI and Data. These guidelines defined data contracts as *'contracts relating to the utilization, processing, transfer and other handling of data'*.[3] The United Nations Commission on International Trade Law's (UNCITRAL) Working Group IV on electronic commerce defined data contracts as *'contracts for the control or processing of data for commercial purposes'*.[4] Also, recently, the American Law Institute and the European Law Institute came together to publish their mutual principles for a data economy which contains default rules for different types of data contracts (ALI-ELI Principles). Accordingly, data contracts are broadly defined as *'a contract the subject of which is data'*.[5]

All the aforementioned documents are non-binding documents that aim to provide legal guidance on the realm of the data economy. Their varying definitions demonstrate that there is not a universal understanding of what data contracts are and how they should be categorized. In order to avoid delving into details of different categories, this article does not make any preference on any of the abovementioned definitions. However, to be clear, data contracts within the meaning of this article are

[2] Regulation (EU) 2023/2854 of the European Parliament and of the Council of 13 December 2023 on harmonised rules on fair access to and use of data and amending Regulation (EU) 2017/2394 and Directive (EU) 2020/1828 (Data Act) (2023).

[3] Ministry of Economy, Trade and Industry of Japan (2018), p. 1.

[4] United Nations Commission on International Trade Law (2022), p. 7.

[5] ALI-ELI Principles for a Data Economy: Data Transactions and Data Rights (ELI Final Council Draft) Principle 3(j).

those contracts where one party gives access to data that it holds (data holder) to the other party (data recipient).

2.1 Data Contracts' Status in the Digital Economy

Data is a significant asset in the digital economy.[6] Data can have an economic value in its raw or processed form. Enterprises collect and store data for reasons including improving internal operations and controlling and monitoring enterprises' activities along with monetizing data through selling it.[7] According to the European Data Market Study, the value of the data market[8] in the 27 EU countries is estimated to reach 118 billion Euros in value in 2030.[9] On the other hand, the value of the data economy[10] in the 27 EU countries is estimated to be worth 544 billion Euros in 2023.[11]

A very significant challenge of the data economy is the reluctance of data holders to share their stored data with third parties. According to a 2022 study, more than ¾ of enterprises in Europe report that they do not share their data with non-profit organizations, businesses or individuals.[12] From an economic analysis of the data economy, it has been observed that high transaction costs, information asymmetries and asymmetry of bargaining power of parties make it hard to have an efficient market where data holders voluntarily share data with requesting parties.[13] For this reason, legislatures have been seeking ways to oblige enterprises to share their data. Without such an intervention, data holders insist on exclusive control of data and preserve dominance in the market.[14] To diminish the effects of this reluctancy and ensure a more equal distribution of power in the data market, the EU introduced its Data Act which imposes a right to access and use data.[15] Within the scope of this regulation,

---

[6] Graef (2015).

[7] For enterprises' motivations to store data *see* European Commission (2022), p. 61.

[8] Data market is defined as "*the marketplace where digital data is exchanged as "products" or "services" as a result of the elaboration of raw data*". International Data Corporation, Lisbon Council (2024), p. 19.

[9] *Ibid* 20.

[10] Data economy is defined as "*the overall impacts of the data market on the economy as a whole*". *Ibid.*

[11] *Ibid* 21.

[12] *Ibid* 64.

[13] Schweitzer/Metzger (2023), p. 340.

[14] *Ibid*. Previously, *Graef* and *Prüfer* argued that data sharing should be made obligatory only for enterprises which have a market share more than 30% in data-driven markets and that gatekeepers should be able to access data of others. Graef/Prüfer (2021), p. 3.

[15] Data access rights already existed under different legal instruments. For example, right to access personal data was already granted under the General Data Protection Regulation (GDPR) Article 15 (Right of access by the data subject). Also, right to access ranking, query, click and view data generated by online search engines offered by gatekeepers was granted under the Digital Markets Act

companies that collect data through connected products can no longer refuse requests for sharing such data. This is a small step in ensuring a flow of data in the market between parties with varying bargaining power.

Voluntary or non-voluntary data sharing gives rise to a contractual relationship between the data holder and the data recipient (an individual or an enterprise). Contracts have a significant role in these transactions as parties only have contracts to rely on in case a dispute arises because of the lack of binding default rules for data contracts. Unlike the sale of goods where there are national laws and even an international convention (i.e. the United Nations Convention on Contracts for the International Sale of Goods (CISG)) regulating all default provisions in detail, there is no instrument with similar effect regarding data contracts. Therefore, data contracts play a crucial role in determining transactions involving data in the data economy.

Another reason why contracts are significant in the data economy is the absence of non-contractual rights in data. The question of whether a person has any kind of exclusive right in data that is held under control is a complicated question that sparked discussions among academics and legislatures. The possibility of data ownership and a new IP right on data have been proposed.[16] In the EU and in a few countries that followed the EU, parties who invested in creating databases with their accumulated data can enjoy the *sui generis* protection of databases.[17] Even this sui generis protection is not sufficient to create exclusivity in data as it only protects whole or parts of a database and not the data on its own. Therefore, most individuals rely on trade secrets protection to enjoy de facto exclusivity. To that end, they keep such data confidential which also incentivizes them not to share data with others. In case a data holder decides to share data, as non-contractual remedies are not available, they try to reflect all remedies in a contract with the data recipient. For this reason, contracts have an extra layer of importance in the data economy.

2.2 General Characteristics of Data Contracts

Data contracts that deal with provision of data have some commonalities. Some enterprises hold great amounts of data collected through the offering of their services

(DMA) Article 6(11). Regulation (EU) 2022/1925 of the European Parliament and of the Council of 14 September 2022 on contestable and fair markets in the digital sector and amending Directives (EU) 2019/1937 and (EU) 2020/1828 (Digital Markets Act). The Data Act introduced a data access right with a broader scope as it applies to all types of data (i.e. personal or non-personal) and also does not depend on the market power of the data holder (Cf. also on the "contractualization" of data law Hennemann et al. (2024); For an analysis of existing data access rights *see* Schweitzer/Metzger (2023).

[16] For critical analyses of these proposals *see* van Erp (2020); Hilty (2018); Drexl (2020).

[17] Directive 96/9/EC of the European Parliament and of the Council of 11 March 1996 on the Legal Protection of Databases, Official Journal of the European Communities No L 77/20. Outside the EU, a few other countries implemented the sui generis database protection in their laws. For example, Turkey amended its Law on Intellectual and Artistic Works (Law no. 5846) and added Additional Article 8 on the protection of databases in 2004.

and therefore also have a powerful position in the data market.[18] These actors also have great leverage in determining how or if this data will flow between different actors in the digital economy. Enterprises that do not hold big chunks of data need to collect or access the already collected data to be able to enter this market. Yet, they are not able to do so easily as there are entry barriers awaiting them. Therefore, they need to ask enterprises that already hold big amounts of data to share that data with them. Negotiations do not advance smoothly due to the challenges of the data economy.

First, asymmetry of bargaining power and information asymmetries have a particularly strong impact on the formation of data contracts. The powerful players in the data market have a disproportionately high bargaining power against the data requestors, independent of the size of the latter. Data requestors have no other choice but to convince the data holders as there are generally not a lot of alternatives in the market. Also, as data monetization is recently being diversified and objective criteria for data valuation do not exist, data holders are the only ones who may have information on the real or potential value of data. Data requestors are unable to determine what is the data's real value and extreme pricing can easily take place which is one of the consequences of information asymmetry.[19] Second, high transaction costs are another challenge in the market. Data sharing is not (yet) an established practice. Initiating and progressing negotiations require to establish the market practice and demand time and money. Especially since data holders are reluctant to share their data, contacting all data holders and attempting to convince them raise transaction costs.

In addition to these challenges that data contractors face, there are also other common characteristics of data contracts. As a consequence of the lack of a property-like right over data, as discussed above, data contracts have an extra layer of significance between parties. Therefore, contractual provisions are crucial and constitute one of the few or, even, the only remedy available to parties in case there is a mishandling of data.[20] As a result, parties give importance to contractual provisions and are inclined to reflect every detail of their relationship in contracts. Any problem with contractual provisions may have amplified effects on the relationship between the parties.

Also, provision or processing of data usually accompany an existing relationship between parties. This is an important characteristic that perhaps also supports the asymmetry of bargaining power as parties will not want to risk an ongoing relationship by insisting on amending a provision of the draft contract. It also shows that any imbalances in risk and obligations distribution under the contract might have long-term effects on the parties. As data has a dynamic nature, provision of data usually

---

[18] The European Commission announced on 6 September 2023 that they designated six companies as gatekeepers under the Digital Markets Act. These are Alphabet, Amazon, Apple, ByteDance, Meta and Microsoft. See European Commission (2023)

[19] Ciuriak (2018).

[20] United Nations Commission on International Trade Law (2023), A/CN.9/WG.IV/WP.183, p. 7 ("*The absence of a comprehensive property-like regime for data rights means that contractual rights are relied upon to secure the use of data*").

entails supply of data for a long period of time to allow for updating and improving of data for enhanced accuracy. Therefore, problems with the contract might cause damages to the data requestor for a long span of time.

In sum, there are some characteristics of data contracts that are derived from the nature of data. First, there is an asymmetry of bargaining power and information asymmetry between parties to data contracts. This, along with high transaction costs, causes an unhealthy negotiation phase before the conclusion of the contract. Second, parties heavily depend on contract provisions as non-contractual remedies are rarely available. As a result, data contracts are detailed and cover a wide range of possibilities that parties may face. Third, there is usually a long-term relationship between parties and therefore parties are risk averse. This factor also weighs against data requestors who may feel the need to please data holders regardless of the unfairness of the proposed terms and conditions.

3 Protection Against Unfair Terms in Contract Law

3.1 An Outcome of Contractual Justice

Contractual freedom is a long-established principle of contract law. The philosophical grounds for this principle can be grouped into two: (1) individual autonomy and hence self-determination; and (2) public interest from the viewpoint of utilitarian theory.[21] Regarding individual autonomy, contractual freedom allows individuals to negotiate and determine the rules that will govern their relationships which is a major difference compared to how narrow an individual's autonomy was in feudal times. On the other hand, the public interest view argues that contractual freedom is the best way to ensure that the limited resources are allocated to those who value them the most and therefore such allocation serves the best interest of the society.[22]

With the Industrial Revolution, contracts started to be used as tools similar to what feudal lords used against their vassals. This analogy was made because of how enterprises started dictating their terms to other parties with the use of standard terms. Contracts were no longer texts that were a result of negotiations between parties. More and more, the majority of contracts were comprised of terms dictated by one party and submitted to by the other party.[23] This one-sidedness of the drafting of contracts led to the introduction of new constraints to contractual freedom. As a result, contractual justice became a rising principle confining contractual freedom.[24]

Contractual justice comprises of procedural fairness and substantive fairness. One of the ways to ensure a contractual relationship is substantively fair is to protect

[21] Zweigert/Kötz (1998), pp. 325-326.

[22] *Ibid* 326.

[23] *Ibid* 334.

[24] *Ibid.*

contracting parties against unfair terms.[25] Examples of unfair terms include exclusion and limitation clauses which lead to lack of liability of one party in case of violation of contractual obligations. The extent of such protection against unfair terms depends on each jurisdiction's approach to this concept.[26]

Legislatures' approach to protection against unfair terms depends on certain criteria. These criteria include (1) types of contracts that are subject to these rules (i.e. whether they apply to B2B or B2C contracts); (2) clauses that are subject to these rules (i.e. whether negotiated or core terms are subject-matter of rules against unfair terms); (3) the strictness of these rules (i.e. whether there are any black or gray lists of clauses that are accepted or presumed to be unfair).

The first criterion is an important factor determining the scope of protection against unfair terms. Most of these rules only apply to consumer (B2C) contracts.[27] Main reason of this choice is the fact that consumers are generally accepted as parties who have inferior bargaining power and need to be protected against enterprises that might exploit their lack of experience in the concerned business. This preference of consumer contracts relies on the presumption that B2B contracts do not have a significant imbalance of power between parties. However, it is possible that enterprises that do not have a lot of experience or presence in a market may be as inexperienced and vulnerable as consumers when facing enterprises with more experience or dominance in the market. For this reason, some jurisdictions adopted rules that protect against unfair clauses in B2B contracts as well.[28]

3.2 *Rules on Fair Terms in Data Contracts*

With the rise of technology, a new revolution is happening which will have as major effects as the Industrial Revolution had in the past.[29] The emergence and development

---

[25] Beale/Fauvarque-Cosson/Rutgers/Vogenauer (2019), p. 811.

[26] Protection against unfair contract terms has been applied by judges for a long time even when statutory protections were not in place. Long standing doctrines like the doctrine of offer and acceptance and doctrine of misrepresentation have been invoked to declare unfair terms imposed on a party as non-binding. Additionally, rules of interpretation and rules of good faith have also been used to interpret and curb the unfairness of the imposed terms. *See* Beale/ Fauvarque-Cosson/ Rutgers/Vogenauer (2019), p. 813.

[27] One impactful example is the EU's Directive 93/13/EEC of 5 April 1993 on unfair terms in consumer contracts.

[28] Germany adopted unfair terms protections for B2B transactions in §§ 305 ff. BGB where unfair terms protection applies to contracts regardless of whether there is an imbalance of power between the parties (i.e. provisions also apply to commercial contracts) MüKoBGB/Fornasier, 9. Aufl. 2022, BGB § 305 Rn. 4. Turkey, England and France also adopted statutory rules expanding unfair terms protections to B2B contracts. Turkish Code of Obligations Art. 20-25; England's Unfair Contract Terms Act 1977 applies to businesses that act as a consumer in a contract (*see* Beale/ Fauvarque-Cosson/Rutgers/Vogenauer (2019), p. 853).

[29] Schweitzer and Metzger call this transformation as a time "*from industrial capitalism to informational capitalism*". Schweitzer/Metzger (2023), p. 337.

of data markets and data economy is one of the outcomes of this revolution. Data markets are closely linked to digital markets as companies that are active in the digital sector are able to accumulate data and then use such data as the subject of other transactions. In the newly emerging data markets, certain actors quickly gained dominance as is the case in the digital markets.

The EU's Digital Markets Act (DMA) recognized the imbalance of economic power in the digital markets and the European Commission designated certain actors as gatekeepers in accordance with its article 3. The DMA is focused on taking *ex ante* measures against these gatekeepers in order to preserve competition in the markets. The DMA is focused on ensuring fairness and contestability of the market where gatekeepers are present and is complementary to competition rules.[30] A few years after the DMA, the Data Act was accepted. The Data Act's main objective is to ensure sharing of data on a horizontal level under fair terms. This objective differentiates the Data Act from the DMA as the former targets all big players in data markets, regardless of whether they qualify as a gatekeeper, and takes precautions outside the realm of competition law.[31] For example, protection against unfair contract terms under Chapter IV Article 13 of the Data Act applies to all data holder enterprises, regardless of their size, and to all data contracts, regardless of whether they are above the threshold for dominance in the market.

Data Act's Chapter IV Article 13 is an important example of an attempt to ensure fair terms in data contracts. To start with, these rules are applicable to terms that are unilaterally imposed by an enterprise on another enterprise. In general, 'unfair contract terms' is defined as '*of such a nature that its use grossly deviates from good commercial practice in data access and use, contrary to good faith and fair dealing*' (Art. 13(3)).[32] The following paragraphs include lists of terms that shall be accepted as or presumed to be unfair which is very useful to illustrate examples of unfair terms.

Data Act's provisions on unfair terms is a good starting point for establishing contractual justice in the context of data contracts. Nevertheless, it has some aspects that are open to criticism. Most importantly, the subject-matter of Article 13 of the Data Act is very limited as it only applies to '*unilaterally imposed*' terms which is defined as terms that are '*supplied by one contracting party and the other contracting party has not been able to influence its content despite an attempt to negotiate it.*'[33] This definition leaves terms that are not made subject of negotiations outside its scope and parties to a data contract who do not have a strong market power may not even be able to ask for negotiations as they are in a take-it-or-leave-it position.[34] Such terms

---

[30] Digital Markets Act Recital (11), Art. 1(1).

[31] Despite these differences, both instruments aimed for "*rebalancing the digital economy in favour of smaller economic players and of empowering the users of digital services*" Commission Staff Working Document (2022), p. 6.

[32] In the Recitals, "*grossly deviating from good commercial practice*" is stated to include "*inter alia, objectively impairing the ability of the party upon whom the term has been unilaterally imposed to protect its legitimate commercial interest in the data in question*". Data Act Recital (61).

[33] Data Act Art. 13(6).

[34] Drexl/Banda/González Otero/Hoffmann/Kim/Kulhari/Moscon/Richter/Wiedemann (2022), para. 122 – 123; Wiebe (2023), p. 1575; Hennemann et al. (2024), p. 143.

will hence never be considered for being negotiated and thus will not be subject to fairness control under the Data Act's Article 13.

Data holders do not need to have a dominant market position to be subject to data sharing obligations under the Data Act. The Commission acknowledged that even if a competition law problem (such as dominant position in the market) does not exits regarding a data holder, that data holder can still enjoy '*de facto exclusivity over the data collected by its devices*' as data requestors cannot obtain that data from any other supplier.[35] The balancing of data markets is in this way beyond competition law's realm and the Data Act tries to fill this lacuna.

4 Need for Fair Terms in Data Contracts on a Global Level

Contractual freedom is one of the main principles of contract law. On the other hand, contractual justice requires intervention to contractual freedom. For this reason, contractual justice is a concept that needs to be addressed carefully so as not to tarnish entrepreneurial freedom.[36] Contractual justice for data contracts addresses an important problem in the data markets: lack of incentives for data holders to share data voluntarily under fair terms. As explained, even if data holders are obliged to share data with other enterprises, there is a risk of abuse of contractual imbalance and extreme pricing to make data sharing impossible in practice.[37]

If it is accepted that unfair terms control in B2B data contracts is a useful and necessary tool, this paper argues that rules with similar effect should be in effect on a global level. Otherwise, merely protecting European small players will only ensure sharing of data in the European market and pose bigger problems for small players outside the European data market.[38] The data economy already poses significant risks to developing countries as global value chains are not formed which was the case after the Industrial Revolution.[39]

The size of data economies of countries outside the EU demonstrates that data contracts are also executed frequently outside the EU. In 2022 and 2023, the United States had the world's strongest data economy in the world.[40] China is home to nearly

[35] Commission Staff Working Document (2022), p. 6.

[36] The Data Act's intervention to contractual freedom was criticized for limiting entrepreneurial freedom.

[37] Commission Staff Working Document (2022), p. 11. The report lists the following as examples of abuse of contractual imbalances: '*exclusion or disproportionate limitation of warranties and liability of the data holder, restrictions of data access and use, lock-in effects and conditions surrounding the termination of a data-sharing contract*'. Commission Staff Working Document (2022), p. 18.

[38] Article 1(3) of Data Act determined the territorial scope of the Regulation. Data recipients or users of connected devices outside the Union who request data from data holders outside the Union are outside this scope.

[39] Ciuriak/Ptashkina (2019), p. 6.

[40] International Data Corporation, Lisbon Council (2024), p.151.

two-thirds of the international data supplier companies.[41] Regardless of where data is collected from, data holders keep data exclusively under their control and data creators cannot benefit from the value of their data.[42] If a user of a connected device which stores data in China or the US resides in the EU, this user or a third party acting in agreement with the user will be covered by the Data Act and will be able to insist on fair terms for data contracts. The same will not be possible for users or third parties who are not residing in the EU. For example, non-EU resident users of connected devices manufactured by non-EU companies or third parties may continue to face unfair contract terms when they request data that is collected by these manufacturers, if they manage to convince these manufacturers to share data in the first place.

Regarding cases where the Data Act is not applicable, domestic rules on unfair terms protections may still protect the party with weaker bargaining power. Naturally, data holders, which are usually the party with the stronger bargaining power, may prefer to select a governing law that will not have such protections. Data recipients may have to submit to these choices of law. Therefore, having local protections will not suffice to ensure fairness in the data market. For example, an ongoing problem with such choice of governing law clauses concerns intellectual property protection of social media users. Some social media platforms' terms of use governing law clauses indicate laws of countries where copyright license agreements are not subject to written form. This way, users' works that are uploaded to these platforms are automatically licensed to social media companies without the need to obtain users' consent every time a new work is uploaded. Written form for all contracts affecting the author is a requirement in most of the civil law countries. However, this requirement which aims for the protection of authors is overcome by the choice of governing law where rules are less strict. Users are not able to argue for the change of governing law clauses as the terms of use are not open to negotiations.

Going back to general rules on unfair terms in contract law, a global regime concerning unfair terms in B2B transactions does not exist. Attempts on local or international levels to harmonize contract law through non-binding soft law documents aimed at harmonizing unfair terms protections as well. For example, Article 4:110 of the Principles of European Contract Law's (PECL) entitled '*Unfair Terms not Individually Negotiated*'[43] and Article 2.1.20 of the UNIDROIT Principles of International Commercial Contracts entitled '*Surprising terms*'[44] contain rules related to the validity of standard terms in B2B transactions. Yet, international instruments with binding effect do not contain provisions on unfair terms control. For example, under the CISG, there is no provision on protection against unfair terms.[45] This problem is

---

[41] *Ibid* 163.

[42] This problem has been linked to the concept of 'data sovereignty'. de Bastion/Mukku (2020), p. 29.

[43] Principles of European Contract Law.

[44] UNIDROIT Principles of International Commercial Contracts (2016).

[45] Huber/Mullis (2007), p. 33.

left to the discretion of domestic laws as Art. 4(1)(a) openly states that '*the validity of the contract or of any of its provisions*' is not governed by CISG.[46]

Guidance on data contracts is available in soft law documents like the ALI-ELI Principles. These principles refrained from providing any unfair terms protections.[47] A game-changer might be UNCITRAL's ongoing work on default rules for data provision contracts. However, the most recent draft of these rules and the meeting notes of the working group suggest that this will not be the case. UNCITRAL's ongoing work is heavily influenced by CISG, which was also drafted by UNCITRAL.[48] Following CISG's footsteps, these default rules, so far, refrain from intervening in the material validity of contracts. Although CISG is a successful example of an international treaty on the sales of goods, it should not be taken as an outright model for rules on data provision contracts.

Data has many characteristics that distinguish it from the traditional notion of goods. Data is non-rivalrous which means that data's utility can be shared by different people and resembles public goods in this way.[49] Especially, the problem of power imbalance between parties is a problem that seems to be different than what exists regarding sales of goods. As there are a few actors that collect data, data requestors have little bargaining power against data holders.[50] Lack of any provisions on this matter in CISG was compensated by competition law mechanisms that already provide solutions against market concentrations and dominant players. As explained above, the power imbalance between parties in a data contract is not a problem that competition law can, at least for now, solve. Therefore, data and data market's unique nature should be taken into consideration by the Working Group IV of UNCITRAL which is currently debating the draft rules which are intended to form model legislation or model contract clauses in the future.[51]

Another alternative might be sector-specific guidelines on data contracts that promote fair terms. Data markets have different dynamics in different sectors and finding one-size-fits-all solutions is not realistic as each sector has different needs, actors and priorities. The EU's Code of Conduct (CC) on Agricultural Data Sharing by Contractual Agreement is a good example of this.[52] This early example of a CC which was published in 2018, before the publication of the Data Act's draft, called for

---

[46] Although the content of standard terms is not governed by CISG, it is accepted that the question of whether standard terms are a part of the contract in the first place is indirectly governed by CISG under Article 8 (*Interpretation*). *Ibid.*

[47] It is explicitly stated in the ALI-ELI Principles commentary that the principles do not aim for changing anything related to a jurisdiction's approach to a general contract law notion like unfairness in B2B transactions. ALI-ELI, Principles 18.

[48] For example, the most recent draft "Default rules for data provision contracts" commentary on the draft articles frequently makes reference to CISG (eg. Art. 6 & 7). It is also acknowledged in UNCITRAL's meeting report that CISG was accepted as a starting point for their ongoing work on default rules. United Nations Commission on International Trade Law (2023), p. 11.

[49] Purtova/Maanen (2024).

[50] Data Act, Recital (27).

[51] United Nations Commission on International Trade Law (2023) A/CN.9/1132, p. 13.

[52] EU Code of conduct on agricultural data sharing by contractual agreement (2018).

fair contract terms.[53] For example, a farmers' right to transmit the collected data to other users is recognized and protected under this code of conduct.[54] The usefulness of these sector-specific examples was recognized in the Data Act's Recitals.[55]

Similarly, in March 2023 the European Travel Commission published its Code of Conduct on Data Sharing in Tourism.[56] After explicitly referring to the Data Act in its Introduction, this CC contained recommendations on having fair terms including a call for fair renumeration for data and inclusion of liability provisions in case the supplied data is erroneous.[57] Needless to say, the signatories of these CCs are European associations/enterprises active in these sectors. Accepting the fact that a binding document (e.g. an international treaty) on material invalidity of contracts might be unrealistic, sector-specific and global CCs can fill the gaps and serve the objective of ensuring fair terms between players from different data markets.

5 Conclusion

Fair access to data is one of the goals of today's data strategies. In addition to problems that exist vis-à-vis players with big market shares in digital markets (such as gatekeepers), other problems also need to be addressed to ensure that more and more data is reused in the data economy. Power imbalance between parties and therefore inequality of bargaining power is an important problem that weaker parties face. Recognizing this challenge, the EU's Data Act addressed the problem of unfair terms due to power imbalance between parties to data contracts under its Chapter IV, Article 13. The relevant provisions are not perfect but do a good job in shedding light on what problems weaker parties face if and when they convince a data holder to share data.

Unfair terms protections are a limitation on contractual freedom. The EU legislature made the decision to limit contractual freedom in the case of data transactions. This paper argues that unfair terms protection for B2B data contracts is a significant step in ensuring a more balanced data market and this objective can only be achieved if such protections are adopted on a global level. Otherwise, only the EU data market will become balanced, and current problems will continue to exist, perhaps by amplifying, in the remaining data markets. Non-binding model rules can evolve to binding legislatures in the remaining jurisdictions.

Due to business concerns, some legislatures may refuse to intervene in entrepreneurial freedom so much. Nevertheless, soft law documents such as codes of conduct (CCs) may at least raise awareness on the issue and create incentives for parties to negotiate in a fair way. The CCs on EU's agricultural and touristic

[53] *Ibid* 3.

[54] *Ibid* 9.

[55] Data Act, Recital (27).

[56] European Travel Commission (2023).

[57] *Ibid* 11.

data sharing sectors are good examples in this regard. CCs by stakeholders from a global circle should be adopted so that data is reused globally, not only in the EU. Doubtlessly, the UNCITRAL's ongoing work on default rules for data provision contracts can also set an example by including rules on unfair terms protections.

References

ALI-ELI principles for a data economy: data transactions and data rights. https://www.principlesforadataeconomy.org/fileadmin/user_upload/p_principlesforadataeconomy/Files/Principles_for_a_Data_Economy_ELI_Final_Council_Draft.pdf. Accessed 22 Feb 2025

Beale H, Fauvarque-Cosson B, Rutgers J, Vogenauer S (2019) Cases, materials and text on contract law. Hart, Oxford

Ciuriak D (2018) The economics of data: implications for the data-driven economy. https://www.cigionline.org/articles/economics-data-implications-data-driven-economy/. Accessed 22 Feb 2025

Ciuriak D, Ptashkina M (2019) Leveraging the digital transformation for development: a global south strategy for the data-driven economy. Center for International Governance Innovation Policy Brief No. 148. https://www.cigionline.org/static/documents/documents/PB%20no.148%20web.pdf. Accessed 22 Feb 2025

Commission Staff Working Document (2022) Impact Assessment report accompanying the document proposal for a Regulation of the European Parliament and of the Council on harmonized rules on fair Access to and use of data (Data Act) SWD (2022) 34 final

de Bastion G, Mukku S (2020) Data and the global south: key issues for inclusive digital development. Heinrich Böll Stiftung. https://us.boell.org/en/2020/10/20/data-and-global-south-key-issues-inclusive-digital-development. Accessed 22 Feb 2025

Drexl J (2020) The (lack of) coherence of data ownership with the intellectual property system. In: Bruun N, Dinwoodie GB, Levin M, Ohly A (eds) Transition and coherence in intellectual property law: essays in honour of Annette Kur. Cambridge University Press, Cambridge, pp 213–223

Drexl J, Banda C, González Otero B, Hoffmann J, Kim D, Kulhari S, Moscon V, Richter H, Wiedemann K (2022) Position statement of the Max Planck Institute for Innovation and Competition of 25 May 2022 on the Commission's Proposal of 23 February 2022 for a Regulation on harmonised rules on fair access to and use of data (Data Act). https://pure.mpg.de/rest/items/item_3388757_4/component/file_3395639/content. Accessed 22 Feb 2025

EU Code of conduct on agricultural data sharing by contractual agreement (2018). https://cema-agri.org/images/publications/brochures/EU_Code_of_conduct_on_agricultural_data_sharing_by_contractual_agreement_2020_ENGLISH.pdf. Accessed 22 Feb 2025

European Commission, Directorate-General of Communications Networks, Content & Technology (2022) Survey of businesses on the data economy. https://ec.europa.eu/newsroom/dae/redirection/document/88634. Accessed 22 Feb 2025

European Commission (2023) Digital markets act: commission designates six gatekeepers. https://ec.europa.eu/commission/presscorner/detail/en/ip_23_4328. Accessed 22 Feb 2025

European Travel Commission (2023) Code of conduct on data sharing in tourism. https://etc-corporate.org/reports/code-of-conduct-on-data-sharing-in-tourism/. Accessed 22 Feb 2025

Graef I (2015) Market definition and market power in data: the case of online platforms. World Compet 38(4):473–506

Graef I, Prüfer J (2021) Governance of data sharing: a law & economics proposal. Res Policy 50:104330

Hennemann M, Ebner G K, Karsten B, Lienemann G, Wienroeder M (2024) Data act: an introduction. Nomos [Open Access]

Hilty R (2018) Big data: ownership and use in the digital age. In: Seuba X, Geiger C, Pénin, J (eds) Intellectual property and digital trade in the age of artificial intelligence and big data. Global perspectives for the intellectual property system, CEIPI-ICTSD (5), pp 85–94
Huber P, Mullis A (2007) The CISG: a new textbook for students and practitioners. Sellier, Germany
International Data Corporation, Lisbon Council (2024) European Data market study 2021–2023 CNECT/LUX/2020/OP/0027–VIGIE 2020–0655, contract number: LC-01568518, D2.7 Final report on facts and figures. https://ec.europa.eu/newsroom/dae/redirection/document/101694. Accessed 22 Feb 2025
Ministry of Economy, Trade and Industry of Japan, 'Contract Guidelines on Utilization of AI and Data: Data Section' (2018)
Picht PG (2023) Caught in the acts: framing mandatory data access transactions under the data act, further EU digital regulation acts, and competition law. J Eur Compet Law Pract 14(2):67–82
Principles of European Contract Law. https://www.trans-lex.org/400200/_/pecl/. Accessed 22 Feb 2025
Purtova N, van Maanen G (2024) Data as an economic good, data as a commons and data governance. Law Innov Technol 16(1):1–42
Regulation (EU) 2022/1925 of the European Parliament and of the Council of 14 September 2022 on contestable and fair markets in the digital sector and amending Directives (EU) 2019/1937 and (EU) 2020/1828 (Digital Markets Act)
Regulation (EU) 2023/2854 of the European Parliament and of the Council of 13 December 2023 on harmonised rules on fair access to and use of data and amending Regulation (EU) 2017/2394 and Directive (EU) 2020/1828 (Data Act) (2023), *Official Journal L Series*
Schweitzer H, Metzger A (2023) Data access under the draft data act, competition law and the DMA: opening the data treasures for competition and innovation? GRUR Int 72(4):337–356
UNIDROIT Principles of International Commercial Contracts (2016). https://www.unidroit.org/wp-content/uploads/2021/06/Unidroit-Principles-2016-English-bl.pdf. Accessed 22 Feb 2025
United Nations Commission on International Trade Law (2022) Fifty-fifth session, 'Legal issues related to digital economy—proposal for future work on data transactions: Note by the Secretariat', A/CN.9/1117
United Nations Commission on International Trade Law (2023) Default rules for data provision contracts (first revision), A/CN.9/WG.IV/WP.183
United Nations Commission on International Trade Law (2023) Report of Working Group IV (Electronic Commerce) on the work of its sixty-fifth session, A/CN.9/1132
United Nations Commission on International Trade Law (2023) Report of Working Group IV (Electronic Commerce) on the work of its sixty-sixth session, A/CN.9/1162
van Erp S (2020) Management as ownership of data. In: Lohsse S, Schulze R, Staudenmayer S (eds) Data as counter-performance – contract law 2.0?, 1st ed. Nomos/Hart, pp 77–94
Wiebe A (2023) Der data act – innovation oder illusion? GRUR 22:1569–1648
Zweigert K, Kötz H (1998) An introduction to comparative law, 3rd ed. Oxford

Dr. Zeynep Ülkü Kahveci is a lecturer and research assistant at Istanbul Bilgi University's Faculty of Law. She has an LLM degree from Harvard Law School and has been a part of Harvard Law School-Berkman Klein Center's CopyrightX project as a teaching fellow. She completed her PhD at Istanbul University Social Sciences Institute in 2024 after defending her thesis entitled "Evaluation of Legal Rights in Data".

Future-Proofing the Global CBPR Forum

María Vásquez Callo-Müller

Abstract This chapter puts into perspective the establishment of the Global Cross Border Privacy Rules (CBPR) Forum, launched in April 2022 as a major initiative to promote trusted cross-border flows of personal data. The importance of the Global CBPR Forum should not be underestimated. Since its establishment, it has already attracted the attention of at least a dozen countries worldwide. The Forum is expected to build upon the APEC CBPR System. However, policy and scholarly analysis on the functioning and success of this system is scarce. This article seeks to fill this gap by explaining the origins, functioning and performance of APEC CBPR System so far. The discussion of these aspects serves a constructive purpose: to future-proof the Global CBPR Forum and its associated privacy certification. Considering the relevance of facilitated cross-border data flows for the digital economy, the analysis of the Global CBPR Forum in light of its predecessor is not only important but necessary to implement global data privacy certification systems on the ground.

Keywords Global CBPR · APEC CBPR · APEC privacy framework · Accountability agents · Cross-border data flows

1 Introduction

An important instrument to facilitate cross-border flows of personal data was launched in April 2022—The Global Cross Border Privacy Rules (CBPR) Forum.[1] As its name suggests, the Global CBPR Forum has worldwide ambitions. It seeks to enable the interoperability, though a privacy certification, of different privacy regimes. To that extent, it intends to be an alternative to other mechanisms for facilitating cross-border data flows, including adequacy decisions.

[1] U.S. Department of Commerce (2022a, b).

M. Vásquez Callo-Müller (✉)
University of Lucerne, Lucerne, Switzerland
e-mail: maria.vasquez@unilu.ch

J. Drexl et al. (eds.), *Comparative Data Law*, MPI Studies on Intellectual Property and Competition Law 32, https://doi.org/10.1007/978-3-031-91401-0_14

While the Global CBPR Forum has been catapulted into global privacy governance conversations,[2] it is largely based on a mechanism that has been flying under the radar so far: the Asia–Pacific Economic Cooperation (APEC) CBPR System. The System, which has been fully functioning for over a decade, operationalizes the APEC Privacy Principles embedded in the APEC Privacy Framework,[3] and allows companies that join the system to transfer data across borders. Nevertheless, scholarly publications on the APEC CBPR system are limited. This lack of in-depth scholarly analysis is troublesome as the Global CBPR Forum will be based on the APEC CBPR system. The overall goal of this article is to contribute to filling this scholarly gap. It puts into context what the launch of the Global CBPR Forum means for global data governance, and what lessons can be extracted from the functioning of its predecessor—the APEC CBPR System—lessons which may offer insights for the development of future global or regional government-backed privacy certification systems.

This article proceeds as follows. Part two will outline the emergence of the Global CBPR Forum and how it fits into the current global privacy governance. Part three will explain the CBPR in the context of APEC, focusing on three aspects: its history, functioning, and performance to date. The fourth and final part will discuss the challenges that the APEC CBPR System has faced so far, challenges which should be considered as the Global CBPR Forum is operationalized.

2 The CBPR Goes Global

On April 21, 2022, Canada, Singapore, Japan, the US, the Republic of Korea, Chinese Taipei, and the Philippines released a joint declaration announcing the creation of a Global CBPR Forum.[4] The goal of the Global CBPR Forum is to "establish an international certification system based on the APEC Cross Border Privacy Rules (CBPR) and Privacy Recognition for Processors (PRP) Systems."[5] The hope of the initial Global CBPR Forum participants is that this forum could become an instrument in helping to achieve interoperability of data protection laws, particularly as it is not restricted to APEC membership. Such global ambitions should facilitate "trade and international data flows" and promote "global cooperation, building on our shared data privacy values while recognizing the differences in our domestic approaches

[2] Zweifel-Keegan (2021); JD Supra (2022); Crowell & Moring LLP (2022).

[3] APEC (2015).

[4] U.S. Department of Commerce (2022a, b) Global Cross-Border Privacy Rules Declaration [hereinafter Global CBPR Declaration]; U.S. Department of Commerce (2022a, b) Statement by Commerce Secretary Raimondo on Establishment of the Global Cross-Border Privacy Rules (CBPR) Forum; Australia joined the initiative on August 17, 2022. See: Australian Minister for Trade, Tourism and Investment (2022) Australia joins the Global Cross-Border Privacy Rules Forum.

[5] Global CBPR Declaration.

to protecting data privacy."[6] This highly desirable goal contrasts with the approach undertaken by other regions, such as the European Union (EU), whose adequacy decisions are taken unilaterally and require an equivalent level of privacy protection.

More recently, on January 29, 2024, the US Federal Trade Commission announced its participation in the Global CBPR Forum and the Global Cooperation Arrangement for Privacy Enforcement (Global CAPE).[7] This follows developments in 2023, a year in which countries such as the United Kingdom (UK) received Associate Status in Forum,[8] while others have expressed increased interest in joining.[9] 2023 also marks the year in which other operational aspects of the Global CBPR forum were clarified. These includes details on the functioning of the Global CAPE[10] and that, importantly, the basis for certification will be the Global CBPR Privacy Principles, which closely resemble the nine privacy principles found in the APEC Privacy Framework.[11] In addition, in 2023, other important documents were released, such as the Forum's Terms of Reference[12] and template letters to participate as an Associate as well as to participate in the Global CAPE.[13] Moreover, in 2023, Singapore was appointed as Deputy Chair of the Global Forum Assembly—the policy-making body of the Forum.[14]

While the rolling out of the Global CBPR Forum is ongoing, it is important to revisit the functioning and performance to date of the APEC CBPR System. The System, already launched in 2011,[15] has been slow to take off and has been fully implemented by only a handful of countries. This has raised questions about its benefits and the business case for CBPR certification.[16] The next section takes a closer look at the APEC CBPR System, its history and functioning in order to gather insights about aspects that could be improved and incorporated in the Global CBPR Forum.

---

[6] U.S. Department of Commerce (2022a, b) Statement by Commerce Secretary Raimondo on Establishment of the Global Cross-Border Privacy Rules (CBPR) Forum. (In commenting about the newly created Global CBPR Forum, US Secretary of Commerce Gina Raimondo said that the move "reflects the beginning of a new era of multilateral cooperation in promoting trusted global data flows that are critically important to our modern economy." This approach will facilitate "trade and international data flows" and promote "global cooperation, building on our shared data privacy values while recognizing the differences in our domestic approaches to protecting data privacy.").

[7] FTC (2024).

[8] UK Government (2023).

[9] Privacy Commissioner of Bermuda (2022).

[10] On October 17, 2023, the Global Cross Border Privacy Rules (CBPR) Forum published the Global Cooperation Arrangement for Privacy Enforcement (Global CAPE). See Global CBPR (2023d), Global Cooperation Arrangement for Privacy Enforcement.

[11] Global CBPR (2023a) Global Cross-Border Privacy Rules (CBPR) Framework (2023).

[12] Global CBPR (2023b) Global CBPR, Global CBPR Forum Terms of Reference.

[13] See Global CBPR (2023c).

[14] IMDA (2023).

[15] APEC (2011a, b) 19th APEC Economic Leaders' Meeting 2011 - The Honolulu Declaration [hereinafter The Honolulu Declaration].

[16] See Greenleaf (2021).

3 The APEC CBPR System

Scholarly literature on the APEC CBPR System is scarce, with only few exceptions.[17] Yet the APEC CBPR system exits for more than 10 years and it was initially conceptualized much earlier than that, in the APEC Privacy Framework of 2005.[18] At that point it was proposed as a mechanism for "mutual recognition" or "acceptance" of different domestic privacy laws, which would allow for effective privacy protection without creating unnecessary barriers to cross-border information flows.[19] The link between trade and privacy emerges clearly from this conceptualization and from the forum from which the CBPR stems: APEC.

APEC is an organization composed of 21 "economies" in the Asia–Pacific.[20] The use of the word "economies" instead of "countries" is fundamental to understand the nature of cooperation within APEC processes, which are mainly restricted to trade and economic issues, and are based on soft-law and non-binding decisions.[21]

APEC economies engage in substantive policy discussions through dedicated working groups. The APEC CBPR system was developed within one of these working groups; the Data Privacy Subgroup (DPS), part of the Committee of Trade and Investment (CTI). The DPS itself was established in 2003 and work undertaken by this forum led to the creation of the APEC Privacy Framework in 2005[22] and to the APEC Data Privacy Pathfinder of 2007,[23] which lay the foundations of a data protection accountability-based,[24] later crystallized by the APEC CBPR system endorsed by APEC leaders[25] in November 2011.

The APEC CBPR System certifies that a company fulfills a set of nine information privacy principles contained in the APEC Privacy Framework.[26] These principles are: preventing harm; notice; collection limitation; use choice; integrity; security safeguards; access and correction; and accountability. These principles are concretized in the APEC CBPR Program Requirements[27]; and the Intake questionnaire, which is applicable to companies applying for CBPR certification.[28]

---

[17] Vásquez Callo-Müller (2018); Sullivan (2019), p. 380–397; and Greenleaf (2022).

[18] APEC (2005), APEC Privacy Framework (2005) [hereinafter APEC Privacy Framework 2005].

[19] Id. at 36.

[20] The reader should notice that APEC membership includes Chinese Taipei and the Peoples Republic of China, and both "economies" are represented and hold membership at the same time.

[21] Hsieh (2021), p. 197.

[22] APEC Privacy Framework 2005.

[23] The APEC Data Privacy Pathfinder was established by Ministers in 2007 to enable participating APEC member economies to work together to develop a framework for accountable flows of personal data across the region. APEC (2007), *APEC Data Privacy Pathfinder* [hereinafter APEC Data Privacy Pathfinder].

[24] Ibid.

[25] Honolulu Declaration.

[26] APEC (2015) APEC Privacy Framework.

[27] CBPRs (2019a, b, c) APEC Cross-Border Privacy Rules System Program Requirements.

[28] CBPRs (2021) APEC Cross-Border Privacy Rules System: Intake Questionnaire.

The functioning of the APEC CBPR System has been governed by the Charter of the Cross-Border Privacy Rules Joint Oversight Panel (Charter of the CBPR JOP), which establishes the JOP as the body in charge of engaging in consultations with economies that have indicated an intention to participate in the System, make recommendations for the recognition of Accountability Agents (AAs), consider and recommend their suspension, verify that AAs fulfill the re-certification criteria, among others.[29]

The JOP is composed of three members and decisions are taken by simple majority.[30] The current JOP members are representatives of the US, Singapore and Japan.[31] The functions of the JOP are developed in the Protocols of the APEC CBPR System JOP.[32] The protocols establish the process for: (i) economy participation, (ii) AA application, (iii) ongoing engagement, (iv) the determination of an AA continued recognition, and (v) additional provisions, such as the establishment of working teams.

According to Charter of the CBPR JOP, when an economy wishes to participate in the CBPR framework, it must meet three conditions: (a) participate in the Cross-border Privacy Enforcement Arrangement (CPEA), (b) express the intention to use at least one APEC-recognized AA, and (c) explain how the economy meets CBPR program requirements and how the system can be enforced domestically.[33]

Once an applicant economy fulfills the above requirements, and its participation is approved by JOP and the respective APEC forums, companies acting as data controllers can apply for CBPR certification. To obtain this certification, companies self-assess that they comply with APEC's nine Privacy Principles, by completing an intake questionnaire composed of 50 questions.[34] Then a third party (the AA) will certify the applicant companies after an assessment of their privacy policies. It is in this context that the availability of AA in an economy has been critical in the operationalization of the APEC Privacy Framework so far. AAs not only certify that participating firms are compliant with the CBPR system but they are also in charge of handling frontline dispute resolution between individuals and CBPR-certified firms.

The process of becoming an AA is also detailed in the Charter of the CBPR JOP. Prospective AAs are expected to submit their application to the relevant domestic authorities in charge of privacy enforcement (i.e., PEA), but it will be the JOP the entity assessing the AA application and recommend its certification. It is important to highlight that the recognition of an AA is limited to one year and that subsequent re-certifications are valid for two years.[35]

---

[29] CBPRs (2019) Charter of the APEC Cross-Border Privacy Rules and Privacy Recognition for Processors System Joint Oversight Panel [hereinafter JOP Chapter].

[30] Ibid. at para. 6.2.

[31] APEC (2021) Summary Report - Data Privacy Sub-Group Meeting.

[32] APEC (2019), Protocols of the APEC Cross-Border Privacy Rules System Joint Oversight Panel.

[33] Ibid. at p. 2.

[34] CBPRs (2021) APEC Cross-Border Privacy Rules System: Intake Questionnaire.

[35] CBORs (2019) APEC Cross-Border Privacy Rules System: Policies, Rules and Guidelines. para 36.

To date, only nine out of 21 APEC economies participate in the APEC CBPR system— Australia, Canada, Japan, Korea, Mexico, the Philippines, Singapore, Chinese Taipei, and the US.[36] But only five have fully implemented the System by having an AA. Moreover, only four jurisdictions have companies that have effectively been CBPR-certified—the US, Korea, Japan and Singapore. In 2021, an initiative to broaden CBPR membership to include non-APEC economies was met with resistance by some economies.[37]The stalemate on expanding the APEC CBPR System beyond APEC economies is probably the reason behind the creation of the Global CBPR Forum, which is expected to be open to every country that meets CBPR standards, not only APEC economies.[38]

The CBPR system has also been incorporated in domestic privacy legislation in Japan and Singapore. Japan's Amended Act on the Protection of Personal Information (APPI) provides for internationally recognized certification mechanisms as one of the cross-border transfer tools.[39] The Guidelines of the APPI stipulate that CBPR is one such internationally recognized certification mechanism.[40] In the case of Singapore, the Personal Data Protection Commission recognizes the CBPR as a transfer mechanism in its own right under the Personal Data Protection (PDP) regulations 2021.[41] This allows firms in Singapore to transfer personal data to an overseas recipient that is CBPR-certified, without any additional requirements. Some concerns were raised regarding the EU-Japan adequacy decision and whether Japan's participation in the CBPR system could lead to it bypassing GDPR standards of protection. Such concerns led to a carve-out in Japan's data protection law, by which EU citizens' data cannot be transferred to other CBPR-participating economies using CBPR.[42] A similar situation may follow with Korea, which is also a CBPR member and has recently received an adequacy decision from the EU.[43]

Regarding enforcement, there have been very few cases to date, leading to some suspicion among privacy scholars as to whether the APEC CBPR by design leads to weaker levels of enforcement. Chander et al. point to the limited number of cases

---

[36] CBPRs.

[37] APEC ECSG-DPS (2011) Summary Report - Data Privacy Sub-Group Meeting.

[38] U.S. Department of Commerce (2022a, b) Statement by Commerce Secretary Raimondo on Establishment of the Global Cross-Border Privacy Rules (CBPR) Forum.

[39] See Act on the Protection of Personal Information (Act No. 57 of 30 May 2003, as amended) art. 24 [hereinafter APPI].

[40] Guidelines on the APPI (for transfers to third parties in foreign countries), Sect. 4.3.

[41] Singapore's Personal Data Protection (PDP) Regulations allows firms in Singapore to transfer personal data to an overseas recipient that is CBPR or PRP certified, without additional requirements. Section 12 (2).

[42] Commission Implementing Decision (EU) 2019/419 of 23 January 2019 Pursuant to Regulation (EU) 2016/679 of the European Parliament and of the Council on the Adequate Protection of Personal Data by Japan under the Act on the Protection of Personal Information (notified under document C (2019) 304) 2019 O.J. (L 76). para. 79.

[43] Commission Implementing Decision (EU) 2022/254 of 17 December 2021 pursuant to Regulation (EU) 2016/679 of the European Parliament and of the Council on the adequate protection of personal data by the Republic of Korea under the Personal Information Protection Act (notified under document C(2021) 9316, 2022 O.J. (L 44).

that have been brought up before the US Federal Trade Commission (FTC),[44] while Peng contends that "public enforcement under the CBPR is very limited".[45] These elements as well as other aspects that can help to future-proof the Global CBPR are explored in the next section.

4 Future-Proofing the Global CBPR Forum

4.1 Improving Credibility

One of the main critiques that has been raised about the APEC CBPR certification is that it falls short in comparison to the contemporary standards for data protection, and that the basis of the CBPR system, which is the APEC Privacy Framework, is no longer adequate.[46] While this is a valid critic, it needs to be complemented by explaining why the APEC information privacy principles or the APEC CBPR program requirements, in which these are reflected, have not been updated so far.

A fundamental issue that poses a roadblock for any kind of update of the APEC Privacy Framework is related to the nature of how decisions are adopted within APEC, which requires consensus by all APEC economies.[47] That is to say that to modify the APEC Privacy Framework, consensus among 21 APEC economies (including the US, Russia and China, the latter two are not part of the APEC CBPR System) is necessary. However, by leaving the APEC Forum, nothing prevents Global CBPR members to agree on improved privacy principles and raise the level of protection set by the APEC Privacy Framework.

However, another point to consider is that the common principles in which the Global CBPR Forum is based upon, can only be upgraded as long as a proposed new obligation is already included in each member's domestic law, and it is enforceable. This is due to the bottom-up approach to interoperability that Global CBPR forum embraces, and it is a reflection of how to achieve both interoperability (in the sense of all having the same minimum standards) and enforcement (in the sense of ensuring compliance with domestic laws). Low hanging fruits that could be incorporated in the Global CBPR Forum include elements such as data breach notification, existing in many domestic data protection laws, among others.

But even if the Global CBPR included new elements that are common to all its members, there would always be the question of how it fares when compared to laws that offer even higher standards of protection (i.e., the GDPR or similar). If

---

[44] Chander and Schwartz (2023), p. 49–136.

[45] Peng (2022), p. 9.

[46] See, for instance, Greenleaf (2009), p. 29.

[47] APEC. About APEC. ("In APEC, all economies have an equal say and decision-making is reached by consensus. There are no binding commitments or treaty obligations. Commitments are undertaken on a voluntary basis and capacity building projects help members implement APEC initiatives.").

in the future the Global CBPR Forum will seek interoperability with EU privacy certifications, the gaps between the Global CBPRs and the GDPR will have to be resolved, and there is precedent that such exercise may require mapping the elements of both systems.[48]

But a deeper look into comparisons into the two data protection mechanisms not only reveals legal but also business considerations. One could question, for instance, why would firms, which are already complying with more stringent requirements as a consequence of domestic laws that resemble GDPR standards of protection, need to apply for Global CBPR certification? In practical terms, would firms still need to fulfill domestic data privacy law requirements separately even after obtaining Global CBPR certification? What then is the value-added of Global CBPR certification? This question presumes, of course, that either there is a law comparable to the GDPR to which a company already abides or that the company at stake is engaged in cross-border data transfers to/from Europe, but this may not always be the case.

4.2 *Creating Incentives to Promote Uptake*

Fostering APEC CBPR uptake—after an economy joins the system—is key not only for the success of the system in a particular economy, but also for creating incentives for other jurisdictions and for more firms to join. In order to increase business uptake, some economies have offered incentives to companies to become CBPR-certified. For example, Singapore provides funding support to encourage firms to apply for relevant certifications. These include subsidies of up to 70 percent to cover fees charged by AAs for APEC CBPR certification and any third-party consultancy services.[49]

Another aspect that plays a role in increasing the appeal to be CBPR certified is the validity of the certification. The term of validity of a CBPR certification is shorter than of other privacy certifications, which in some cases are valid for up to three years, while CBPR certification is only valid for one year.[50] This leads to consider that increasing the appeal for CBPR Certification also demands increasing the validity of such certification.

A related aspect is how a Global CBPR Forum certification will fare in comparison to Standard Contractual Clauses (SCCs)—which are being adopted by many countries and regions in the world. The key question is, why would a firm decide to obtain Global CBPR certification, with all the related costs, when it can use SCCs to transfer data overseas? SCCs do not entail certification costs and do not involve an

48 APEC, Joint work between experts from the Article 29 Working Party and from APEC Economies, on a referential for requirements for Binding Corporate Rules submitted to national Data Protection Authorities in the EU and Cross Border Privacy Rules submitted to APEC CBPR Accountability Agents. See also: Article 29 Working Party, Opinion 02/2014 on a referential for requirements for Binding Corporate Rules submitted to national Data Protection Authorities in the EU and Cross-Border Privacy Rules submitted to APEC CBPR Accountability Agents.

49 IMDA, APEC Cross Border Privacy Rules (CBPR) System.

50 See, for instance, JIPDEC PrivacyMark System.

AA. Once approved by the relevant authority, they can be used by any company to facilitate transfers of data to other companies.[51] The potential value added of a Global CBPR Forum certification could be to not only enable cross-border transfer of data among certified companies, but among jurisdictions—at least for those jurisdictions that recognize the CBPR as a valid mechanism for cross-border data transfers in their domestic laws.

Finally, the business case to be, and to remain, CBPR certified could also increase if the interoperability of the Global CBPR system with other regional cross-border data transfer mechanisms is resolved. This is key in fostering the desired networks effects that would make the system appealing to firms, even more so considering that the current pool of CBPR-certified firms are sophisticated enterprises, often with cross-border operations across different continents. For them, interoperability with other regions, not limited to the EU, would be important in increasing the appeal for CBPR certification.

5 Conclusions

This article has explained and put into perspective the launch of the Global CBPR forum, which is expected to build upon the APEC CBPR System. In light of this, this article has explained the origins the APEC CBPR System and its performance to date. Considering the lessons learned from the roll-out of the APEC CBPR System on the ground, this article has also discussed some elements to future-proof the Global CBPR Forum and the privacy certification that will emerge from this initiative. Considering the complexity of the regulatory frameworks for cross-border transfers of personal data, and their importance for digital trade, the promise of a Global CBPR forum is a welcomed one.

References

APEC (2005) APEC privacy framework (2005). https://www.apec.org/publications/2005/12/apec-privacy-framework. Accessed 22 Feb 2025

APEC (2007) APEC data privacy pathfinder. http://www.asianlii.org/apec/other/agrmt/adpp221/. Accessed 22 Feb 2025 [hereinafter APEC Data Privacy Pathfinder]

APEC (2011) 19th APEC economic leaders' meeting 2011—The Honolulu declaration—toward a seamless regional economy. http://mddb.apec.org/Pages/BrowseLeadersDeclarations.aspx?Setting=browseLeadersDeclaration&DocType=%22Leaders%27%20Declaration%22. Accessed 22 Feb 2025 [hereinafter The Honolulu Declaration]

APEC (2011) Summary report - data privacy sub-group meeting 2011—2011/SOM3/ECSG/011. http://mddb.apec.org/Pages/search.aspx. Accessed 22 Feb 2025

[51] On SCCs in the EU context, see: Kuner (2020). Article 46. Transfers Subject to Appropriate Safeguards. In Kuner, Bygrave and Docksey (2020), p. 799–806.

APEC (2015) APEC privacy framework. https://www.apec.org/Publications/2017/08/APEC-Privacy-Framework-(2015). Accessed 22 Feb 2025

APEC (2019) Protocols of the APEC cross-border privacy rules system joint oversight panel. http://cbprs.org/wp-content/uploads/2021/02/3.-JOP-Protocols-CBPR-updated-17-09-2019.pdf. Accessed 22 Feb 2025

APEC (2021) Summary report—data privacy sub-group meeting—2021/SOM3/DESG/DPS/SUM. http://mddb.apec.org/Documents/2021/DESG/DPS2/21_desg_dps2_summary.pdf. Accessed 22 Feb 2025

Joint work between experts from the Article 29 Working Party and from APEC Economies, on a referential for requirements for Binding Corporate Rules submitted to national Data Protection Authorities in the EU and Cross Border Privacy Rules submitted to APEC CBPR Accountability Agents. https://www.apec.org/docs/default-source/Groups/ECSG/20140307_Referential-BCR-CBPR-reqs.pdf. Accessed 22 Feb 2025

About APEC. https://www.apec.org/about-us/about-apec. Accessed 22 Feb 2025

Article 29 Working Party, Opinion 02/2014 on a referential for requirements for Binding Corporate Rules submitted to national Data Protection Authorities in the EU and Cross-Border Privacy Rules submitted to APEC CBPR Accountability Agents. https://ec.europa.eu/justice/article-29/documentation/opinion-recommendation/files/2014/wp212_en.pdf. Accessed 22 Feb 2025

Australian Minister for Trade, Tourism and Investment (2022) Australia joins the global cross-border privacy rules forum. https://www.trademinister.gov.au/minister/don-farrell/media-release/australia-joins-global-cross-border-privacy-rules-forum. Accessed 22 Feb 2025

CBPRs (2019) APEC cross-border privacy rules system: policies, rules and guidelines. http://cbprs.org/wp-content/uploads/2019/11/4.-CBPR-Policies-Rules-and-Guidelines-Revised-For-Posting-3-16-updated-1709-2019.pdf. Accessed 22 Feb 2025

CBPRs (2019) Charter of the APEC cross-border privacy rules and privacy recognition for processors system joint oversight panel. http://cbprs.org/wp-content/uploads/2019/11/2.-JOP-Charter-updated-17-09-2019.pdf. Accessed 22 Feb 2025

CBPRs (2019) APEC cross-border privacy rules system program requirements. http://cbprs.org/wp-content/uploads/2019/11/5.-Cross-Border-Privacy-Rules-Program-Requirements-updated-17-09-2019.pdf. Accessed 22 Feb 2025

CBPRs (2021) APEC cross-border privacy rules system: intake questionnaire. http://cbprs.org/wp-content/uploads/2021/02/Cross-Border-Privacy-Rules-Intake-Questionnaire.pdf. Accessed 22 Feb 2025

CBPRs. http://cbprs.org/government/. Accessed 22 Feb 2025

Chander C, Schwartz P (2023) Privacy and/or Trade. Univ Chicago Law Rev 90(1):49–136

Commission Implementing Decision (EU) 2019/419 of 23 January 2019 Pursuant to Regulation (EU) 2016/679 of the European Parliament and of the Council on the Adequate Protection of Personal Data by Japan under the Act on the Protection of Personal Information (notified under document C (2019) 304) 2019 O.J. (L 76)

Commission Implementing Decision (EU) 2022/254 of 17 December 2021 pursuant to Regulation (EU) 2016/679 of the European Parliament and of the Council on the adequate protection of personal data by the Republic of Korea under the Personal Information Protection Act (notified under document C(2021) 9316, 2022 O.J. (L 44)

Crowell & Moring LLP (2022) Global data transfer developments: taking the APEC CBPR system global, Lexology. https://www.lexology.com/library/detail.aspx?g=b6d772f2-4cf8-4fe2-a0e8-8a6c595bd8b4. Accessed 22 Feb 2025

FTC (2024) FTC signs on to multilateral arrangement to bolster cooperation on privacy and data security enforcement. https://www.ftc.gov/news-events/news/press-releases/2024/01/ftc-signs-multilateral-arrangement-bolster-cooperation-privacy-data-security-enforcement. Accessed 22 Feb 2025

Global CBPR (2023) Global cross-border privacy rules (CBPR) framework. https://www.globalcbpr.org/wp-content/uploads/Global-CBPR-Framework-2023.pdf. Accessed 22 Feb 2025

Global CBPR (2023) Global CBPR, global CBPR forum terms of reference. https://www.globalcbpr.org/wp-content/uploads/Global-CBPR-Forum-Terms-of-Reference-2023.pdf. Accessed 22 Feb 2025

Global CBPR (2023) Template letter of intent for associate status and template letter of intent for global CAPE. https://www.globalcbpr.org/documents/. Accessed 22 Feb 2025

Global CBPR (2023) Global cooperation arrangement for privacy enforcement. https://www.globalcbpr.org/wp-content/uploads/Global-CAPE-2023.pdf. Accessed 22 Feb 2025

Greenleaf G (2009) Five years of the APEC privacy framework: failure or promise? Comput Law Secur Rev 25(29):28–43

Greenleaf G (2021) Global data privacy laws 2021: uncertain paths for international standards. Privacy Laws & Business International Report 169

Greenleaf G (2022) Global CBPRs: a recipe for failure. Privacy Laws & Business International Report. https://papers.ssrn.com/sol3/papers.cfm?abstract_id=4180516. Accessed 22 Feb 2025

Guidelines on the APPI (for transfers to third parties in foreign countries) https://www.ppc.go.jp/personalinfo/legal/guidelines_offshore/. Accessed 22 Feb 2025

Hsieh PL (2021) The marginalization or rejuvenation of APEC. In: Hsieh PL (ed) New Asian regionalism in international economic law. Cambridge University Press, Cambridge, p 197

IMDA (2023) Singapore appointed as Deputy Chair of the Global Cross-Border Policy Rules (CBPR) Forum's Global Forum Assembly. https://www.imda.gov.sg/resources/press-releases-factsheets-and-speeches/press-releases/2023/singapore-appointed-as-deputy-chair-of-the-global-cross-border-policy-rules-forums-global-forum-assembly. Accessed 22 Feb 2025

IMDA. APEC cross border privacy rules (CBPR) system. https://www.imda.gov.sg/programme-listing/Cross-Border-Privacy-Rules-Certification. Accessed 22 Feb 2025

Japanese Act on the Protection of Personal Information (Act No. 57 of 30 May 2003, as amended) https://www.ppc.go.jp/en/legal/. Accessed 22 Feb 2025

JD SUPRA (2022) New global cross-border privacy rules forum established by APEC CBPR members. https://www.jdsupra.com/legalnews/new-global-cross-border-privacy-rules-7751638/. Accessed 22 Feb 2025

JIPDEC PrivacyMark system. https://privacymark.org/ Accessed 22 Feb 2025

Kuner C (2020) Article 46. Transfers subject to appropriate safeguards. In: Kuner C, Bygrave LA, Docksey C (eds) The EU general data protection regulation (GDPR). Oxford University Press, Oxford, pp 799–806

Peng S (2022) Public-Private Interactions in Privacy Governance. Laws 11(80):9

Privacy Commissioner of Bermuda (2022) Privacy commissioner leads at digital trade agreement discussions. https://www.privacy.bm/post/privacy-commissioner-leads-at-digital-trade-agreement-discussions. Accessed 22 Feb 2025

Singapore's Personal Data Protection (PDP) Regulations allows firms in Singapore to transfer personal data to an overseas recipient that is CBPR or PRP certified, without additional requirements. Section 12 (2) https://sso.agc.gov.sg/SL/PDPA2012-S63-2021?DocDate=20210930&ProvIds=P13-#pr12-. Accessed 22 Feb 2025

Sullivan C (2019) EU GDPR or APEC CBPR? A comparative analysis of the approach of the EU and APEC to cross-border data transfers and protection of personal data in the IoT era. Comput Law Secur Rev 35(4):380–397

U.S. Department of Commerce (2022) Global cross-border privacy rules declaration. https://www.commerce.gov/global-cross-border-privacy-rules-declaration. Accessed 22 Feb 2025

U.S. Department of Commerce (2022) Statement by Commerce Secretary Raimondo on establishment of the global cross-border privacy rules (CBPR) forum. https://www.commerce.gov/news/press-releases/2022/04/statement-commerce-secretary-raimondo-establishment-global-cross-border. Accessed 22 Feb 2025

UK Government (2023) Press release: UK gets new status in global data privacy certification programme. https://www.gov.uk/government/news/uk-gets-new-status-in-global-data-privacy-certification-programme. Accessed 22 Feb 2025

Vásquez Callo-Müller M (2018) GDPR and CBPR: reconciling personal data protection and trade. https://www.apec.org/Publications/2018/10/GDPR-and-CBPR---Reconciling-Personal-Data-Protection-and-Trade- Accessed 22 Feb 2025

Zweifel-Keegan C (2021) A globalized CBPR framework: peering into the future of data transfers. https://iapp.org/news/a/a-globalized-cbpr-framework-peering-into-the-future-of-data-transfers/. Accessed 22 Feb 2025

Dr. María Vásquez Callo-Müller is a researcher and consultant on digital trade issues. She is part of the Trade Law 4.0 project, working as a post-doctoral fellow at the University of Lucerne. Her research focuses on the regulation of digital technologies and trade, particularly in the areas of intellectual property rights (copyright and trade secrets), data governance, and cybersecurity. She regularly consults international organizations on digital trade and data policies. María holds a Ph.D. in Law from the University of Bern, as well as an LLM in Intellectual Property Law from the Munich Intellectual Property Law Center (Max Planck Institute for Innovation and Competition) and a Master of Advanced Studies in International Law and Economics (MILE) from the World Trade Institute, University of Bern. She is admitted to practice law in Peru.

The manufacturer's authorised representative in the EU is Springer Nature Customer Service Centre GmbH, Europaplatz 3, 69115 Heidelberg, Germany. If you have any concerns regarding our products, please contact ProductSafety@springernature.com

Printed and bound by CPI Group (UK) Ltd, Croydon, CR0 4YY
01/10/2026
02225864-0011